D1714759

The
Psychoanalytic
Study
of the Child

VOLUME SIXTY-TWO

Kindly submit seven copies of new manuscripts by post
or as an email attachment in MS Word to

Robert A. King, M.D.
Yale Child Study Center
230 South Frontage Road
P.O. Box 207900
New Haven, CT 06520-7900
Phone: (203) 785-5880
E-mail: robert.king@yale.edu

The
Psychoanalytic
Study
of the Child

VOLUME SIXTY-TWO

Yale University Press
New Haven and London
2007

Designed by Sally Harris
and set in NewBaskerville type.
Printed in the United States of American by
Vail-Ballou Press, Inc., Binghamton, N.Y.

Library of Congress catalog card number: 45-11304
ISBN: 978-0-300-12540-5
A catalogue record for this book is available from the British Library.

The paper in this book meets the guidelines for
permanence and durability of the Committee on
Production Guidelines for Book Longevity of the
Council on Library Resources.
10 9 8 7 6 5 4 3 2 1

Contents

TREATMENT OF CHILDREN OF TRAUMA AND DISRUPTION

CHILD PSYCHOANALYTIC TECHNIQUE

ADULT DEVELOPMENT

CELEBRATING THE 150TH
ANNIVERSARY OF THE BIRTH
OF SIGMUND FREUD

A Forward View

Celebrating the 150th Birthday of the Founder of Psychoanalysis

SAMUEL ABRAMS, M.D.

The author notes that the two principal goals of psychoanalysis have always been the development of a general psychology and the enhancement of its clinical theories. Integrating the two would certainly be profitable to both, but the integration has been difficult to achieve. Teaching and learning are burdened by ambiguous terms, clinical controversies, the inclination to favor reductionism while putting constructivist thinking aside, and the sheer weight of the complexities of the human mind. Many of the writings of Sigmund Freud and Anna Freud provide opportunities to overcome these obstacles.

FOLLOWING GUIDELINES ESTABLISHED BY SIGMUND FREUD AND ANNA Freud, psychoanalysis has produced two desirable products: a way of helping people get better and a more broadly applicable general psychology. The centerpiece of the first is the psychoanalytic process; a core feature of the second is the developmental process. Obviously, it would be advantageous to effectively coordinate that unique thera-

Clinical Professor, The Psychoanalytic Institute Department of Psychiatry at N.Y.U. Medical Center; Editor, *The Psychoanalytic Study of the Child.*

Originally presented in a different form at the Psychoanalytic Association of New York in February, 2004, under the title "Coordinating the Developmental Process with Clinical Psychoanalysis." Comments by Drs. Leonard Shengold and Herbert J. Schlesinger at the time were stimulants for refining some of the proposals. Dr. Robert King's comments about earlier versions of this paper inspired additional modifications.

The Psychoanalytic Study of the Child 62, ed. Robert A. King, Peter B. Neubauer, Samuel Abrams, and A. Scott Dowling (Yale University Press, copyright © 2007 by Robert A. King, Peter B. Neubauer, Samuel Abrams, and A. Scott Dowling).

peutic modality within a general psychology, but it has proven difficult to do so. Partly, this reflects a division of labors. Sigmund Freud's preferred focus was clinical, and he collected his data primarily from the adult population. Anna Freud undertook the task of sculpting a comprehensive general psychology, while her research efforts were focused mostly upon children. A practitioner can claim Freudian status without being too informed about psychoanalytic psychology, while many who are preoccupied with the growth and development of the human mind are allied to Anna Freud's innovative ideas without having to be too rigorously immersed in traditional clinical technique.

Traditional clinical technique underscores looking backward to find earlier pathogenic components. Anna Freud's therapeutic and research attentiveness stresses looking forward toward new structures. This difference in perspective furthers the difficulties encountered in attempting to integrate the two domains. Consequently, to date, the effective coordination of the analytic and the developmental processes remains elusive. It would be useful to consider the many obstacles that stand in the way of what would certainly be a landmark achievement. A 150th birthday celebration of the founder of psychoanalysis provides an opportunity for trying to delineate those impediments as a step toward overcoming them.

The Definitional Obstacle

An immediate imposing obstacle is a *definitional* one. As matters rest today—to paraphrase George Bernard Shaw—psychoanalysis can be described as a group of affiliated disciplines separated by the same language. Analytic educators immersed in tribal wars assign different meanings to the same high maintenance words. Consequently, it is necessary to begin by describing how the phrases "psychoanalytic process" and "developmental process" will be used in these pages. For those who have strong leanings toward other meanings, it may require more than a certain degree of forbearance to endure both this introductory passage and the journey through the subsequent sections.

The Psychoanalysis Process and the Developmental Process Defined

The psychoanalytic process describes those steps in a treatment designed to access and integrate the psychologically unrecognized. The

phrase "psychologically unrecognized" includes—but is not necessarily limited to—the dynamic unconscious, where earlier unresolved conflicts and disordered relationships reside. Technically, clinicians are expected to acquire the skill of floating their attention so
that it may be attuned to the *continuing* links between what happened
then and what's happening now, however obscure the links might appear to be. The required perspective is a linear one. During the treatment the unrecognized past components are discovered and differentiated so that they might be re-combined in a more felicitous way.
The process is accelerated as the past is increasingly brought to life
on the stage of the ongoing present therapeutic relationship.

The nature of the re-combinations is not inconsequential. For example, re-arranging the old components may result in a new compromise between the constituents or in a transformation—and these
are very different yields. Interpretations—especially historical (genetic) interpretations—and reconstructions are major technical
tools that abet such an analytic effort, an effort implemented by the
cognitive argument known as reductionism. While there is considerable consensus about this way of defining the psychoanalytic process
(sometimes labeled "classical" analysis and not always with esteem),
there are many clinicians who would challenge at least some of the
features in this model.

The definition of the developmental process is likely to evoke an
even greater dissent. This is understandable because there are many
models of development in use and because some schools of psychoanalysis owe their very clinical existence to one developmental variant or another—self-psychology and attachment psychology, to cite
two examples, some separation-individuation theorists to cite a third.
Furthermore, the word "developmental" is sometimes used as a substantive noun and sometimes simply as a modifier, without recognition of the significance of such differences. This only furthers the ob-
fuscation.

Sigmund Freud provided the oldest conceptualization of the psychoanalytic developmental process. It may still be quite serviceable.
It has the advantage of having been initiated by the founder of the
field who inferred it from clinical settings. However, as it has grown,
it has the greater advantage of bridging concepts that are applicable
to other disciplines such as embryology, evolutionary biology, and
the neurosciences. Borrowing from Freud's proposal, this definition
regards the developmental process as a sequence of progressive hierarchical steps in the organization of the mind. The progression is fueled by an inherent biological blueprint and becomes actualized

through ongoing experiences and interactions with people and things. The yield is a set of transformed (and transforming) organizations and structures, stages or phases, which may also be called emergent structures. "Emergent" is an appropriate term since it suggests entirely new entities, neither predictable by what has preceded nor reducible to their antecedents. This singles out the larger superordinate structures of the mind from the several sub-categories that are subsumed within it that harbor self and object-relations, instincts and the defense organization, and the more autonomous set of functions.

However, this developmental model instantly underscores the orientation problem for many clinicians. In contrast to the linear way in which analysts "floatingly" attend to empirical data, clinicians concerned with matters of development are required to recognize *discontinuities*. To put it a bit differently, they are expected to look at present data as potential expressions of *emerging* new structures not only as *resultants* of antecedent ones. Development is more than the sum of its preceding parts and since growth is not linear, a constructivist way of thinking is necessary to do justice to the clinical realities. By contrast, some other developmental models underscore continuities, seriously limiting the understanding of mental growth since they focus upon resultants, not emergents.

There is an important empirical marker that can be used to distinguish resultants from emergents. George Henry Lewes, an English philosopher of the nineteenth century, proposed a metaphor to emphasize that distinction. He contrasted the combining of sand and powder with the combining of sodium and chlorine. The sand and powder, he explained, yields a *resultant* mixture; its characteristics reflect the consequence of the proportions of each component, components that retain their distinctive characteristics within the mixture. However, sodium and chlorine combine to produce salt, a true emergent, i.e., a yield with qualities that bear virtually no relationship to the components that created it. It is a transformed product, in George Lewes's terms, an emergent.[1] It would not be possible to derive the characteristics of sodium and chlorine by examining salt, nor would it be possible to predict what salt is like by simply assessing the characteristics of its component parts. In a parallel way, it is not possible to predict the novel expressions of latency merely by studying antecedent structures.

---

1. A parallel can be seen in some substantive distinctions between Newtonian physics and quantum mechanics.

To be an adept Freudian psychoanalyst has always required nurturing an orientation to the components of the *past* as determinants of the pathologic present so as to promote more useful *resultant* compromises. For many analysts, the phrase "new compromise-formations" is a principal measure of achievement in clinical work. However, if Anna Freud's developmental concepts are to be more adequately absorbed, clinicians are required to also attend to the ways in which a set of *present* components may be brought together to produce an emergent, i.e., an innovative unexpected outcome.

Such an extension of technique may be comfortably embraced by some, but it is likely to initiate confrontational challenges in many others. One way of addressing these challenges is to reflect upon a useful guide passed down into this century by the father and daughter of psychoanalysis.

Sigmund Freud and Anna Freud's Guide
for Twenty-First Century Analysts

Freud introduced both orientations—reductionism and constructivism—, the first as a clinician, the second when he proposed psychoanalysis as a general psychology. When Freud said that hysterics suffer from unrecognized reminiscences he established the basic orienting foundation for the growth of clinical work, the aim of literally linking present symptoms with embedded stealth pathogenic components laid down in the past. He fostered the value of reducing the now to the then—that's why he called his new discipline psycho*analysis* and not psycho*synthesis*. His approach revolutionized the entire field of psychology, not to mention a few other disciplines along the way. Discovering what is not known remains the indispensable quest for psychoanalytic clinicians. If Sigmund Freud had done nothing else he would have assured himself a prominent position in the pantheon of scientists.

However, as the cartographer of a general psychology, he did do something else. He described the developmental process. Close on the heels of the recognition of the importance of looking *backward* to fantasies and experiences, Freud offered a conceptual outline for growth from the standpoint of looking *forward*. He described libidinal development modeled upon epigenetic formulations—epigenetic, meaning a series of new births over time. Libidinal development, he said, proceeds in accordance with an inherent biologically determined blueprint that yields a sequence of hierarchical phases—oral, anal, phallic, genital—each new libidinal phase ushering in empirical and conceptual novelties. The novelties, while somewhat influenced by antecedents, bore a *discontinuous* relationship to what had occurred before; they were emergent phases, not merely resultants. Sublimations were transformations of instinctual aims, not compromise-formations, perhaps not even truly defenses. Nothing about the quality of oral pleasure-seeking would lead anyone to predict adolescent sexuality; nothing about adolescent sexuality would lead anyone to reconstruct those distinctive experiences that accompany antecedent oral pleasure-seeking. Emergence is contingent upon an inherent maturational blueprint actualized by way of experiences.

The cognitive psychologists have extensively mapped out particular landmarks in the transformation of thinking, and some who labor in the field of moral development have staked similar claims. The more these and other epigenetic sequences are brought into psychoanalysis, the more vital its general psychology and its clinical applications are likely to become.

While Freud introduced both continuities and discontinuities into psychoanalysis, his preference led him to the clinical application of the continuities and to a technique that features reconstruction and historical interpretation. Perhaps this was abetted because he worked exclusively with adults. It was up to his daughter, Anna Freud, who also found herself constructing a general psychology, to attempt to bring the developmental process with its emphasis upon discontinuities into clinical work.

This proved relatively easy with children. Many of the principles of child analysis implicitly address the discontinuities of the developmental process. For example, the aim of child analysis is to bring children to the point where they can optimize the prospects of the next pull forward, not simply to reduce the influences of antecedent pathogens. That is, the goal of analysis in children is the freeing of bound components so that they can optimally participate in the next innovative re-birth. Obstacles to the freeing are addressed, especially those resistances created by internalized or continually present external pathogens, but also those that arise from variants within the program itself. When neurotic features are the principal obstacle then analysis—with its attention to repressed antecedents—is the treatment of choice. But neurosis is not the only obstacle. It follows that child analysts are expected to be aware of the characteristics of each succeeding phase so as not to confuse an ongoing emergent with a resultant derived from a pathogen in residence. Child analysts quickly learn that while much of their clinical activities contain the look backward, many others require their attention to the pull forward. Indeed, there are occasions when an analyst's insistence on the past may blunt the pull forward—an unhappy technical slip.

Parsing the Analytic Relationship

All this stresses how important it is to distinguish empirical data as potential expressions of a linear phenomenon from those that arise as an expression of discontinuities. One illuminates the present/past orientation, the other the present/future orientation. Happily, this distinction also helps to parse several features of the analytic relationship and this serves the task of integrating general psychology with clinical applications.

The term *transference* is often used globally to cover all aspects of what transpires within the treatment setting. This poses a dilemma for the teaching and learning of our discipline.

Strictly speaking, the word was invented to convey something quite narrow, namely, the assigning of a feature of some past person upon the current analytic exchange. The "past" transference attribution provides what may be the most valuable path to the pathogenic components continuing from an earlier time. In fact, the design of the treatment setting facilitates the analyst becoming such a *transference* object. Analysts who ignore this feature, do so at their own and their patients' peril.

However, the analyst is a *real* person also. In all analyses, some of the actualities of the analyst may leverage the treatment action. For example, the real traits of caring, tolerance of affects, a readiness to attend to a broad range of thoughts that are not part of the customary social dialogue, the withholding of personal judgments, and the preference for knowing rather than denying are all actualities that regularly steer analytic work along its productive path. Many patients are likely to recognize these real attributes, and when they identify with them it usually has a beneficial influence upon the outcome. Some analytic educators urge their students to actively leverage the potential of the real traits of the analyst for the sake of the treatment, for example, those who favor theories of therapeutic action that stress inter-subjectivity and the promotion of object relationships. So, in addition to being seen as a transference (past) object, the analyst is a real object. Unfortunately, this real feature often is labeled transference also. This is likely to be confusing to students and practitioners of our discipline.

In addition—and Anna Freud stressed this—the analyst can repre-

sent *externalized* elements of parts of the patient's current self organization, so that intra-psychic dilemmas appear in the form of concrete
personal exchanges. This is not quite classical (past) transference
and certainly not a *real* exchange, but it can be readily assimilated
into the technique of those who tap the past or the present. Several
schools of psychoanalysis regard work with the externalizations as the
core of the treatment process, some Kleinians, for instance. Regret-
tably, this externalization of aspects of the self is often called transference as well. Such free play with a basic term is particularly unfortunate because the differentiation of past, real, and externalized is
heuristically useful and can have direct concrete therapeutic applications.

Child analysts, like the analysts who confine their work to adults,
regularly face these three components of the therapeutic interaction,
but they are also required to consider an important fourth one.
When child patients stand at the threshold of a fresh organizational
pull forward, their analysts may be used as *new* objects to actualize
the expected pull forward into the next step of the hierarchy. When
a child enters the threshold of that mental organization that ushers
in triadic complexities and oedipal conflicts, for example, he
searches the surround for figures to engage the newly emerging configuration; when he enters latency he needs people and things to
promulgate those new transformations known as sublimations; in
adolescence he requires figures to facilitate a new emerging feature
of relationships, object removal. So, the analyst who has been educated to recognize the therapeutic influence of her *real* traits, trained
to appreciate the pull backward with the concomitant *past* attribution, accepts the idea of the *externalized* representation of an aspect of
her patient's self, now has to recognize an entirely fresh way of being
represented—a *new* object in the service of promoting developmentally fueled structural transformations.[2] Balancing the old with the
real and the externalized self is difficult enough—and occurs in
adult analyses as well; adding the component of *new* can be particularly taxing, especially because it requires a mode of attending that is
quite different than what is needed for all the others. The complexity
of it all represents another serious obstacle to the teaching and learning not to mention the doing of clinical work informed by advances
in psychoanalytic psychology.

---

2. In this sense the word "new" reflects the anticipated novel emergent rather than
something real or actual in the behavior of the analyst.

EXPANDING THERAPEUTIC ACTION

The awareness of these distinctions inspired by our general psychology can help in designing more effective technical strategies. Each attribution provides a different approach to helping people get better, to searching out different modes of therapeutic action. The past-object analyst illuminates the infantile embedded pathogens while the real analyst provides traits for identification and useful inter-subjective exchanges. The analyst as an externalized aspect of the self assists in matters of comprehending self-regulation and self-coherence. The new object analyst taps into the forward pull, providing leverage for the creative burst that arises as new hierarchies evolve.

Children in analysis get better in the classical way, i.e., they newly integrate discovered pathogens from the past and find more effective compromises to deal with them. They also use modes of identifications to buttress traits that are useful for the treatment and also profit from a beneficent personal exchange. Children can be helped to recognize features about themselves within the externalized setting, and this awareness can lead to more stable regulatory apparatuses and a greater sense of coherence. And children get better when they are afforded the opportunity to fully engage the freshly emerging organization by using the analyst as a new object in the service of progressive transformations.

As is evident from this brief summary, the complex prospects of balancing different forms of therapeutic action can be daunting. Furthermore, each approach may not always be technically compatible with one or more of the others, precipitating all kinds of clinical dilemmas—yet another obstacle to teaching and learning.

This view of the components of therapeutic interaction may seem agreeable to some and perhaps intuitively useful to others. However, despite the fact that these perspectives are rooted in Sigmund Freud's views and that Anna Freud promoted their application in childhood and adolescence, the impression remains that they still have little currency in our current psychoanalytic endeavors. The core of a general psychology and the centerpiece of practical therapeutic applications continue to dwell in somewhat different plains of existence. It is appropriate to wonder why the guide left by the founder and his daughter has not been more vigorously exploited.

One obstacle, already cited, is definitional. The conceptual framework for the psychoanalytic process just described would be rejected out of hand by a considerable number of practitioners today, but would still be less controversial than what might be raised about the phrase *the developmental process.* The existence of such ambiguities and controversies and complexities is bound to make effective teaching and learning even more challenging than they customarily are.

But even if we could arrive at a definitional consensus and somehow simplify and differentiate the terms, there would still be other obstacles. Every analyst knows how serviceable the orientation toward continuities has been—especially with adults—and acknowledges the effective therapeutic results achieved with reductionism. Would our discipline truly be enhanced were we to add discontinuities and constructivism?

This question blends into a third obstacle to teaching and learning. Is the consideration of discontinuities truly an *analytic* matter altogether, or is it an entirely different way of observing data that may be incompatible with what clinicians do everyday? Those who articulate this question in the form of an objection regard developmental considerations to lie outside the field of analytic inquiry, and, consequently, an encumbrance to the expected free-floating attention. They feel that the developmental threatens our field by confusion and distraction, and what's more it threatens our very identity.

This blends into the most daunting obstacle of all. If awareness of the developmental process is truly useful for clinical analysts, the additional way of attending should have applications with adults not only with children. What are those applications? Could they be utilized without bending the practice completely out of shape?

APPLICATIONS TO ADULT ANALYSIS

Does an orientation that encompasses the view of the mind as a result of progressive super-ordinate hierarchal organizations—so eminently useful in analytic work with children—have any applications for working with the psychological organization found in adults?

The obstacles arising from this question, paradoxically, can be characterized as either overly complex or too simplified.

THE OVERLY COMPLEX OBSTACLE

Introducing the developmental process provides a new way of exploring that super-ordinate organizing and integrating structure, the adult mind. The adult mind suddenly surfaces not merely as a resultant of a continuous growth but as a final emergent organization arising after a sequence of newly created antecedent minds. This mind has certain configurations that are more complex and serve adaptation and survival more effectively than those that have preceded it. Such a view establishes a somewhat different observational perch from the standpoint of diagnostic appraisal and for designing therapeutic strategies. Diagnostics would now include some appraisal about the nature of this final form. Has it proceeded in an expectable way or are there special proclivities or dispositions that have induced unexpected derailments? For example, we assume that the different subordinate systems of mind grow in equivalent paces, but what if the growth is not so harmonious? What if there is an unevenness between the growth of autonomous ego functions and instinctual development, for example? We know that one consequence can be a disorder that very much resembles obsessive-compulsive disorder, yet has little to do with anal phase issues. We also are inclined to assume that the major infantile conflicts peak equivalently in everyone, but what if an earlier conflict is more dominant and a later one is simply incorporated within it? How can we diagnostically assess the presence of such a configuration, and what role would it play in our approach to conflict resolution? Indeed, do different conflicts arising during different phases sometimes co-exist with one another, or overlap, or remain sharply differentiated rather than progressively transform in the course of growth? What innovations in technique would be necessary to deal with one kind rather than another, assuming we perfected the tools that would permit us to recognize such distinctions? And what of the role of dispositional differences as it impacts upon the entire developmental sequence? Does an inherent orientation toward things rather than people have sufficient impact upon subsequent development that it requires a re-evaluation of ways of proceeding in the treatment? Certainly when thing-orientation overwhelmingly dominates the relationships to persons, as in autistic disorders, the resulting havoc upon psychological organization makes analytic treatment impossible, at least as we customarily understand it. But in less extreme cases can the treatment be creatively modified to suit that kind of strained configuration?

Asking practitioners to freshly revisit the conventional diagnostic categories is not likely to bring forth a hearty endorsement unless there is clear evidence that such an effort is worth the undertaking. The prevailing diagnostic categories appear to work, or at least we make them work. And there is a historical reason for being pessimistic about trying to expand our diagnostic thinking about psychological disorders in this particular way. Anna Freud proposed a careful profile for study along such lines and delivered a remarkably elaborate empirical and conceptual outline useful for the diagnosis and treatment of children. However, the task of implementing her profile proved so complex that few child analysts elected to go there, while some adult analysts demonized her for fleeing from conventional views. It's not that it wasn't useful; it just was too different and too difficult. Bringing a developmental assessment into adult clinical work opens up research opportunities into a vast still relatively unexplored psychological terrain, but trying to grasp it with the depth it deserves would be a strain for educators and students alike.

The application of these basic features of developmental hierarchies to clinical work with adults also comes upon a second obstacle. While the first leads us toward near-daunting complexities that seem more than routinely difficult to overcome, this second obstacle arises from what might be characterized as a somewhat oversimplification of the concepts, thereby prematurely dismissing the many potential benefits that might come with greater probing. The journey along this path is much easier, but the treasure lies in another direction.

One form of oversimplifying derives from some theorists who argue that the blueprint that informs the steps in progressive developmental hierarchies does not end in young adulthood but continues throughout life. They envision different evolving super-ordinate embracing systems and consequently different configurations within its subordinate systems. Adults "develop" as they grow older, they argue, so why not encompass that fact within the developmental process?

As adults, persons change their patterns of love, work, and play. They seek different jobs, they marry, they have children, they go to war, they grow older. If these activities truly reflect the influence of a developmental blueprint throughout life, clinicians might be in a position to usefully function as facilitators with adults in the same way they do with children.

There are many examples in the literature that support this view. These include the proposal that marriage and parenthood are developmental phases, or owning a home is a developmental phase, or that grandparenthood is a developmental phase, or even that death is a developmental phase—suggestions that such life events represent empirical markers for new psychological organizations as a whole. This point of view leans upon an analogy between organizational novelties during childhood and adolescents such as triadic relationships or object removal. The adherents of this extended developmental perspective suggest that analysts can provide for grown-ups what child therapists provide for children. Surely, they contend, there are biological influences upon pairing, partnering, and parenting that can be equivalently tapped. If we assist children into novel phases, we may equivalently assist adults into forming suitable alliances or acquiring property.

Biological concomitants do accompany these and other adult activities. Biology, as measured by endocrine or neurotransmitter levels, gene activation, or functional brain scans, is recognizable in acts of love and war, work and play. Sometimes they act as stimulants for such behavior; certainly they occur as associated measurable phenomena. Unlike the function of the developmental process in childhood, however, at least some of these biologically referenced interests—such as the readiness to be marshaled into combat—do not necessarily best serve personal survival or societal coherence. Perhaps, therefore, it is not useful to characterize such biological influences in adult life in the same terms as those that fuel the inherent timetable that accounts for progressive changes in the psychological organization as a whole, changes that promote adaptedness and adaptation. When doing so, adherents of that position globalize the words "biology" and "development" rather than differentiate them and thereby introduce unnecessary pedagogic problems.

However, there is a more important clinical limitation of this perspective aside from its resting on a logical fallacy. This technique of "assisting" adults toward specific aims brings clinicians to the threshold of altering the fundamental nature of the psychoanalytic enterprise altogether. Prominent social and political figures regularly call up some affiliated psychological and biological theorists to augment positions they have arrived at from entirely different sources. They do this to promote specific contemporary interests and values. In contrast, the biological factors that fuel progressive hierarchical superordinate structures are neutral in respect to the choices selected from within the three subordinate systems. Falling in love does not only mean heterosexual pairing; partnering and parenting do not necessarily imply establishing the nuclear family; employment does not lean on inevitable biologically determined aggressive competitive affects, although hormonal or neurotransmitter level changes are measurable in all of these instances. Progressive hierarchical organizations only honor the value of more complex and diverse possibilities, a greater range of choices, and the prospect of exercising innovative solutions to pre-existing difficulties. To conflate the assisting of what may be more socially and politically inspired goals with those determined by the biological time-table may turn clinical psycho-analysis into a tool of adjustment to the prevailing social order, rather than a method of tapping innovative ways of thinking, being, and doing by discovering unrecognized obstacles to all three. An oversim-plified view of the developmental process—one that fails to differ-entiate the meanings of "developmental" and obscures the distinc-tion between those "biological" factors that fuel the growth of the super-ordinate system of the mental organization as a whole from those that affect features of the subcategories—these are threats and obstacles to the growth of psychoanalysis as a general psychology and as a distinctive approach to helping people get better. And attempt-ing to coordinate the two under such circumstances would become even more difficult.

Therefore, in respect to the application of Sigmund Freud's and Anna Freud's concept of the developmental process to adult analysis, contemporary matters can be summed up in this way. Certain appli-cations of their developmental principles to adult analysis are possi-ble and may prove extraordinary useful, but because of their com-plexity they are very difficult to teach, learn, and research. These include attention to unevenness in development, to dispositional ex-cesses, to variants in emergent conflicts. It remains unclear if the ef-forts would be as rewarding as some imagine. But if they proved re-warding it would place a general psychoanalytic psychology in the center of our interests and expand therapeutic possibilities.

Other approaches—those that I've characterized as too simpli-fied—fail to distinguish the different modes of biological influences or fail to discriminate super-ordinate structures from the functions and systems encompassed within them; these failures permit a fur-ther blurring of the word "developmental" while potentially subvert-ing the most fundamental features of the psychoanalytic process—discovering the unconscious and the unrecognized.

SUMMARY

I believe it is useful to bring together the two principal goals of psy-choanalysis: its way of getting people better and its general psychol-ogy that encompasses pathology but extends beyond it. Significant centers of each are the psychoanalytic process and the developmen-tal process respectively.

I have tried to explain how I define each of those. I've suggested that it is useful to add the orientation of discontinuous development to the prevailing one about growth that underscores linearity. The yield can include enhanced approaches to diagnosis, to technical strategies, to theories of therapeutic action. On the way, I paid special attention to the treatment relationship, noting that a differentiation of the components that make up the therapeutic exchange is far more preferable than having them encompassed within a single global term.

Listing the obstacles to teaching and learning these views, I've pointed out definitional ambiguities, ongoing clinical controversies, global thinking, the sheer weight of complexities and some overly simplified analogies that may seductively undermine rather than clarify.

In all of this, I hope I've conveyed the idea that our discipline is closer to the beginning of its useful discoveries than the end. Further clinical research is in order to tap the opportunities of the guides left by the founder and his daughter. Coordinating Sigmund Freud's comments about transformational potentials and Anna Freud's developmental concepts with established clinical practice may be one way to harness those opportunities. This should invigorate our enterprise and provide additional benefits for our patients.

LITTLE HANS REVISITED

Updating Little Hans

An Introduction to the Section

SAMUEL ABRAMS, M.D.

IT IS ALTOGETHER FITTING THAT *THE PSYCHOANALYTIC STUDY OF THE Child* publish these up-to-date reflections about Little Hans. For one thing, the release of new data about Hans and his family by the Sigmund Freud Archives has stirred considerable interest among analysts. There are also ceremonial reasons: we have just passed the 150th birthday of the founder of the field and are fast approaching the 100th anniversary of the publication of the Little Hans study. And there is another justification, perhaps the most compelling of all. The disputes that characterize current ways of thinking in our discipline may be more sharply illuminated by a detailed focus upon this case from the past.

For any enterprise, the discovery of new information is bound to evoke mixed responses. Some may simply ignore the new data and stay their conceptual course; others address it in ways that suggest that a paradigm shift may be in order. This was the setting, for example, in seventeenth-century embryology. At the time, scientists were in dispute. Some were inclined to examine the accumulating data of their discipline from the framework of continuity. They held that the adult was a child that had grown larger, just as a child had risen from a fully formed embryo whose structures were simply too tiny to be discriminated. Development was by accretion. They were preformists. They assumed that if it were possible to look more closely at the teeny creatures their theory would be completely affirmed. Consequently, improvements in the microscope were greeted with a certain enthusiasm since much more of the spermatozoa was suddenly visi-

The Psychoanalytic Study of the Child 62, ed. Robert A. King, Peter B. Neubauer, Samuel Abrams, and A. Scott Dowling (Yale University Press, copyright © 2007 by Robert A. King, Peter B. Neubauer, Samuel Abrams, and A. Scott Dowling).

ble. This instantly introduced new observational data for embryologists to consider. Many of the preformists peered at the specimens
and eagerly described little completely intact human beings; some of
the keener observers could even determine gender differentiation.
The homunculus really existed! For them, the new information affirmed what they already believed to be true: embryos were preformed little persons residing in spermatozoa that grew bigger as
they received necessary nutrients.

Another point of view was voiced by a group of embryologists who
fashioned themselves epigenesists. By contrast, they held that only
the potential for adulthood existed within the embryo, a potential
that was actualized over a sequence of steps. Growth was discontinuous, an orienting perspective quite distinctive from the preformists.
While the preformists examined adults from the point of view of reducing elements to their equivalent antecedents, the epigenesists examined them as products of new ways of organizing the antecedents
and of transforming them into something else. Over time, the epigenesists prevailed. It became clear that embryonic development proceeds in a series of sequential discontinuous steps, characterized by
periodic emergences of new structures, transforming earlier elements while setting the stage for future ones. To be sure, at certain
points in the course of growth, continuity became dominant, that is,
a small heart became a big one rather than transforming into another kind of structure. Continuous and discontinuous features
would need to be integrated to fully comprehend the phenomenon
of human growth and development. This tale is not without interest
for psychoanalysis, preoccupied as it is with the study of the growth of
the human mind.

The new information recently provided to psychoanalysts adds further information about the life and childhood of Little Hans (Herbert Graf was his real name). Little Hans is one of the few case histories that Freud described as his discipline grew in complexity. The
original narrative he left us suggested that the young boy's phobic
components could be reduced to specific antecedents. This was a
valuable finding for Freud. A year or two earlier, he had hypothesized
the existence of an infantile sexual life simply on the basis of inference and reconstruction, a position that attracted considerable opposition if not downright condemnation. Consequently, the direct
observations of Little Hans's sexuality proved something of a tri-
umph. Freud found what he was looking for; the infantile disorder
was formed from earlier specific libidinal antecedents.

It did not take long for some other analysts to claim that there were
even earlier determinants for the phobia or determinants of an en-

tirely different nature. It is not without interest that the resultant challenge was to the nature of the antecedents and not particularly to the explanatory framework of continuity. These different schools accepted the fundamental role of antecedents and the use of reductionism to unearth them; they simply probed deeper or elsewhere. In these early assaults on Freud's views of Little Hans, the central role of precursors, the concept of continuity, and the use of reductionism to discover the first and apply the second stood unchallenged.

The veritable feast that follows illustrates what has changed since then and what has remained the same. Happily, for the serious student of psychoanalysis, it reflects both old interpretations of new data and new interpretations of old data. Consequently, data and framework come under review.

Elisabeth Young-Bruehl's text describes different data and different frameworks although it is presented simply as a historical paper. She emphasizes the unique role of the Little Hans case history. As a "founding" text, she notes that it conveys not only Freud's view of a phobic boy at the turn of the last century but of his concepts of child development at the time, especially of the centrality of sexuality and the Oedipus complex. She describes how much the case can be linked to the struggle between Anna Freud and Melanie Klein, apparently over the roles of Oedipal and pre-Oedipal determinants as pathogens. When the history of the Freud/Klein struggle is framed in this way, both appear to adhere to preformist and reductionistic frameworks. However, Young-Bruehl transcends this usual argument. She cites a later work of Anna Freud in which constructivism and contextualism offer an entirely different framework (consistent with epigenesis) that establishes a foundation for understanding child development differently. However, the attempt to shift the debate to this level of conceptualization has not proven very successful. Differences between Anna Freud and Melanie Klein continue to be shaped in terms of differences in precursors rather than in their cognitive frames of reference, as if both of them are preformists rather than one being equally planted in epigenesis. Young-Bruehl's contribution is well worth a close read.

This is equally true of Harold Blum's. His is an overview of the Little Hans case. As we have come to expect from his many other contributions, Blum extracts the essentials of the literature and organizes them systematically. He collates the old and new information. He appreciates that advances in understanding of technique and in the development of the mind also require new ways of looking at the old as well as the freshly revealed events. The bulk of his paper is a rich harvest of the different reconstructions made in the course of time in the quest to discern the seminal antecedent pathogens. His work will reward a careful reading, summarizing, as it does, the breadth of psychoanalytic reductionism and speculations. For those who have also had mothers in their etiologic cross-hairs, Olga, Hans's mother, is uncovered as the veritable anti-mother. She had a dreadful childhood of her own. She lost her father at eleven months, two of her brothers killed themselves, and a sister attempted suicide at least once. Poetically, Blum speaks of "the black thread of depression and regression" that runs through her life. As a parent she was rejecting, abandoning: she threatened her son with castration, beat her daughter often (the daughter committed suicide as an adult). Blum speculates that she suffered from a post-partum psychosis, implemented toilet-training poorly, and notes that she exhibited tantrums and jealous rages and seethed with chronic envy. She took her son into bed with her often. Pre-oedipal adherents and attachment theorists are sure to shudder with horror as Blum relates these and other details, while the emphasis on her seductiveness is likely to be targeted by the Oedipal hunters. Many a skilled practitioner of our discipline might well look upon this information and wonder why, in view of the nature and quality of his early life, Hans did not grow up to be the DSM equivalent of a raving lunatic. But Blum tells us that didn't happen. Hans grows devoid of a nervous disorder and ends up with a successful, even creatively tinged career in the arts. In other papers we are to learn that he marries and has a child. Given the nature of the antecedent components, how was this possible? Had he been successfully analyzed after all, at a time when virtually nothing was known about psychoanalytic technique? Blum labels the therapy as a protoanalytic experience of the "heroic" period of our discipline. Noting the good outcome, he wonders if it might be partly attributed to endowment and the young boy's identification with his father.

   If Blum sorts the details, others are to probe them with greater depth. Jerome Wakefield is one of those. He argues that the newly released documents about Little Hans conclusively demonstrate the validity of Bowlby's earlier speculation that Hans suffered from anxious attachment. As Wakefield puts it, the data reflects *real* pathogenic factors in the boy's early life, not merely products of fantasies. These real factors, interweaving with the Oedipal dynamics, are crucial for understanding Hans's disorder. While Bowlby had speculated in an earlier paper that two of five hypothesized antecedent pathogens were present to account for the existence of anxious attachment, Wakefield demonstrates that all five were present by using the newly derestricted data. He calls this approach not reductionism but "retrodictive" thought. Wakefield skillfully pulls events together into causal relationships as he expands the arguments that real experiences, not merely fantasies, produce early phobic states. The skill lies in his cognitive versatility as he searches for "truth" and scientifically sound "causes." There are moments in his essay where he accepts that psychodynamic features can influence the nature of those experiences, but his heart is in the failed real mother-child world. Hans's mother was an "avoidant personality" who "under-indulged" her child.

Wakefield's paper is an important read for any student for several reasons. Firstly, it competently describes another class of antecedents, those that derive from the real world rather than the world of fantasy. Integrating the two worlds is one of the continuing tasks in all analyses. Secondly, it provides a clear summary of Bowlby's views about the early determinants of anxiety, the subsequent elaborations by Ainsworth and Main, and brings us up to date on contemporary points of view. Finally, it underscores how similarly analysts think when they look backward, quite aside from whatever differences they may have about the real or imagined nature of the reconstructed elements. Wakefield is taken with how well Hans does later in life and offers various possibilities, including the idea that the mode of therapeutic action in the initial treatment he received as a little boy helped move him toward a more competent attachment state. Perhaps it is in this way that intense Oedipal conflicts arising from within and all five sources of anxious attachment arising from without may be remedied with relatively few consequences.

Joseph Bierman is prepared for a different answer to the mode of therapeutic action that yields such a successful outcome. He believes that the treatment offered the little boy was more effective than may have been realized. In fact, he is prepared to suggest that the treatment may even conform to certain standards of some modern conceptual outlines of what child analysis is all about.

He describes one such contemporary conceptual outline. Adult analysis is characterized by the sequence of steps established as a patient looks back to uncover the pathogenic components and put them together differently. The analyst is entrusted with certain tasks to guard the integrity of the process. A child analysis succeeds in doing that, but it is particularly important that the analyst also be the guardian of the developmental process by assisting the move forward into new organizational hierarchies. The paper Bierman leans up is a complex one.[1]

Bierman carefully reviews the data on Little Hans to determine to

---

1. Full disclosure: I wrote it.

what degree the case history conforms to contemporary frameworks. It is unlikely that any future paper on the subject will so carefully detail the events that occurred during that time and the roles taken by the primary players. He establishes a sequence of steps that appear to satisfy the criteria he embraces. He doubts if Max, the "father-analyst," or Freud, the "supervisor," could be seen as adequate guardians of the psychoanalytic process and is uncertain as to whether such a process fully materialized. However, he cites one particular intervention, the explanation to Hans that all children have Oedipal feelings, as setting it into motion. In Bierman's judgment there is enough there to suggest that however modest, the analytic treatment was successful. Readers will be able to examine both the conceptual overview that informs his thinking as well as the data that he extracts to determine how convincingly the one fits the other. Can this framework provide a basis for assessing other child work as he implies?

Eugene Halpert's paper enriches by providing another contextual lens. His is an attempt to understand the case by more closely examining the specifics of the familial and societal elements that existed at the time. We cannot, he explains, understand what it was like to live in Vienna at the end of the nineteenth century by thinking of that city the way it exists today. Vienna was the cultural hub of a large empire, a center of the arts and a crucible of intellectual fervor. It was also a place where anti-Semitism was endemic. To be a Jew was a considerable disadvantage and the Grafs were Jewish. Halpert traces the Graf family through generations, demonstrating especially the father-son interaction as it passes down over time. His paper is intended to place Little Hans within the societal and familial contexts of the period. And it certainly succeeds. It contains some carefully researched biographical data of both father and son, Max and Herbert, interspersed with suggested interpretations—at first tentative, then more bold—directed toward Max's unconscious aggression toward his own father and the influence of marital discord upon the erotized rivalry that Herbert had with his parents. Psychoanalysts need to be reminded that their patients are influenced by the abiding societal values and the way those values are implemented by families, and Halpert reminds us. He is not unaware of the maternal side of the pathogenic equation, of course. And in spite of the many flaws in technique (that he repeatedly documents), he concludes that some kind of treatment process must have occurred since Hans did so well in later life. The treatment may have focused upon Oedipal elements, but, he assumes, pre-Oedipal pathogens might have been effectively swept in as well. Thus, while Wakefield takes similar data to point out the importance of anxious attachment as a determinant of Herbert's childhood phobia, Halpert retains the intra-psychic Oedipal emphasis, augmented by the new information about the actualities of the family situation.

The three contributors, Wakefield, Bierman, and Halpert, are concerned with uncovering the antecedent real and fantasized components of the disorder as a way of accounting for the original phobia and—at least for Bierman and Halpert—for explaining the way the treatment worked. Peter Neubauer proposes a decidedly different argument. If the others are the preformists in this metaphoric tale, Neubauer is the epigenesist. Eschewing what he calls the "retrospective reevaluation" (i.e., reductionism) of Little Hans, Neubauer emphasizes the developmental transformations. Citing the same Anna Freud paper that Young-Bruehl had referenced, he proposes that Freud guided Max into tracking the unfolding of the Oedipal conflict, not merely into confirming the antecedent determinants of pathology. This tracking helped Hans transform many of the earlier real and imagined pathogens into a newly emerging phase organization. It is this facilitating that Neubauer regards as analytic and, for him, accounts for the successful outcome. Neubauer credits Freud with having applied the psychoanalytic method to confirming his earlier published theory of mental development as well as for discovering an approach to promote the expected developmental progression in a clinically useful fashion. At times, he is prepared to take to task those who lean too heavily merely upon antecedents. "[A]ll theories which take the first years of life as the basis of normality or pathology will arrive at a simple developmental model. . . . [They] reduce development to basic core-constellation and reduce thereby therapeutic intervention strategies." In his brief contribution, Neubauer presents an entirely different view of the treatment of Little Hans and the ways of conceptualizing child analytic work. Both his view and those ways deserve careful reflection.

As the reader travels along in the section that follows, it will become increasingly evident that it contains a bounty of *contemporary* struggles about theories and findings. How do clinicians integrate the real and the imagined, the preformed and the developmental? Many historical reviews—and this one is certainly destined to become memorable—often have more to say about the present than they do about the past. For the future of psychoanalysis, it may be worth our while to carefully attend to its messages.

Little Hans in the History
of Child Analysis

ELISABETH YOUNG-BRUEHL, Ph.D.

This article places the Little Hans case in the history of child analysis by considering Anna Freud's reflections on the case at various moments in that history and the way in which she took the case as a touchstone while she developed child analysis in directions the case did not point: beyond the infantile neurosis. Her direction is contrasted briefly with Melanie Klein's and the relative lack of attention to adolescent analysis in Freud's work and in Klein's is noted. In a brief biographical sketch of Little Hans in his adolescence, constructed from interview material in the Sigmund Freud Archive, the question is taken up of how an infantile neurosis, even if more or less cured, can suffuse an adolescent character consolidation process.

SIGMUND FREUD'S "ANALYSIS OF A PHOBIA IN A FIVE-YEAR-OLD BOY," first published in 1909, has a unique status in the history of child analysis, which is a history that has hardly begun to become a written history.[1] It also has a unique role in the history of psychoanalysis gen-

---

1. Recently, two European histories of child analysis have been translated into English: Claudine and Pierre Geissmann, *A History of Child Psychoanalysis* (1998; French original 1992) and Alex Holder, *Anna Freud, Melanie Klein, and the Psychoanalysis of Children and Adolescents* (2005; German original 2002). But there are biographies and studies of key figures in the history (Anna Freud, Melanie Klein, Donald Winnicott, etc.), several autobiographies, and many brief studies of particular moments or aspects of the history, mostly in English, French, Spanish, and German (e.g., W. Rehm

---

Elisabeth Young-Bruehl has a private practice in Manhattan where she is on the faculty of the Columbia Center for Psychoanalytic Training and Research. She is the author of many books, including a biography of Anna Freud.

The Psychoanalytic Study of the Child 62, ed. Robert A. King, Peter B. Neubauer, Samuel Abrams, and A. Scott Dowling (Yale University Press, copyright © 2007 by Robert A. King, Peter B. Neubauer, Samuel Abrams, and A. Scott Dowling).

erally, which is a history that has only recently begun to evolve beyond Freud biography.

Der kliene Hans is, on the one hand, a foundling text, with all of the authority that belongs to a beginning. It was the first extended statement by Freud of his ideas about child development referencing any other source than psychoanalytic work with adults.[2] Little Hans's story, as it appears in the case study, is not a reconstruction; it is a narrative of development in process and an infantile neurosis *in statu nascendi*. Hans's Oedipus complex is played out before Freud's eyes as the father rival reports it to him and as the ardently desired young mother (one of Freud's patients, so quite intimately known and quite protected in the text from too much revelation[3]) looms in Hans's thoughts, alluring and frighteningly threatening. His Oedipus complex and his castration anxiety are seen through the lens of what Freud had learned in adult analyses, and to him and his followers at the time they confirmed his theory of neurosis and the map of development that Freud was making.

Since 1909, the case has been the first encounter with child analysis of all who study psychoanalysis, and it has been the introductory text for all child analytic candidates. Throughout the history of child analysis, its huge influence has, however, led some to find it the chief anchor for conservativism within child analysis and within psychoanalysis generally. Melanie Klein and her followers, for the most prominent example, struggled to reveal the pre-oedipal (or as she initially said, the early oedipal) domains that the case did not explore, and her struggle, particularly with Anna Freud, then virtually became the history of child analysis, to the exclusion until recently of almost all other contributors (except Winnicott) and topics. Currently, even some of those who followed Anna Freud have needed to take distance from the case, to the point where a prominent New York child analyst, Samuel Abrams, an editor of the premier journal

---

[1968]). And key figures in the history have written historically, particularly Anna Freud and Melanie Klein.

2. There are, of course, references to child observation in Freud's earlier writings—his use of one of his little daughter Anna's dreams in *The Interpretation of Dreams* is perhaps the most famous example—and he made effective use of pediatric literature in *Three Essays on the Theory of Sexuality*. In the minutes of the Vienna Society before World War I, there are many notes about child observations made by the members, often on their own children. It is important to remember that before the invention of psychoanalysis Freud the neurologist had been on staff seeing child patients at the Kassowitz Institute.

3. On Little Hans's mother, see Jean Bergeret, *La Petit Hans et la Realite* (1987), a book which references his earlier study *La Violence fondamentale* (1984).

in the field, *The Psychoanalytic Study of the Child,* could call the case "the Hansian encumbrance."[4] Abrams was alluding to the psychoanalyst Robert Fliess's wry remark that many medical students, because their first training patient was a cadaver, have an "autopsic encumbrance" as they try to deal with whole, living people.

The encumbrance of the case study, as Abrams presents it, is twofold. First, Hans's Oedipus complex and his castration anxiety dominated Freud's understanding to such an extent that little else appeared; and, then, *Der kliene Hans* became such a lens over many later analysts' eyes that they could see and treat little else in their child cases. By implication, the case is also a technical encumbrance. Little Hans was, of course, not Freud's patient, but his own father's, so psychoanalytic child analysis was launched with a treatment arrangement that was at the time coming into currency in American child guidance centers: a disturbed child is helped through his parents. From that moment forward, child analysis was without a clear method of its own, distinct from child guidance. All later child analysts have had to wrestle with questions about how a child analysis is distinct from child guidance and then child psychotherapy, and later still with questions about how it is distinct from a growing range of technical interventions with children and their families. In the 1920s, and ever since, there have been technical questions about the relationship between child analysis and adult analysis.

These debates within psychoanalysis about child analysis had the further consequence that adolescent analysis was completely overshadowed and was very slow to emerge theoretically and technically. Despite the work of Siegfried Bernfeld and August Aichhorn in the 1920s, there was no founding case for adolescent analysis (and Freud's Dora case was never viewed as such, partly because it was concerned with a particular neurosis, hysteria, partly because it was concerned with a female, which meant that it galvanized debates about female psychology, not female adolescence, and mostly because what Freud had called "the transformations of puberty" were not stressed in it). In 1958, half a century after the publication of *Der kliene Hans,* Anna Freud said (V, p. 136) quite accurately that "adolescence is a neglected period, a stepchild, where analytic thinking is concerned."[5] Since then, while adolescence itself has been changing so

4. My thanks to Samuel Abrams for supplying me with a copy of his unpublished lecture "The Hansian Encumbrance: Therapeutic Action in Child Psychotherapy."

5. I will quote from *The Writings of Anna Freud* by indicating volume and page number in my text.

dramatically in the EuroAmerican world, there has been a great deal of important work by Erik Erikson, Peter Blos, and many more recent contributors, but there was not and still is no text comparable to *Der kliene Hans* in influence or as a foundation for investigation.[6]

As a kind of prolongedly adolescent science, child analysis has a history of identity search, and of balance between acknowledgment of the great achievement of *Der kliene Hans* and exploration of its limitations and delimiting influence. I would like to take up this complex history by examining closely just one strand of it: the history of how Anna Freud read her father's case study and both built upon it and went beyond it—individuated from it. I will proceed by weaving together Anna Freud's responses to the case at different historical vantage points, comparing her prospective and retrospective assessments of it. My primary purpose is to show—as I think it still needs showing—that Anna Freud was not fixated to the stage of child analysis represented by the case. But I also want to turn to an interview with Little Hans, conducted in 1959, and recently made available by the Sigmund Freud Archives, to apply several of Anna Freud's observations about his childhood to his adolescence.

LITTLE HANS'S "INFANTILE NEUROSIS" AND MECHANISMS OF DEFENSE

Three years before her death in 1982 at the age of eighty-seven, Anna Freud wrote a Foreword to a new German edition of her father's case study, which had first appeared when she was fourteen and just beginning to take an interest in the Wednesday meetings in her home of the group that became the Vienna Psychoanalytical Society. Anna Freud took stock of *Der kliene Hans* near the end of her long career, during which she, who had herself been Freud's first multi-year long adolescent case, had emerged as the crucial figure in child analysis's identity search.

In her Foreword, she, naturally, presented the case as the trailblazing work that it was. But she also chose to ignore all questions about it and describe the trail it had blazed as having become a highway, *the* highway. Each of Freud's other case studies, she observed, had focused on a specific form of pathology (a form of neurosis, a perversion, a psychosis), offering interpretation, psychodynamic formula-

---

6. Late adulthood or old age was also overshadowed by the concentration on adulthood and childhood (until Erikson created his lifespan developmental approach) and by the fact that older people were so seldom treated analytically.

tion and suggestion for treatment. But the child study was different, she argued, because it pointed toward a general theory of development (VIII, p. 278):

> What the analysis of Little Hans opened up is a new branch of psychoanalysis, more than the extension of its therapy from the adult to the child—namely, the possibility of a new perspective on the development of the individual and on the successive conflicts and compromises between the demands of the drives, the ego, and the external world which accompany the child's laborious steps from immaturity to maturity.

With this careful formulation, in which she attributes to her father founding authority over the branch of psychoanalysis that she herself had actually established, she was admitting that the case did not found child analysis as a technique. Later (VIII, p. 281–82) she made this limitation explicit:

> we must also be prepared to acknowledge that his statements about the insuperability of the technical difficulties in the way of conducting an analysis in early childhood have not proved to be true. Since 1909, a considerable number of analysts have learned to adapt the method of psychoanalysis to the intrinsic nature of the child and to replace the factor of "authority of a father and a physician [being] united in a single person, and . . . both affectionate care and scientific interest [being] combined" in him by their own interest in the developmental processes and their own empathy with the different modes of expression used by the child. Freud remains right in asserting that the technique so laboriously gained in the analyses of adults is not directly applicable to children; that children are unwilling or unable to associate freely; that they neither make nor keep a contract with the analyst to be candid and honest; that they are unreliable collaborators; that they shun insights offered them through interpretations; that they rebel against renunciations; and that they prefer to act out transferences rather than use them to gain understanding of past emotional relationships. That despite these obstacles it was possible to forge an analytic-therapeutic access to the child could not be predicted more than half a century ago.

Implicit in this statement is Anna Freud's long-running disagreement with Melanie Klein about the differences between adult analysis and child analysis, which she always stressed, while Melanie Klein proceeded from the assumption that child analysis and adult analysis do not differ fundamentally.

Even though she presented her father as the founder of the new branch of psychoanalysis—the branch dealing with development generally—Anna Freud could state clearly (VIII, p. 279) that Freud's intention in writing the case had been quite focused and specific: he had looked to Hans's neurosis, his phobia, for confirmation of a hypothesis about how infantile sexuality's components are the "motive forces of all the neurotic symptoms of later life." This crucial admission connects to her clear retrospective understanding that her father's intention—an intention that was shared by all adult analysts for decades—implied that behind every adult neurosis lies a child neurosis completely comparable to the adult neurosis in its psychodynamics. The similarities between child neuroses and adult neuroses were consistently stressed in all the work that immediately succeeded the Little Hans case and the later case of the Wolf Man (1918) as well as in Freud's revisiting of the Little Hans case in *Symptoms, Inhibitions and Anxiety* (1926), where he used the case to revise his definition of anxiety and bring the new definition to bear on his theory of the neurosis. As Anna Freud pointed out in a 1970 retrospective statement "The Infantile Neurosis," which takes the second anxiety theory into account (VII, 191):

> what was demonstrated in the [Little Hans and Wolf Man case histories] was the fact that both, the adult and the infantile disorder, shared the same motivation by conflict, the same construction, the employment of the same mechanisms, and that their symptoms represented identical attempts at conflict solution, inadequate as the latter may be if viewed from the aspect of reality adaptation. What I am describing here is the well-known formula which covers the formation of neuroses in general: conflict, followed by regression; regressive aims arousing anxiety; anxiety warded off by means of defense; conflict solution via compromise; symptoms.

Anna Freud herself had made one of the most important contributions to study of "the formation of neuroses in general" by combining the insights of the Little Hans case and the review of it in *Symptoms, Inhibitions, and Anxiety* with her own first decade of work as a child analyst to produce a catalogue of the mechanisms of defense that are common to child and adult neuroses. When she wrote her 1982 Foreword to *Der kleine Hans*, she noted that her father had shown how the boy's inner life was a tissue of "painful and anxiety-arousing contradictions"; that he was an "amiable, affectionate, easily moved, compassionate" boy, attached to and dependent upon his parents, but also in the grip of his defenses against his drives and death wishes. She offers a veritable summary of *The Ego and the Mechanisms of Defense* (1936), the book she had given to her father as a gift on his 80th birthday, by describing as follows what Freud had seen:

Here the observer—and the reader—witnesses for the first time, not by way of reconstruction but directly from the child, the struggle to transform the drives, and learns about the means at the disposal of the human ego and superego for the socialization of the individual. In the case of Little Hans, it was the task of *repression* to remove the aggressive wishes (stemming from the anal-sadistic phase); it is the task of *reaction formations* to transform jealousy of siblings[7] into love for them, exhibitionism into modesty, pleasure in soiling into disgust. *Displacement* from humans (father, mother) to animals (lions, giraffe, horse) is the order of the day, at the same time as attempts are made to divert threatening instinctual dangers from the parental home to more distant parts of the external world. *Identification with the aggressor* determines the role play in which the child takes on the part of the dangerous, biting, kicking horse. *Projection* externalizes his own bad impulses and makes him experience them as coming from his father. *Denial in fantasy* or *in action* serves to assuage the narcissistic injury sustained by the realization of the better physical equipment of the father and the child's own inferiority in relation to the bigger, stronger, and perhaps omnipotent and omniscient man.

But, at the same time that Anna Freud was doing so much with her systematic approach to the defenses both to establish the "formation of the neuroses in general," and to supply the detailed inquiry into the defenses that helped her colleague Berta Bornstein's pioneering work in analyzing children's defenses, her work in the late 1920s and early 1930s was also directed at, on the one hand, distinguishing between normal (not neurotic) childhood symptomatology, and, on the other hand, revealing the kinds of child pathology that lie outside of "the neuroses in general," and that were not part of Little Hans's story.

Taking up the first of these topics, she was able to make even in her early work a very important revision of her father's case study and his commentary upon it in *Symptoms, Inhibitions and Anxiety*.[8] Freud had argued that what distinguished Hans with his neurosis from a normal boy with typical mother-love and father-fear was "the replacement of his father by a horse." Anna Freud had questioned this formulation in a paper (II, 71–82) entitled "A Counterpart to the Animal Phobias of Children," which was later incorporated into *The Ego and the Mech-*

7. Hans had, of course, only one sibling, his little sister, but Anna Freud, who had five bigger ones, tended to think in plurals.

8. In the next two paragraphs, I am repeating an observation I made in *Anna Freud: A Biography*, p. 182.

anisms of Defense (where its questioning of her father's work was very understated but nonetheless very far-seeing and ambitious). She compared Little Hans to a nevenyear old patient of her own who hated and feared his father as a rival in relation to his mother. This boy had produced not a phobia but a fantasy in which he had a tame lion—a substitute for his father—which loved him and frightened everybody else. Another patient, ten years old, had not just a tame lion but an entire circus of animals that he had trained to be good to one another and not to attack humans. In this circus master's fantasy, the father was turned into the animals, and their tamed and appropriated strength protected him against any renewal of his anxiety about his father. If fantasies such as these are successful in denying reality, Anna Freud argued, the ego has no need "to resort to defensive measures against its instinctual impulses and to the formation of a neurosis."

Freud's formulation—"the replacement of his father by a horse"— had, Anna Freud implied (II, p. 74), obscured a key difference between normal and neurotic displacements. A normal boy could also replace his father with a horse; something more has to happen for a phobia to result. "The efforts of the infantile ego to avoid unpleasure by directly resisting external impressions belong to the sphere of normal psychology. Their consequences may be momentous for the formation of the ego and of character, but they are not pathogenic." In Anna Freud's estimation, the two fantasies that Little Hans had produced as his phobia was clearing up, one about a plumber fitting him with bigger buttocks and penis and one about himself as caring for a number of children—fantasies about being equal to his father and like his mother—"belong to the sphere of normal psychology." With this kind of distinction, Anna Freud was moving child observation and analysis in the direction of study of normal development and founding the "new branch of psychoanalysis."

NORMAL DEVELOPMENT AND DEVELOPMENTAL LINES

But, at the same time, as I noted, Anna Freud was exploring pathologies that were not "the infantile neurosis," which she took to be centered on the Oedipus complex, just as her father had argued in Little Hans: "the child, unable to solve either the oedipus complex or the castration complex, or a combination of both, regresses to earlier fixation points" (V, 302). Her exploration came about when psychoanalytic clinics for treating children were set up, like the child guidance clinic attached to the Lehrininstitut of the Vienna Psychoanalytic Society in 1924. In a 1956 paper (V, 303) entitled "The Assessment of Borderline Cases," Anna Freud wrote as a historian:

> What came as a surprise were the types of cases with which clinics were confronted [when they opened]. The majority of the children who were referred did not fit the picture of the infantile neurosis. Many children were seen whose difficulties or conflicts were far removed from the oedipal scene, who had in fact never reached the oedipal level and consequently could not be described as having regressed from it. It was far from easy to bring order into the chaos of clinical pictures.
>
> There are, for one, children who suffer from disturbances of their vital functions, such as eating, sleeping, later on learning; or who show unusual delays in acquiring vital capacities such as movement, cleanliness, speech. There are many whose development has been arrested, especially at the points of transition between one developmental phase and the next. Cases of this kind crowd out those with phobias and incipient obsessional neuroses, even though the later two are not completely absent.

Unlike many who write about the history of child analysis, Anna Freud was always careful to set the general historical context and to emphasize that different historical circumstances (like wartime conditions) produce different clinical populations and that different populations come to clinics in different circumstances, too. Little Hans himself was the child of progressive, analytically informed parents who had tried to provide him with "sexual enlightenment" and to refrain from severe restrictions (although his mother was unable to refrain from threatening to send him to the doctor to have his widdler cut off if he continued to touch it). As psychoanalytic ideas about child-rearing spread, they had an impact upon the population brought to psychoanalytic clinics and the problems characteristic of them, as Anna Freud noted in this same paper: "We know that the absence or the mitigation of the masturbation conflict has done a great deal to change the picture of the infantile neurosis. On the other hand, this does not explain why we see the disturbances so much earlier now." The relative infrequency of Little Hans–like infantile neuroses in the clinic population could be taken as a sign of progressivism in child-rearing, but what factors influence difficulties and conflicts "far removed from the oedipal scene"?

Anna Freud pondered the question in the 1930s but did not write about it then as she went on to address the disturbances she saw by making a second fundamental contribution: her systematization of her father's (unelaborated) notion of "developmental lines." It was the framework of "the developmental lines" that, she hoped, would bring order into the chaos of clinical pictures she encountered in those children who were not like Little Hans.

She was able, as her experience gathered and as she worked collaboratively with other child analysts in her various clinic settings, to come to three conclusions that are tacit in the 1956 paper I have just quoted, but which came out more clearly in her 1965 summa *Normality and Pathology in Childhood*. The first was that, while in adults individual symptoms usually have a sure place in a personality structure, the same is not true for children. As she explained (VI, p. 151): "In children, symptoms occur just as often in isolation, or are coupled with other symptoms and personality traits of a different nature and unrelated origin. Even well-defined obsessional symptoms such as bedtime ceremonials or counting compulsions are found in children with otherwise uncontrolled, restless, impulsive, i.e., hysterical personalities; or hysterical conversions, phobic trends, psychosomatic symptoms are found in character settings which are obsessional. Single delinquent acts are committed by children who are well adapted and otherwise conscientious. Children who are out of control at home submit to authority at school and vice versa."

A second conclusion was that there is no certainty that a particular type of infantile neurosis will be the forerunner of a same type of adult neurosis, while there is much evidence pointing in the opposite direction. Early delinquent and impulsive behavior does not lead to later delinquency or criminality and may, on the contrary, lead to obsessionality. Many hysterical children grow into obsessionals. Many children who have obsessional symptoms that resemble adult obsessional symptoms develop not an obsessional neurosis in later life but a schizoid or schizophrenic state. The course a child takes depends on how the child's ego and superego develop, on how strongly early symptoms remain as residues in a later configuration, or on whether early ambivalence conflicts and compulsions are signs of splits and disharmonies in an evolving structure that may give way to psychotic disintegration.

Thirdly, and most generally, Anna Freud concluded that "the field of mental disorders in childhood is more extensive than expected from experience with adult psychopathology" (VI, 153). She explained that (non-organic) somatic disturbances and developmental delays and retardations, the early disturbances of narcissism and object relations, and the states caused by uncontrolled aggression and sexual drives can be described as failures to reach the phallic-oedipal stage (where infantile neuroses start), or as distorted and chaotic defense organizations, or as reflections of underdeveloped superego structuration. But, generally, she kept open the question of whether these explanations, which framed the disturbances as pre-stages of infantile neuroses, were sufficient or whether the disturbances should sometimes be framed in other terms, for example as "abortive neuroses, i.e. unsuccessful, incomplete, short-term attempts of the ego agencies to come to terms with and modify the drives" (VI, 154).

By making a thorough map of developmental lines that embraced physical, development, ego and superego development, affect regulation and object relations development, developmental capacities for various activities, and so forth, Anna Freud hoped to be able to guide clinicians to more detailed and exact assessments and to techniques that would be appropriate to the non-infantile neurotic disturbances. She did not assume that the kind of child analysis—growing from the Little Hans prototype—that could cure an infantile neurosis was appropriate for a developmental disturbance or what would later be called a "developmental pathology."

The technical implication of these conclusions was the very one that Samuel Abrams came to in arguing that child psychotherapy free of the Hansian encumbrance—that is, of the idea that therapy must uncover a child's Oedipus complex and castration anxiety to cure the child—can focus on the disturbance uncovered in a therapy without assuming in advance that the disturbance is an infantile neurosis, even if the symptoms look like those of an infantile neurosis. The therapist, then, does not have to operate as the recipient of an infantile neurotic transference—as an oedipal object—but can be free to supply just what the child needs in order to overcome developmental disturbances not of the Hansian type.

Anna Freud's extension of her work beyond the infantile neurosis came about as she and her collaborators treated disturbed children of Little Hans's age or older (latency children) but not suffering from an infantile neurosis. That is, she proceeded by distinguishing these children from the Little Hans prototype and vastly extending the psychoanalytic nosology to include other types of disturbance than the infantile neurosis. As her work developed, she and her colleagues were able to treat children younger than five. Her route was, thus, quite different than Melanie Klein's; for Klein, whose work was so decisively influenced by the decision she made early in her practice (which was not conducted in clinic settings) to analyze children younger than Little Hans, rejected the Little Hans prototype. For her, all children, no matter what their later symptomology, start off with a trauma—"the weaning trauma"—and develop, then, in reaction to that trauma. The weaning trauma (and later what she called "the paranoid—schizoid position") became, for her, what the Oedipus complex and castration complex had been for Freud, the nucleus of the neuroses and psychoses.

In very simple terms, Anna Freud and Melanie Klein had different ambitions in the period that has been called "the golden age of child analysis,"[9] the 1930s, and these ambitions led the two in very different directions. Anna Freud saw a vast range of infant and childhood disturbances beyond the Hansian infantile neurosis and wanted to "bring order" to that field by establishing a richly elaborated series of normal developmental lines against which to understand every variation in that vast range. Melanie Klein, by contrast, wanted to relocate the nucleus of all pathologies—to move it into the preoedipal—and center it on the weaning trauma and all of the innate aggression mobilized in and by the weaning trauma. This ambition eventually led her to look at each child as moving (or failing to move, or moving incompletely or distortedly) from "the paranoid-schizoid position" to "the depressive position." Because of the intensive and extensive study that Melanie Klein and her followers gave this one (in Anna Freud's terms) developmental line, her cases have had an importance in modern psychoanalysis almost equal to Freud's study of Little Hans's Oedipus complex and castration anxiety. But from the Anna Freudian perspective, Klein focused on one transition along one developmental line, which meant that the Kleinian theory was right and illuminating and therapeutic for some children but not others—and not for a *Der kliene Hans.*

DIAGNOSTIC PROFILES FOR CHILDREN, ADULTS, AND ADOLESCENTS

It was in the inaugural time of child analytic practice and the first work with children in clinics that Little Hans, Herbert Graf, presented himself, age 19, to Sigmund Freud. "I am Little Hans," he an-

9. This phrase was used by Helen Ross and Bertram Lewin in their *Psychoanalytic Education in the United States,* which contains (in Chapter XXIV) the first effort to write a history of child analysis (although only in America). This important history makes it very clear why child analysis, after its golden age in the 1930s, had such a slow and troubled development within American psychoanalysis, where the vast majority of American Psychoanalytic Association psychoanalysts were medically trained analysts of adults who treated child analysis like an unruly child with no technique or standards of its own. Ross and Lewin viewed the history of child analysis in America between the golden age and the 1950s in developmental terms: "The early vigorous infancy of child analysis was thrust into the rule-making of the latency period, which continued until 1958 with the setting up of standards by the [American] Board of Professional Standards." Not until the latency ended was child analysis taught in American institutes with any regularity or rigor.

nounced in 1922, and proceeded to tell Freud the story of how he
had come across his case in his father's library while it was being
packed up to be moved. His parents were divorcing, and he acknowledged to Freud that their divorce had been very hard on him, although he had come through it, as through his adolescence "without
any damage," as Freud estimated in his Postscript to the case, where
he also remarks, generally, that the "strapping youth" was "perfectly
well and suffered from no troubles or inhibitions." (Later documen-
tation makes it clear that Herbert Graf's younger sister, who eventually committed suicide in America after the failure of her own marriage, had not fared so well, either at the time of the parental divorce
or in her childhood, when she had suffered from her mother's fa-
voritism toward her brother and relative indifference to her.[10])

In this Postscript, Freud was also making the first longitudinal or
follow-up study of a treated child who had reached his adolescence.
That Herbert Graf was so "perfectly well" seemed confirmatory of
Freud's theory about his phobia and of the (adult) analytic technique for making the unconscious conscious. Critics who had railed
against the case by foretelling a terrible future for a child who had
been "robbed of his innocence" by his father's offer of sexual enlightenment and psychoanalysis would, Freud hoped, be silenced by the
Postscript.

But what is apparent in the story of Herbert Graf, as he revealed it
in his 1959 interview with Kurt Eissler, representing the Sigmund
Freud Archives, and then in his 1972 autobiography *Memoirs of an Invisible Man,* is that more understanding of adolescence and the transition to early adulthood would have helped Freud himself and the
early analysts, so mesmerized by *Der kliene Hans* and by the focus on
childhood, to see how an infantile neurosis, even one "cured," can
translate into character and shape a life, even a very professionally
successful and rich one.

In his late adolescence, at the beginning of a career that eventually
led him to be the operatic stager (*Opern Regisseur*) at some of the
world's greatest opera houses, including the Metropolitan in New
York (1936–1950), Herbert Graf, had needed to "flee" Vienna, which

10. The sister's story is told—or alluded to—in interviews that Kurt Eissler conducted (December 16, 1952) with the father, Max Graf, and (October 22, 1959) with
Herbert Graf. Both father and son speak of the mother's attitude toward the sister as
troubled, distant, and of the mother, generally, as asocial, afraid (perhaps phobic?) to
go out. Max Graf speaks of her hysteria and says that she was depressed after sexual
intercourse. Both interviews are available through the Sigmund Freud Archives web-
site.

he considered "a very decadent place" at the end of the Austrian Empire. "The misery of the Austrian," he told Eissler in his rather broken German sentences (translated here), was for him:

> a personal misery because of the divorce of the parents, a certain amount of poverty . . . And all these pictures of Hofmannsthal and Schoenberg and Freud, and all this . . . somehow we young people left Vienna in an opposition and went to Germany for that reason. As far away from Vienna as possible! . . . I went to Muenster in Westphalia, for instance, to begin with. So we had a sort of aversion against the whole [Viennese] world . . . [Psychoanalysis] included, practically [symbolizing the Viennese world] . . . But that, even if it was a positive reaction, still it was all too complicated . . .

This reminiscence led Graf to a reflection on psychoanalysis, which he said was "the most wonderful thing on earth as, as a thought, as a science and everything, but it is too easily . . . I mean the hands of the people who handle it are often not worthy . . . of handling it . . . " He had had his attitude toward Viennese psychoanalysis complicated later by seeking out a psychoanalyst during a difficult period in his marriage and finding that "I didn't like it at all!" He claimed that it was the common sense of his wife that helped him, not his analyst.

As an adolescent, he had to stay away, he said, from that Viennese sensibility that he described as too full of *Schadenfreude* for his taste— although he often returned to Vienna, where his mother lived. Further, he explained that in his work, too, he had needed to stay away from what he called the "floating emotionalism" of Romanticism. "I am afraid now of Tristan." He preferred Bach, Mozart; he preferred to "feel more solid": and thus he could appreciate the longing for system in Schoenberg, Berg, even though he acknowledged that most people could not hear in their music the control, the structure. In his field of opera, he said, he was engaged in a battle between styles of conducting, too, with his own mentor, Toscanini, who "first let us study the letter of the thing and then to come back to the spirit of the thing by analysis," contrasted to those who were all for "the great emotional experience," like Furtwangler or even Bruno Walter (whom he nonetheless considered "a good father"). As an opera stager, he abhorred self-aggrandizing people who insisted on doing things their own way, while he preferred and followed "the Toscanini principle" of analyzing a work carefully and then coming to the form of the production. His father, he said, was a very controlled man, sometimes to the point of being detached in a Goethean manner, aloof, but his mother was "much less controlled," even hysterical.

When Herbert Graf was invited to become the general manager at the Zurich opera house in the year that he spoke with Eissler, 1959, he viewed the opportunity as a kind of new beginning, a chance to make "an embryo model opera house." He imagined that he might, in a small house with a good subsidy, be free of "the star system" and the kinds of over-bearing egos that had made his professional development conflictual—that had forced him to put artistic decisions aside and obey administrative orders from the men who were his bosses. He liked the idea that in Zurich there were no resident conductors or permanent directors, only visitors; that he might try out the idea of an ensemble company, "a new principle, new things." He was, it seems, still wrestling with the question of his adolescence: how to be like his father, a professional man of the musical world, but with an identity of his own, in control, and not swept over by too much emotion, or too much egoism.

One can imagine Anna Freud reading this interview (as she may very well have in 1959, since Eissler shared so much of his research with her) and hearing in it the adolescent process of seeking control over frightening drives, seeking rationality and service to a model of good analysis (in the musical and the psychoanalytical senses of the word) and avoiding (but not to the point of cool detachment) emotionalism of the sort he associated with his mother—although he always returned to her, and to Vienna, for visits. Like so many adolescents, he set up a parental binary in himself and associated it with places: exhibitionistic and emotional Vienna vs. modest and controlled Westphalia. His character then became an orchestration of these two major identificatory chords and their minor chords (the lovable in motherly Vienna that drew him back, the over-controlled or aloof qualities in fatherly Westphalia that repelled him).

After her work on the mechanisms of defense, the developmental lines and the developmental disorders, Anna Freud made her fourth major contribution, that is, The Diagnostic Profiles for doing psychoanalytic assessment. She began with a Profile for children, but then in the 1960s, working with colleagues at the Hampstead Center, she supervised the creation of profiles for babies, adults, and adolescents. Out of the work on adolescents came the European Association for Adolescent Psychoanalysis (EAAP), initiated by her colleagues Moses Laufer and Egle Laufer. In her profiles, Anna Freud consistently took up the strand of her commentary on *Der Kliene Hans* that had been her first original contribution to psychoanalysis: the strand of identifying normal fantasies of the sort through which Herbert Graf came to organize his life—he who had had childhood normal fantasies of having big, strong equipment like that of his controlled father and caring for babies like his emotional mother.

Anna Freud's Diagnostic Profiles, which have provided generations of clinicians with thorough guidance in assessment and directions for treatment, were being used with adolescents at her clinic by the late 1960s, so she would have had that work on her mind when in 1970 she, age 75, was in Geneva, Switzerland, and a distinguished looking man of 67 came up to her and introduced himself: "I am Little Hans."[11]

BIBLIOGRAPHY

BERGERET, J. (1984). *La violence fondamentale*. Paris: Dunod.

——— (1987). *Le Petit Hans et la Realite*. Paris: Payot.

EISSLER, R. ET AL., ED. (1977). *Psychoanalytic Assessment: The Diagnostic Profile*. New Haven, CT: Yale Univ. Press.

FREUD, A. (1936). The Ego and the Mechanisms of Defense. *The Writings of Anna Freud*, vol. 2. New York: International Universities Press, 1966.

——— (1970). The Infantile Neurosis: Genetic and Dynamic Considerations. *The Writings of Anna Freud*, VII, pp. 189–203.

——— (1980). Foreword to "Analysis of a Phobia in a Five-year-old Boy." *The Writings of Anna Freud*, VIII, pp. 277–282.

FREUD, S. (1909). Analysis of a Phobia in a Five-year-old Boy. *Standard Edition*, 10: 3–152.

——— (1926). Inhibitions, Symptoms, and Anxiety. *Standard Edition*, 20: 77–178.

GEISSMANN, C. & P. GEISSMANN (1998). *A History of Child Psychoanalysis*. New York: Routledge.

HOLDER, A. (2005). *Anna Freud, Melanie Klein, and the Psychoanalysis of Children and Adolescents*. London: Karnac Books.

KLEIN, M. (1932). *The Psycho-analysis of Children*. London: Hogarth.

REHM, W. (1968). *Die psychoanalytische Erziehungslehre*. Munich: Piper.

ROSS, H. & B. LEWIN (1960). *Psychoanalytic Education in the United States*. New York: Norton.

YOUNG-BRUEHL, E. (1988). *Anna Freud: A Biography*. New York: Summit Books.

11. Geissmann (1998), p. 21, referencing Bergeret (1987).

Little Hans

A Contemporary Overview

HAROLD P. BLUM, M.D.

The case of Little Hans, an unprecedented experimental child analytic treatment, is re-examined in the light of newer theory and newly derestricted documents. The understanding of the complex over-determination of Hans's phobia was not possible in the heroic age of psychoanalysis. Distance and de-idealization of the pioneer past have potentiated current reformulation of the case. Trauma, child abuse, parental strife, and the pre-oedipal mother-child relationship now emerge as important issues. With limited, yet remarkable help, Little Hans nevertheless had the ego strength and resilience to resume progressive development and to forge a successful creative career. The new knowledge about Little Hans, his family, culture and child development provides new perspectives and raises new questions and challenges to the century-old pioneer report and formulations confirming and largely limited to the child's positive Oedipus complex.

INTRODUCTION

LITTLE HANS'S PHOBIA CAN NOW BE ELABORATED AND REFORMU-
lated in the light of contemporary psychoanalytic thought. The newly
de-restricted interviews of Max Graf (1952) and of Herbert Graf
(1959) contribute to the new data and inferences, which add to, ex-

---

Clinical Professor of Psychiatry and Training Analyst, N.Y.U., Executive Director of The Sigmund Freud Archives, and the former editor of *The Journal of the American Psychoanalytic Association*.

The Psychoanalytic Study of the Child 62, ed. Robert A. King, Peter B. Neubauer, Samuel Abrams, and A. Scott Dowling (Yale University Press, copyright © 2007 by Robert A. King, Peter B. Neubauer, Samuel Abrams, and A. Scott Dowling).

tend, and modify the original case report and raise questions about the initial conclusions. Little Hans was written before many of Freud's major theoretical advances, for example, anxiety in response to danger, dual drives, structural theory, and non-defense ego functions. Countei-transferences to parent and to child were not yet appreciated during the treatment of Little Hans, January through April 1908. Contemporary theory and a longitudinal life perspective over the many years after the case report (1909) have afforded opportunities to update understanding beyond what was then possible. In particular, the relationship of Little Hans's mother with her husband and children began to emerge as a significant influence on her son's development and phobic disorder. In the light of new information her influence is seen as even more central to our understanding of Little Hans. The present reconsideration illustrates the value of historical reconstruction in the ongoing development of psychoanalytic theory. With all of its pioneering limitations, Little Hans then becomes psychoanalytic theory in progress rather than only of historical interest, a relic of a bygone era. Fascinating to generations of psychoanalysts, this reconsideration of Little Hans is particularly appropriate for the 150th anniversary of Freud's birth (1856–2006).

Freud's case history of Little Hans marked the inception of child psychoanalysis. Though child analysis was not then recognized, Freud later referred to "this first analysis of a child"(1909, p. 148). Psychoanalysis was then in its own childhood and psychoanalytic studies of infant and child development were just being contemplated. Freud's Wednesday night study group had been initiated in 1902, and Freud had asked his first students and adherents to observe their own children and to take notes about their development. Max Graf, one of the earliest members of the group, followed Freud's advice and with his notes provided the data for Freud's case history of his son's treatment. Freud assisted the father and in effect supplied the analytic principles, knowledge, direction and "supervision" that allowed the treatment to progress to a successful conclusion. The brief treatment, essentially from January through April 1908, was thus the first application of psychoanalysis to the understanding and treatment of a young child, the first supervised psychoanalysis (Glenn, 1980), a first form of analytic family therapy and child guidance.

Freud's reconstructions about the childhood origins of adult neurosis were now validated in a paradigmatic case report of "Little Hans." Freud could not be charged with suggesting, selecting, or fabricating the data since the clinical material was almost entirely provided by the five-year-old boy's father. This was important in the circumstances where Freud was treated with derision in academia and the media. Despite possibly distressing self-revelation, and anticipated public opprobrium, Max Graf gave his consent to Freud to publish the case.

BACKGROUND

Before Little Hans, Freud had relied on reconstruction from adult cases for his formulations of the infantile neurosis and childhood sexual conflict and trauma. Here was complementary data and verification of psychoanalytic findings directly from a child. "Surely there must be a possibility of observing in children at first hand and in all the freshness of life the sexual impulses and wishes which we dig out so laboriously in adults." (Freud, 1909, p. 6). Freud noted that the parents of Little Hans had been among his closest adherents, and he had received regular reports from them about their son. Freud had met Little Hans only once during the treatment and relied entirely upon the father to conduct the analytic work. He revealed that Olga, the mother of Little Hans, had been his patient for an indeterminate length of time. We learn from the Eissler interview of Max Graf in 1952, that two of Olga's brothers shot themselves to death, and one talented sister attempted suicide before the marriage. This information now confirms D. Abrams' (2005) identification of Olga as "the nineteen year old girl with almost pure obsessional ideas" whom Freud wrote that he took into treatment in the summer of 1897. Freud reported to Fliess, July 7, 1897, that her father died "before the child was 11 months old, but two brothers, one of them three years older than the patient, shot themselves." Her father's death and her brothers' suicides could well have traumatized Olga and her entire family. The youngest of five children, suicide and repeated object loss was a dark cloud in the life of "Little Hans's" mother, with possible biogenetic as well as traumatic determinants. Freud, therefore, had knowledge of the mother's personality and the disorder for which she sought his help, even before the birth of "Little Hans," on April 10, 1903. Analytic comments on Little Hans's earlier life had been published by Freud in his paper, "The Sexual Enlightenment of Children" (1907), in which the patient is referred to by his later English name of "Little Herbert." Little Hans is also briefly mentioned by Freud in "On the Sexual Theories of Children" (1908). These two papers were followed by the long 142-page report and discussion of "Little Hans." Later, Freud referred to the phobia of Little Hans in his comments "On Animal Phobias in Totem and Taboo" (1913) and his discussions of anxiety after the introduction of the structural theory (1926). Freud thought that only a parent's special knowledge of his own childhood would make it possible to correctly interpret the child's remarks. Freud stated, "it was only because the authority of a father and a physician were united in a single person, and because in him both affectionate care and scientific interest were combined, that it was possible in this one instance to apply the method" (1909, p. 5). Retrospectively, we might attribute these remarks to the naiveté and then limited experience of the founder of psychoanalysis, except that in another decade, he would undertake the analysis of his own daughter. In the subsequent development of psychoanalysis, a deeper understanding of the interplay between transference and counter-transference and the real relationship between analyst and patient gradually evolved.

The analysis of Little Hans occurred in its own time, place, and culture. When Max Graf met his future wife, Olga Honig, circa 1897, he learned from her that she was in psychoanalytic treatment with Sigmund Freud. He was intrigued with her regular descriptions of her treatment sessions, which led him to personally meet Freud. (Max would later repeat the pattern and regularly report to Freud about his own treatment experience with Little Hans.) Max married Olga in 1898 and Freud became a friend of the couple, who were both violinists with shared musical interests. He went to dinner many times at their apartment and was personally acquainted with Little Hans from the time he was born. Freud would then see Olga in treatment as well as at home with Max. He saw Max also at the Wednesday Night Society meetings and for some individual chats. Moreover, Max had become an admired, popular music critic, evoking Olga's envy. Actually, Freud's remarkable pioneering essay (1905), "Psychopathic Characters on the Stage" foreshadowed Max's applied psychoanalytic interpretation of music and Little Hans's career as a stage director. Freud analyzed the relationship between forms of art, especially drama, and their effect on the audience. This paper was never published during Freud's lifetime but was given by Freud to Max Graf. Max Graf then arranged for its publication in English in 1942. Freud then clearly had a high regard for Max Graf, and in 1909 suggested that Max work analytically on Mozart's relationship with Don Juan.

When Max, like Dora, considered not bringing up his child as Jewish in an anti-Semitic milieu, Freud advised against conversion, emphasizing the value of a Jewish identity and not being intimidated. In a far reaching footnote pertinent to Little Hans's castration anxiety,

Freud first connected circumcision to social anti-semitism. Freud
(1909, p. 36) averred, "The castration complex is the deepest source
of anti-semitism, . . . little boys hear that a Jew has something cut off
his penis . . . and this gives them a right to despise Jews." In an un
canny foretoken of the boy's analysis, Freud bought a rocking horse
as a gift for the third birthday of Little Hans (or possibly for a later
birthday, according to the inconsistent memory of Max Graf).

MARRIAGE

There were problems in the parents' marriage to begin with, only
hinted at in the case report, yet clearly stated in the Eissler interviews
of Max and Herbert Graf. Freud stated that the parents would use no
more coercion than necessary in their parenting. Freud, however,
did not comment about the fractious marriage or the disturbed, unstable, dysfunctional personality of Olga Graf, the mother of Little
Hans. Rather, Freud (p. 36) remarked, "We must say a word or two
on behalf of Hans' excellent and devoted mother." What was Freud
thinking when a statement about her parenting required much more
depth? Freud was preserving the confidentiality of his patient, but
the case report is indicative of unrecognized transference-counter-
transference complications involving the parents and Little Hans. As
in all of Freud's case histories, the mother was in relative eclipse compared to the role of the father. In addition, the written data was entirely from the father with his own agenda, although Freud had other
information from the mother. Currently, her very significant influence is apparent, in contrast to her minimal importance in the interpretations of the 1909 paper. The possible effect of the maternal
black thread of depression and regression is overshadowed in the
oedipal framework of Freud's formulations. In the interview of Little
Hans in 1958, Herbert Graf confirms that his mother was always very
nervous. This comment is a son's understatement of his mother's
fragility and instability. Little Hans was exposed to threats of abandonment and rejection by his mother and to her actual rejection of
his sister. In the case report, Little Hans heard his sister Hanna's
screams as she was beaten by their mother. When Hans later states
that he would like to whip horses, his father asked if he would like to
do it as Mummy beats Hanna. Hans denied that the horses would be
harmed, but when his father asked which person he really wanted to
beat, Hans responded that he wanted to hit his mother. His father
was transiently attuned to his son's aggression toward his mother, but
mainly kept to Freud's and his own interpretation of the oedipal

son's rivalry and aggression toward the father. The rejection, neglect, and beating of her six-month-old infant daughter may well constitute unacknowledged child abuse. It was simultaneously emotional abuse of Little Hans. The implied maternal abuse and neglect of Hanna were not addressed by Max Graf nor by Freud. Freud's silence about Olga Graf's probable traumatic child abuse of Hanna, and seductive, intrusive over-stimulation of Little Hans is all the more remarkable in view of his previous emphasis on the pathogenic importance of "seduction trauma." Seduction trauma had been renounced as the exclusive basis of later psychopathology, but the importance of psychic trauma had been retained. While avoiding published criticism of his former patient, Olga Graf, Freud seems to have had an overriding interest at that time in establishing oedipal conflict as central to the etiology of neurosis. Anticipating later theory, Little Hans's experience of maternal seduction could be conceptualized as a phase specific oedipal trauma. Witnessing the abuse of his sister would likely have intensified the guilt of Little Hans's own hostile sibling rivalry. His own wishes to eliminate his sister were shared with his mother, and her abusive behavior would have exacerbated his father's conflicts with his mother. We do not have information about the pregnancy, delivery, or the pre-oedipal development of "Little Hans," but the developmental data suggest problems in both attachment and separation individuation. His mother was very likely distressed during her pregnancy with Hanna. Max Graf later reported that his wife had been upset after intercourse during the pregnancy. Her rejection of Hanna immediately after birth is compatible with an agitated postpartum depression, continuing pre-partum disturbance. In the interview, Max Graf described his wife as shy, not feeling well, and socially avoidant; she could not get along with anyone. She would tear up the professional manuscripts of her husband, an eminent musicologist, further indicating tantrums and jealous rage reactions. Given her own musical talents, her being socially disadvantaged as a woman and Jewish could well have intensified her envy of males.

Because of Little Hans's habitual masturbation, his mother directly threatened castration, warning that she would have the doctor cut his off his "widdler." His father also reinforced castration anxiety by indicating that Little Hans would not overcome his phobia unless he stopped masturbating, conveying that masturbation was indeed a bad, injurious activity which was forbidden. The view of masturbation as a noxious activity, a damaging "bad habit" was shared by Freud, his early adherents including Max Graf, and the medical profession. Prohibition and punishment for masturbation was then prevalent in the

child rearing practices of the wider culture. His father's disapproval
of Little Hans's being in bed with his mother intensified his unconscious fear of castration. The mother of Little Hans would not only
threaten him repeatedly with separation (and his little sister as well)
but would also cuddle him in bed when he was upset about separation. Thus, Little Hans was threatened with both maternal seduction
and desertion. His mother allowed him into the bathroom when she
toileted and bathed with him, and told him she had a widdler. Significantly, two years before his phobic symptoms, Little Hans had asked
his mother if she too had a widdler (p. 7). Her equivocal comments
and exhibitionistic exposure were critical factors in his confusion
and denial of reality, his assumption that she had a "'widdler' like a
horse." He asked his mother to touch his penis, and, exhibitionistic
like his mother, he wanted little Berta and Olga to watch him urinate
(p. 19). (Olga was also his mother's name.) Little Hans had fantasies
of a phallic woman, both reassuring against castration, and overtly
threatening castration. Hans later fantasied that his sister's widdler
would be the same as his, but bigger. The apparent mis-information
conveyed by his mother was compounded by his father's lack of clarity in response to his son's questions. His father explained that men
and women had different "widdlers" (p. 62). However, if widdler is
better translated here as wee-wee maker, then his mother may have
correctly meant that she too had a urinary apparatus. In Freud's
phallocentric model of child development, females were defined by
their lack of a penis, without indication of their own genital and urinary organs (Rudnytsky, 1994). Little Hans thoughtfully asked, "But
how do little girls widdle, if they have no widdlers?" (p. 31). Certainly,
enlightenment about sex was expected to be an important part of
treatment, particularly about the anatomical difference between the
sexes and the origin of babies. Little Hans was exposed to the pregnancy, delivery, and the pain and blood associated with the birth of
his sister, which must have been a shock trauma for the three-and-a-
half-year-old boy with persisting strain. In addition, he may well have
been exposed to the primal scene since he was in the parental bedroom for almost the first four years of his life. Indeed, there is evidence that cumulative traumatic experience was a major determinant of Little Hans's phobic disorder. The tonsillectomy preceded by
the mother's castration threat and an attack of influenza (which may
have precipitated a pharyngo-tonsillitis), combined with a presumed
lack of preparation for the surgical procedure, contributed to Hans's
separation and castration anxiety. With the emphasis on the act of
masturbation at that time, the significance of masturbation fantasies

and the associated anxiety and guilt were scarcely appreciated. Freud (1909, p. 28) concurred with Little Hans's parents that it was not right for him to be preoccupied with widdlers, even his own.

Although there were symptomatic phenomena prior to the appearance of the phobia of horses in January 1908, Little Hans's tonsillectomy resulted in increased distress (Slap, 1961). Marital strife, culminating in a divorce when Little Hans was a teenager, took its own toll on the early development of Little Hans. The parents of Little Hans did not agree about having children, rearing children, parental controls, roles, and responsibilities. When interviewed in 1952 Max denied the significance of his wife being socially avoidant and readily provoked in relation to the phobia of "Little Hans," Little Hans could well have been identified with his relatively reclusive mother. However, his mother did take him to the park and she did shopping and bicycling trips (pp. 56–57). Horses and horse drawn carriages were prevalent on the city streets and in the countryside and Little Hans's avoidance of horses of course kept him inside close to his mother, staying inside with her in the apartment. He lacked playmates, but that hardly explains his sitting for hours on the apartment balcony to observe and admire a seven- to eight-year-old girl below (p. 15). Did his mother leave him there, similar to a modern child neglectfully left watching television? Was his mother unable to engage him in play and conversation? The lonely voyeuristic behavior of Little Hans suggests inner conflicts between attachment and separation, between dependency and independence. Object constancy would have to be consolidated before Hans could firmly confront the challenges of the oedipal phase. The seductive, intrusive, and abandonment threats of Little Hans's mother were recognized by Fromm (1968) and Garrison (1978). Bowlby (1973) stressed Little Hans's separation anxiety and problematic attachment, further elaborated by Ornstein (1993) in the context of pathogenic parental influence. His ambitious, busy father appears to have been generally fond of his son, but often absent, especially during the summer prior to the outbreak of Hans's phobia. His father had little awareness of his own conflicts or of the impact of his wife's disturbance on the family. The Eissler interviews and the case report suggest that Max Graf was limited in his capacity to buffer and protect his children from their mother's dysfunctional behavior. The intense incestuous attachment and guilt of Little Hans suggested an oedipal victory since he joined his mother in bed while eliminating his father from the scene.

His father took Hans to visit his own parents without his wife because of strife between his wife and his parents. Perhaps it was hoped that the employment of a Nanny for a time during Hans's second year would alleviate his mother's emotional instability. Max Graf seemed unaware of the effect on his son of the sudden departure of the Nanny to whom Little Hans was affectionately attached. Freud had noted the difficulty of delineating the precise content of a phobia, and was himself anxious at travel departure. It is of interest that just as the treatment of Little Hans was about to begin, Freud had declined the first invitation to travel to Clark University in Massachusetts for an honorary degree and lectures.

On March 30, 1908, Freud saw Little Hans for the only time during his treatment. On the way to meet Freud, Hans had bumped his father and then his father slapped him. This is strongly suggestive of the reciprocal oedipal conflict of the father, as he approached the idealized father, Sigmund Freud. His son and wife competed with Max for Freud's therapeutic interest and affection. At the same time Max was aware of his wife's emotional lability, and tried to shield his son by opposing his wife's seductive, exhibitionistic behavior.

Identifying with his father, Hans also had idealized Freud. After leaving his meeting with Freud, Little Hans asked, "Does the professor talk to God?" Did Little Hans think that Freud, or his father, could read his mind? His idealization of the two fathers, his own and Freud, probably helped in the educational aspects of his treatment. Freud and Max Graf believed that enlightened education would not only be therapeutic but possibly prophylactic. Freud hoped that treatment of a constricting neurotic symptom in childhood would favor progressive development and possibly prevent more serious neurotic disturbance in later life. In a discussion of the case one year after termination, May 1909, in a discussion of sexual enlightenment, Freud paradoxically proposed that parents might not be best suited for such education of the child. He thought that children should have sex education in school. At that time, referring to the conditions in Little Hans's home, Freud (1967, p. 235) wrote, "not *that* many mistakes were made, and those that did occur did not have *that* much to do with the neurosis. The boy should only have been refused permission to accompany his mother to the toilet. For the rest, neurosis is essentially a matter of constitution." Max Graf was present during this Wednesday night group discourse. Anonymity, confidentiality, neutrality, and counter-transference were not then considered. Graf's (1909, p. 235) comments were reported, "about the case of [Little] Hans, that it is a progressive process of curiosity in the boy. Referring to Freud's remarks that [Hans's] enlightenment was not carried through without anything being left over, Graf says that the boy should have been told the last fact too, with a certain degree of clarity. The child now feels that several pieces are missing and asks his father more and more for explanations of natural events. In the course of time this will accumulate and demand an answer. In matters of sexuality, he has detached himself from his parents. . . . Hans' illness developed, in Graf's opinion, on the basis of his strong sexual predisposition (*Anlage*), which awoke a premature need for love; this in turn became too strongly linked with his parents." His own role as father and therapist of Little Hans and that of Freud as supervisor and teacher permeated the affective atmosphere of the exchange.

Little Hans did become productive and creative in his chosen musical career. The stage manager of the Metropolitan Opera for many years, he held similar important positions in the operas of San Francisco, Salzburg, Geneva, Zurich, Prague, and others. His Godfather had been Gustav Mahler, and "Little Hans," Herbert Graf, was a friend of many of the great opera conductors and singers of his era. For a time Herbert and Max were together in Tanglewood in Massachusetts during Max's stay in America, safe from the Nazi terror.

Herbert's career was deeply influenced, though not overshadowed by the eminence Max had achieved as a musicologist, author, critic, and journalist. But his first marriage was deeply troubled as his parents' marriage had been. We know little of Hans's adolescence when his parents divorced, undoubtedly a very turbulent period in his life. There is confusion about the date of the actual divorce, but there may well have been a separation before the formal divorce. The strains were likely present early, even before the marriage, when Max vacillated and Freud encouraged him to marry Olga. Freud was repeatedly consulted about their having children, indicating their concerns about parenthood, especially on the part of Olga after Little Hans was born. If Freud advised in favor of the Graf's having another child or failed to recognize how internally conflicted Olga was about motherhood, whether he was neutral or took any position at all, may have been a factor in their subsequent ambivalent attitudes toward Freud. Olga appears to have remained disturbed and resentful regarding her marriage and expanded motherhood.

Very disappointed and dissatisfied with the results of her treatment, Olga distanced herself from Freud and befriended Alfred Adler. Max, too, was supportive of Alfred Adler and left Freud's group with Adler in 1911. Widowed after his second marriage, Max again remarried. Max's father had not gotten along with his own father, and this may have been a determinant of Max's proposal to write a play about oedipal conflict after his father died (possibly be-

fore the outbreak of his son's phobia). When Freud saw Herbert after his parents' divorce, the adolescent conflicts were hidden behind
a friendly, curious, and thoughtful Herbert. Herbert Graf was hurt
and disappointed by the parental quarrels and divorce. Regularly visiting his mother, there were periods when he was quite detached
from his father. However, his endowment and identification with his
father were always evident in the great musical and synthetic gifts utilized in his prolific opera productions. He was fond of including animals in some of his productions, not excluding horses on stage.

The influence of Freud and Max on each other did not simply dis-
sipate and disappear. Max had preserved Freud's paper on drama
and later published it. In 1911 Freud had kept and published the paper of Max's on an analysis of Wagner's "Flying Dutchman" opera.
Retaining admiration and respect for his genius, Max also wrote an
appreciation of Freud for Freud's 70th birthday in 1926. It is of interest that the year before, Herbert wrote "The Psychological Roots of
the Art of the Theater" for his doctoral thesis. Herbert, no less than
Max, appears to have been influenced by his treatment, by later reading about his treatment, and perhaps by reading additional Freud papers.

Max's conflicts with his own father were evident in relation to his
son just after the end of World War II in 1946. Max was still in America as was his son Herbert, who had the foresight to immigrate to the
United States in 1934. Uneasy with their Jewish identity, neither Max
nor Herbert was vocal about the danger of Nazism. As a corresponding music critic, Max sent reports to the Vienna media that were critical of the Metropolitan Opera management and artistic performance. Since his son Herbert was stage manager of the Metropolitan
Opera, the incisive criticism clearly included his son. Hurt and embarrassed at the time, Herbert Graf defended himself with the classic
comment, "my father is responsible for me, but I am not responsible
for my father."

Beyond the formulations in Freud's case of Little Hans, largely
centered on the positive Oedipus complex, contemporary understanding would also include the negative oedipal constellation, pre-
oedipal antecedents, and narcissism, which had not yet been conceptualized. The treatment of Little Hans occurred at the dawn of
organized psychoanalysis. Freud's Wednesday Night Society eventually became the Vienna Psychoanalytic Society. The year after the
publication of the case of "Little Hans," Freud, with the help of Ferenczi and Jung, founded the International Psychoanalytical Association. The case belongs to the heroic period of psychoanalysis, when

all of Freud's adherents were novices, who interpreted each other's dreams, slips, associations, and fantasies. This spontaneous mode of analysis lacked anonymity, confidentiality, and a therapeutic alliance Little Hans could be discussed by his father's colleagues and friends, sometimes in his father's presence. The pioneers attempted to analyze themselves, and sometimes their own children, and their own spouses. Max Graf is reported to have transiently engaged in self-analysis by associating to internalized melodies. Carl Jung initially supported Freud's findings in the analysis of Little Hans in a clinical report, which was actually an analysis of his own child. Jung's daughter also became symptomatic after the birth of a sibling rival.

The early relatively small contingent of psychoanalysts was actually an avant-garde movement. Dazzled by the insights that psychoanalysis offered, they were eager to promulgate analytic ideas and to win new Freudian followers in the service of the psychoanalytic "cause." Analytic practice could be an exciting adventure with a daring, experimental character. Intra-psychic boundaries, intra-familial boundaries, clinical boundaries, and the psychoanalytic framework were in statu nascendi, unformulated or barely delineated. Many patients identified with their analysts and psychoanalysis and became analytic therapists. Some analytic couples were formerly, or even simultaneously analyst and patient without formal recognition at the time of analytic or ethical contra-indication. Though Max Graf was an important pioneer of applied psychoanalysis, he never analyzed anyone before or after his own son. Thus his son's treatment was his sole clinical endeavor and accomplishment. After leaving Freud's Wednesday evening analytic group, Max Graf remained ambivalent to psychoanalysis and no longer wrote about applications of psychoanalysis to the arts. Max Graf later wrote (1942) that psychoanalysis was organized like a religious orthodoxy, alternately criticizing and praising Freud. The ambivalence is reminiscent of the behavior of Little Hans who could pinch his father and then kiss the point of impact on his father.

Though the treatment of Little Hans by his father with Freud's supervision was clearly limited and soon outdated, it was remarkably innovative and therapeutically effective. Even in contemporary clinical child analysis, extra analytic contact between parent and analyst is essentially unavoidable and in many respects desirable. Provided that the focus is on the child's problems and for the benefit of the child, the parent may be the source of important data. The parent may supply vital information concerning endowment, development, and traumatic experience. Through contact with the parent the analyst

56 Harold P. Blum

may infer how the parent may participate or collude in the child's difficulties. Relevant to Little Hans, what is enacted at home may not appear in the transference, especially since the child's defenses and gratifications are shared with the original objects. Further, Little Hans was exposed to parental discord, parental nudity, primal scene, pregnancy, and aspects of childbirth. He was witness to the traumatic abuse and neglect of his infant sister by his mother. Hans had trouble with toilet training, which was stormy from the very first (p. 55). His anal pre-occupation and anal birth fantasies were fortified by his mother giving him enemas and laxatives, although possible constipation was not elaborated. His father did not enlighten Little Hans about pregnancy or childbirth, and told him that his baby sister was born like a lumpf, that is, a fecal object. His mother wanted to eliminate her upon birth, if not in utero. (His sister Hanna's suicide as an adult can be interpreted as an acting out of the internalized maternal abuse and rejection. The early death of Olga's father and the suicides of her brothers were likely determinants of her own conflicts over separation and traumatic loss.) The case of Little Hans's sister illuminates what could not likely have been reconstructed in the adult analysis of a suicidal patient—the maternal rejection and aggression toward the patient from birth.

Currently, parents would be questioned about the child-rearing practices depicted in the case report, for example, permitting the child in the parental bathroom or bedroom, the enemas, and the indications of child abuse. The traumatic potential of surgery such as "Little Hans's" tonsillectomy would be discussed. Parents could be helped to prepare the child for surgery and to assist the child's psychological recovery from surgery. Hans's play with the rubber doll in which he pushed a knife through the doll (p. 84) between her legs, probably referred to his tonsillectomy, and his retaliatory rage at his parents for their castrating, punitive threats. Overdetermined, the assault on the doll also represented an attempt at mastery through play of his castration, impregnation, and birth anxieties.

Little Hans apparently had fantasies of being impregnated by a domineering phallic mother, as well as by his father. This presumably intensified his feminine fantasies of bearing and caring for children. The negative Oedipus complex had not yet been formulated, so the case stresses the positive Oedipus complex. Complementary constructions regarding Hans's bisexuality are found in the case report, and in the later literature on the case (Silverman, 1980). His father was a vital object of love and identification, providing a far more benevolent, alternate relationship to that of his mother. During the treatment, Max Graf benefited from the relationship with Freud, a benefit transmitted to his son.

For Freud and Max Graf, the biting horse was almost always the feared father, the falling horse was the dying, killed father. Little Hans was afraid to touch a horse because it might bite his hand, but his father interjected that he meant "widdler" rather than horse. Hans objected that a "widdler" doesn't bite, but the father responded, "Perhaps it does, though" (Freud, 1909, p. 30). The interpretation that the horse-cart and coal cart (the "stork cart") were the pregnant mother was not entirely overlooked. Freud inferred that the loaded carts or stork carts and Hans's anxiety about defecation were related to his mother's past pregnancy; the fallen horse also referred to birth. The horse making a row and the horse threatening to ride away would now also be interpreted as the angry mother who threatened abandonment, the quarrels between the parents, and his mother's beating of his sister. The horse was also Little Hans himself who made a row and stamped his feet during toilet training. Hans used the giraffe, a reference to the family name, as a substitute horse, which was again regarded as a father figure. However, as Max departed, he said to Olga on at least one occasion, "Goodbye, big giraffe" (Freud, 1909, p. 40). The giraffe then also represented mother and the crumpled giraffe, Hans's rejected sister. When Hans proposed his own active separation and non-incestuous erotic choice of sleeping downstairs with his little girl friend, his mother inveighed, "If you really want to go away from Daddy and Mummy, then take your coat and knickers and good-by" (p. 7). Her response was seemingly jealous and possessive, as well as determined by her own narcissistic needs. She could be punitive and vindictive, rather than empathically sensitive to her son's needs and interests. Her reaction resembles her apparent jealousy of her husband's writing instead of his attending to her. For Little Hans, her narcissism, seduction, and instability would have impeded separation-individuation and added to fear of his own hostile impulses. Her aggression provoked Hans's conscious and unconscious rage as well as regression (Frankiel, 1992). Hans was over-controlled and over-stimulated, with induced loss of control of bodily functions through enemas given over an indeterminate period of his childhood. Hans had also abruptly lost a Nanny to whom he was attached for an indeterminate time. His mother could not be described as calm, cheerful, and tolerant, a mother who was oriented to the developmental challenges of her children.

Freud actually supplemented and concluded the May 1909 discus-

sion in his Wednesday night group with a very different emphasis
from the incestuous conflicts of Little Hans. He then asserted the pathogenic importance of the child's unconscious aggression toward the
mother in the phobia. Freud's overlooked addendum has emerged
as a critically important dimension of the case. The hostile aggression of Little Hans may now be regarded as exacerbated by the reciprocal aggression of his mother toward her children as well as her husband and herself. Little Hans was fond of his parents, but because of
his mother's ambivalent threats of desertion he was anxious that if
his father left he would not return. Father and Little Hans played
horse and little Hans's play and playfulness with selected associations
were interpreted in a restricted, conflicted paternal sphere. His father could direct the child's attention and supplied verbal expression. From a contemporary viewpoint, Hans's fear of his father was
partly a displacement from his fear of his mother's aggression, and
his aggression toward his mother.

Awareness of pre-oedipal problems of attachment and separation-
individuation enrich the reconstruction of pathogenic determinants
as well as sources of resilience. Bowlby (1973) postulated that Little
Hans was anxiously attached; this remains a significant open question, not suggested by the available data of his adult life. Herbert
Graf was able to travel internationally and frequently to opera houses
and concerts. However, the current designation of insecure attachment would apply to Little Hans's sister. Impaired attachment would
be entirely consistent with the severely disturbed relationship of his
mother and sister, culminating in his sister's later suicide.

OUTCOME

Little Hans became involved in the treatment effort with growing curiosity, increasing grasp of cause and effect, and integrative capacity.
When his father admonished him for expressing death wishes toward
his baby sister, Hans replied that he could think it. Unlike his father,
he made the crucial distinction between thought and act. He used
his preoccupation with "wee-wee machers" to differentiate animate
from inanimate, since he deduced that only the living urinated. He
sensed parental evasion and hypocrisy when he was misinformed. His
powers of observation, cognition, reality testing, and affect expression progressed during the treatment, despite the phobia. When Little Hans arrived at this imaginative solution to his incest conflicts by
proposing that he and his father each marry their own mother, he
was not afraid of paternal prohibition and punishment. In his second

plumber fantasy, the plumber had finally given him the phallic equipment symbolic of being prepared for mature attainment of his adult
life goals. Hans appeared to be on track for progressive development
without phobic interference (A. Freud, 1980). Freud and his father
supported the little boy's desire to understand and be understood.
There was an unarticulated therapeutic alliance of patient, parent,
and analyst-supervisor. Hans had joined his father in dictating the
near verbatim notes sent weekly to Freud. Alongside interpretation
and education, the inter-relationship of Freud, Max Graf, and Little
Hans importantly contributed to the treatment progress. His father,
Max, was a very important love object with whom Hans was strongly
identified; his father provided a crucial alternate relationship to that
of his mother. Considering the historical context, the brief treatment, and the parent/therapist's lack of any formal psychoanalytic
education, the case was an inevitably flawed, yet most impressive pioneering proto-analytic experience. Little Hans remained free of phobia and led an extraordinarily productive and innovative professional
life.

Would Little Hans have become Herbert Graf, a prodigy of opera
production in his early twenties and later stage manager of major
opera houses throughout the world, without his treatment? The very
fact that it is a treatment case report, first analysis of a childhood
phobia, and a prototype of child analysis, appropriately focuses on
pathogenesis, as well as emerging psychoanalytic theory and technique. Though ambivalent, his mother had a sustained affection for
her son, and she wrote to Freud of her joy at her son's recovery. But
an overview of the case must also encompass the resourcefulness and
resilience of Little Hans and the bold therapeutic innovation of "Little Hans's" father, and Professor Freud. Both Max and Herbert Graf
made valuable contributions to musicology, to music and song, and
to the music and words of analytic therapy integrated by Freud. Studied by successive students of psychoanalysts, the newly enlarged picture of Little Hans in the context of his family, his work, his culture
and new theoretical perspectives, builds on prior formulations and
inspires further psychoanalytic inquiry. Little Hans will remain on
stage in the science and art of psychoanalysis.

BIBLIOGRAPHY

ABRAMS, D. (2005). *Olga Honig: The Mother of Little Hans*. Unpublished pa-
    per. Publication pending.

BOWLBY, J. (1973). *Attachment and Loss. Vol II.* New York: Basic Books.

EISSLER, K. (1952). Interview of Max Graf. *The Freud Collection,* Library of Congress.

———— (1959). Interview of Herbert Graf. *The Freud Collection,* Library of Congress.

FRANKIEL, R. (1992). Analyzed and unanalyzed themes in the treatment of Little Hans. *Internat. Review Psychoanal.,* 19: 323–333.

FREUD, A. (1980). Foreword to "Analysis of a phobia in a five year old boy," *The Writings of Anna Freud, VIII,* pp. 277–282.

FREUD, S. (1905). Psychopathic characters on the stage. *Psychoanal. Quart.,* 11: 459–475, 1942.

———— (1908). On the sexual theories of children, *S.E.,* 9.

———— (1909). Analysis of a phobia in a five year old boy. *S.E.,* 10.

———— (1913). Animal phobias in totem and taboo. *S.E.,* 13.

———— (1926). Inhibitions, symptoms, and anxiety. *S.E.,* 20.

———— (1985). *The complete letters of Sigmund Freud to Wilhelm Fliess, 1887–1904,* ed. and trans. J. M. Masson. Cambridge: Harvard University Press.

FROMM, E. (1968). The Oedipus complex: Comments on the case of Little Hans. *Contemp. Psychoanal.* 4: 178–188.

GARRISON, M. (1978). A new look at Little Hans. *Psychoanal. Rev.* 65: 523–532.

GLENN, J. (1980). Freud's advice to Hans' father: The first supervisory sessions. *Freud and His Patients,* eds. M. Kanzer and J. Glenn. New York: Aronson, pp. 121–127.

GRAF, M. (1952). Reminiscence of Professor Sigmund Freud. *Psychoanal. Quart.* 11: 465–476.

ORNSTEIN, A. (1993). Little Hans, his phobia and his Oedipus complex. *Freud's Case Studies. Self Psychological Perspectives,* ed. B. Magid. Hillsdale, N.J.: Analytic Press, pp. 87–106.

RUDNYTSKY, P. (1994). "Mother, do you have a wiwimaker, Too?," Freud's representation of female sexuality in the case of Little Hans. In *One Hundred Years of Psychoanalysis,* eds. A. Heynal and E. Falzeder, pp. 121–133.

SILVERMAN, M. (1980). A fresh look at Little Hans. *Freud and His Patients,* eds. M. Kanzer and J. Glenn. New York: Aronson, pp. 95–120.

SLAP, J. (1961). Little Hans's tonsillectomy. *Psychoanal. Quart.* 30: 259–261.

Little Hans and Attachment Theory

Bowlby's Hypothesis Reconsidered in Light of New Evidence from the Freud Archives

JEROME C. WAKEFIELD, PH.D., D.S.W.

Bowlby (1973), applying attachment theory to Freud's case of Little Hans, hypothesized that Hans's anxiety was a manifestation of anxious attachment. However, Bowlby's evidence was modest; Hans was threatened by his mother with abandonment, expressed fear of abandonment prior to symptom onset, and was separated from his mother for a short time a year before. Bowlby's hypothesis is reassessed in light of a systematic review of the case record as well as new evidence from recently derestricted interviews with Hans's father and Hans in the Freud Archives. Bowlby's hypothesis is supported by multiple additional lines of evidence regarding both triggers of separation anxiety preceding the phobia (e.g., a funeral, sibling rivalry, moving, getting his own bedroom) and background factors influencing his working model of attachment (mother's psychopathology, intense marital conflict, multiple suicides in mother's family) that would make him more vulnerable to such anxiety. Bowlby's hypothesis is also placed within the context of subsequent developments in attachment theory.

IT IS NOW APPROACHING A HALF-CENTURY SINCE JOHN BOWLBY'S PUB-lication (1960) of the third in a trilogy of articles presenting the

---

Professor at New York University.

The Psychoanalytic Study of the Child 62, ed. Robert A. King, Peter B. Neubauer, Samuel Abrams, and A. Scott Dowling (Yale University Press, copyright © 2007 by Robert A. King, Peter B. Neubauer, Samuel Abrams, and A. Scott Dowling).

elements of attachment theory to the psychoanalytic community (Bowlby, 1958, 1959). That article provoked considerable criticism by mainstream psychoanalysts (Freud, 1960; Schur, 1960; Spitz, 1960). Propelled by ongoing empirical research as well as by Bowlby's masterful 3-volume summary (Bowlby, 1973; 1980; 1982), attachment theory has since become accepted as a vital part of the modern multi-theoretical psychoanalytic endeavor.

If these multiple theoretical perspectives each reveal an additional aspect of the truth about the human mind, then they should be capable of retrospectively providing new insights into past cases, including the very ones used to support the classic theory when it was held to be the exclusively correct approach. Just such a demonstration of the retrodictive usefulness of attachment theory was attempted by Bowlby (1973) when, in *Separation: Anxiety and Anger,* the second volume of his "Attachment and Loss" trilogy, he offered an attachment-theoretic interpretation of Freud's (1909) case of Little Hans.

In a nutshell, Bowlby argued that Hans's phobia is partially explained by separation anxiety brought about primarily by Hans's mother's threats to leave him if he did not behave, conjoined with Hans's actual separation from her during her confinement when having Hans's sister Hanna a year before. In offering this interpretation, Bowlby was incurring on what amounted to sacred territory for classic theory. Freud's case history of the treatment of Little Hans's horse phobia at age 5 by Hans's father with Freud's guidance was the first recorded case of the psychoanalytic treatment of a child, thus the beginning of child analysis. It was also the first recorded description of psychoanalytic supervision. More importantly the case has been studied by generations of students of psychoanalysis as the exemplar of classic Oedipal dynamics. Indeed, Freud presented the case as his most direct evidence for the Oedipal complex, arguing that Hans's horse phobia and other problematic behavior, including his intense desire to cuddle with his mother, were due to longings of a specifically sexual, even inchoately genital, nature exacerbated by excessive intimacy with the mother. The case, as Bowlby noted, also provides a prototype for classic accounts of phobias.

In this paper, I reconsider Bowlby's hypothesis about the Little Hans case. I go beyond Bowlby's discussion in two ways. First, I more systematically harvest the evidence available in the case record, showing that more evidence is available than Bowlby allowed. Second, I present fresh evidence about family dynamics and history from newly derestricted interviews in the Freud Archives. The result is a substantially stronger case for the attachment-theoretic account than Bowlby himself anticipated.

I assume throughout the discussion that multiple levels of interpretation are possible and that attachment theory may illuminate one level of meaning of the Little Hans case material within an overall understanding that may include other elements. For example, the evidence that components of childhood sexuality play a role in the Little Hans case is overwhelming, as in his preoccupation with "widdlers," but will not be reviewed here. Instead, I focus on the evidence that attachment theory also has a role to play in explaining the case record.

BOWLBY ON THE ROOTS OF ANXIOUS ATTACHMENT

Bowlby (1973) made three central claims with respect to anxious attachment. First, "when an individual is confident that an attachment figure will be available to him whenever he desires it, that person will be much less prone to either intense or chronic fear" (p. 202). Correspondingly, anxious attachment predisposes to developing phobias, especially school refusal, animal phobias, and agoraphobia, for three reasons: the child is more likely to experience the traumatic levels of fear that can produce phobias; the function of attachment is partly to protect from predators, so there might be a direct link between reduced attachment figure availability and increased vigilance and fear directed toward animals; and school and animal phobias perform the function of keeping the child close to the attachment figure, as when Hans's horse phobia keeps him at home.

Second, "confidence in the availability of attachment figures, or a lack of it, is built up slowly during the years of immaturity" (p. 202). This suggests the need to explain anxious reactions in terms of longer term factors, not just proximate causes.

Third, "the varied expectations of the accessibility and responsiveness of attachment figures that different individuals develop during the years of immaturity are tolerably accurate reflections of the experiences those individuals have actually had" (p. 202). Bowlby thus "attributes what a child fears to his real experiences" (p. 272). Noting that it is "most unwise to adopt an explanation solely in terms of unconscious wishes before an explanation in terms of experience has been thoroughly investigated and shown to be inadequate" (p. 272), Bowlby concluded that "evidence suggests that in an overwhelming proportion of cases the eventualities a child fears can be understood wholly, or at least in part, in terms of his actual experiences" (p. 272). It was this claim, that real experiences shape the child's working model and thus its response to attachment disruption, that led to the accusation that attachment theory is not really psychoanalytic.

On the basis of the research literature and clinical experience, Bowlby (1973) identified five particularly potent factors from real experience that may bring about anxious attachment and consequent phobias (N.B.: Throughout the discussion that follows, I use "mother" as a shorthand for the attachment figure):

(1) Actual separation from the mother: Bowlby noted that even brief separations can have substantial effects on attachment security (p. 220).

(2) Threats of abandonment by the mother: "Clinical experience suggests that threats of these kinds, especially threats to abandon . . . , play a far larger part in promoting anxious attachment than has usually been assigned to them" (p. 226; cf. pp. 235, 272).

(3) Maternal threats of suicide, death, or illness: "A child may come to fear some disaster after hearing his mother make alarming threats about what may happen to her in certain circumstances. For example, if her child does not do what is asked of him, she will become ill; or . . . she will desert the family or commit suicide" (p. 272); "Threats to abandon, including threats to suicide, play a far larger part in promoting anxious attachment than has usually been assigned to them" (p. 226).

(4) Intense spousal arguments: "When parents quarrel seriously a risk that one or the other will desert is always there. Not infrequently, moreover, it is made explicit. In such conditions children usually hear a great deal more than parents like to believe" (p. 235).

(5) Knowledge of actual suicide, death, or illness: "For example, a child may come to fear that his mother may become seriously ill or die after seeing or hearing about the illness or death of a relative or neighbor, especially when the mother is herself in ill health. . . . When a grandmother or neighbor dies suddenly, it is not unnatural for a child to fear that mother may die equally suddenly" (pp. 272–273). Bowlby postulated a toxic interaction between maternal threats and such actual events: "Another factor, and one likely to enhance to a much higher degree a child's anxiety about harm befalling his mother, is his having been threatened that, if he is not good, she will fall ill or die. In such a case, . . . a friend's death is taken as a lesson that mother's predictions are not idle ones; illness and death are real and may strike mother at any time" (p. 274).

BOWLBY'S ACCOUNT OF THE LITTLE HANS CASE

Having argued that anxious attachment due to real experiences plays a role in virtually all childhood phobias, Bowlby (1973) considered whether such anxiety likely played a role in Little Hans's case. He claimed "there is clear presumptive evidence that it did" play a larger role that Freud recognized (p. 283), indeed that "it seems probable that anxious attachment was indeed contributing a great deal to Little Hans's problem. Most of his anxiety, it is suggested, arose from threats by his mother to desert the family" (p. 284). Thus, of several family-dynamic patterns Bowlby identified as common in cases of school refusal or animal phobia, he proposed that Hans's family fits into his pattern B: "The child fears that something dreadful may happen to mother, or possibly father, while he is at school and so remains at home to prevent it happening" (p. 264).

One of the challenges in evaluating Bowlby's hypothesis is that manifestations of Oedipal desires of the kind described by Freud and manifestations of anxious attachment of the kind hypothesized by Bowlby can overlap in superficial ways even if the motivational sources are different. Many features that Bowlby might list as characteristic of childhood attachment relationships might equally well be found in a list of behaviors characteristic of sexual bonding, such as desire for proximity to the object, pleasure in cuddling with the object, and the ultimate goal of contact and clinging bodily to the object. Due to this overlap of superficial manifestations, it is possible, for example, for Hans and his father to be directly in competition for access to the mother despite being driven by very different motivational systems. The way Bowlby addressed this issue was to focus on showing not that the goals of the desire are attachment-like rather than sexual but rather to demonstrate that the kinds of causal factors that are known from research and clinical work to activate attachment needs are present in the case.

In sum, Bowlby offered a two-part hypothesis: Childhood animal phobias are caused by anxious attachment; and anxious attachment is caused by real experiences that undermine the perceived availability of the mother. Thus, his view predicts: (1) Hans should manifest anxious attachment prior to the phobia's onset; and (2) the anxious attachment should be preceded by a substantial amount of the identified five triggering experiences.

Bowlby offered the following evidence in support of his account: (1) Attachment anxieties immediately preceded the horse anxieties, suggesting a possible causal relationship. ("Hans [aged four and three-quarters] woke up one morning in tears. Asked why he was crying, he said to his mother: 'When I was asleep I thought you were gone and I had no Mummy to coax with'" [*SE* 10: 23]).

(2) Six months before the onset of symptoms, Hans had also ex-

pressed concern that his mother might leave. ("I had already noticed something similar at Gmunden in the summer. When he was in bed in the evening he was usually in a very sentimental state. Once he made a remark to this effect: 'Suppose I was to have no Mummy,' or 'Suppose you were to go away,' or something of the sort." [*SE* 10: 23]) However, such earlier expression of insecurity is reported to have occurred only once.

(3) Hans's own report to his father that he was afraid of being left by his parents and that his mother threatened to leave if he was naughty. (*"Hans:* 'When you're away, I'm afraid you're not coming home.' *"I:* 'And have I ever threatened you that I shan't come home?'" *"Hans:* 'Not you, but Mummy. Mummy's told me she won't come back.'" (He had probably been naughty, and she had threatened to go away.) *"I:* 'She said that because you were naughty.'" *"Hans:* 'Yes.'" [*SE* 10: 44–45])

(4) An entirely speculative suggestion (at the time Bowlby wrote) that the parents' later divorce might mean that there was spousal conflict at the time of the phobia onset at a level that caused Hans attachment anxieties.

(5) Hans's forced separation from his mother during her pregnancy with Hans's sister, Hanna. Bowlby observed that the father himself suggests that the disruption of attachment at the time his wife was giving birth could be responsible for Hans's anxiety: "At the time of my wife's confinement he was of course kept away from her; and his present anxiety, which prevents him from leaving the neighbourhood of the house, is in reality the longing for her which he felt then" (*SE* 10: p. 96). Elsewhere, the father asserts that Hans suffers from "fear of not finding his parents at home because they have gone away" (*SE* 10: p. 45). But, as Bowlby noted, the father soon refocused on the Oedipal interpretation. However, this separation occurred more than a year before the phobia; consequently, Bowlby did not place much weight on it.

Bowlby thus easily demonstrated that Hans had anxiety about attachment, specifically fear of losing his mother, prior to or contemporaneous with the phobia, although the evidence is not overwhelming in amount—a statement by Hans six months before the phobia, another at the outset of the phobia, and a third during the course of the analysis. However, there are a host of reasons why an animal phobia and anxiety about attachment might occur together (e.g., anxious temperament, unconscious hostile wishes, Oedipal dynamics). To make a persuasive case, Bowlby had to show that Hans's attachment anxiety could be plausibly attributed to the kinds of real experiences he identifies as potential triggers.

Bowlby was able to show from the case material that one of his five triggers, maternal threats of abandonment unless Hans behaves, did occur; Hans tells us this. Other than that, Bowlby mentioned that there was an actual separation when Hans's mother was confined during the end of her pregnancy with Hans's little sister, Hanna, a year and a quarter before. Bowlby also noted that the parents ultimately divorced and that there may have been spousal arguments at the time of the case, but the date of the divorce was unknown and the inference unsupported.

In sum, it must be admitted that Bowlby's argument is not entirely compelling, for two reasons. First, only one proximal triggering factor for anxiety about attachment is adequately documented in Hans's case; most of the other cases he cites in his discussion involve demonstrably more severe and often multiple triggering factors. Second, the longer-term experiences emphasized by Bowlby that would lead to a working model of attachment prone to yield severe anxiety under stress are not identified or supported, so it remains mysterious what deeper roots within Hans's earlier-formed working model might make him vulnerable to proximal triggering factors at age five.

Perhaps these limitations are part of the reason for Bowlby's caution in avoiding direct criticism of Freud's account. He concluded merely that the attachment-theoretic approach is at least as plausible as the Oedipal account, implicitly allowing that perhaps both have a portion of the truth: "There it must be left since there is no way of knowing which of the alternative constructions is nearer the truth. . . . The hypothesis advanced here seems no less plausible than the one adopted by Freud" (p. 287).

FURTHER EVIDENCE FROM THE CASE

A systematic culling of the case evidence reveals several additional strands of support for the attachment account, unnoticed by Bowlby (1973) but consistent with his view:

(1) A crucial piece of information mentioned only incidentally in the report is that Hans had seen his first funeral at Gmunden the summer before the phobia began (p. 90). In the case history, the father comments that Hans "often recalls it," but he dismisses it as a "screen memory" covering over an Oedipal death wish (p. 90). At another point in the case report, Hans suddenly asks whether there are people buried under the sidewalk as in a cemetery (p. 69). Recall that the father reports that Hans had expressed his first concerns about his mother leaving him during that same summer at Gmunden as the funeral, saying something like "Suppose I were to have no

Mummy" or "Suppose you were to go away," statements easily inter-
pretable as reactions to the funeral.

(2) At the very end of the report, in an addendum, the father
notes that about eight months before the phobia, Hans was moved
out of his parents' bedroom into his own room (p. 99), a disruption
of attachment access and increase in aloneness. Because of the summer holidays at Gmunden, this would have had its full impact only
four months before the phobia. This fact offers an additional way to
understand Hans's frequent attempts described in the case report to
return to the parental bedroom. It also places in a new perspective
Hans's fears of being in his room because, he said, a horse might
come into the room and bite him; this appears to have been the first
time in his life that he was regularly alone in a room at night by himself, a situation that easily conjures up fear.

(3) About six months before the outbreak of the phobia, the family moved to a new flat (p. 15), where Hans had no friends (p. 16).
Again, due to the summer holidays during which he had familiar
companions to play with at Gmunden, the full impact on Hans would
have occurred about four months before the phobia. After that,
Hans displayed his longing for peers in his frequent fantasies about
the children at Gmunden noted in the case report. The move not
only deprived Hans of friendly contact leaving him more prone to
fear, but also demonstrated that those near to him could disappear.

(4) During the summer preceding the phobia, while the family
resided at Gmunden, Hans's father had spent considerable time
working in the city, separated from the family. Freud interprets this as
having taught Hans that the absence of the father is associated with
more access to the mother, but in light of the funeral and its impact,
an equally salient meaning might have been that even a parent can
leave.

(5) In addition to Hans's separation from mother at Hanna's birth
noted by Bowlby, Hans also noted and was concerned about the
blood in the basins after the mother gave birth (he observes to his father that blood does not similarly come out of his widdler). The
blood may have suggested his mother's potential for dying or getting
ill. Moreover, while Hans's mother was in confinement, Hans would
likely have been threatened with the potentially dire consequences
to his mother of his misbehaving or making noise; and the blood he
saw afterward could only be a confirmation of his worries that something horrible could befall his mother. (We noted earlier Bowlby's
recognition of the potentially toxic combination of threats and actual evidence of illness.) The funeral in Gmunden had then reinforced the notion that people do die.

(6) A further potent factor is of course that after the birth Hans was permanently unable to have the kind of ready access he had had to his mother before. In my view, Bowlby tends to overemphasize the confinement separation itself rather than the subsequent chronic difficulty of access due to the new baby. Bowlby observes that disruption of an attachment relationship can yield anger, and it is surely the case that Hans's anger and rivalry toward his sister is due in part to her real role in taking away his access to mother.

(7) There appears to be another, more subtle source of disruption to Hans's attachment access to his mother in the period before the onset of the phobia. In the course of the case report, it becomes clear that the father, driven in part by his Freudian understanding of the mother-son relationship, has what amounts to a "Laius complex"–type reaction in which he consistently disapproves of and resists intimate contact between the mother and Hans. Thus, for example, in the morning, when Hans comes into the parental bedroom to cuddle with his mother, the father objects; and in general, the father tends to blame the mother for being overly affectionate and indulgent of Hans. The anger reported in the case record by Hans toward his father could be partly the result of the real interference by the father in Hans's attachment to his mother.

(8) Finally, it can be speculated that some additional factors made the topics of death, illness, and separation due to hospitalization more salient to Hans in the time preceding the outbreak of his phobia. In particular, we know, from comments in the minutes of the Vienna Psychoanalytic Society (Nunberg and Federn, 1967), that Max's father (Hans's grandfather) was apparently seriously ill for some time and died on June 3, 1908, just one month after the phobia was cured. The phobia had lasted only three months, so it seems likely that the grandfather's terminal illness could well have been a factor in arousing thoughts of illness and death in the months following Hans's witnessing of the funeral and prior to the phobia.

In addition, Hans had a tonsillectomy just one month into his phobia. The tonsillectomy experience and any attendant separation could not itself therefore have been a cause of the heightened anxiety that led to the phobia.[1] But, as Frankiel (1992), following Slap (1961) and Silverman (1980), observes: "Hans' tonsillectomy, which was performed one month after the outbreak of the phobia, may well

---

1. Louis Breger (2001), in his biography of Freud, mistakenly places the tonsillectomy prior to the phobia and thus falls into the error of suggesting it was causative: "Shortly before his phobia appeared, he had a tonsillectomy, with the characteristic fears that such an operation sets off in a young child" (p. 184).

have been under discussion at this very time" (p. 326), that is, at the
very time that preceded the beginning of the phobia.

In sum, the case record is substantially more supportive of proximal causes of anxious attachment than Bowlby suggested. Hans had
attended his first funeral, moved apartments, and been placed alone
in his own bedroom, all within the months preceding the phobia.
Moreover, his access to mother was disrupted both by Hanna, a baby
needing priority of care, and the father, concerned about Oedipal
over-stimulation by the mother. Together, these factors help explain
Hans's heightened uncertainty and anxiety about access to mother,
and add powerfully to the weight of Bowlby's hypothesis.

NEW EVIDENCE FROM THE FREUD ARCHIVES

Even after scouring the case record, one kind of evidence that would
strengthen Bowlby's claims remains lacking; there is no hint of why
Hans's earlier experiences within the family might have yielded a
working model of attachment that would predispose him to react to
such proximal causes with a relatively severe reaction of the sort he
had. Recently derestricted interviews in the Freud Archives offer just
such evidence. It is rare to have such fresh evidence regarding one of
Freud's cases.

The Archive interviews, carried out by Dr. Kurt Eissler, are with
Max Graf (interviewed in 1952), Little Hans's father who was an early
follower of Freud and who conducted the analysis with Freud's guidance; Herbert Graf (1959), Little Hans himself; and Herbert's wife
(1960), who as daughter-in-law was familiar with Herbert's mother.[2] I
consider three areas addressed by the interviews that are postulated
by Bowlby to be important factors in the causation of insecure attachment: the mother's personality and attachment responses; spousal
conflict; and family history of suicide, illness, or death that might
have been known to Hans or used by the mother in threats.

2. The interviews are primarily in German. I take some liberties with my translations to smooth out discontinuities and awkward phrasing in ways that do not affect
the substance relevant to my argument. For a fuller translation and citation of many
of the passages I mention, see the article by Eugene Halpert on "The Grafs" in this issue. A full translation of the interviews by Dr. Harold Blum, M.D., Director of the
Freud Archives, is now available at the Archives at the Library of Congress. I thank Dr.
Blum and the Freud Archives for providing access to the interviews considered in this
analysis. I also thank Frederick W. Bauman, Jr., M.A., former Manuscript Reference
Specialist for the Sigmund Freud Collection in the Library of Congress (the "Freud
Archives"), who gave invaluable assistance with translating the Graf interviews.

MOTHER'S PERSONALITY AND ATTACHMENT RESPONSES

In assessing Bowlby's hypothesis, a critical issue is the nature of the mother's responses to Hans. Freud, in his commentary in the case history, says of Hans's mother that she was an "excellent and devoted" (pp. 27–28) mother who cannot be blamed for Hans's phobia because, in virtue of her inevitable Oedipal role, she "had a predestined part to play" (p. 28) in its genesis. In later comments to the Vienna Psychoanalytic Society (Nunberg and Federn, 1967), Freud asserts that, other than the mother's taking Hans into the toilet with her, the parents made no errors that can be held responsible for Hans's neurotic condition, which must be laid to constitution. At one point in his Archives interview, Max, too, portrays his wife favorably as a mother who "had a good attitude toward" Hans, unlike her attitude toward Hanna, from whom, according to Max's interview, the mother turned away permanently at birth.

However, in the case history, Max asserts that the mother's excessive affection was responsible for Hans's problem. In his commentary, Freud agrees that "the father accuses her, not without some show of justice, of being responsible for the outbreak of the child's neurosis, on account of her excessive display of affection for him and her too frequent readiness to take him into her bed" (1909, p. 28), thus accepting her overindulgence as a factor in Hans's neurosis. The mother's claimed seductiveness has been a theme of much subsequent commentary on the case.

If the case is interpreted in attachment-theoretic terms, the notion that the mother's excessive affection or spoiling of Hans is a factor in Hans's heightened separation anxiety goes directly against one of Bowlby's (1973) signature claims, that it is virtually never overindulgence (except where generated from certain kinds of maternal anxieties leading to problems such as overprotectiveness or parentification of the child), but instead almost always lack of sensitive responsiveness, that triggers anxious attachment and separation anxiety in the child. The Archives interviews in fact support a third possible understanding of the mother's role, other than inadvertent participant in inevitable Oedipal dynamics or overindulgent seductive stoker of her son's libidinal desires.[3] Instead, consistent with

3. Or even seductive stroker of Han's penis, according to Frankiel, 1992. She baselessly infers that a footnote of Freud's (1909, p. 23) that includes a comment about how parents sometimes stroke the genitals of their children must be about the Graf family itself, despite contrary evidence in the case history that the mother takes care not to touch Han's penis.

Bowlby's prediction, the interviews reveal inadequate sensitivity and responsiveness as a potential factor in the genesis of Hans's attachment insecurity.

The Archive interviews consistently reveal personality features of the mother that would be expected to limit the sensitivity of her responses to Hans and encourage Hans to develop a working model that predisposed him to anticipate possible loss and to have intensely anxious reactions when the attachment bond was perceived as threatened. One thing on which the three interviews agree is that Hans's mother was a highly anxious, emotional, neurotic individual.[4] Max says, "She is without a doubt a hysterical woman"; Herbert says, "she is a very nervous person and always was a very nervous person"; and Herbert's wife affirms, "Herbert's mother's nerves are not so good and never were. She exaggerates." Recent developments in attachment theory research suggest that such anxieties and self-involvement are often accompanied by distracted, dissociated, or anxious states that frighten and confuse the child as to the availability of the parent for protective attachment functions, leading to insecurity, conflict, and even a disorganized/disoriented, unintegrated insecure attachment response (Hesse and Main, 2006; Main and Hesse, 1990; Main and Solomon, 1986, 1990).

Max, in discussing his and Hans's regular visits to his mother on Sundays in his Archives interview, notes that his wife did not go with them because there was tension between his mother and his wife, and he adds that there was tension between his wife and everybody.[5] This suggests that the mother's anxieties extended to intimates, and was sufficiently intense to interfere with her ability to spend time with Hans even on the weekends.

Max also makes it clear in his Archives interview that his wife's primary problem was neither depression nor a specific phobia like Hans's nor agoraphobia. What he describes appears on the surface

---

4. Here and elsewhere in my use of the Archives interviews, in the absence of reasons to the contrary, I generally take the interview reports as accurate reflections of the family's reality. However, given the subsequent divorce and the schism in the family over psychoanalytic theory itself with the mother siding with Adler and the rest with Freud (see the text below), it must be kept in mind that the reports could be biased and imputing unreasonableness to the mother where in fact there is a difference of preference or belief.

5. "*Eissler:* Did your wife go along, or were you alone?
Graf: Usually not.
Eissler: Was there a tension between your wife and . . .
Graf: And my mother, Yes. . . . There was a tension between my wife and everybody."

to resemble rather a generalized social phobia or avoidant personality. He says she was shy and did not want to socialize, not because she was anxious or afraid, but simply because she was of an unsocial nature.[6]

The mother's social anxiety could shed light on her behavior toward her children. Some social phobics report anxiety even when amongst family members. Thus, it seems possible that one reason the mother did not spend more time with Hans (see below) was because her social anxieties were experienced even in his presence. This could be part of the reason why she complained that Freud's advice to the couple to have children had not been sensitive to the emotional burden children placed on her.

Bowlby emphasized that it is not just literal physical access but the quality of attention and emotional response given the child that influences a working model. The interviews, like the case material, do not suggest that the mother grossly neglected Hans (indeed, the father asserts that his wife "had a good attitude toward" Hans and did not neglect him, unlike her attitude toward Hanna), but do suggest limited physical access (Max states in his interview that she did not spend much time with Hans) as well as emotional distraction and unavailability that would be likely to create a working model prone to yield anxiety when stressed: "She was an hysteric, and she was focused completely on herself. . . . Did she really pay attention to him the way a mother pays attention to a child? I don't really want to say that.").

Diagnostic hypotheses must remain highly speculative at this historical distance, given the limitations of the available information and the fact that the descriptions in the interviews are by individuals who had complex, contentious relationships with the mother. Nonetheless, the description of the mother's "hysterical" character in the interviews in fact suggests a potential personality disturbance of more severity than social anxiety or even avoidant personality disorder. The degree of the mother's early losses, including her father and two brothers (see below), the emotional intensity and ambivalence of her reactions to her spouse (see below), and her general tensions

6. "*Graf:* "She had shyness [*Hemmungen*] around people, so she didn't want to go out."

   Eissler: "Was she also afraid [*Angst*] to go out?"

   Graf: "No, not in that sense. At least not as something that would be really striking. No, she was just generally of an unsocial nature."

   Eissler: "Yes. But nevertheless there was a certain similarity to the symptoms of the child?"

   Graf: "Yes, but not from fear.""

and constrained relationships with everyone else reported by Max in his interview, could suggest a borderline pathology in consequence of early trauma. The case report indicates that she beat her daughter, and this, as well as her threats of abandonment and castration to Hans also reported in the case history, could be indicative of the emotional dysregulation and excessive intensity associated with borderline personality disorder. All the new lines of evidence, combined with the hints from the case history, suggest less capacity for unambivalent, emotionally empathic, and balanced interaction with Hans than was suggested by the case history.

Thus, contrary to Max Graf and Freud's suggestion that Hans's need for contact with the mother was the result of overindulgence and spoiling by the mother, the interviews seem to provide an example of Bowlby's opposite claim that it is underindulgence, not spoiling, that generally brings about clinging. Of course, seductive overindulgence and dissociated unavailability can occur in the same relationship. However, the interviews provide no substantial evidence of the former. Also, it should be kept in mind that the mother's behavior when she does respond to Hans "indulgently" as described in the case, for example, in letting him come into her bed in the morning when he seeks soothing, or in personally taking him out on a walk to see what was causing his newly reported anxiety, seems on the surface to be exactly what Bowlby suggests, namely, a natural maternal caregiving response despite her inhibitions and anxiety, rather than evidence of a generalized overindulgence or seductiveness.

MARITAL CONFLICT

Bowlby placed great weight on spousal arguments in causing anxiety in the child. However, marital argument has not generally been a salient part of interpretations of the Little Hans case, simply because there is little evidence within the case report for such conflict at a sufficient level of intensity at the time preceding the phobia to suggest such harm. Bowlby, like others who have studied the case report for hints of family conflict, noted the mention in the report that the parents subsequently divorced. But the case record offers no date for the divorce; we only know that it occurred before Hans's "follow-up" visit to Freud thirteen years after publication of the case. Thus, it has been unclear what can be inferred about the marriage at the time of Hans's phobia.

The timing of the divorce is revealed in the interviews with Max and Herbert Graf; Max reports that the divorce occurred about 18-

and-a-half years into the marriage, and Herbert reports that his parents separated when he was about 16–17 years old, thus about 19 or 18 years after the phobia. The separation was in fact not much before Herbert's visit to Freud.[7] So, the date of the divorce offers no reason to postulate intense family strife prior to or at the time of the case, over a dozen years earlier.

However, such inferences and speculation are no longer needed because the interviews provide a direct window into the state of the marriage at the time prior to the phobia. They reveal a striking picture of intense marital tension and active spousal conflict over a variety of issues starting from the beginning of the marriage. We learn that Max, 27 years old when he married, although smitten with the beauty and brains of his 23-year-old bride (he describes her as "very interesting, very intelligent, and very beautiful"), already had serious concerns prior to the marriage, observing that his wife is "without a doubt a hysterical woman." Despite obtaining Freud's prior approval of the marriage (the wife was in treatment with Freud), Max's concerns unfortunately turned out to be amply warranted. Recalling Freud's advice, "Marry her, and you'll have your fun," Max can only comment, "Well, I didn't really have fun." In addition to the social-phobic and agoraphobic symptoms described earlier, Max reports that his wife suddenly became jealous of his work to the point of tearing up some of his manuscripts.

The fact that his wife went so far as to tear up Max's manuscript at a time when he was laboring to realize his aspirations as a writer (and irrespective of the fact that the focus, time, and isolation needed to write can easily cause conflict in a family), suggests intense conflict with emotional acting-out of a kind that could surely have been visible to a child. Although these problems are described as occurring before Herbert's birth (indeed, having a child was an attempt to save the marriage from these conflicts), the conflicts over work and socializing presumably would have been chronic.

In addition, the couple had severe sexual problems that were a source of marital conflict. The wife's ambivalence about sex may be one reason Max described her as "hysterical." At one point in the interview, Max hints of sexual problems but backs off: "There were

---

7. This is not coincidental; it was upon the parents' separation that a teenage Herbert, still ignorant of his identity as "Little Hans," while helping his father to pack his books in preparation for moving, discovered a copy of Freud's book on his case that provoked his curiosity and eventually led to his discovery that the case report was about him, and thus his visit to Freud!

other things about which I don't wish to speak any further which did
not fit well into a young marriage in which one would have some
erotic pleasure." Later, he returns to the topic and explains. "The cir
cumstances of the depression, to the extent that she had them, were
always after sex. . . . I only know that after each night of lovemaking
[*Liebesnacht*], that early in the morning she would have some outburst or other." Whatever pathological status such outbursts or depression after sex may have reflected, in fairness it should be kept in
mind that Max's wife desperately wanted to avoid having further children, and that at the time the available birth control was of limited
effectiveness and pregnancy and birth in themselves were still quite
dangerous to the woman. Nonetheless, such outbursts and the associated arguments could easily have impacted Hans.[8]

The interview also reveals that the couple's psychological and sexual problems became entwined with a theoretical divergence as well
over psychoanalysis, in which the mother turned against Freudian
doctrine and embraced Adler's rival views. The mother's friendship
with Adler is mentioned by Herbert in his interview, and Herbert's
wife (here denoted *FG* for "Frau Graf") describes these allegiances of
her mother-in-law's as continuing even decades later:

> *FG:* "My mother-[in-law] had broken with Freud, and then she went to
> Adler. . . . And whenever you see her, she still talks about Freud and
> Adler."
> *KE:* "But against Freud?"
> *FG:* "Against Freud!"

Indeed, in a letter written to Kurt Eissler in 1953 refusing to be interviewed, Olga Hoenig refers to a comment of Adler's about such
an interview, so she must have been in active contact with him still at

---

8. It appears that Freud relied on this very possibility in inferring how it was that
Hans arrived at a sadistic theory of coition. In his paper on the sexual theories of children, which is largely about the Graf case, Freud (1908) observed that children may
pick up the notion that sex is violent from observing marital interactions: "In many
marriages the wife does in fact recoil from her husband's embraces, which bring her
no pleasure, but the risk of a fresh pregnancy. And so the child who is believed to be
asleep (or who is pretending to be asleep) may receive an impression from his
mother which he can only interpret as meaning that she is defending herself against
an act of violence. At other times the whole marriage offers an observant child the
spectacle of an unceasing quarrel, expressed in loud words and unfriendly gestures;
so that he need not be surprised if the quarrel is carried on at night as well" (pp. 221–
222). Given what the interviews reveal about the Graf's quarrel-filled marriage, intense conflict over sex, and Olga Hoenig's reluctance to have children, this description seems likely to be Freud's reconstruction of Hans's experiences.

that time, in her mid-70s (Ross, 2006). Although Herbert's wife says she does not know why the mother turned away from Freud, Herbert offers a startling explanation in his interview: his mother complained that Freud's bad advice had harmed and ultimately destroyed the marriage: "My mother still has complaints, saying that Freud was not good in her life, and advising father to have children, and so forth, etc. It ultimately more or less broke up the marriage." Herbert sensibly observes that the notion that Freud broke up the marriage is likely incorrect: "I would think all these things develop rather normally and it was a different cause why this marriage broke up." But Herbert also says of the effect of Freud's advice (or perhaps of his mother's rejection of Freud; it is ambiguous in the interview) that "it was not good for [his parents'] private living."

It is worth noting that, whatever the causes of the marriage's failure, the mother's claim that Freud recommended having children is not without some factual basis. In Max's Archives interview, although he does not state explicitly that Freud recommended having children, Max does obliquely offer support for the mother's claim in his description of a consultation he had with Freud after a year of marriage:

> After a year, I went to Professor Freud. And I said to him, "Herr Professor, this marriage isn't working." He was very surprised, and I made another effort. I thought, maybe children will change the circumstances. But that didn't happen, and nevertheless I lasted eighteen and a half years in this marriage until the children were so big that I could easily leave the marriage without disturbing their development.

Freud apparently did not support ending the marriage, and the passage at least suggests Freud's acquiescence in Max's plan to have children to fix the situation. The degree to which the wife was consulted is not stated.[9] In any event, as noted earlier, according to Herbert, the mother felt that for her, having children "was too much of a burden on her mind."

In sum, the marriage was characterized, even prior to the case rec-

---

9. That the father took Freud's advice on important and sensitive matters of family life is also suggested by an anecdote reported in both Graf (1942) and in the interview that reveals that Freud influenced Hans's life in a remarkable way. The interview version is as follows: "When my son was born, I had to decide whether to let him grow up as a Jew, or I wondered if to make life easy for him, I should have him baptized. I went to Freud and asked his advice; he said raise him as a Jew, because the boy will gain a lot from having to do twice as much as anyone else."

ord, by intense and pervasive conflict over sex, work, family (e.g., not visiting Max's mother), and child-rearing (how to respond to attachment needs), and the conflict even extended to psychoanalytic theory itself!

REALITY OF SUICIDE AND DEATH IN THE FAMILY HISTORY

Bowlby emphasized that maternal threats of suicide or death, or knowledge of the suicide or death of others, can exacerbate the effect of parental threats on anxious attachment. However, except for the recent funeral at Gmunden, there is no hint in the case record that any such theme exists in the family or that such topics would have come up in the family.

The Archive interviews in fact reveal a staggering history of familial suicidality and death within the mother's family of origin. In particular, the interview with Max Graf reveals that, prior to the marriage, the mother's family had suffered from multiple suicides. The mother lost her father while an infant, and two brothers had shot themselves to death (we are told that one did so after receiving a medal for saving someone's life) when she was a girl. A younger sister of the mother had infantile paralysis, and it appears from the interview that yet another sister had attempted suicide. This overwhelmingly traumatic history could hardly have entirely escaped Hans's notice. In any event, the mother's tendency to use extreme threats (e.g., castration, abandonment) and to exaggerate suggests that she might have used suicide or death as a threat to Hans at some point. If the mother ever did threaten suicide or illness, there existed ample reason for Hans to worry that the threat was real.

Of course, events subsequent to the time of the case record cannot have been a causal factor in Herbert's anxiety. However, striking later events might reveal earlier latent dynamics. There is, sadly, a tragic event of such a kind described in the interviews: The fate of Hanna, although her death occurs long after the case record, was also suicide. The father was in fact visiting America, the home of both his children at the time, when the daughter committed suicide. His report contains heartrending elements:

> I lost the daughter. She died here in America. She committed suicide in America. She had married and lived in an unhappy marriage, and my god somehow she wanted to replace that with other men, and then she came across a man with whom she experienced the same thing as with the other one whom she divorced, and that seems to have been decisive. And the tragic part was that three days after this

event, a letter from her man came in which he asked me if I could bring about a reconciliation. It was already too late.

In regard to the general issue of Hans's anxiety in relation to death, there is a final speculative point worth making about Hans's reaction to the funeral he attended in Gmunden. For Hans to experience separation anxiety as a result of the funeral he attended would not be surprising, but it would be particularly expectable if a parent had unusual anxieties about death and funerals. And this, we learn from the Archives material, was the case with Hans's father. According to Herbert, the father had a remarkably intense ambivalence about death and funerals (Herbert describes it as a "wonderful ability . . . to push things away") that kept him away even from his own daughter's funeral and burial after her suicide. A similar kind of denial seems to have occurred when Max's second wife died, when he smilingly told Hans that she died "beautifully" and it was "wonderful."

We are not told whether the father was present at the funeral in Gmunden that was attended by Hans. But whether or not he was there, the father's anxieties about death (as well as the mother's, given her earlier family experiences) could easily have been communicated to Hans.

HANS FROM THE PERSPECTIVE OF CONTEMPORARY ATTACHMENT THEORY

I now turn from Bowlby and the Archives evidence to the task of placing that evidence in the perspective of post-Bowlby attachment theory. Bowlby (1973) considered "anxious attachment," "overdependency," "clinging behavior," and (chronically high or excessive) "separation anxiety" to refer to roughly the same phenomenon, namely, attachment behavior that is greater in frequency or urgency than is usual (or, in a wry vein, greater than what the therapist thinks is proper) (p. 212). He disputed the common notion that anxious attachment is triggered by excessive physical affection, spoiling, or overindulgence by the caregiver (the view adopted by Freud and Hans's father about the origins of Little Hans's anxiety), suggesting instead that it is the lack of attachment access or responsiveness, or the threat of such, that leads to anxious attachment.

When Ainsworth and her colleagues (Ainsworth, 1979; Ainsworth et al., 1978; Ainsworth and Wittig, 1969) later studied children's responses to separation and reunion in the Strange Situation, she divided insecure attachment into insecure-avoidant (typically the child might ignore the mother upon reunion) and insecure-ambivalent (or resistant; typically the child might approach the mother upon reunion but then resist soothing, back off, and perhaps express anger). Still later, Main and her colleagues (Main and Solomon, 1986) presented evidence for a more clearly pathological insecure state, disorganized/disoriented, in which there exists no consistent strategy for coping with separation and reunion. Many recent writers use "anxious attachment" interchangeably with "insecure attachment" to refer to the three standard Ainsworth-Main categories.

In addition, Main and her colleagues created a parallel adult classification of secure-autonomous, avoidant-dismissive, and enmeshed-preoccupied attachment, partly based on how coherently and reflectively adults represent their earlier attachment relationships (Main, 2000a, 2000b; Main, Kaplan, and Cassidy, 1985). The enmeshed-preoccupied category, analogous to the resistant-ambivalent child category, indicates constant concern about the attachment figure's availability and difficulty being fully soothed and exploring away from the secure base, closely paralleling Bowlby's notion of anxious attachment. Brennan, Clark, and Shaver (1998) organized four attachment categories around the two dimensions of anxiety and avoidance, making room for a similar enmeshed category having high anxiety and low avoidance. Eagle (1997) contributed the important argument that Bowlby was mistaken to assume that the internal working model of attachment was a veridical representation of early parenting, for in fact various psychodynamic and interactional factors could influence how the child represents the relationship, thus bringing psychodynamics back into the heart of attachment theory. Although Hans does not clearly display either ambivalence or avoidance, from a theoretical perspective the central feature of the resistant-ambivalent and enmeshed-preoccupied pattern is impaired ability to be comforted and use the caregiver as a secure base due to hyperarousal of attachment needs. Such children show exaggerated fear responses, heightened monitoring of the caregiver, and inhibited exploration (Shamir-Essakow et al., 2005). These features surely do characterize Hans. Thus, Hans would likely be classified as resistant-ambivalent during the case period. Notably, the resistant-ambivalent pattern is often associated with anxiety disorders (Bradley, 2000; Cassidy and Berlin, 1994) and tends to result from the sort of inconsistent availability of the caregiver that seems to have characterized Hans's mother. Also, recalling that Hans was recently placed in his own bedroom in a new home without his usual friends, it is noteworthy that such anxiety may be triggered by an unfamiliar environment (Shamir-Essakow et al., 2005).

There is an instance in the case record in which Hans goes out accompanied by his mother and remains anxious nonetheless, unable to be soothed by her presence. Freud ponders how to explain this within the framework of his libido theory of anxiety. Such inability to be soothed is typical of insecure-ambivalent children. Their working model is such that they are chronically concerned about the reliability of the caregiver's future availability when needed, and experience anticipatory separation anxiety as a result.

Suggestions about Hans's likely development prior to the case record must remain speculative; it is impossible to know how Hans might have reacted to the Strange Situation at age 1. The parents do not report any unusual anxiety prior to the case report, and Hans appears to have been a normal, cheerful, and robust boy. He certainly did not possess an inhibited temperament, a risk factor for insecure attachment (Kagan, Reznick, and Gibbons, 1989; Kagan, Snidman, Zentner, and Peterson, 1999).

But based on the Archives evidence, it seems likely that Hans's working model contained the seeds of vulnerability to anxiety. Prior to the case record, Hans would likely have manifested a subclinical form of resistant-ambivalent attachment, or conceivably might have qualified as secure but with a working model that left him vulnerable. Research indicates that caregiver pathology, especially anxiety disorder, likely in Hans's mother, is associated with various forms of insecure attachment (Manassis et al., 1995), although the coherence and perspective of the caregiver's later representation of early attachment experiences also influences what is transmitted to the child (Main, 2000). Contemporary theory also suggests that caregiver sensitivity and responsiveness is central to attachment security, and such features have been found to be stable over time (Goldberg, MacKay-Soroka, and Rochester, 1994). The Archives interviews suggest that the mother's sensitivity to Hans was limited. Clearly, her own history in losing multiple older siblings under shocking and unexpected circumstances suggests she would have her own difficulties trusting relationships (Freud observes that she entered treatment for something that happened in her girlhood, and we can speculate that her siblings' suicides may well be related to her concerns), and the father emphasizes the mother's ambivalence about children. Nonetheless, the case record does display the mother's fairly consistent responsiveness to Hans's needs, even against the wishes of her husband, to the point that the father and Freud worry about maternal overstimulation as the cause of Hans's aroused sexuality. Even if not perfectly attuned and not entirely available and consistent, and even if driven by her own anxieties, she is yet neither markedly rejecting nor hostile to Hans.

Hans's vulnerability, we may speculate, was due to his working model derived from features of his relationship to his mother (e.g., threats to leave, mention of suicide and death, marital quarrels with threats to divorce, etc.). These features yielded potential scenarios of object inaccessibility, unresponsiveness, and loss. Such scenarios remained distant enough that no problems occurred during Hans's early years. Then, under the demanding circumstances indicated earlier—within a few months, the funeral, competition with a new sibling, renewed threats from his mother, the confinement separation, the move to a new neighborhood and a new bedroom, etc.— the model's schemas of potential loss were activated. One of the most solid and replicated findings of attachment research is that a confluence of such negative environmental events is predictive of changes in attachment status from secure to insecure (Hamilton, 2000; Lewis, Feiring, and Rosenthal, 2000; Shamir-Essakow, Ungerer, and Rapee, 2005; Waters et al., 2000; Weinfield, Sroufe, and Egeland, 2000). A child without the burden of Hans's working-model schemas might have withstood the circumstances without heightened anxiety.

HANS AND DISORGANIZED ATTACHMENT

The recent attachment literature contains important developments that potentially shed further light on the Hans case. A watershed achievement in recent attachment theory has been the systematic measurement and study of the disorganized/disoriented variant of insecure attachment in the Strange Situation (Main and Hesse, 1990; Main and Solomon, 1986, 1990). This classification applies to cases where there is, at least momentarily, no discernible organized strategy to express attachment needs under stress, hence confusing, unpurposeful behavior. Such behavior can be the response of securely or otherwise insecurely attached infants to particularly stressful circumstances. However, infants who display such behavior as an integral even if fleeting part of their Strange Situation response can be classified as disorganized in attachment style. Because this behavior is only a small part of overall attachment behavior except in highly pathological cases, such infants are generally provided also with an alternative classification describing their predominant behavior as secure or insecure avoidant or ambivalent.

The disorganized attachment pattern has become a focus of research, partly due to the fact that ample research demonstrates that it is a risk factor for later psychopathology (Kobak, Cassidy, Lyons-Ruth, and Ziv, 2006; Liotti, 1992; Lyons-Ruth, Alpern, and Repacholi,

1993; Nakash-Eisikovits, Dutra, and Westen, 2002; van IJzendoorn, Schuengel, and Bakermans-Kranenberg, 1999). Moreover, while research on the stability of attachment over time has generally revealed less stability than theoretically predicted and expected, disorganized attachment (and its later forms of controlling behavior; see below) has displayed somewhat more stability than other insecure patterns, and thus can be projected over time with somewhat more confidence.

Light has been shed on the life-span course and intergenerational transmission of attachment styles through studies involving the Adult Attachment Interview (AAI), which provides a reliable method of assessing adult attachment status. If a death or abuse experience during childhood is identified by the adult respondent being administered the AAI, then the interview is assessed for possible "unresolved" status, as evidenced in the interview by lack of reasoned resolution about the loss or abuse, loss of reasonable self-monitoring or coherent discourse about the loss, unreasonable feelings of responsibility, or excessive preoccupation with details of the loss or trauma. Like disorganized behavior in the infant, these sorts of features of parent discourse are generally not global but rather brief momentary failures of coherence within an overall cogent interview. A link between adult caregivers unresolved status on the AAI and the child's disorganized attachment status in the Strange Situation has been supported by replications and in a meta-analysis (van IJzendoorn, Schuengel, and Bakermans-Kranenberg, 1999), which found that on average 53% of disorganized infants had unresolved mothers. (Obviously, the remaining 47% implies that there are other pathways to disorganized attachment.) These findings take on particular significance in light of the fact that disorganized attachment is significantly associated with later child psychopathology.

Main and Hesse (1990) proposed an influential theory to explain the observed link between, on the one hand, unresolved adult attachment status indicating unresolved or reflectively unintegrated early trauma, loss, or abuse in a parent, and, on the other hand, disorganized attachment status in the infant indicating a breakdown of integrated, coherent attachment strategy. These were linked via a hypothesized intermediary of frightening, frightened, or dissociated behavior on the part of the parent. The theory postulated that the mother's unresolved status led to anomalous (frightening etc.) caregiver behavior when the infant seeks closeness. Thus, the infant is placed in the untenable position of looking for safety with a caregiver who herself appears unavailable, incomprehensible, or a threat. This resulting irresolvable approach-avoidance conflict dysregulates the infant's attachment system, allows disorganized behavior momentarily to break through the overall purposeful organization of the infant's behavior, and yields conflictual representations and unintegrated working models. Disorganized attachment was thus conceived as a second-generation transmitted effect of the parent's trauma (loss or maltreatment) and failure to resolve it emotionally (for a review, see Hesse and Main, 2006).

Another research development particularly relevant to Hans is the extension of attachment measures to quasi–Strange Situation reunion processes in preschool and school-age children, revealing various nuances and subcategories of the traditional infant categories of secure, avoidant, and ambivalent (Cassidy and Marvin, 1992; Crittendon, 1992; Main and Cassidy, 1988). In addition, corresponding to the greater capacity for complex strategies of the growing child, several new categories of attachment behavior emerge by ages 4–6. Under the general category of "controlling" behavior aimed at the attachment figure, the preschool or school-age child tries to control the parent's attention and behavior and may assume a judgmental or caregiving role that is more appropriate for a parent than a child. Two salient forms were noticed: a punitive-hostile type and an excessively-cheerful caregiving type (Main and Cassidy, 1988).

These recent developments seem potentially illuminating of Hans's case. Although his mother had been in analysis for some years and thus one might have thought "reflective" about her losses, her behavior suggests lack of resolution of her traumas and thus a high probability of producing some disorganization in Hans. Relevant to speculations above about her possible borderline pathology, this form of maternal psychopathology has also been found to be strongly associated with child disorganized attachment patterns (Hobson, Patrick, Crandell, Garcia-Perez, and Lee, 2005). Recall that Herbert says in his Archives interview that his mother was always a very nervous person, suggesting that as a child he may have perceived her as distracted and dissociated due to her own internal anxieties, and unavailable for soothing, a maternal style quite consistent with recent models of the genesis of disorganized attachment. Hans's father's description of mother strongly reinforces such a picture. From the perspective of this recent literature, Hans's mother's severe early losses as well as some of her threatening and frightened behavior strongly argue for the transmission of some degree of disorganized attachment to Hans—perhaps, as suggested, within a broader secure or resistant pattern—yielding vulnerable, less fully integrated internal working models and thus a tendency to respond pathologically to stresses.

Despite this neat fit of Hans's risk factors with current theory, and the consequent ease with which such theory can be imposed on the data, it must be said that it remains unclear from the case report and interviews whether Hans actually did develop a disorganized pattern to any pronounced degree. His described behavior in seeking his mother's soothing appears well-organized, purposeful, unambivalent, and even thoughtfully defended against his father's objections. Despite all that he has suffered from his mother, Hans thus seems anxious, not disorganized, at the time of the case. However, detection of disorganized behavior, even in the Strange Situation, is a subtle matter, and perhaps the relevant behaviors are just not reported in the case.

However, for reasons not yet fully understood, early disorganization is often replaced in children of Hans's age by quite well-organized controlling patterns of behavior, with either punitive or caregiving predominant elements. Hans clearly does not evidence a controlling-punitive approach. An argument for a controlling-caregiving pattern can be made, not only on theoretical grounds but also based on Hans's fantasies about taking care of children as well as the fact that Hans is repeatedly described as a cheerful child. His precocious adult-like cheerful behavior is sufficiently notable to be a target of Freud's amusement. This is a hallmark of the controlling-caregiving child's attempt to regulate chaotic or painful marital and family interactions. If, understandably, Hans did have an early element of disorganized attachment, he may have transformed it by the time of the case into the caregiving strategy. Note also that the caregiving type of controlling pattern may be more associated with families who have experienced losses (Moss, Cyr, and Dubois-Comtois, 2004).

On the other hand, a controlling-caregiving pattern of behavior often represents some degree of failure, due to conflict, of the usual attachment soothing-seeking behaviors, leading to a compromise formation: the child does not get direct soothing but gets to stay close to the attachment figure by offering caregiving, and thus receives indirect soothing without explicitly seeking it. Yet, Hans seems to have the standard behaviors and capacity for soothing-seeking for himself aplenty, as described in the case record. Whether Hans adapted to his mother's unreliable soothing with a controlling-caregiver pattern thus remains a tantalizing but speculative possibility.

CONCLUSION

I have argued that, by closely examining the Little Hans case record and assessing the trove of information now available through the de-restricted interviews at the Freud Archives, dramatic new evidence emerges in support of Bowlby's attachment-theoretic account of Hans's anxiety. The interviews offer surprising confirmations of Bowlby's speculations, a rather unusual event in psychoanalytic clinical theorizing that comes as close to successful "bold predictions" as is likely. In particular, the Little Hans case record contains much more evidence of proximal causes of Hans's anxious attachment than Bowlby himself suggested. Moreover, in contrast to the case record, which reveals little about background problems in the family, the Archives interviews offer dramatic confirmation of the kinds of problems that, according to Bowlby's theory, would yield a brittle working model in Hans. Instead of two out of five possible triggers of anxious attachment as Bowlby claimed, there is arguable evidence in the case record and the Archives interviews for all 5 factors in the Little Hans case: actual separation from the mother, albeit brief; threats of abandonment by the mother; intense spousal arguments involving threats of divorce and separation; knowledge of actual death, suicide, and illness; and likely threats of suicide or illness by the mother.

From an attachment-theoretic perspective, the success of the treatment of Little Hans is likely related to the way the treatment influenced his attachment security. Here it may be speculated that the fact that the treatment was provided by Hans's father may have had a therapeutic impact for reasons unrelated to the Freudian theories that guided the father's intervention, but rather because the father served as a benign attachment figure, a point that has often been raised (e.g., Frankiel, 1992; Juri, 2003). As attachment theory has evolved, the notion that attachment needs must be satisfied by one unique individual to whom the child is attached has been gradually replaced by the idea that the child may attach in varying degrees to more than one adult, although the exact relations among attachments within the family remain controversial (van IJzendoorn and De Wolff, 1997). It has long been known that sources of risk with respect to parenting can be buffered by sources of support, and protective factors can reduce the impact of risk factors (Belsky, 1984; Belsky and Jaffe, 2006; Cicchetti and Rizley, 1981). The treatment clearly afforded Hans greater opportunity for closeness to his father and for reassurance that his parents—or at least his father—would be emotionally available. Thus, it is conceivable that the intimacy attendant on the treatment of Hans by his father led to Hans's reassurance that his attachment needs would be met and thereby relieved some of the anxiety from which he suffered

The results of this exploration of the Little Hans case underscore the fact that today's multiple levels of psychoanalytic interpretation can be justified by the added explanatory power and novel insights they can provide, even in regard to such classic cases as that of Little Hans. Yet, the case also illustrates the ease with which different theoretical models and conceptual frameworks may be applied to case material, either by selective attention to certain evidence or by shaping the interpretations of the same evidence (Midgley, 2006). Thus, from the perspective of history and philosophy of science, the case brings home the limited power of case-history confirmation in selecting among theories. Despite Freud's claim that the Hans case provides "direct" evidence for the Oedipal theory, Bowlby's challenge and the success of many of the predictions that can be derived from his theory illustrates that what appears direct evidence for a theory to one generation may be ambiguous for another in the context of a new theoretical understanding, or may even appear to be direct evidence for a rival theory. In the end, the case supports the need for humility and open-mindedness, while yet confirming the value of critical mindedness in preventing premature closure of our theoretical understanding.

BIBLIOGRAPHY

AINSWORTH, M. D. S. (1979). Infant-mother attachment. *American Psychologist*, 34, 932–937.

AINSWORTH, M. D. S., BLEHAR, M. C., WATERS, E., & WALL, S. (1978). *Patterns of attachment: A psychological study of the strange situation.* Hillsdale. N.J.: Erlbaum.

AINSWORTH, M. D. S., & WITTIG, B. A. (1969). Attachment and exploratory behaviour of one-year-olds in a strange situation. In B. A. Foss (Ed.), *Determinants of infant behaviour* (Vol. 4). London: Methuen.

BELSKY, J. (1984). The determinants of parenting: A process model. *Child Development*, 55, 83–96.

BELSKY, J., & JAFFEE, S. R. (2006). The multiple determinants of parenting. In D. Cicchetti and D. J. Cohen (Eds.), *Developmental psychopathology, 2nd Edition* (vol. 3) (pp. 38–85). Hoboken, N.J.: Wiley and Sons.

BOWLBY, J. (1958). The nature of the child's tie to his mother. *International Journal of Psycho-Analysis*, 39, 350–373.

BOWLBY, J. (1959). Separation anxiety. *International Journal of Psycho-Analysis*, 41, 89–113.

88   *Jerome C. Wakefield*

BOWLBY, J. (1960). Grief and mourning in infancy. *The Psychoanalytic Study of the Child*, 15, 3–39.
BOWLBY, J. (1973). *Attachment and loss. Vol. 2: Separation: Anxiety and anger.* New York: Basic Books.
BOWLBY, J. (1980). *Attachment and loss. Vol. 3: Loss, sadness and depression.* New York: Basic Books.
BOWLBY, J. (1982). *Attachment and loss. Vol. 1: Attachment* (rev. ed.). New York: Basic Books.
BRADLEY, S. (2000). *Affect regulation and the development of psychopathology.* New York: Guilford.
BREGER, L. (2001). *Freud: Darkness in the midst of vision.* New York: Wiley and Sons.
BRENNAN, K. A., CLARK, C. L., & SHAVER, P. R. (1998). Self-report measurement of adult romantic attachment: An integrative overview. In J. A. Simpson and W. S. Rholes (Eds.), *Attachment theory and close relationships* (pp. 46–76). New York: Guilford Press.
CASSIDY, J. (1988). Child-mother attachment and the self in 6-year-olds. *Child Development*, 59, 121–134.
CASSIDY, J., & BERLIN, L. J. (1994). The insecure/ambivalent pattern of attachment: Theory and research. *Child Development*, 65, 971–991.
CASSIDY, J., & MARVIN, R. (1992). Attachment organization in 3- and 4-year-olds: Procedures and coding manual. Unpublished manuscript, Attachment Working Group, Department of Psychology, University of Virginia, Charlottesville.
CICCHETTI, D., & RIZLEY, R. (1981). Developmental perspectives on the etiology, intergenerational transmission and sequelae of child maltreatment. New Directions for Child Development, 11, 31–56.
EAGLE, E. (1997). Attachment and psychoanalysis. *British Journal of Medical Psychology*, 70, 217–229.
FRANKIEL, R. V. (1992). Analysed and unanalysed themes in the treatment of Little Hans. *International Review of Psycho-Analysis*, 19: 323–333.
FREUD, A. (1960). Discussion of John Bowlby's paper. *The Psychoanalytic Study of the Child*, 15, 53–62.
FREUD, S. (1908), On the sexual theories of children. SE 9: 205-226.
FREUD, S. (1909). Analysis of a phobia in a five-year-old boy. *SE* 10: 5–149.
GOLDBERG, S., MACKAY-SOROKA, S., & ROCHESTER, M. (1994). Affect, attachment, and maternal responsiveness. *Infant Behavior and Development*, 17, 335–340.
GRAF, MAX, Interview by Kurt Eissler. (1952). Box 112, Sigmund Freud Papers, Sigmund Freud Collection, Manuscript Division, Library of Congress, Washington, D.C.
GRAF, HERBERT, Interview by Kurt Eissler. (1959). Box R1, Sigmund Freud Papers, Sigmund Freud Collection, Manuscript Division, Library of Congress, Washington, D.C.
GRAF, FRAU, Interview by Kurt Eissler. (1960). Box R1, Sigmund Freud Pa-

pers, Sigmund Freud Collection, Manuscript Division, Library of Congress, Washington, D.C.

HAMILTON, C. E. (2000). Continuity and discontinuity of attachment from infancy through adolescence. *Child Development,* 71, 690–694.

HESSE, E., & MAIN, M. (2006). Frightened, threatening, and dissociative parental behavior in low-risk samples: Description, discussion, and interpretations. *Development and Psychopathology,* 18, 309–343.

HOBSON, R. P., PATRICK, M., CRANDELL, L., GARCIA-PEREZ, R., & LEE, A. (2005). Personal relatedness and attachment in infants of mothers with borderline personality disorder. *Development and Psychopathology,* 17, 329–347.

JURI, L. J. (2003). Revisiting Freud in the light of attachment theory: Little Hans' father—oedipal rival or attachment figure? In M. Cortina and M. Marrone (Eds.), *Attachment Theory and the Psychoanalytic Process* (pp. 227–241). New York: Wiley and Sons.

KAGAN, J., REZNICK, J. S., & GIBBONS, J. (1989). Inhibited and uninhibited types of children. *Child Development,* 60, 838–845.

KAGAN, J., SNIDMAN, N., ZENTNER, M., & PETERSON, E. (1999). Infant temperament and anxious symptoms in school age children. *Development and Psychopathology,* 11, 209–224.

KOBAK, R., CASSIDY, J., LYONS-RUTH, K., & ZIV, Y. (2006). Attachment, stress, and psychopathology: A developmental pathways model. In D. Cicchetti and D. J. Cohen (Eds.), *Developmental psychopathology, 2nd Edition* (vol. 1) (pp. 333–369). Hoboken, N.J.: Wiley and Sons.

LEWIS, M., & FEIRING, C. (1989). Infant, mother, and mother-infant interaction behavior and subsequent attachment. *Child Development,* 60, 831–837.

LEWIS, M., FEIRING, C., & ROSENTHAL, S. (2000). Attachment over time. *Child Development,* 71, 707–720.

LIOTTI, G. (1992). Disorganized/disoriented attachment in the etiology of the associative disorders. *Dissociation,* 5, 196–204.

LYONS-RUTH, K., ALPERN, L., & REPACHOLI, B. (1993). Disorganized infant attachment classification and maternal psychosocial problems as predictors of hostile-aggressive behavior in the preschool classroom. *Child Development,* 64, 572–575.

MAIN, M. (2000a). The adult attachment interview: Fear, attention, safety and discourse processes. *Journal of the American Psychoanalytic Association,* 48, 1055–1096.

MAIN, M. (2000b). The organized categories of infant, child, and adult attachment: Flexible vs. inflexible attention under attachment-related stress. *Journal of the American Psychoanalytic Association,* 48, 1055–96.

MAIN, M., & CASSIDY, J. (1988). Categories of response to reunion with the parent at age 6 predictable from infant attachment classifications and stable over a 1-month period. *Developmental Psychology,* 24, 415–426.

MAIN, M., & HESSE, E. (1990). Parent's unresolved traumatic experiences are related to infant disorganized/disoriented attachment status: Is frightened and/or frightening parental behavior the linking mechanism? In M. Greenberg, D. Cicchetti, and E. M. Cummings (Eds.), *Attachment in the preschool years. Theory, research, and intervention* (pp. 161–182). Chicago: University of Chicago Press.

MAIN, M., KAPLAN, N., & CASSIDY, J. (1985). Security in infancy, childhood, and adulthood: A move to the level of representation. In I. Bretherton and E. Waters (Eds.), *Growing points of attachment theory and research.* Monographs of the Society for Research in Child Development, 50 (1–2, Serial No. 209), 66–104.

MAIN, M., & SOLOMON, J. (1986). Discovery of an insecure-disorganized/disoriented attachment pattern. In T. B. Brazelton and M. Yogman (Eds.), *Affective development in infancy* (pp. 95–124). Norwood, N.J.: Albex.

MAIN, M., & SOLOMON, J. (1990). Procedures for identifying infants as disorganized/disoriented during the Ainsworth strange situation. In M. Greenberg, D. Cicchetti, and E. Cummings (Eds.), *Attachment in the preschool years: Theory, research, and intervention* (pp. 121–160). Chicago: University of Chicago Press.

MANASSIS, K. (2001). Child–parent relations: Attachment and anxiety disorders. In W. K. Silverman and P. D. Treffers (Eds.), *Anxiety disorders in children and adolescents: Research, assessment and intervention* (pp. 255–272). New York: Cambridge University Press.

MANASSIS, K., BRADLEY, S., GOLDBERG, S., HOOD, J., & SWINSON, R. P. (1995). Behavioral inhibition, attachment and anxiety in children of mothers with anxiety disorders. *Canadian Journal of Psychiatry,* 40, 87–92.

MANASSIS, K., BRADLEY, S., GOLDBERG, S., HOOD, J., & SWINSON, R. P. (1994). Attachment in mothers with anxiety disorders and their children. *Journal of the American Academy of Child and Adolescent Psychiatry,* 33, 1106–1113.

MIDGLEY, N. (2006). Re-reading "Little Hans": Freud's case study and the question of competing paradigms in psychoanalysis. *Journal of the American Psychoanalytic Association,* 54, 538–559.

MOSS, E., CYR, C., & DUBOIS-COMTOIS, K. (2004). Attachment at early school age and developmental risk: Examining family contexts and behavior problems of controlling-caregiving, controlling-punitive, and behaviorally disorganized children. *Developmental Psychology,* 40, 519–532.

NAKASH-EISIKOVITS, O., DUTRA, L., & WESTEN, D. (2002). Relationships between attachment patterns and personality pathology in adolescents. *Journal of the American Academy of Child and Adolescent Psychiatry,* 41, 1111–1123.

NUNBERG, H., & FEDERN, E. (Eds.). (1967). *Minutes of the Vienna Psychoanalytic Society, Volume 1: 1906–1908.* New York: International Universities Press.

ROSS, J. M. (2006). The truth about Little Hans: Weep for baby Hanna. Paper delivered to the New York Psychoanalytic Society, March 27, 2006.

SCHUR, M. (1960). Discussion of John Bowlby's paper. *The Psychoanalytic Study of the Child,* 15, 63–84.

SHAMIR-ESSAKOW, G., UNGERER, J. A., & RAPEE, R. M. (2005). Attachment, behavioral inhibition, and anxiety in preschool children. *Journal of Abnormal Child Psychology*, 33, 131–143.

SILVERMAN, M. (1980). A fresh look at the case of Little Hans. In M. Kanzer and J. Glenn (Eds.), *Freud and his patients* (pp. 95–120). New York: Jason Aronson.

SLAP, J. W. (1961). Little Hans's tonsillectomy. *Psychoanal. Q.* 30: 259–261.

SPITZ, R. (1960). Discussion of John Bowlby's paper. *The Psychoanalytic Study of the Child*, 15, 85–94.

THOMPSON, R. A. (2006). The development of the person: Social understanding, relationships, conscience, self. In Damon, W., and Lerner, R. M. (Eds.), *Handbook of child psychology, 6th edition* (vol. 3, *Social emotional and personality development*) (pp. 24–98). Hoboken, N.J.: Wiley & Sons.

VAN IJZENDOORN, M. (1995). Adult attachment representations, parental responsiveness, and infant attachment: A meta-analysis on the predictive validity of the adult attachment interview. *Psychological Bulletin*, 117, 387–403.

VAN IJZENDOORN, M., & DE WOLFF, M. (1997). In search of the absent father: Meta-analysis of infant-father attachment: A rejoinder to our discussants. *Child Development*, 68, 604–609.

VAN IJZENDOORN, M. H., SCHUENGEL, C., & Bakermans-Kranenberg, M. J. (1999). Disorganized attachment in early childhood: Meta-analysis of precursors, concomitants, and sequelae. *Development and Psychopathology*, 11, 225–249.

WATERS, E., MERRICK, S., TREBOUX, D., CROWELL, J., & ALBERSHEIM, L. (2000). Attachment security in infancy and early adulthood: A twenty-year longitudinal study. *Child Development*, 71, 684–689.

WEINFIELD, N. S., SROUFE, L. A., EGELAND, B. (2000). Attachment from infancy to early adulthood in a high-risk sample: Continuity, discontinuity, and their correlates. *Child Development*, 71, 695–702.

The Psychoanalytic Process
in the Treatment of Little Hans

JOSEPH S. BIERMAN, M.D.

This paper studies the psychoanalytic process in the treatment of Little Hans, using Samuel Abrams's 1988 paper in which he defines the psychoanalytic process as the sequence of steps which appears within the mind of the patient as the treatment proceeds. As with the adult, the child can affectively recall or reenact the past in the transference, but the child also tries to promote whatever developmental phase is being clocked in. In January 1908 Max Graf, Hans's father and a member of the Vienna Psychoanalytic Society who was a musicologist, wrote Freud that his son had developed a fear that a horse would bite him in the street. Freud first suggested that the father give his son some enlightenment in the matter of sexual knowledge, such as his mother and other females have no "widdlers." The enlightenments only increased Hans's anxiety, prompting Freud to meet with Hans and his father and interpret the fear of the horse as fear of the father. While Max Graf was able to help Hans understand some dreams and fantasies, he exhibited a punitive attitude toward Hans's masturbation, which was reinforced by Freud's attitude that it was harmful. The father did not promote his son's development when he withheld knowledge of how babies are born, neither did Freud when he withheld any contrary suggestions from the father.

IN 1908 FREUD CONSIDERED THE TREATMENT OF FIVE-YEAR-OLD LITTLE
Hans, Herbert Graf, by his father with some supervision by Freud to
be an analysis of a phobia. Obviously, the concept of analysis and

---

Baltimore-Washington Institute for Psychoanalysis.

The Psychoanalytic Study of the Child 62, ed. Robert A. King, Peter B. Neubauer, Samuel Abrams, and A. Scott Dowling (Yale University Press, copyright © 2007 by Robert A. King, Peter B. Neubauer, Samuel Abrams, and A. Scott Dowling).

child analysis has changed and developed in the almost century that has passed. While this treatment might well be considered today a type of treatment via the parent, Freud and Max Graf conceived of it as a necessary groundbreaking analysis in 1908 terms.

What was the psychoanalytic process like in this first ever version of the analysis of a child?[1] To study it I will examine Freud's case report using a generally accepted modern definition of the process. Samuel Abrams' 1988 paper, "The Psychoanalytic Process in Adults and Children," is especially relevant because in it he discusses how both a twenty-three-year-old woman and a not yet five-year-old boy in the course of their analytic work developed a relationship to a stuffed animal, a rhino and a teddy bear respectively, which became a vehicle for the analytic process, much as the horse and giraffe carried various meanings in that process for Little Hans. Abrams defines the analytic process as "the sequence of steps which appears within the mind of the patient as the treatment proceeds" (p. 245). Abrams comments on the similarities and differences between adults and children. "An adult has the task of reviving and consolidating the infantile neurotic constellation within the transference, while affectively recalling or reenacting the pathogenic past. A child patient does this as well but has an additional task: he searches for ingredients within the setting that will promote whatever developmental phase is being clocked in by maturation" (p. 259).

Abrams stresses how "the analyst is the guardian of the psychoanalytic process. The treatment is facilitated with children when the analyst is mindful not only of the transference, but also of the requirements of development, so that he may attend to the concomitant task of facilitating phase progression" (p. 259). As we shall see, this will be quite important in the treatment of Little Hans.

Leo Rangell in his 1968 paper on "The Psychoanalytic Process" is of the opinion that the analytic process begins when the analyst passes the test of being viewed by the patient "as objective and nonjudgmental" and not critical (p. 22).

How do these definitions and elaborations on the psychoanalytic process apply to the treatment of a not yet five year old boy in 1908? What was the core of the psychoanalytic process like, when, on one of the first days of January, 1908, Hans woke up crying from an anxiety dream (Freud, S., 1909a, p. 23)? What was the state of analytic tech-

---

1. A previous version of this paper was presented on April 2, 2004, at the Association for Child Psychoanalysis annual meeting in Cleveland, Ohio.

94 *Joseph S. Bierman*

nique, especially with children, of knowledge about children's development, including sexual development and very much including the function and effects of masturbation, and of analytic theory and metapsychology as the year 1908 began?

On October 30 and November 6, 1907, Freud presented the "Beginning of a Case History" to the Vienna Psychoanalytic Society. He had started the treatment of the "Rat Man" on October 1. In his minutes Otto Rank summarized what Freud had to say about how "the technique of analysis has changed to the extent that the psychoanalyst no longer seeks to elicit material in which he is interested, but permits the patient to follow his natural and spontaneous trains of thought." In a footnote the editors of the *Minutes*, Herman Nunberg and Ernst Federn, comment that "here for the first time we have a report of an analysis which was carried out with the help of *free associations*" (I, 1962, p. 227) instead of the urging method—insistence, encouragement, and giving conscious direction—for overcoming resistance. The report of this change in technique occurred two months before Hans would awake with the anxiety dream, which presaged the onset of the fear of horses by only a few days. Little Hans's father and future analyst, Max Graf, Ph.D., an eminent musicologist and a member of the Vienna Psychoanalytic Society, had been present at both of Freud's case history presentations. He had attended roughly 40 percent of the meetings that year.

While Freud had published the first edition of his *Three Essays on the Theory of Sexuality* in 1905, in which he set forth his hypotheses about his adult patients' infantile sexuality being connected to the formation of their neuroses, he realized that there was not much known—by him or others—about the sexual lives of children. In order to observe "in children at first hand and in all the freshness of life the sexual impulses" (Freud, 1909a, p. 6), he had asked friends and pupils to collect observations on the sexual lives of their children. The first reports on Herbert-Hans by Dr. Graf dated from when he was not quite three. Freud utilized these reports in a 1907 article on "The Sexual Enlightenment of Children." I quote from Freud's account of Herbert-Hans's intellectual interest in the riddles of sex, his desire for sexual knowledge.

"I know a delightful little boy, now four years old, whose understanding parents abstain from forcibly suppressing one part of the child's development. Little Hans has certainly not been exposed to anything in the nature of seduction by a nurse, yet he has already for some time shown the liveliest interest in the part of the body which he calls his 'widdler.' When he was only three, he asked both his mother and father if they had widdlers. He considered his seven day old sister's widdler 'still quite small but thought it would grow" (Freud, 1907, pp. 134–135).

Freud went on to talk in general about the question in a child's mind about the origin of babies that "is usually started by the unwelcome arrival of a small brother or sister. It is the oldest and most burning question that confronts immature humanity" (p. 135).

Freud stated that "there does not seem to me to be a single good reason for denying children the enlightenment which their thirst for knowledge demands," but he was rather pessimistic about how parents customarily keep all sexual knowledge from children as long as possible and "then on one single occasion a disclosure is made to them in solemn and turgid language, and even so is only half the truth and generally comes too late" (pp. 136–138).

On December 18, 1907, the last meeting of the year and just two weeks before little Hans started to develop his symptoms, the topic discussed at the meeting of the Society was on "Sexual Traumata and Sexual Enlightenment." Dr. Graf was in attendance. Freud formulated the basic question for the day's discussion: Is it possible to gain from enlightenment a kind of protective inoculation against sexual trauma? Dr. Eduard Hitschmann opened the discussion by stating he did not think that enlightenment could provide protection against the childhood traumata; for example, it would be hard to convey the full meaning of the perversions. He also stated that an "overly severe injunction against masturbation may have just as injurious an effect as a trauma" (Nunberg and Federn, 1962, p. 271). Freud agreed with Hitschmann about the trauma inflicted by the prohibition of masturbation. While Freud thought that enlightenment could no doubt accomplish something, he did not think that it was a panacea.

Graf asked: "to what extent can enlightenment succeed in diminishing or preventing the harmful consequences? Complete sexual enlightenment may perhaps be more dangerous than the 'natural' enlightenment which, as a rule, occurs gradually" (p. 272).

Masturbation, and especially whether it was harmful or not, was an oft recurring theme not only in the minutes but also with Hans and his parents. When Hans was three and a half, his mother found him with his hand on his penis. She threatened to call the doctor to cut off his widdler (Freud, 1909a, pp. 7–8). On January 15, seven days after Hans first said that he was afraid that a horse would bite him and was asked by his mother if he put his hand to his widdler to which he answered "yes," and six days after he was warned by her before his afternoon nap not to put his hand to his widdler, Stekel and Freud disagreed about whether masturbation was harmful. Stekel viewed masturbation as harmless. It was only the struggle against masturbation and the ideas connected with it which were injurious because of the sense of guilt which he thought was at the core of most neuroses. Freud was by no means convinced of the harmlessness of masturbation. Dr. Max Graf attended that meeting.

We can get a picture of the persistence of these 1908 views on masturbation by jumping ahead to 1911 and 1912 when a series of discussions on masturbation was held in the Society. Freud and Stekel continued to differ, as did many others, around the question of whether masturbatory activity per se could be harmful with Freud answering in the affirmative, and Stekel in the negative. Annie Reich in her review article of the 1912 discussion stresses how "at that time ego psychology had not yet been introduced into analysis, the Oedipus complex had just been accepted as a universal human fate, and the role of castration anxiety as the core of neurotic anxiety was not yet fully understood" (Reich, 1951, p. 80).

I have tried to summarize here what theoretical and knowledge background was available to equip little Hans's analyst(s). What kind of guardians of the psychoanalytic process would they be? What were some potential interferences for both the father and Freud in carrying out the function of the guardian of the psychoanalytic process?

It would obviously be essentially impossible for any father, even a well trained and well analyzed analyst father, to be the "objective and non-judgmental" guardian of the analytic process.

For well over seven years before the start of Hans's phobia, there had been several kinds of contact between Freud and Hans's parents. Freud said that the beginning of the connection with the parents was when Hans's "beautiful mother" (Freud, 1909a, p. 141) was in treatment with him for a neurosis in 1900. It was through his future wife that Max Graf met Freud. She would tell him "after her sessions with Freud of the remarkable treatment by means of questions and answers" (Graf, 1942, p. 467). The ideas about the unconscious and dreams affected him with a "psychological fermentation" (p. 467), and he wanted to know Freud personally. He was invited to his office and soon after was invited to join the circle of his first pupils for weekly meetings as one of the representatives from different fields of endeavor, such as art, writing, and music (p. 470). Graf's Reminiscences, written forty years after meeting Freud and twenty-two years after divorcing his wife, reveal his abiding anger at her when he describes her only as "a lady I knew" (p. 467) and not as his former wife.

We know from Max Graf in an article published in 1942 on his reminiscences of Freud that "a personal contact had developed between Freud and my family which made Freud's human warmth particularly valuable" (p. 472) Graf consulted Freud when his son was born as to whether to bring him up Jewish or Christian. Freud was described as taking "the warmest part in all family events in my house" (p. 472). In this 1942 article Graf stated that on the occasion of little Herbert's third birthday, Freud brought him a rocking horse which he himself carried up four flights of stairs (p. 474). But in his 1952 interview with Kurt Eissler he said that Freud delivered the rocking horse on his son's fifth birthday. Freud had certainly become very involved with his past patient and her family which included a future patient and a pupil colleague. What kept Freud from suggesting that he supervise another analyst in the treatment of Max Graf's son? Or that another analyst treat little Herbert without any supervision by or consultation with Freud? Freud was of the opinion that no one except the father "could have prevailed on the child to make any such avowals. . . . It was only because the authority of a father and a physician were united in a single person, and because in him both affectionate care and scientific interest were combined" (Freud, 1909a, p. 5). I am reminded of the "urging method" for overcoming resistance by insistence and encouragement that Freud started to give up with the analysis of the Rat Man. I also wonder if the same concern about authority and prevailing wasn't still present ten years later when Freud took his twenty-three-year-old daughter Anna into analysis (Gay, p. 435).

In mid-January, 1908 the father wrote Freud that he is sending "a little more about Hans—but this time, I am sorry to say, material for a case history. As you will see, during the last few days he has developed a nervous disorder, which has made my wife and me most uneasy, because we have not been able to find any means of dissipating it. I shall venture to call upon you tomorrow, . . . but in the meantime . . . I enclose a written record of the material available.

"No doubt the ground was prepared by sexual overexcitation due to his mother's tenderness; but I am not able to specify the actual exciting cause. He is afraid *a horse will bite him in the street,* and this fear seems somehow to be connected with his having been frightened by a large penis. . . . I do not know what to make of it. Has he seen an exhibitionist somewhere?" (Freud, 1909a, p. 22).

Before reviewing the account of Hans's anxiety and phobia and the course of his treatment, a few words about Strachey's translation are in order. There are several instances relevant to the matter of

Hans's sexual overexcitation in which I believe his translation either
needs explication or is in error.

The first instance is his translation of the anxiety dream that her-
alded the phobia:

"When I was asleep I thought you were gone and I had no Mummy
to coax with" (p. 23). In the original 1909 publication, the sentence
reads, "Wie ich geschlafen hab,' hab' ich gedacht, du bist fort und
ich hab' keine Mammi zum Schmeicheln (= liebkosen)."(p. 14) By
using the past tense Strachey loses the immediacy and anxiety of the
dream which Hans relates in the present tense "you are gone and I
have no Mammi. . . ." In his chapter on "A Psychoanalytic Translation
of Freud" Mahoney (1992) comments that Strachey habitually translated dreams in the past tense, whereas Freud tended to write about
them in the present tense to preserve their hallucinatory nature
(pp. 37–39). The explication of the translation of "zum Schmeicheln
(=liebkosen)" seems incomplete. "Schmeicheln" connotes the verbal: flatter, compliment, coax, cajole and fawn upon. "Liebkosen,"
which the father added in parentheses, connotes the physical: caress,
pet and fondle. Perhaps it seemed defensively safer for Hans and
maybe also his mother to treat what was going on when he was in bed
with her as verbal rather than physical or both.

The father commented that during vacation the previous summer
when he was at times absent, the mother would take Hans into bed
with her when he would talk about her going away.

On January 5, he came into his mother's bed and told her that
Aunt M. had said, "Er hat aber ein liebes Pischl." (Freud, 1909, p. 14)
which Strachey translated as "'He has got a dear little thingummy"
(Freud, 1909a, p. 23). Even though Freud's original footnote for "Pischl" equates it to "Genitale" or penis and Strachey in his footnote
says "meaning his penis," he translates "Pischl" incorrectly as "thingummy," which is defined as something hard to classify or whose name
is unknown or forgotten, rather than as the Viennese diminutive of
the penis that pisses and wiwis.

On January 7 Hans went to the Stadtpark, the city public gardens,
with his nursemaid, but began to cry and asked to be taken home so
he could coax with his mother from whom that evening he could not
be separated.

On January 8 he reluctantly went to the zoo at Schoenbrunn with
his mother but became uneasy there at the sight of a horse, and on
the return trip he said, "I was afraid a horse would bite me" (p. 24).
He said that a horse would come into his room that night.

That same day his mother asked him if he put his hand to his widdler. He answered: "Yes, every evening, when I'm in bed" (p. 24). The next day, January 9, he was warned before his afternoon nap not to put his hand to his widdler, but when asked about it, he said that he had put it there for a short time anyhow. Hans must have felt in a dilemma. It was exciting to be in bed with mother and coax and caress with her and exciting when his aunt would praise his penis, but when he would put his hand on his widdler because of being excited by mother or Auntie M. or in an attempt to relieve anxiety, he would receive a severe injunction against masturbating.

Freud soon "arranged with Hans's father that he should tell the boy that all this business about horses was a piece of nonsense and nothing more" (p. 28). "Dummheit" was the word Freud used. It is variously translated as ignorance, stupidity, blunder, and folly. Within a month after the Vienna Society had discussed whether sexual trauma could cause neurosis and whether enlightenment could prevent neurosis, Freud was advising Hans's father to give several types of enlightenment as the opening therapeutic move.

"The truth was, his father was to say, that he was very fond of his mother and wanted to be taken into her bed. The reason he was afraid of horses now was that he had taken so much interest in their widdlers. He himself had noticed that it was not right to be so very much preoccupied with widdlers, even with his own, and he was quite right in thinking this. I further suggested to his father that he should begin giving Hans some enlightenment in the matter of sex knowledge. The child's past behavior justified us in assuming that his libido was attached to a wish to see his mother's widdler; so I proposed to his father that he should take away this aim from Hans by informing him that his mother and all other female beings (as he could see from Hanna) had no widdler at all. This last piece of enlightenment was to be given him on a suitable occasion when it had been led up to by some question or some chance remark on Hans's part" (p. 28).

It seems to me that Freud was trying to set the stage for the treatment and help the not yet five year old who developmentally would have some difficulty distinguishing between dream, fantasy, fear, and reality. Freud was letting Hans know through his father that his father recognized how his feelings about his mother and his preoccupation with his and horses' widdlers were very important and were connected to his fear of horses. Freud tried very hard to talk evenhandedly about Hans's conflict over his interest in widdlers, but seemed to me to come down on the side of "it's not right."

The father sent his next batch of news to Freud after March 17. He had straightaway enlightened Hans as to the meaning of his anxiety, but not about women having no widdlers. This was followed, according to the father, by a fairly quiet period without difficulty walking in the Stadtpark. However, his fear of horses became transformed more and more into a compulsion to look at them and then he would become frightened. It seemed necessary for Hans not to decrease but instead to defensively increase his interest in horses and their widdlers. But then the fear may have arisen from his doing something he thought he was forbidden to do.

Two added complications then intervened. He caught the flu which kept him in bed for two weeks. After this, his phobia increased so that he could not be induced to go out. I wonder if Hans imagined that getting the flu was a punishment for doing something he shouldn't have been doing and about which he was feeling guilty. This is often the case with immobilizing illnesses such as polio but also with many other physical ailments such as respiratory infections (Robinson et al., p. 978).

The second complication followed on the heels of the first, which may have been the impetus for it. Hans had a tonsillectomy which kept him indoors for yet another week after which his phobia grew very much worse. In his article on Hans's tonsillectomy Slap (1961) wonders why Freud didn't make more of this procedure that was bound, at least as we see it now, to produce much castration anxiety. Could Hans have thought that the operation was the punishment threatened by his mother, just as one of the four-year-old boys in a study by Jessner did, whose mother had similarly threatened him (1952).

After the tonsillectomy the father put pressure on Hans not to put his hand to his widdler. Hans said that his "nonsense" was bad not because he had been ill and couldn't go out for walks like father had suggested, but because he still put his hand to his widdler every night. The father would supply a bag for Hans to sleep in to keep him from even wanting to put his hand on his widdler. Hans was quite willing to comply to get rid of his "nonsense." Freud commented that Doctor and patient were at one in ascribing the chief factors in the pathogenesis of Hans's fears to his habit of masturbation. That Freud agreed with them is explicit in his comment that there were also "other significant factors" (Freud, 1909a, p. 30).

Ten days earlier the Grafs had gotten a new maid who let Hans ride on her back while she cleaned the floor. He would call her his horse while holding on to her dress and crying "Gee-up." On March 10 his wish to see the maid's widdler came up in a punishment fantasy that he told her. If she did something wrong, she'd have to undress altogether and even take off her chemise which would be shameful because people could then see her widdler.

On March 15 the father took the opportunity to give the second hit of sexual enlightenment that Freud had suggested, but not when it had been led up to by some question or some chance remark on Hans's part. He told Hans that "little girls and women . . . have no widdlers: Mummy has none. . . ." "But how do little girls widdle, if they have no widdlers?" "They don't have widdlers like yours. Haven't you noticed already, when Hanna was being given her bath" (p. 31)?

The next morning Hans awoke early with a frightening masturbatory fantasy, very similar to the one that he had had about the maid-horse. "I put my finger to my widdler just a very little. I saw Mummy quite naked in her chemise, and she let me see her widdler. I showed Grete, my Grete, (a little girl at Gmunden) what Mummy was doing, and showed her my widdler. Then I took my hand away from my widdler quick" (p. 32). This fantasy follows the enlightenment that females do not have widdlers. I see this as a defensive fantasy designed to avoid the threat of castration anxiety. Mummy still has her widdler, and Hans can reassure himself that his widdler is still rooted in by not only touching it but by showing it to Grete. But the castration anxiety breaks through. He had better take his hand away from his widdler quickly.

In his next weekly report to Freud, the father documented how Hans was getting more phobic. On March 22nd he had taken Hans to the zoo at Schoenbrunn. There he was afraid of all the large animals, especially the giraffe, elephant, and pelican which he had never been afraid of before. Freud knew that the enlightenment about women not having wiwimachers was bound to arouse his castration complex. Hans's fears increased. He hardly ventured out the front door now. Father asked for a consultation with Freud that was to include Hans.

Two nights before coming to see Freud, Hans had a fantasy in the middle of the night after which he came into his parents' bed where he fell asleep after telling the father he would tell him in the morning why he came in. The father took the fantasy down in shorthand. "In the night there was a big giraffe in the room and a crumpled one; and the big one called out because I took the crumpled one away from it. Then it stopped calling out; and then I sat down on top of the crumpled one" (p. 37). Hans asked the father why he was writing everything down. "Because I shall send it to a Professor, who can take away your 'nonsense' for you." Hans retorted, "Oho! So you've written down as well that Mummy took off her chemise, and you'll give that to the Professor, too" (p. 38). Father immediately went back to wondering how a giraffe can be crumpled up, and did not do anything with Hans's addition about his Mummy taking off her chemise and how eager Hans was to write that to the Professor. Did this signal the start of what we shall see is a continuing pattern of ignoring evidence of the Professor's importance to Hans and his treatment?

That same day the father "discovered the solution of the giraffe phantasy. 'The big giraffe is myself, or rather my big penis (the long neck) and the crumpled giraffe is my wife, or rather her genital organ. It is therefore the result of the enlightenment he has had'" (p. 39). It seemed to him to be a reproduction of the scene that had been going on for a few mornings. Hans would come in, and his mother would take him into bed with her. The father would warn against it, and mother would reply that it was "nonsense" (not Dummheit but Unsinn) "one minute is of no importance" (p. 39). Father realized that the matrimonial scene was transposed into giraffe life instead of horse life. However the next morning the father changed his interpretation when he jokingly said "Good-bye, big giraffe" (p. 40) to his wife. Hans agreed with this and immediately added that Hanna is the crumpled giraffe. Hans could thus join his father in the defensive fantasy that mother did have a big widdler in spite of the enlightenment and seeing her with her chemise off.

The morning of the visit with Freud Hans told his father about a fantasy about both of them being at the Schoenbrunn zoo where the sheep are, crawling under the ropes, and telling the guard at the entrance that they had done that, and getting seized by him. After the visit Hans related a similar fantasy about a guard. I would think that these fantasies have to do with the visit to Freud who was perhaps seen by Hans as the Wachmann, the guard, who would apprehend the two of them for breaking the rules, for doing the forbidden and telling him about it.

The father opened the first parent-child session we know of by "remarking that, in spite of all the pieces of enlightenment we had given Hans, his fear of horses had not yet diminished. We were also forced to confess that the connections between the horses he was afraid of and the affectionate feelings towards his mother which had been revealed were by no means abundant" (pp. 41–42). The worried father is, so to speak, saying to Freud, "What you prescribed isn't working! My son is still very phobic. In fact, I'll tell you about some new puzzling symptoms. Hans is now particularly bothered by what horses wear in front of their eyes and by the black round their mouths, and these are certainly not to be explained from what we know." And how did Freud react to this not-too-veiled criticism? Like the ideal guardian of the psychoanalytic process, he analyzed. Seeing the father and phobic son sitting in front of him, he realized something that he thought the father would have a hard time seeing. The blinders and the black round the horses' mouths represented the father's eyeglasses and moustache. After pointing this out to Hans, he interpreted to Hans that he was afraid of his father, precisely because he was so fond of his mother. "It must be, I told him, that he thought his father was angry at him on that account; but this was not so, his father was fond of him in spite of it, and he might admit everything to him without fear. Long before he was in the world, I went on, I had known that a little Hans would come who would be so fond of his mother that he would be bound to feel afraid of his father because of it; and I had told his father this" (p. 42).

What Freud said must have touched a very sensitive, defensive spot in the father. He interrupted Freud to ask Hans why he thinks that he, the father, is angry at him. Has he ever scolded or hit him? The father can't remember at first that he had hit little Hans that morning reflexively, when Hans butted his head into his belly. Freud commented in his paper that it was remarkable that the father had not brought this into connection with the neurosis. In his 1952 interview with Kurt Eissler, Max Graf gave some possible insight into that when he told how his own father, due to his old fashioned rearing, would give a thrashing when somebody would act up. He was afraid of his father.

Hans was impressed with Freud's prescience and omniscience. "Does the Professor talk to God" Hans asked his father on the way home "as he can tell all that beforehand" (pp. 42–43)?

Freud had enabled the treatment process to begin in earnest—"a possibility had now been offered him of bringing forward his unconscious productions and of unfolding his phobia" (p. 43). Freud has paved the way for Hans, as much as possible, to see his father-analyst as reacting to what he says and does in, as Rangell says, "an objective and non-judgmental way" both by his interpretation and, I think, by his example of analyzing. Unlike the Wachmann guard and more like the guardian of the analytic process Freud did not arrest Hans for wanting to make the same illegal, forbidden entry as his father.

The father began to send almost daily reports to the Professor. Three days after the consultation Hans came into bed with his father whom he told that when he is not in bed with him he is frightened. He then berated his father. "Why did you tell me I'm fond of Mummy and that's why I'm frightened, when I'm fond of you" (p. 44)? Freud

comments that Hans was bringing to notice that his love for his father was wrestling with his hostility toward him in his capacity of rival
with his mother. In addition and related to that I wonder if Hans
wasn't defending against his still unanalyzed fear that father will kill
or castrate him for his anger and rivalry by stressing his love for him
and denying the love for the mother, using his negative oedipal feelings to defend against his positive oedipal anxieties.

When he told his father that he was afraid father wasn't coming
home in the same way that mother threatened to not come back
home if he were naughty, he was still defending against his castration
anxiety. It's you that I miss, not Mommy. When the father got up
from the breakfast table, Hans said, "Don't trot away from me," and
laughed when the father sensitively replied, "Oho! So you're afraid
of the horse trotting away from you" (p. 45). The father saw Hans's
fear of his going away as evidence for his "hostile wishes . . . for then
he would be the father" (p. 45). The father agreed with Freud that
this new hostile phase could come out only after Hans knew that his
father was not angry because he was so fond of his mother.

We will see to what extent, in Abrams' words, the transference with
the father and Freud was able to consolidate and embody the pathogenic past. We will also see to what extent the concomitant task of facilitating phase progression was attended to by the father and his supervisor.

Very quickly after the session with Freud new additions to fears
concerning horses emerged in Hans's mind. These mostly concerned a warehouse which was across the street from the Grafs'
home, "with a loading dock at which carts are driving up all day long
to fetch away boxes, packing cases, etc." (p. 46). Hans became afraid
that a horse would fall down when a cart turned. He would become
frightened when a cart would start moving and even more frightened
of large horses and vehicles driving past quickly. Freud commented
"that, in consequence of the analysis, not only the patient but his
phobia too had plucked up courage and was venturing to show itself"
(p. 47).

After he defied father by stating he would come into the parents'
bedroom, he developed a fear that a parked cart would drive off with
him if he tried to climb over it. Father again ignored Hans's asking if
the Professor would know about the fear.

Hans revealed to his father that he got the "nonsense" when he saw
a horse in a bus fall down. He became afraid that a horse would fall
down and bite, especially because the bus horse made a row with its
feet, which Hans demonstrated by lying down on the ground and

kicking. Hans started to play horses in his room. He would trot
about, fall down, kick about and neigh. Once he tied on a nose-bag
He repeatedly ran up to his father and bit him. And he would defy father in the most decided manner

The father did consult again with Freud and told Hans the next
day that the Professor wanted to know on what occasions Hans himself would make rows with his feet. Hans was now bringing in the past
by means of the rows which he would make "when I'm cross, or when
I have to do 'lumf' (feces) and would rather play" (Freud, 1909a,
p. 54). The father added that Hans would kick when he would have
to widdle and would rather keep on playing. Hans interrupted at that
point to say that he must go widdle. I would see this not only as confirmation of the thought but perhaps a transference manifestation,
i.e., regressing to an earlier time with an earlier version of father. After this talk, Hans revealed a fear of heavily loaded coal carts.

What followed this reemergence of lumf anality was Hans experiencing disgust at his mother's yellow drawers. The preoccupation
with yellow and then black drawers led the father to find out from his
wife that Hans would pester her until she would let him go to the
W.C. with her.

When Hans soon began to prance like a horse, his father asked
many questions, especially about horses: Did he play at horses in
Gmunden? Was he the horse? etc. When Hans interrupted to ask the
father if his nonsense will be over if he writes everything to the Professor, the father again ignored this, but continued his questions, especially about going to the W.C. with Mummy. Some of Hans's answers were that black drawers are like lumf and yellow ones are like
widdle. Freud commented that the father was asking too many questions and pressing the inquiry along his own lines rather than allowing the little boy to express his thoughts.

The next day Hans brought up a fantasy, the translation of which
by Strachey I believe to be incorrect. "I was in the bath, and then the
plumber came and unscrewed it. Then he took a big borer and stuck
it into my stomach" (p. 65). The word that Strachey translates as
plumber is "Schlosser" (Freud, 1909, p. 47) which means "locksmith." Bohrer is probably better translated as drill. The father interpreted the fantasy as follows, "I was in bed with Mommy [who gave
him the baths]. The Daddy came and drove me away. With his big penis he pushed me out of my place by Mummy" (p. 65). Especially
with this fantasy following the father pressuring Hans while talking
about lumf and widdle and horse matters, I would think that the fantasy had to do with a regression to an anal struggle around lumf and

widdle. The locksmith unlocks the dirty water in the bath tub and unlocks the lumf in the belly with the enema. The father had noted that Hans had had trouble with his stools from the first, and that aperients and enemas had frequently been necessary. At one point the constipation was so bad that a doctor had to be consulted who recommended a more moderate diet. But recently the constipation had become more frequent (p. 56). The frequent enemas, some of which might well have been administered by the father, would stimulate passive anal erotism and fixation at the anal-sadistic level. A passive homosexual penetration fantasy would stem from this. The father had earlier reported that it was mostly he who would unbutton Hans's knickers and take his penis out to make Hans widdle and that it was a pleasurable process for Hans which gave "the child an opportunity for the fixation of homosexual inclinations upon him" (p. 20). The father thought that the fear of defecation and of heavily loaded carts was equivalent to the fear of a heavily loaded "Bauch"—a belly or stomach.

Freud commented that Hans was now beginning to bring fuel to the analysis in the shape of spontaneous utterances of his own. He introduced his fear of sitting or lying in the bath tub and then the fear of falling in because his mother would let go of him and ultimately his wish that Hanna would fall in after her mother would let go of her.

On April 14 the father wrote that "the theme of Hanna is uppermost" (p. 68). Freud comments in a footnote that the Hanna theme immediately succeeded the lumf theme. Hanna was a lumf herself, and babies were lumfs. For the next week and more Hans gave many different versions of how Hanna was conceived, carried and born, such as she had traveled in a box to Gmunden with the family, and she was taken out of the box by Mummy and Hans or the stork. Freud thought that these versions were Hans's revenge on father for not telling him what was going on during the pregnancy. Hans continued to "stuff" his father, as Freud put it, with stories about the stork. There certainly was a past to these stories. When Hans said the stork got her from the stork box which was painted red, he said it came from his first picture book which had a picture of a stork's nest with storks, on a red chimney and on the same page there was a picture of a horse being shod. Later, Hans said that the stork opened the stork box to take Hanna out with his beak that could turn the key in the lock. Immediately the father asked if a bus didn't look like a stork-box. Yes. And a furniture-waggon? Hans replied "And a scallywaggon" (p. 79), which the father defined as a term of abuse for naughty children. Hans in his droll way could continue teasing the father as he had been doing for some few days with all of his Hanna stories.

A fear that he would tease horses was soon followed by a wish to beat Mummy with a carpet beater just as she had threatened to do that to him. Soon after, he told his father that buses, furniture-vans and coal-carts were stork-boxes, that is, pregnant women.

On April 22 Hans played all morning with an India-rubber doll which he called Grete (a girl at Gmunden). *"He had pushed a small penknife in through the opening to which the little tin squeaker had originally been attached, and had then torn the doll's legs apart, so as to let the knife drop out. He had said to the nurse-maid, pointing between the doll's legs: 'Look, there's its widdler!'"* When his father questioned him about what he had done with the doll, he was very vague and didn't know. When his father asked him if he thought the knife was a baby, he answered, "No, I didn't think anything at all; but I believe the stork got a baby once—or some one" (p. 84). After being literally the obstetrician, Hans felt it necessary to regress to, or conceal his knowledge behind, the familiar stork theory. It was as if Hans felt that it would be dangerous to let the father know that he knew there was an opening in the mother's body that the baby came through, an opening that he thought was made by tearing. His father then, instead of being the guardian of his developmental push, switched from talking about the stork to talking about chickens laying eggs, as if he thought that to talk about how human babies are made and are born was dangerous. He had said exactly that to the Society four months earlier. Freud called the talk about chickens and eggs a payment on account. Hans continued to be perplexed about what the role of the father was, how Hanna belonged to father, and what father meant when he said that Hanna belonged to him, Mummy, and Hans.

Two days later the father and the mother made another partial payment. They "enlightened Hans up to a certain point: we told him that children grow inside their Mummy, and are then brought into the world by being pressed out of her like a 'lumf,' and that this involves a great deal of pain" (p. 87). This partial enlightenment, that there *was* a baby growing in Mummy's stomach, was followed by "visible improvement in his state" (p. 88). However, when Hans asked about more babies in Mummy, the father said that if God did not want it, none would grow inside of her.

But the partial enlightenment also equated babies with lumf. The evening of that day a sleepy Hans started talking about his children. The next day Hans started to have fantasies of having children. When he would sit on the chamber and a lumf came, he thought he was having a baby and this got connected with the bus-horse falling down. He would play at loading and unloading packing cases. Frankiel (1991) in a note on Freud's inattention to the negative oedipal in Little Hans comments on how Freud disavowed the presence of a feminine strain of desire in Hans for having children, a strain of passivity, feminine identification, and erotic receptivity and pleasure. Freud approached but did not reach negative oedipal interpretations.

Four days later, on April 30th, he told his father that his wish had changed from wanting to be a mummy to wanting to be a daddy. The children's mummy would be his Mummy, and his father would be their granddaddy. Freud comments how the little Oedipus allowed his father to become a big Oedipus instead of putting him out of the way.

Two days later Hans had a fantasy, the translation of which Strachey does not give the fullest meaning. He translates "der Installateur"(Freud,1909, p. 74) as the *"plumber"* who *"came; and first he took away my behind with* 'einer Zange'" (which he translates as *"a pair of pincers"* and which can also be translated as pliers), *and then gave me another, and then the same with my widdler.* He said: 'Let me see your behind!' and I had to turn round, and he took it away; and then he said: 'Let me see your widdler'" (p. 98). Hans agreed that it was a bigger widdler and behind that would be given. The word "Installateur" that Hans used means any installer, not only a plumber but also a gas or electricity installer and a fitter. The fantasy continues the theme of the conflict between the negative and positive oedipal. While this fantasy was indeed wishfulfilling, I wonder if from a paternal transference point of view it might have been an indication of what Hans thought about his father as analyst and especially as the guardian of his development. There was both something castrating and growth fostering about his father. An installer of bigger organs would express the growth fostering aspect of father. The withholding of sexual knowledge could have been the way the father acted out his castrating anger toward his son for his sexual interest in his wife.

On May 2 when Hans was able to go to the Stadtpark for the second day in a row, the father regarded his illness as cured. Freud was not consulted about this. Could the fear of fire, present from childhood, that Herbert Graf described to Kurt Eissler in 1959, have been overlooked or could his conflicts over his impulses have taken another form after the ending of the treatment?

The mother wrote Freud more than once to thank him for her boy's recovery.

A week later Freud received a postscript informing him of several important matters that the father had withheld from him during the course of the treatment. Among these was the fact that "Hans was about four years old when he was moved out of our bedroom into a room of his own" (p. 99). The father said, "I have no direct evidence of his having, as you suppose, overheard his parents in the act of intercourse" (p. 100). We might also add to the denial-"overseen." The parents had been sexually overexciting their son by exposing him to their baby making, and the father had been keeping this information from his supervisor, Freud, who had inquired about it, in the same way that he had continued to keep enlightening information from his son-patient about making babies.

In the postscript the father described the trace of Hans's disorder that still persists, his need to ask questions about what things like machines are made of and who makes them. An unsolved residue remained behind; he keeps cudgeling his brains to discover how he belongs to father too.

There is overall some sense of process in the treatment of Little Hans which Freud termed the analysis of a phobia and the presence of impediments. It is possible to follow many of the steps that were appearing in his mind, especially in response to Freud's interventions: suggestions to the father for enlightenment, interpretation to Hans of the fear of a horse as fear of father and reassurance that father wasn't angry at him, and his question about Hans's rows with his feet. There were times when Hans's father was on the mark with fantasy and dream interpretation, and at times not. But his punitive attitude toward masturbation reinforced by Freud's concern that it was harmful did not allow Hans to more fully explore his fantasy life and castration anxiety. Freud's question about the history of the rows led to what might be considered a transferential anal regression. The father did not promote his son's development when he essentially withheld knowledge of how babies are made, a move that Freud disagreed with but made no active attempt to influence.

BIBLIOGRAPHY

ABRAMS, S. (1988). The psychoanalytic process in adults and children. *Psychoanal. Study Child*, 43: 245–261.

FRANKIEL, R. V. (1991). A note on Freud's inattention to the negative oedipal in Little Hans. *Int. Rev. Psa.*, 18: 181–184.

FREUD, S. (1907). The sexual enlightenment of children. In: *S.E. IX*. pp. 130–139.

———— (1909). Analyse der Phobie eines 5jaehrigen Knaben. In *Jahrbuch fuer Psychoanlytische und Psychopathologische Forschungen,* 1, pp. 1–109.

———— (1909a). Analysis of a phobia in a five-year-old boy. In: *S.E. X.* pp. 3–149.

———— (1909b). Analyse der Phobie eines fuenfjaehrigen Knaben. In *Gesammelte Werke VII:* pp. 243–377. (1941).

GAY, P. (1988). *Freud: A Life for Our Time.* New York: Norton.

GRAF, H. (1959). Interview [of Herbert Graf] by Kurt Eissler. Box R1, Sigmund Freud Papers, Sigmund Freud Collection, Manuscript Division, Library of Congress, Washington, D.C.

GRAF, M. (1942). Reminiscences of Professor Sigmund Freud. *Psychoanal. Q.* 11: 465–476.

———— (1952). Interview [of Max Graf] by Kurt Eissler. Box 112, Sigmund Freud Papers, Sigmund Freud Collection, Manuscript Division, Library of Congress, Washington, D.C.

JESSNER, L., BLOM, G. E., & WALDFOGEL, S. (1952). Emotional implications of tonsillectomy and adenoidectomy on children. *Psychoanal. Study Child,* 7: 126–169.

MAHONEY, P. (1992). A psychoanalytic translation of Freud. In *Translating Freud,* ed. D. G. Ornston, Jr. pp. 24–47.

NUNBERG, H., & FEDERN, E. (Eds.) (1962). *Minutes of the Vienna Psychoanalytic Society.* I: 1906–1908. New York: Int. Univ. Press (1962).

RANGELL, L. (1968). The psychoanalytic process. *Int. J. Psa.,* 49: 19–26.

REICH, A. (1951). The discussion of 1912 on masturbation and our present-day views. *Psychoanal. Study Child,* 6: 80–94.

ROBINSON, H. A., FINESINGER, J. E., & BIERMAN, J. S. (1956). Psychiatric considerations in the adjustment of patients with poliomyelitis. *N. Engl. J. Med.* 254: 975–980.

SLAP, J. W. (1961). Little Hans's tonsillectomy. *Psychoanal. Q.* 30: 259–261.

The Grafs

Father (Max) and Son
(Herbert a.k.a. Little Hans)

EUGENE HALPERT, M.D.

Herbert Graf's childhood neurosis and treatment are viewed through the prisms of his and his father's life histories, the context of the time and the place they and Freud lived and worked and new material not available at the time of the original publication of his case. These approaches provide additional ways of thinking about and understanding the first child analytic patient and his treatment.

IT IS ALMOST ONE HUNDRED YEARS SINCE FREUD (1909) PUBLISHED "The Analysis of a Phobia in a Five-Year-Old Boy." With the passage of time, this seminal case study can be assessed in various contexts that were not available then. Though Freud let it stand unchanged, his own theoretical and clinical points of view changed over time. Certainly, theory and clinical practices in psychoanalysis have changed since Freud's time. In addition, pertinent material not included in the published report is now available. We know the identities of the two remarkable people who were, each in his own way, Freud's collaborators in the work: Herbert Graf (Little Hans) and his father, Max Graf. Both were so prominent and productive in their own fields that there are public records available that provide material to place Freud's pioneering paper in different contexts. In addition to viewing Herbert Graf's childhood neurosis and treatment backward

---

Training and supervising analyst in adult psychoanalysis at the NYU Psychoanalytic Institute, Clinical Professor of Psychiatry, NYU School of Medicine.

The Psychoanalytic Study of the Child 62, ed. Robert A. King, Peter B. Neubauer, Samuel Abrams, and A. Scott Dowling (Yale University Press, copyright © 2007 by Robert A. King, Peter B. Neubauer, Samuel Abrams, and A. Scott Dowling).

through the prism of his and his father's life histories, I will review his illness and treatment in the context of the time and place they and Freud lived and worked. Since context is always a guide to meaning, I thereby hope to provide some new understanding of this first attempt at child analysis.

Analysts such as Silverman (1980), Glenn (1980), and Slap (1961), while acknowledging that this was indeed a pioneering effort, stressed that the child would be treated quite differently currently and offered additional interpretations they felt Freud either omitted or missed. They also raised all the problems connected to a parent making interpretations, particularly id interpretations, to his child. While many of their points have validity, the context in which Freud published this case, the reasons he wanted to publish it, and the fact that this was the first time a child had ever been "analyzed" cannot be stressed enough. Any criticisms today involving the method or content of Max Graf's interventions, the problems entailed in a father probing his own child's psyche, or Freud, his supervisor, having preexisting thoughts that focused only on certain areas of the child's psyche, have to be seen in the context of Freud and Graf traveling in uncharted waters in a hostile environment. The disbelief, the anger, and the mockery Freud's findings and ideas aroused were rampant not only in medical circles but with the general public. Max Graf (1942) described the scene vividly. "The neurologists were enemies of Freud. The Viennese society laughed at him. In those days when one mentioned Freud's name in a Viennese gathering, everyone would laugh, as if someone had told a joke. Freud was the queer fellow who wrote about dreams. . . . More than that he was the man who saw sex in everything. It was considered bad taste to bring up Freud's name in the presence of ladies. They would blush." (p. 466–67)

It was in this setting that Freud (1909) expressed his wish for a more direct proof of infantile sexuality than that obtained in the analysis of adults. He wrote, "With this end in view I have for many years been urging my pupils and my friends to collect observations of the sexual life of children—the existence of which has as a rule been cleverly overlooked or deliberately denied." (p. 6) One of those friends and pupils, Max Graf, complied with Freud's urgings and began noting down such observations about his son, who was born April 15, 1903. When, during the course of Graf's reporting these observations, the little boy developed a phobia of going out of the house lest he be bitten by a horse, the opportunity presented itself for Freud to attempt something that had never been done before, to treat (via the father) a child's neurotic suffering with analysis. Given the tenor of the times, this act was not only novel but also daring. It also indicated Freud's utter conviction in the correctness of his theories. Freud was well aware of what he might be accused. He wrote, "Did the little boy proceed to take some action as regards what he wanted from his mother? Or did his evil intentions against his father give place to evil deeds? Such misgivings will no doubt have occurred to many doctors, who misunderstand the nature of psychoanalysis and think that wicked instincts are strengthened by being made conscious." (p. 144)

Just as Freud was courageous in having Max Graf treat his son in a way that was untested in a child, Graf himself displayed daring, courage, and a strong conviction in Freud's theories. After all, the elder Graf was not a physician and had no training in any form of therapy. No matter how differently the boy might be treated today, the wonder is that Graf was able to do it as well as he did. We may also wonder about the effect of the father's personality and psyche on the son during the course of the treatment and the effect of the treatment on the course of Herbert's life. To explore these issues I will review the arc of their lives beginning with its setting in the Vienna of Herbert Graf's childhood. The importance of Herbert's mother in his development, conflicts and fantasies cannot be overestimated, but the focus of this study will be on the father and the son.

VIENNA IN THE FIRST DECADE OF THE 20TH CENTURY

Vienna at the time of Herbert Graf's childhood phobia in 1908 was a far different city than it is today. Then, it was the capital of a large empire stretching eastward into what is now Russia, southward into parts of Italy and the Balkans, and in a northerly direction into what is now the Czech Republic and Slovakia; now it is a capital city of a small country. Then it had a population of two million with about one hundred and fifty thousand or more Jews, now it has a population of 1.6 million and fewer than seven thousand, mainly post–World War II immigrant Jews. Then it was "a city so brimming with culture, science and scholarship that visitors came from all over the world to hear its concerts, consult its doctors and study under its professors" (Berkley, 1988); now most of those who visit are tourists who come not because of what it is now but what it was then.

Most importantly for the lives of Herbert Graf and his father, Max, Vienna then was the universally acknowledged musical capital of the Western world. In the century prior to Herbert's birth, Beethoven, Brahms, Handel, Schubert, Johann Strauss, Anton Bruckner, and many other greats had all lived and/or worked in Vienna. During the decades of Herbert's birth through his teens, Gustav Mahler, Alexander von Zemllusky, Arnold Schoenberg and Richard Strauss all lived, composed and conducted in Vienna. Max Graf (1946) wrote, "The city seemed to have been created for music as other cities seem to be created for business, for things of the intellect, or for religion. Music was in the air . . . When we wandered with a girl in the outskirts of Vienna on fresh summer evenings, it was along the rustling brook of Beethoven's Pastoral that we sauntered . . . We drank our sour wine in little inns where Schubert once sat . . . Musical history was bound up with the life of Vienna and with our lives." (pp. 18–20) If music was in the air, Max Graf breathed it in deeply, as did his son, Herbert.

However music wasn't the only thing in the air in Vienna at that time; it also had reeked of anti-Semitism for centuries. A commemorative plaque to the mass burning of Jews in the fifteenth century which implies that the Jews themselves were to blame for the massacre because of their refusal to accept baptism has never been removed from a building on the Judenplatz. While the Vienna of Herbert Graf's childhood and youth still awaited the Nazi fiery furnace to come, it none-the-less burned with the old hatred of the Jews, which flourished officially and unofficially. The Catholic Church still had a say in secular appointments and promotions and barred the way for non-Christians. Carl Luger, a vicious anti-Semite, was mayor of Vienna for many years. Adolf Hitler returned to Vienna in 1909, the year of the publication of the case history, to breathe in more of the air of Jew hatred that he so relished. This atmosphere deeply affected the lives of Viennese Jewry. Berkley (1988) noted, "By 1900 . . . Viennese Jews had the highest conversion rate of any Jewish community in the world . . . One half of all the Viennese Jews who left Judaism became Catholics, one quarter became Protestants, while the remaining quarter simply declared themselves without religion." (p. 54) The world of Viennese music, in which so many of the musicians, conductors, composers, and critics were Jewish, was noticeably affected. Mahler for one had himself baptized when he realized that his ambition to conduct the Vienna Opera would be thwarted if he remained a Jew. The outcry against his possible appointment to the post was led by Wagner's widow, who publicly expressed outrage at the idea of a Jew conducting her husband's music from such a prestigious podium. The Grafs, father and son, did not escape the effects of living in such a world.

MAX GRAF (1873–1958)

Max Graf was born in Vienna on October 1, 1873. He was the oldest of three children of a Jewish couple, Regina (nee Lederer) and Josef Graf, cousins who had come from Bohemia. His father was a political writer and editor whose own father was described by Max as a Jewish religious teacher in Pilsen, Bohemia. Max's maternal grandfather was the owner of a large Czech estate and a postmaster. When Max Graf, then age 79, was interviewed by Eissler (1952) his fear of his father was still palpable. "I was afraid of my father . . . Unfortunately, I did not have a good relationship . . . I mean, there was nothing at all . . . He was still one of the old school. You received a beating—no?—when you had done something. I was always somehow afraid of my father." (p. 24) In this vein his father had banished his younger brother to America, " . . . because my father, according to the views of that time, believed that one had to send someone who was no good to America." (p. 28) The reason his brother was judged "no good" was that as a teenager, "he had an affair with a lady from the theater." Thus Max Graf's domineering, physically punitive father bred not only fear, but also defiance or submission in his children.

While he was aware of his fear of his father, Max did not seem to have been as aware of his own anger. Though his books contain many personal incidents of his life in Vienna, he did not report any anti-Semitism acts directed at him. On rare occasion he did mention anti-Semitic actions toward others. In 1945 Graf expressed "bewilderment" that the composer Carl Goldmark, "who represented, in his personality, the best Jewish traditions, wanted to escape his Judaism . . . Even if Goldmark did not want to recognize the Jewish heritage in his creative faculty, he certainly was intimidated by the anti-Semitic students who stood in the gallery of the Opera House and hissed at a performance of the 'Queen of Sheba.' The music critics of anti-Semitic Viennese newspapers did not fail to deprecate Goldmark's music as that of a Jew." (pp. 122–23) Graf was puzzled by Goldmark's wish to deny his Jewishness, even as he recognized the blatant anti-Semitism directed at the composer. Yet, it is likely that the ambitious, talented Graf suffered multiple anti-Semitic insults and abuses akin to those suffered by Goldmark. When Graf asked Freud whether he should have Herbert baptized to "remove him from the prevailing anti-Semitic hatred" (Graf 1942, p. 473), he perhaps was asking in a displaced way about protecting himself as well. The anti-Semitic reality perhaps, also unconsciously, evoked the terror and hatred he had felt when his father had threatened, bullied, and beaten him as a child. As he may have done in his childhood, he defended himself with a distancing denial of the danger of their rage and his own. Despite his awareness of the anti-Semitism in Vienna, his descriptions of the city and its people were most often tinged with fond nostalgia. In an insightful comment to Eissler (1952) he said, "It was my nature to find the good in everything." (p. 7) His son commented on Max's distancing to Eissler (1959): "Father had this wonderful time to push things away . . . He could also do it in private affairs . . . all his life . . . His second wife died when he was rather young . . . and I came to him . . . He was sitting there with a smiling face. He said she died so beautifully, so wonderful! . . . Enormous strength in turning things to the positive or to forget them . . . My sister committed suicide in this country. Father was here when that happened. I don't know really how he could manage that situation. But he wouldn't have gone to a cemetery." (pp. 26–27)

So it was that he tended to find only the good in the Viennese, even at the time of the Nazi Anschluss. Graf (1945) wrote, "On March 13, 1938, the soldiers of the German Reich . . . marched into peaceful Vienna . . . In the streets, no rejoicing greeted the victorious army . . . a national fanaticism, imported from Germany, murderously stormed through this city which had never been fanatical, but always humane, gay and friendly." (pp. 3–4) Yet others have described that the reaction of many, many if not most Viennese to the Anschluss was one of rejoicing and glad hearts. The murderous fanaticism had not just marched in from the outside, as Max Graf wanted to believe. This denial possibly reflected not only his wish not to see murderous feelings in many of his neighbors but also unconsciously not to have seen them in his father or himself.

In other areas of his life Max Graf dealt with his unconscious anger at his father in adaptive sublimated ways. In *Composer and Critic* (1946) he wrote of the beginnings of his career.

> I wanted to fight against the sensual conservatism of Vienna, which tried to bar the great musicians of our day . . . Conservative music criticism—there was no other in the great Viennese dailies of that period—tried to place all modern music under interdict . . . So I fitted my first arrow to the bow and began shooting . . . It was a little and insignificant weekly that first published three articles of mine under the promising title 'Musico-critical raids.' The editor . . . was happy to have found for his shooting gallery a young David who hit the bull's-eye with his first three shots. The first article attacked Eduard Hanslick with ridicule, making a scarecrow of the celebrated music

critic. The second made fun of Max Kalbeck, the friend and later the
biographer of Brahms . . . The third article was an analysis of the
great French critic, Sainte Beuve, whom I opposed to my Viennese
colleagues as the model of a wise and objective critic. The articles
against Hanslick and Kalbeck ran through the streets of Vienna like
foxes with burning brushes . . . After a short time I was sitting as a
music critic in the office of one of the greatest newspapers of Vienna
and writing my reviews day by day, always with the aggressive courage
of youth, enthusiastic and eager to clear the way for great musicians."
(pp. 23–24)

This passage suggests a sublimated expression of his unconscious
pleasurable fantasy of ridiculing and killing his conservative, intimi-
dating father, himself a writer and critic. The expression of Max's aggression in this manner helped launch his career as a musical critic.

The same intra-psychic elements played a role in both his relationship with Freud and his interpretations to his son during the analysis.
He said he left the Wednesday evening psychoanalytic meetings because he felt Freud was dogmatic in his dispute with Adler. Freud's
insistence on the correctness of his views in this dispute probably
touched on Max's feelings toward his father who had tried to beat
him into submission. Despite his disappointment and anger at Freud
and his hurt and anger when Freud rebuffed his attempts to reestab-
lish a warm personal relationship, Graf never lessened his respect for
and appreciation of the man and his genius. For example, in 1947 he
wrote, "Only within the past four and a half decades have we had an
insight into the dark recesses of the soul where works of art give their
first signs of life. It was Sigmund Freud who descended into the deepest districts of the soul." (p. 86)

In his analysis of Herbert, Max Graf may well have come to recognize at least some part of his own patricidal fantasies as he interpreted such feelings to his son. His initial acquiescence to Freud's request that his pupils observe their children, as well as his initial
interest in analysis, was based in part on curiosity about himself. The
notes of the Feb. 10, 1909 meeting of the Vienna Psychoanalytic Society indicate he attempted self-analysis: "GRAF tells about his self-
analysis of 'spontaneously emerging melodies' which he regularly
found to be associatively linked to the text." (p. 151) His acceptance
of Freud's theories about unconscious murderous wishes and incestuous erotic desires and his ability to interpret such feelings to his
son suggest that, to some degree, he had recognized them in himself.
He did not want to repeat with his son what his father had done to
him. Rather, he tried to treat his son with loving respect and equality,

and largely succeeded. Herbert told Rizzo (1972), "Typically my father neither pushed me nor held me back." (p. 20)

There is evidence that his analytic work with his son was emotionally trying because it so trenched on his own frightening unconscious murderous fantasies. Four decades later, in 1947, he wrote,
"However psychic material does not deposit itself in the unconscious
only around tenderness and love instincts of the child; it also gathers
around sentiments of animosity and hate that are no strangers to
children. Morbid thoughts of death can result from repressed impulses of hostility . . . which return to consciousness in altered forms."
(pp. 122–23) He used the life of the poet Friedrich Hebbel to illustrate the effect of repressed childhood hatred toward a brutal father.
He noted that Hebbel "confesses in his diary: 'My father hated me,
nor could I love him'" and that the diary "abounds in entries about
murder, bloody outrages and bloodiness." (p. 123) Graf then commented, "It is not easy to place oneself in such a trodden, hurt child
where fear, hatred and thoughts of death dwelt side by side; but it
would only be human if, due to the association of all these sentiments, evil desires developed in the boy, desires that descended to
the darkness of the unconscious and later came to light in the guise
of tragedies." (p. 123) His analysis of Hebbel suggests a further reworking of his own childhood murderous feelings and fantasies toward his father and an indication of how even such feelings may be
used in creative productive work. Graf's acknowledgment that it was
not easy to put himself back in the position of the frightened child
applied equally to Hebbel, himself and to his own son. That he was
able to empathically help his son with unconscious murderous feelings indicates that he had worked through his own conflicts sufficiently enough to use them to do productive work with his son and
in his profession.

Another possible factor involved in Max's ability to work as his
son's analyst as well as in his identification with Freud is suggested by
another mention of Hebbel which occurred in the Dec. 9, 1908
meeting of the Vienna Psychoanalytic Society. In that meeting, Graf
reported on his analysis of the draft of a play that he had written the
summer of that year, two months following the death of his father.
The notes of that meeting continue, "In connection with this sketch
memories of Schiller and Hebbel came back to him: both in spite of
living in conflict with their fathers achieved prominence. Thus this
play is his own personal justification." (Nunberg and Federn, 1962,
p. 81) Max's analysis of his own play, which was a response to the

death of his father, gives indication that he had some awareness of both his competition and identification with his writer-critic father. That he admitted a wish to justify himself (most likely to both himself and his father) suggests the possibility that he not only sought to alleviate guilt over a wish to defeat and outdo his father as a writer and critic but that he also wished to win Joseph's love and approval by fulfilling what he might have felt were his father's own ambitions. If this were so, then these wishes and feelings could be contributing factors in Max's seeking out Freud (also a gifted writer) and identifying with him. In this posited identification with Freud, he could not only win Freud's loving approval but could in his role as his son's analyst unconsciously be the father he had wished for, someone who was interested in and accepting of even angry, competitive, and sexual feelings. A wish for a loving father would also help us to understand one possible factor in Graf's attempt at reconciliation with Freud after he left the Vienna Society and his hurt at Freud's rebuff. The fact that Max Graf's father, Joseph Graf, died in the spring of 1908, the year of Herbert's illness, would increase the possibility that Max's feelings and fantasies about his father, conjectured about here, affected his work as his son's analyst.

Max Graf's personality, interests, and career presented positive elements for identification that would stand Herbert in good stead. At age 69, Herbert painted the following glowing portrait of Max during an interview by Francis Rizzo (1972): "He was an extraordinary man, the most extraordinary I've ever known. He's remembered chiefly as a musicologist and critic, but his interests and accomplishments ranged far and wide over many different fields. He was a disciple of Romaine Rolland, whose works he translated into German, and his mentors and teachers included Hans Richter, Eduard Hanslick and Anton Bruckner . . . My father later took his doctorate in law, but he was a formidable scholar of literature and aesthetics and taught both, first at the Vienna Academy and later in this country. He was also an astute political analyst and for years wrote leading articles on the subject for the Neue Freie Presse. He was equally at home in philosophy and science and quite capable of talking mathematics with Einstein, which he did when they met in the United States." (p. 26, 1972) Some might think that Herbert's assessment of his father reflected a continuation of his idealization of his father's abilities expressed at the end of his treatment: "I thought," said Hans, "you knew everything as you knew about the horse." (1909, p. 144) However, Max Graf's books reveal that indeed he knew, if not everything, then a great deal. Herbert's view of his father was not just a remnant of an oedipal fantasy of a father's power, but a realistic assessment as well.

Max Graf's contemporaries also held him in high esteem. When the composer Richard Strauss wanted to write a preface to his opera Intermezzo, he had Max lecture him in detail on the history of the opera recitative. (Graf, 1945, p. 250) When the city of Vienna wanted to put on a music festival on the 50th anniversary of Wagner's death they commissioned Max Graf to oversee it. It was not only the famous and the powerful that admired and appreciated him for his many talents and abilities. Graf (1945) proudly noted, "It was one of the most beautiful moments in my career as critic when, on one of my birthdays, the young people in the fourth gallery presented me with an address which lauded my critical activity with flattering and highly exuberant words." (p. 68)

But it was Max Graf's love of music and his immersion in the world of music in what was then the music capital of the world that most prominently echoed in Herbert. Herbert's childhood home was filled with music and musical personalities. Early in life Max had wanted to be a musician and composer. He (1945) wrote, "As a student in high school, I took my violin every evening and went to other homes and played classical string quartets with minor officials, teachers or business people just as if that were self-understood. On Sundays I played Haydn's or Mozart's masses in church choirs." (p. 67) Of his wish to be a composer Max Graf (1945) wrote, "I was a student at the University of Vienna . . . and ambitious to become a musician—or better still, a composer . . . I had been composing day and night—songs, violin pieces, chamber music—and like many young people, I was obsessed with the one thought of giving utterance to my musical feeling." (p. 106) His mother was a friend of Brahms's landlady and arranged to have Brahms look at some of his work. Brahms was not impressed. After Brahms's discouragement, Max channeled his musical ambitions in another direction, becoming an important and valued critic, musicologist, and teacher.

Over the course of his long and illustrious career, Max Graf knew, intimately, most of the musical greats of his day. At the age of 17 he spent a year in Paris where he got to know Claude Debussy. Brahms, Bruckner, Ravel, Richter, Schoenberg, Mahler, Walter, von Zemlinsky, both Strausses, Wedekind, Goldmark, and many others prominent in the world of music were acquaintances or more. Mahler was Herbert's godfather. While proud of his relationship with these people, Max was also clear eyed. Graf (1946) noted, "I was successful, and as I grew older I became a mandarin myself. Musicians doffed their hats and whispered to me (when no other critic was close by) that I was the only one that understood. The worse they sang, the more tenderly opera singers caressed my hand. At parties hostesses presented me to their guests with pride . . . I have had some of the leading musicians of our time as friends, Gustav Mahler for a while, Felix Weingartner for many years, and Richard Strauss. But I always found friendly relations with these men so ticklish, difficult, complicated, and unstable that they could be destroyed by a few frank words of criticism . . ." (p. 27–29) His ability to get along with these "difficult, complicated, and unstable" people is a testimony to his own patience, astuteness, and psychological acuity. These were traits that Herbert profitably identified with.

These traits contributed to Max's ability to be his son's analyst, as did his work as a music critic. While Herbert was the only person that Max ever treated, a decade of carefully listening to music and trying to understand and interpret it to the public had helped hone faculties necessary to a psychoanalyst. Max Graf saw himself in his work as a critic as primarily an interpreter, an analyst. In *Composer and Critic* (1946) he wrote, "The first and only important dweller in the house of art is the creative artist . . . The structure of an artistic society in which the critic is not the interpreter of the artist to the public, but the spokesman of the public against the artist, is faulty." (p. 27) This attitude of listening and explicating rather than fault finding may have been communicated to Herbert during the course of the analysis of his phobia, and may, in turn, helped enable him to listen to and accept what his father-analyst had to say.

Throughout his life, Max Graf tried to function as an interpreter of the artist to the public. Just as he contributed much to the young field of psychoanalysis and its founder, analysis and Freud benefited him. During the twelve years in which he was a friend and student of Freud's, he was an active and astute participant in the Wednesday-night meetings of the Vienna Psychoanalytic Society. During those meetings Graf's comments were often more astute than those of the analysts around him. For example, in a paper he presented to the group in 1907 on the psychology of poets, he noted that artistic creations cannot be reduced to being merely an expression of their creator's psychopathology; rather, the healthier aspects of the poets' personalities had to be considered as well. He took what he learned about analytic theory during that first decade of the 20th century and used it in his work for the rest of his life. Abrams (1993) noted, "Graf was so aware of his debt to Freud and the Wednesday night group that he wrote in the foreword [to his 1911 paper Richard Wagner in the *Flying Dutchman*] that it 'would be impossible to separate the ideas which I owe to the guidance of Professor Freud and those which should be attributed to several of my colleagues. Thus I dedicate this study to the memory of those stimulating and exciting hours spent in mutual intellectual strivings with this circle of friends.'" (1911, p. ii) Just as he used analytic theory in his earliest attempts to understand the creativity of Wagner, Max used the same tools four decades later to understand and explain the origins of musical creativity in his books, *Modern Music* (1946) and *From Beethoven to Shostakovich* (1947).

Over the course of his long life Max Graf suffered many separations and losses: divorce, the early death of his second wife, the suicide of his daughter, and having to flee his beloved Vienna to escape the Nazis. However, he never lost his ability to work productively or his interest in people and music. When he arrived in New York City in 1938 he began teaching in the music department of The New School for Social Research. He also continued writing, publishing several books, and was invited to teach at Carnegie Mellon and Temple University. He immigrated back to Vienna in 1947 but often visited the United States to see Herbert as well as his own brother and sister. Looking back at his treatment of his son (1952) Max noted with satisfaction, "This analysis of a child caused a great stir, provoked great polemics. That someone had analyzed a four year old boy seemed to be something scandalous. The medical profession predicted that this was a very neurotic child—No?—who would come to nothing. Well, this very boy—No?—actually became something." (p. 9) Max Graf died in Vienna at the age of 86 on June 24, 1958.

HERBERT GRAF (1903–1973)

Herbert Graf (a.k.a. "Little Hans"), the first-born of Dr. and Mrs. Max Graf, was born April 10, 1903. Freud's 1909 case study gives a vivid picture of the first several years of Herbert's life as recorded by his father. Dr. Kurt Eissler's interviews with Herbert in 1959 (when he was 56 years old) and with his father in 1952 (when Max Graf was 79) add significant new material for analytic consideration and understanding of those early years and the years that followed as well.

Freud (1909) had reported that he had become acquainted with Max Graf through the mother, who had been a patient of his. From the Eissler interviews we learn much more about this connection. It was 1900, just after the publication of the *Interpretation of Dreams*, that

Dr. Freud and Dr. Graf met. Dr. Graf was then going for nightly walks with a Miss Olga Hoenig, the woman he would marry. On these walks she told him of her treatment with Freud, including details from the sessions. Graf said, "It was of extraordinary interest to me. I also had the feeling that one might be able to use this analysis of the unconscious for an account of the process of composition and of artistic creation." (Eissler, 1952, p. 1) He expressed his wish to meet Freud. Miss Hoenig, acting as the intermediary, then asked Freud if he would meet with Graf. Rather than making this request a subject of analytic inquiry, Freud agreed to see his patient's boyfriend to discuss analytic theory. Graf remembered Freud as "extraordinarily charming and very warm" at their first meeting and they continued meeting. Such was the state of analysis in those very early years. The concept of boundaries was not then known and the idea of what was appropriate treatment technique was still in a primitive state.

Graf and Freud became friends, often meeting in coffee houses in the evening. (It is unknown whether on the nights they met Graf also saw his girlfriend, Freud's patient.) Freud also would bring along his sister-in-law, Minna. After a while Freud invited Graf to join a new group, men from various fields that would meet regularly in his apartments to "examine the viability of psychoanalytic theory, its significance for the most diverse fields." (p. 2) It is apparent that not only did Freud, age 44, impress Graf; but Graf, then only 27, was already an important figure in the cultural world of Vienna, impressed Freud. Graf did join, becoming a charter member of the Vienna Psychoanalytic Society.

Freud and Graf's relationship deepened to the point where Freud frequently dined at Graf's home. These dinners occurred over a period of time. Graf (1957) reported, "I had married the young woman he had treated, and Freud often climbed the four flights to our small apartment and had simple evening meals with us to which I invited the composer, Eduard Schutt, whom Freud loved as I did." (p. 163) Freud was eating meals prepared and served by an ex-patient in her home while discussing psychoanalytic theory (and who knows what else) with her husband, who was now more the focus of his attention than she. Freud's regular visits to the Graf home may have even continued during her pregnancy and after the birth of Herbert Graf. (We know, for example, that he climbed those four flights of stairs carrying the gift of a rocking horse on Herbert's third birthday.) Thus a whole series of boundary violations were being enacted over a long period of time, causing confusion and conflict in the woman who would be "Little Hans'" mother.

Of all the extra-analytic intrusions with Herbert Graf's parents, perhaps none compromised his mother's treatment more than Freud brokering their marriage while she was in analysis with him. Max Graf was conflicted about whether to marry his 23-year-old girl-friend. "My first wife was or is a very interesting, very clever and very beautiful woman. She was without a doubt a hysteric but I could not see it at all as a young man. To me she was attractive and interesting even in her hysterical moments . . . After a year, before I decided to marry her I went to Professor Freud, whose patient she still was and asked him if . . . her condition was such that one could marry her. Freud said, 'By all means marry her. You will have fun!' Well, fun I didn't really have." (Eissler, 1952, p. 13) Graf's concern about marrying Ms. Olga Hoenig was probably based not only on his observations of her but also on what he knew of her family history. She was the fifth of six children of a Viennese family. Her two older brothers had committed suicide, and her youngest sister had attempted it.

That Freud stepped so far out of his role as an analyst may have contributed to Mrs. Graf having lifelong negative feelings toward Freud. Herbert Graf told Eissler that his mother (who then was about 80) ". . . is very nervous and has always been a very nervous person. I am quite sure in those surroundings where we all lived without that process, analysis could have resulted in some damage. It didn't help my mother at all . . . My mother still has complaints saying that Freud was not good in her life and in advising father to have children [an-other inappropriate intrusion]." (p. 9) Although Herbert also said that his mother blamed Freud for the breakup of her marriage to his father he did not agree. When Eissler asked whether his mother thought she shouldn't have had children, he responded, "She should. Maybe one. Maybe still me. But not my sister who in the meantime has died. She feels that it was too much of a burden on her mind . . . and that it was not good for their private living . . . I have no way of judging it. I think all these things develop normally and there was a different cause for the breakup of their marriage . . . She didn't like Professor Freud because she felt the advice he gave my father was not good." (pp. 9–10)

From the very beginning the marriage was a miserable one for Max Graf. After one year he told Freud that it was not working. He re-called to Eissler (1952), "On the one hand I was at the beginning of my career, a young writer, a young critic. I wanted to advance. I had the ambition of a talented person and had already at age 25 pub-lished two books. On the other hand here was a woman who did not want to socialize or who was insecure in the company of others . . .

and therefore avoided it. One does not have a young beautiful wife in order to be locked into one's apartments . . . Another reason was that this woman suddenly became jealous of my papers and tore them up. Freud was very surprised and I made another attempt. I thought to myself perhaps having children would change these moods of hers. But this did not happen. I lasted for 18½ years in the marriage until the children were old enough for me to leave the marriage safely, without disturbing their development too much. Later I wondered whether it would have been better . . . if I had left earlier. I don't know what the right thing was . . . There were other things that I don't want to talk about anymore, which did not sit well in the marriage of young people. In which one should also . . . take pleasure in the erotic . . . However I did not leave in anger but parted amicably and she got married soon thereafter." (pp. 13–14) Later on, he added that every time he and his wife had intercourse "there was some episode in the morning." What this episode was, what she actually did or felt was never elucidated.

I have related the preceding material in detail because new contexts emerge from it in which to view Freud's 1909 paper. For three years before Herbert's birth in 1903, both his parents were enmeshed with Freud in a web of interrelated, complex enactments that would take an analytic Houdini to untangle completely. Suffice it to say that in the beginning era of analysis no one knew better. Sadly though, no matter what the nature of Mrs. Graf's psychopathology, these enactments compromised whatever she might otherwise have derived from her treatment. Another context which emerges is that Herbert was born to a couple who were already unhappily married and that his father had the fantasy that his birth would resolve his mother's conflicts and lead to a resolution of their marital difficulties. In fact, the marital discord continued through the years described in the 1909 paper and beyond. Herbert's beautiful, histrionic mother, who tore up his father's papers and had "episodes" after sexual intercourse, was likely to have enacted dramatic, "operatic" scenes in front of him. (One of Mrs. Graf's equally beautiful sisters was, in fact, a professional actress.) Such melodrama would have contributed to the many unconscious determinants of his fear of going out of the house lest he see a horse and be bitten by it or that it would fall down and "make a row with its feet." It would likely also have been an unconscious contributing factor to the choice of his life's work as an opera director (as I will discuss in detail below).

While the 1909 paper referred to problems that Mrs. Graf had as a

parent, particularly her seductive behavior toward her son, the Eissler interviews provide more details of the difficulties both her husband and son saw in Mrs. Graf's mothering. In evaluating Max Graf's
memory of the earliest years of Herbert's life, one must take into account that he was 79 years old when Eissler interviewed him. He himself protested at one point, "that was almost 50 years ago." Though
he told Eissler (contrary to what Herbert reported) that his wife had
wanted children when asked if his wife was "very involved with her
son" his response was, "No. This woman was . . . a hysteric. She was
very focused on herself—no?" He added that, while she didn't neglect Herbert, she wasn't involved with him the way a mother should
be. She had even greater difficulty appropriately mothering their second child, Herbert's sister. When the little girl was shown to the
mother immediately after delivery she rejected her. In the father's
words, "When they brought her the girl—no?—She discarded her
like this. (Here Graf must have made a gesture of rejection, of pushing away) . . . She never coped well with the daughter . . . I think it
was jealousy because it was a girl." (Eissler, 1952, p. 20) Herbert also
felt that his mother had not wanted his sister. Freud (1909) commented on Mrs. Graf's reluctance to have children, but did not mention his own role in the decision. He wrote, "It might perhaps have
been possible to make use of Hans' fear of the horse 'making a row
with the legs' for filling up a few more gaps in our adjudication upon
the evidence. Hans, it is true, declared it reminded him of his kicking
about with his legs when he was compelled to leave off playing so as
to do lumpf; so that this element of the neurosis becomes connected
with the problem whether his mother liked having children or was
compelled to have them." (p. 135)

His mother's rejection of his sister may well have played a role in
Herbert's own conscious and unconscious feelings and fantasies
about both his sister and mother during the years described in the
1909 paper. Max Graf described his daughter as very beautiful, even
more intelligent than her brother, and very kind. Though, according
to him, the girl felt slighted by the fact that her brother had gone to
the university and she had not even gone to high school, he also reported that the children got along well together. Herbert's memory
that as an older child, "I began to try my hand at duplicating the wonders I'd seen in the opera house—first with a toy theater I built with
my sister's help at home" supports this contention. (Rizzo, 1972,
p. 28) Though his sister's role in his life and psyche is not the focus of
this study, it is nonetheless important to note that as a grown woman

she committed suicide. This tragic outcome and all that preceded it in her life weighed heavily on Max in his old age and must also have weighed heavily on Herbert.

Though Herbert's mother had had a prior miscarriage, her pregnancy with him was uneventful. He was delivered at home without complications by the family doctor. His father's first impression of him was that he was a beautiful and cheerful infant. By age two, Herbert would walk around the kitchen and sing songs taught to him by an elderly nanny who may have been in the home for about one year. He spent four weeks every summer during his childhood in Gmunden with his mother. His father would join them on weekends. Once he was sent to his father's parents, "for a while because Mama liked him very much." (p. 24) In addition, "Every Sunday I would take him to Lainz where my parents had a villa. We always spent Sunday there, first so that my mother would see him. She liked him. Then one sat in the garden—no?" (p. 29) Father and son made most of these trips without the younger Mrs. Graf because of the tension between her and her mother-in-law. Max Graf added that this was typical of his wife; she was at odds with everybody and reluctant to go anywhere. When Eissler tried repeatedly to draw a parallel between her staying in the house and "Little Hans'" phobia, Graf rejected it. He said that it was different because she wasn't anxious, as Herbert had been, that she stayed at home because she found fault with people. The tension between Herbert's parents from his earliest years onward was evident. His reclusive mother not only refused to go to see Herbert's grandmother, who was so eager to see him, but she also refused to accompany his father, the ambitious man about town, to concerts, plays, or other cultural events. Imagine the bitterness that lay behind Max's comment about Freud's prediction that he would have fun if he married Ms. Hoenig, "Well fun I really didn't have."

How did little Herbert process all of the preceding? Unfortunately the timing, details, or sequence of the separations from his mother are not known. We do not know if he was sent to his paternal grandparents "for a while" before or after his phobia or before or after his sister's birth. We do not know whether "a while" meant a week, a month, or longer. The episode does raise the possibility that his fear of leaving the house may have arisen partly in response to separation from his mother for a period of time. It is hard to imagine that a woman who disliked her mother-in-law and refused to visit her allowed her son to visit her without comment or objection, unless the visit occurred after the sister's birth when the mother possibly had a post-partum depression. Similarly, how did Herbert feel and think about the weekly family visits to his grandparents alone with his father because his mother refused to go? Were there weekly scenes between his parents over these visits? It seems clear that his father found a peaceful refuge once a week sitting in the garden with his mother and his son and away from his wife. Did these weekly separations from his mother contribute to a fear and fantasy of loss that expressed itself in Herbert's fear of leaving the house? In addition, his mother's obvious rejection of his sister may have contributed to a fear of her rejecting him as well.

These contexts and the possibilities they raise of other factors contributing to the unconscious conflicts and fantasies that underlay Herbert's phobia do not refute or replace Freud's findings and conclusions of 1909. Rather, since all symptoms are over-determined, they are possible additions to his findings. In this regard, two paragraphs on one page of Herbert Graf's book, *Opera for the People* (1951), written when he was 48, may be read both as a telling condensation of a series of unconscious images and fantasies that he may have had of his mother and as evidence of the intensity of his identification with his father. "I returned to my native Vienna for a visit with my mother in the spring of 1946. . . . Never will I forget the ghastly experience of . . . seeing the ruins of the famous opera house. . . . Through the huge holes in its bomb-shattered walls one could see the rubble remains of what had been one of the most beautiful auditoriums in the world—a symbol of Europe's musical culture trampled by the evil forces of Hitlerism. My sadness at the sight of these ruins was deepened by the unforgettable memories of my youth. I saw myself night after night, in the company of dozens of my fellow students, storming up the staircase to the 'Fourth Gallery,' after hours waiting in line spent in heated debates. In the gallery we occupied standing room, or, more often, sat on the steps, studying the opera scores while we listened to great performances under the direction of Franz Schalk and Richard Strauss." (p. 4) We do not know how long it had been in 1946 since Herbert had last seen his mother or what he knew about her wartime experiences as he anticipated seeing her again. This memory, in which he appears to associate his mother with a once beautiful opera house that has been violated and left in ruins, hints at what possibly may have been going on in his mind unconsciously. Among those unconscious fantasies and feelings the following are possible: she has been violently castrated; intercourse is a sadistic violent act that leads to castration; the war between my parents led to her destruction; my mother put on violent operatic shows (beating my sister, threatening me with castration, arguing with my father, etc.) that destroyed her as well; what I witnessed of my beautiful, exciting and dramatic mother made me very angry and very sad; I once loved her so and feel sad and angry now about what has become of her; it is so sad to see how destroyed she is by her emotional difficulties.

The other part of Herbert's association to seeing his mother in 1946, the memories of pleasurable excitement running up the stairs of the opera-house to see and hear the opera, seems very much an expressive echo of his excited, erotic childhood attachment to her that was so evident in Freud's 1909 paper. However, it is also a striking echo of his father's erotic fantasies and memories in association with music and the opera house. Compare the wording of Herbert's memory of going to the opera as a teenager reported above with Max's memory of the same (1945). "Thus we prepared ourselves for the holiday when we went for the first time to the Opera palace on the Ring. From noontime on we stood, boys and girls, in front of the small entrance to the Opera House, which still remained locked, with piano scores in our hands, heatedly debating about music. When the door at last opened we would storm excitedly to the box office, and then up four flights of stairs like competing foot-racers up the still dimly lighted passageway to the fourth gallery from where we could look down on the stage . . . When all had become silent and one's heart pounded excitedly, the conductor came, sat at his desk, opened the sorcerer's book and raised his magic wand." (p. 67) That Herbert's description so closely follows his father's suggests Herbert's intense Oedipal identification with Max and a shared unconscious primal scene fantasy in which the young student listener and viewer tries, in the midst of his own mounting erotic excitement, to understand and learn what is going on (studies the score) so that he too, like the phallic conductor father, could make "beautiful music" with mother.

Herbert's identification with his father was most obvious in their shared lifelong devotion to music. Herbert was born with musical ability that came from both parents. A maternal aunt was a professional pianist. His father, who played the violin and piano and had had aspirations to be a composer, lived and breathed music in the musical city of Vienna. Herbert Graf (1951) wrote, "Opera was a truly organic part of the cultural life and musical tradition that pervaded the entire city. My own home and education may serve as an example of this living tradition." (p. 5) Herbert told Rizzo (1972), "Gustav Mahler, my godfather, was a frequent guest at our house . . . I remember Oskar Kokoschka and the architect Adolf Loos, too. Then there was Richard Strauss and Arnold Schoenberg, whose importance my father was among the first to recognize." (p. 27) So nature and nurture conspired to lead the boy into a lifetime devoted to Max's world of music.

However it was more than just a general identification with his father's musical interests or the fact that opera was an organic part of the city in which he grew up that determined the specific role in the world of opera that he chose to play, that of an opera director. He noted to Rizzo (1972), "The profession of opera stage director as we know it simply didn't exist in those days." (p. 27) As director, Herbert controlled everything that went on in the opera. He decided where and when entrances and exits were made; chose costumes, staging, and sets; helped choose and rehearse the cast and worked with the conductor in regard to the interpretation of the opera. This profession allowed him to use his inborn talents in a pleasurable way while permitting him to reenact childhood experiences and fantasies as the person in control rather than as a confused, frightened, or helpless witness. As opera director he could get others to express his passions for him and control the way they did it. The traumatic scenes he had witnessed, whether primal scenes, his mother beating his sister, his parents' quarreling, his mother on the toilet or his mother putting on dramatic displays, and the feelings and fantasies these scenes engendered, could all be replayed under his direction and control. Thus he had an adaptive, sublimated way of reworking and using troubling old memories and the affects and fantasies bound to them.

Herbert Graf (1972) said, "The stage director is opera's invisible man, or should be. It is the very nature of his work to stay behind the scenes and leave the spotlight to the work itself." (p. 26) His wish to make himself invisible consciously subserved another wish, to be an interpreter to the audience of what they were hearing and seeing on the stage. His thesis in "Opera for the People" (1951) is that an opera should be understandable to the audience. To this end he argued that all operas in the United States should be sung in English. In the days when many opera singers were overweight and could not act, he argued for singers who looked the part and had acting skills. He likewise believed the scenery and costumes should serve the purpose of facilitating the understanding of the book. He agreed with his friend and colleague, Toscanini, that the most important attribute of an opera singer was "good diction."

That Herbert's life's work became making operas believable and understandable to the audience suggests that multiple intra-psychic

factors coalesced in it. He believed that if audiences understood operas, opera would become more popular. On another level he may
have identified with the audience as the confused child who could
not understand the scenes to which he had been exposed. He also
may have become an interpreter, or psychoanalyst, in identification
with his father. Max Graf had interpreted and explained things both
during his analysis and as a music critic. Herbert Graf as the stage director not only was able to interpret but to control things in the audience and on the stage.

By Herbert's mid-teens his plan to become an opera director was
set. As the First World War raged, conditions in Vienna deteriorated,
so his parents sent him to spend a summer with his aunt in the sub-
urbs of Berlin. They may also have sent him there to escape the "war"
in the home, since by then they were approaching the end of their
marriage. In Berlin, Herbert saw many dramas directed by Max Reinhardt and was impressed with the realistic details of his productions.
Graf (1972) said, "I felt that it was my mission to do for the opera
what Reinhardt had done for the spoken theater." (p. 27)

With this purpose in mind he entered the University of Vienna to
get a doctorate in musicology (like his father). Simultaneously he enrolled in the School of Arts and Crafts to study scenic design and the
Academy of Music to study composing and singing. His attendance at
three schools at once indicates how certain his ambition was and how
great his intelligence, energy, and abilities were. It may also be that
all this activity served to defensively distance him emotionally from
the tension between his parents. With his doctoral thesis, "Richard
Wagner as a Stage Director: Studies for the History of Opera Staging," Herbert once again expressed his identification with, and competition with, his father. The elder Graf had been a great admirer of
Wagner and had made Wagner the subject of the first paper ever
written that applied psychoanalytic understanding to music. Herbert
received his Ph.D. at the age of 22.

As soon as he had completed his studies he left Vienna. Publicly he
said that he left because Vienna, while a great place to learn, was too
conservative to give beginners a chance. However he revealed more
personal reasons in his 1959 interview with Eissler. "I left a very decadent place . . . but this was the misery of the Austrian at the end of
the Austrian Empire. And there was personal misery because of the
divorce of my parents, a certain amount of poverty. And all these pictures of Hoffmannstahl (Hugo Hoffmannstahl was a great Viennese
poet and librettist for Richard Strauss) and Schoenberg and Freud.
Somehow we young people left Vienna in opposition and went to

Germany for that reason. And as far away as possible. To begin with I
went to Munich. We had a sort of aversion to the whole world
(Eissler asked, 'Psychoanalysis included?') That was included . . . But
still it was all too complicated. So I was quite glad to get away from
everything! That did not mean only psychoanalysis." (pp. 11–12)
Thus, while he tried to rationalize his departure from Vienna on general conditions common to all people of his generation in his field,
there were deeply personal reasons as well. Certainly post–WW I conditions in Germany were as miserable and decadent as in Vienna.
More likely Herbert wanted to get away from the source of the misery
connected to the end of the *other* war, his parents' marriage.

While Max Graf told Eissler that the divorce was amicable, that outcome seems improbable given Mrs. Graf's persona. Many decades
later she was still complaining to Herbert that it was Freud's fault that
her marriage came to an end. Was his mother's blaming Freud for
her failed marriage what Herbert meant when he said, "it was all too
complicated"? Was his mother's lifelong preoccupation with analysis
and Freud part of what he meant when Herbert said he wanted to get
away from analysis? While his mother was given to histrionic displays,
his father was prone to distance himself from conflict, as he had in
leaving the Vienna Psychoanalytic years before. Herbert was probably
made miserable by the scenes of marital conflict and by his mother's
complaints about his father, particularly since he was deeply attached
to both of them. The loss of control and dissolution involved in such
scenes and in the war would have reawakened all the frightening
scenes of his childhood and fears of loss of one or both parents.

Elsewhere in his interview with Eissler, Herbert spoke further
about leaving Vienna, "It is more this reaction against old Austria and
the horror, you see, that we left. . . . I am still very sensitive about Austrian affairs when I go back. I go back frequently because of my
mother or because of my work. But I am jittery in Vienna, much
more so than I am in other cities . . . The mentality of the people is
not a good one to my taste. . . . They are charming, talented. All
these things are positive. But personally . . . I think I find more in-
trigue, and I find more harm done than in any other place in the
world. . . . I mean it's the only city in the world where the harder you
hit a face in an amusement park the better it is and the more they admire you. That's their sense of humor. I was always skeptical of their
sense of humor because there is always a bit of *Schaudenfreude* in it,
a pleasure in hurting the other person. So I am not the best Viennese . . . but I always go back." (pp. 13–14) Here again one cannot
help but wonder, what was the horror from which he tried to get as

far away as possible? Who in particular did he think got sadistic pleasure out of hurting other people? On the most personal level, was he
saying that he had been hurt, as it hit in the face by one or both of his
parents? If so, he was more likely to have felt the victim of his critical,
complaining mother, rather than of his father, who was forever trying
to avoid or deny unpleasantness in others and anger in himself. Such
treatment would have been extremely painful for Herbert because
he was as deeply attached to her as he was to his father. (He continued to visit her in Vienna till her death no matter where in the world
he worked.) In talking to Eissler about his father's ability to distance
himself from and keep control in emotionally painful situations he
said, "I am not that wise because I am also my mother's son. She is
not as controlled as my father was." (p. 26)

Another possibility is that among the horrors and cruelties Herbert wanted to escape was the rampant anti-Semitism of Vienna,
which, again like his father, he did not mention directly. The sadistic
taking of pleasure from other people's misery this certainly would
characterize the numerous anti-Semites in Vienna. In 1925, the year
Herbert left for Munster, he might have believed that anti-Semitism
in Germany couldn't be as bad as it was in Vienna.

Over the next nine years Graf worked his way up from singer and
third opera stage director at the small municipal theater in Munster
in Westphalia to bigger opera stages in Germany, Switzerland, and
Prague. He was only 22 when he began and by emulating his father's
iconoclastic approach Herbert earned a reputation as an *enfant terrible* for his daring and creative staging. His increasing renown earned
Herbert a fellowship to the Julliard School in New York for the summer of 1930. In 1932 he was appointed producer of the Leipzig
Opera and in 1934 was invited to direct operas for the Philadelphia
Orchestra. He eagerly accepted this invitation and his work there
generally met with critical and public acclaim.

What remained unspoken, but probably played a role in Herbert's
eagerness to go to America, was that Hitler and his Nazi party were
then in power in Germany. By 1933, non-Aryans had already been
dismissed from his opera company. Like his father once again, the
younger Graf did not mention any personal anti-Semitic affronts he
may have experienced as part of the spreading Nazi terror, just as he
had omitted mentioning this "horror" as a reason he had earlier fled
Vienna. Yet in all likelihood he must have been concerned both for
himself and his wife and one-year-old son.

Herbert's work in Philadelphia brought him to the attention of
both Toscanini, who enthusiastically approved of his staging, and

Bruno Walter, who invited him to stage a Mozart opera in Florence and Salzburg. Herbert then worked in various opera houses in Europe till he was offered a contract as stage director for the Metropolitan Opera House for the 1936–37 season. He brought his wife and son with him and remained at the Metropolitan for more than two decades. Both in New York and after he left the Met in 1960 to work primarily in Europe, Herbert Graf worked with the greatest conductors, singers, and musicians of the day. During his years at the Met he also guest-directed all over the United States, taught, and even helped found the opera department at The Berkshire Music Center in Tanglewood, Mass. His work became so widely known and applauded that in 1946 he was called to Hollywood to stage some operatic sequences in an MGM movie. He also participated in the early days of television when in 1943 he became director of musical activities for NBC. There were only 5,000 TV sets in America at that time.

After 24 years at the Metropolitan, frustrated that he had never been able to achieve the total control over productions that he craved, he resigned and accepted the post of manager of the State Opera in Zurich. He told Rizzo (1972), " . . . what I wanted was total freedom of choice in repertory, casting, designers and rehearsal time. Unfortunately my freedom proved to be less than total." (p. 27) Frustrated again in Zurich he resigned that post in 1962. However, during his time in Zurich he founded the Zurich Opera Studio, which became a world-renowned institution. He continued to work and teach in the major opera houses on both sides of the Atlantic for the rest of his life.

Herbert summed up his own abilities and talents rather modestly for Rizzo on Feb. 24, 1972, approximately one year before his death. "Look, I'm not a 'brilliant' stage director in the style of a Rheinhardt or a Zeffirelli, and even though I can appreciate that sort of virtuosity, it's neither part of my nature nor my aim. I am a professor's son, an earnest worker, and a know-how man who believes that certain aspects of operatic know-how can be passed along to others. People say that Toscanini was a genius, but for me his ideas, his artistic insights, weren't the stuff of "genius"; that came out in his amazing power to put his ideas across—simple straightforward common sense, conveyed with the thrust and impact of revelation" (pp. 28–29). In this summary of himself in his life's work, Herbert Graf acknowledged his identification with his father and equated him with Toscanini, whose power Herbert felt stemmed from the conductor's ability to interpret things clearly and simply to an audience as his father, Max, had interpreted things to him.

He conveyed the same identification even more explicitly to Eissler. "Many times I wonder why I went into opera, in particular to operatic staging? Whether it has anything to do with all these experiences I had. I cannot prove it but I daresay it has something to do with it because . . . I like to be in the field my father was. I did not feel that I had the talent he had as a writer though I wrote two books very painfully. He wrote easily . . . somehow I wonder whether . . . I am fighting a battle in my field. Maybe that has something to do with it . . . I think it . . . should go back to an analytical way. Toscanini, whose pupil I really am, really went back to the idea first study the letter of the thing and then try to come back to the spirit of the thing by analysis." (p. 27) Here he acknowledged his identification with his father in the choice of his life's work and also his competition with him. Since Herbert could not write as well as Max, he could not compete as a critic and so chose a related field in music. In choosing to be a director of operas, he also appears to have unconsciously lived out an oedipal fantasy replacing father in his relationship to mother since opera, like his mother, is dramatic, histrionic, exciting, pleasurable, and at times difficult to understand. He sought to interpret and control the opera as he wished to understand the scenes his mother enacted so he could help both her and himself feel secure. In the pursuit of these goals he found a musical father in Toscanini, who, like Herbert's real father, tried to analyze and interpret. He also outdid his father, the would-be composer, by becoming a participant in the creative process rather that just a witness to and critic of it.

Little is known of Herbert's life outside of his work. Of the years immediately following his analysis we only know that the symptoms that he had been treated for were gone and that he functioned well. However he told Eissler that he had "always" had a fear of fire. This was never mentioned in the case history. Had Max Graf not reported it? Had Herbert not told his father about it? Had his other fears pushed it aside at that time? Was it not present then? We do not know the reason it was not mentioned. What we do know is that he was deeply affected by what later happened to his city and his family. He told Eissler that with, "The destruction of Vienna and the destruction of our family . . . my parents were divorced and so forth. Then some psychological problems began in our lives. Plenty of them. I don't know if one had to do with the other." (p. 8) Once again, it was never clarified what psychological problems he referred to or who had them. Was it he himself? His mother? His father? His sister? All of them? Whatever he was referring to, as discussed above, it contributed to his fleeing Vienna for Munster. During his nine years in

Germany he married and at age 30 became the father of a little boy himself. Little is known of his marriage except that some "difficulties" arose. He told Eissler, "I mean when we come into our dangerous age, when we sometime have a problem and I am deeply attached to my wife. We had one or two years of a more difficult period. Then I went myself to a psychoanalyst to help me in this situation. But I didn't like it at all! . . . I always had the feeling that psychoanalysis was the most wonderful thing on earth as a thought, as a science. But it is too easily an . . . I mean the hands of the people handling it often are not worthy of handling it." (p. 13) Here again it is unfortunate that Herbert's allusions were never clarified. What did he mean when he said "our dangerous age"? What was the problem? Was he referring to a midlife crisis and or some sexual indiscretion? Was he seen in psychotherapy or in psychoanalysis? What was it that the analyst did or that Herbert felt he had done that evoked such a negative reaction and the metaphor of hands and handling? All that is known is that the marriage did continue on.

Toward the end of the interview by Eissler, Max Graf alluded to some kind of psychopathology in Herbert that had not been revealed. However despite, or perhaps because of, pressure from Eissler, he refused to elaborate. Max appropriately told Eissler that it was his son's business and therefore his son's choice to talk or not to talk about it. What Max Graf had in mind remains unknown.

FATHER AND SON. SUMMARY AND DISCUSSION

I have reviewed the lives of Max and Herbert Graf here, as much as is possible, in their own words, in the hope of elucidating the workings of their minds. In particular I have tried to shed light on how the workings of Max's mind, both as an analyst and as a father, influenced the workings of his son's mind, both during his analysis at the age four and throughout the course of his life. Max Graf had been drawn to Freud and psychoanalytic theory by the hope that psychoanalytic tools offered a key to understanding the sources of musical creativity and composition. Max had once wished to become a creative artist himself, either as a composer or as a musician but became a musicologist, teacher and critic instead. His wish to understand the sources of artistic creativity reflected his wish to understand both himself (and what he lacked) and creative people, so that he could learn their secret, and do what they did. He pursued this attempt to understand the sources of musical creativity throughout his life using what he had learned about psychoanalytic theory from Freud.

Herbert Graf was born into an unhappy marriage. Despite his attraction to Herbert's mother, Max had had grave misgivings about marrying his mother because of her psychopathology and the serious psychopathology in her family. Max turned to Freud for advice and Freud, despite his role as the analyst of the woman in question, unfortunately gave it. Other extra-analytic intrusions went on during and after Freud's treatment of Herbert's mother. In those earliest years of psychoanalysis little was understood about the meaning and consequences of such extra-analytic enactments. That Max Graf, who because of his own controlling and abusive father, had difficulty submitting to authority, asked Freud's advice suggests that unconsciously Max had been searching for a wise, accepting father who would protect him and not reject him because of his sexual desires (as his father had done to his brother).

The marriage was unhappy from the beginning. Max got little or no sexual or social gratification from his wife. Within a year Max was thinking of abandoning the relationship and again consulted Freud. Together they decided that having a child might be a solution to the difficulties in the marriage, despite signs that Mrs. Graf was ambivalent, at best, about having children. It was to this couple in turmoil that Herbert Graf was born. Though Mrs. Graf did not have a nanny for him at birth one was brought in for a year or so sometime in Herbert's second year. We may ponder the reason. Did she become depressed or overwhelmed after his birth or at a later time?

The marital turmoil continued. Max Graf continued going to concerts and shows alone. Mrs. Graf refused to accompany her husband and son to her mother-in-law's house on Sundays. Another, probably more disturbing separation from mother occurred either before or after the birth of Herbert's sister, when he was sent to stay with his paternal grandparents for an unspecified period of time. This separation once again raises the possibility that she was either overwhelmed and/or depressed at the prospect of caring for one or both of her children. In any case feelings, thoughts, and fantasies of separation from mother were likely being stimulated in Herbert and intensified by his observing her rejection of his sister and father. Such feelings and fantasies of loss of mother may have been, in addition to those feelings and fantasies put forward in 1909, contributing factors to his fear of leaving the house.

The 1909 paper described scenes of maternal seduction, loss of control and rage. His mother exposed herself to him in the toilet, took him to bed with her and then told him he was bad and threatened him with castration when he masturbated. She flew into rages and beat his sister, and gave him enemas and laxatives. What the 1909 paper did not describe was the severe marital difficulties that existed between Herbert's parents and the scenes that he must have witnessed expressing those tensions. His mother, described as a hysteric by all (though what her exact diagnosis would be today is unclear), was probably prone to act dramatically. Just as she beat her young daughter it is easy to imagine her arguing, complaining, yelling, threatening and crying at her husband for his going out to concerts and leaving her alone with the children or for taking Herbert to see his mother. It is just as easy to imagine Max Graf, conflicted over his own anger, ever eager to distance himself from such feelings by denial, reacting quietly. Perhaps Herbert's internal fantasies of these scenes also expressed themselves in elements of the fantasy of the horse biting and the horse falling down and making a row with its feet. Feelings of rage, resentment, bitterness and frustration between parents, whether overtly expressed or unconsciously communicated, help undermine any child's sense of safety and stimulate fears that people can lose control and that terrible violent things can happen.

While it is unlikely that the pervasive anti-Semitism of Vienna contributed to the sense of danger evident in the little boy's childhood neurosis, it is possible that it did. Vienna was in reality an ominous and disturbing place for Jews. They were humiliated, insulted, threatened, and held back in many areas. The pervasive anti-Semitism led Max Graf to ask Freud whether he should have his newborn son baptized to protect him. If Herbert was unaware of the danger of anti-Semitism during the time of his phobic anxiety, there is no doubt that he was soon to become aware of it. While his father, on the one hand, was certainly aware of it, at the same time, he tried to deny the hatred by romanticizing Vienna and the Viennese. As a grown man, Herbert, like his father, never wrote of any direct personal anti-Semitic insult or threat even though he ran away from the "horror" of Vienna, and later fled Germany after the Nazi rise to power.

When Herbert's phobic symptoms began and Freud suggested that Max treat him with analysis, even though Max had no prior experience treating anybody Max was nonetheless emotionally prepared. Given the lack of boundaries that he had personally seen in Freud's treatment of his wife and in what he heard and saw in those pioneer meetings of the Vienna Psychoanalytic Society, it probably did not seem unusual or problematic for him to try to treat his own son. He had been drawn to Freud and psychoanalytic thinking not just by his curiosity about others, particularly composers, but also by his wish to

understand himself. Freud's discovery and elucidation of unconscious mental forces and the manifold, disguised expressions of
those forces in fantasy, symptoms and behavior struck him as a possible pathway to that understanding. Even before the outbreak of Herbert's neurosis, Max's close observation of his son, reported to Freud
in weekly letters, unconsciously expressed, through his identification
with his son, his curiosity about himself. As Max observed his son he
became more convinced of the correctness of Freud's findings of the
presence of a rich unconscious fantasy life in children, rife with expressions of erotic desire and murderous hatred. Max became then,
inevitably more aware of that part of his own mental life, preparing
him for the difficult role he was to play as his son's analyst. As we have
seen it was Max Graf who wrote, "It is not easy to place oneself in such
a trodden, hurt child where fear, hatred and thoughts of death dwelt
side by side." (p. 123) It was not easy because the frightened child,
Herbert, roused most strongly the feelings and memories of the
frightened, "trodden" child that Max had been. Yet Max Graf was
able to face those feelings and memories in himself and in his son
and interpret them to them both.

While none of the interpretations Max Graf made to his son dealt
with any of the issues being suggested as contributing causative factors in Herbert's neurosis, Herbert's symptoms disappeared. Does
this result invalidate the suggestion that these factors played a role in
the symptoms? The answer is no. It only suggests that the interpretations that were made were valid and central enough to be sufficient
to help resolve Herbert's conflicts at that time. All symptoms are
over-determined, and in any analysis some intra-psychic threads are
left untouched. In addition, other factors were at work in the analysis
that contributed to the boy's improvement. Max Graf told Eissler
that when Herbert read the case he told him "he was grateful to
me that I took charge of the matter." (p. 42)

Herbert Graf lived his life with no sign of the fear of leaving the
house that had plagued him in his fourth year of life. He moved
freely about the world from city to city and from one side of the Atlantic to the other. While he had another symptom, fear of fire, there
is no indication that this phobia inhibited him in any serious way.
That he should have had some other symptom, as alluded to by his
father to Eissler, is not unusual. Whatever it may have been it did not
interfere with Herbert's ability to work creatively and productively,
one of the measures of psychological maturity. Herbert himself told
Eissler (1959) that, when he visited Freud at age 19, he jokingly told
Freud, "I still will end up in opera which might be proof that all is not

so normal after all." (p. 2) This remark hints at Herbert's recognition that the world of opera is peopled by those who are talented but temperamental, sensitive, narcissistic and given to dramatic emotional outbursts. In short, he consciously or unconsciously seemed to recognize that he would be dealing with people like his mother, people who in his mind were not normal but whom he loved. His experience with his mother prepared him for interacting with them.

However in his role as stage director he could not only be in control of the scenes that these people participated in but he could interpret these scenes for them and the audience. His role as interpreter is but one legacy of his complex identification with his father, who both had interpreted Herbert's childhood fears and who practiced a career that encompassed the role of interpreting artists to their audiences. Herbert not only identified with his father but also competed with him by entering the world of music. By being part of the creative process in opera he both outdid his father and vicariously gratified his father's own wishes to have been a creative artist himself. In that way the oedipal drama that had been lived out in Herbert's work had a happy ending.

We know much less about Herbert Graf's personal life and about his ability to love than we do about his ability to work. Nothing is known about his married life other than he was married twice and had at least one child, a son, by his first wife. We do also know that this first marriage took place when he was a young man in Europe and that he made some loving comments about both this wife and his son in his book *Opera for the People*. Tragically this wife committed suicide. None of the circumstances or events surrounding her death are known. Little is known about his second marriage either other than his second wife was not Jewish. When he spoke to Eissler about a difficult period in his marriage, for which he had sought help from an analyst, it is not known which of the two marriages he was speaking about or what the nature of his difficulty was. However, his work relationships earned him admiration, respect, warmth, and gratitude. Reri Grist (2005), an American soprano of international renown, recalled Herbert Graf with fondness decades after his death: "I went to an audition for Herbert Graf . . . And he invited me to come to Zurich . . . Herbert Graf was a very kind man, a very knowledgeable man and a very capable stage director. I sang in several operas and was successful there. Graf encouraged me to audition for other opera houses . . . I was lucky because people heard me in Zurich and invited me to perform elsewhere: Glyndebourne and Vienna . . . Graf unlike most general managers of an opera house told me that I should accept it and that he would arrange it with Zurich. Most directors would have said no at that point in my career, but he released me." (p. 5) This vignette illustrates Herbert's capacity to love another person, to recognize that person's wishes and needs and to put them before his own. As Grist comments it was a capacity that most in his field and position did not have.

In summary Herbert Graf grew up and lived a life free from the restricting anxiety of his childhood neurosis, a neurosis for which his father treated him under Freud's supervision in the pioneering days of psychoanalysis. Though he had other symptoms, he exhibited a capacity to love and to work. To paraphrase Max Graf's assessment of his son in reference to the dire predictions made in Vienna about what would become of a child treated by psychoanalysis—the boy became something.

BIBLIOGRAPHY

ABRAMS, D. (1993) Freud and Max Graf: On the Psychoanalysis of Music. In *Psychoanalytic Explorations in Music: Second Series*. Feder, S., Karmel, R., and Pollock, G., Ed. Madison, Conn.: International Universities Press.

BERKLEY, G. (1988) *Vienna and Its Jews. The Tragedy of Success*. 1880–1980. Cambridge, Mass.: Madison Books.

EISSLER, K. (1952) Interview With Dr. Max Graf. December 16, 1952. *The Sigmund Freud Archives*. Library of Congress, Washington D.C.

———— (1959) Interview With Dr. Herbert Graf. October 22, 1959. *The Sigmund Freud Archives*. Library of Congress, Washington D.C.

FREUD, S. (1909) Analysis of a Phobia in a Five-Year-Old Boy. *S.E.*, 10.

GLENN, J. (1980) Freud's Advice to Hans's Father: The First Supervisory Sessions. In *Freud and His Patients*, ed. M. Kanzer and J. Glenn. New York: Jason Aronson, 1980, pp. 121–134.

GRAF, H. (1951) *Opera for the People*. Minneapolis: U. of Minnesota Press.

GRAF, M. (1942) Reminiscences of Professor Sigmund Freud. *Psychoanal. Q.*, 11: 465–476.

———— (1945) *Legend of a Musical City*. The Philosophical Library, New York.

———— (1946) *Composer and Critic. Two Hundred Years of Musical Criticism*. New York: Norton.

———— (1946) *Modern Music. The Story of Music in Our Time*. The Philosophical Library, New York.

———— (1947) *From Beethoven to Shostakovich. The Psychology of the Composing Process*. The Philosophical Library, New York.

———— (1957) *Every Hour Was Fulfilled: A Half Century of Life in Music and the Theater*. Wien-Frankfurt: Forum Verlag.

GRIST, RERI. (2005) *Reri Grist: One of a Kind*. Reported by Robert Blue. *U.S. Opera Web*. Online Magazine devoted to American Opera. Aug. 27, 2005.

NUNBERG, H., & FEDERN, E., Eds. (1962) *Minutes of the Vienna Psychoanalytic Society, Vol. 1. 1906–1908.* New York: International Universities Press.
———— (1967) *Minutes of the Vienna Psychoanalytic Society, Vol. 2. 1908–1910.* New York: International Universities Press.
RIZZO, F. (1972) Memoirs of an Invisible Man: A Dialogue with Francis Rizzo. *Opera News:* Feb. 5, pp. 25–28; Feb. 12, pp. 26–29; Feb. 19, pp. 26–29; Feb. 26, pp. 26–29.
SILVERMAN, M. (1980) A Fresh Look at the Case of Little Hans. In *Freud and His Patients.* Ed. M. Kanzer and J. Glenn. New York: Jason Aronson, 1980, pp. 95-120.
SLAP, J. (1961) Little Hans' Tonsillectomy. *Psychanal. Q.* 30: 259–261.

Exploring Little Hans

PETER B. NEUBAUER, M.D.

Freud followed and facilitated the gradual unfolding of Little Hans's developmental course. His concomitant recognition of the transformations of antecedent components into the Oedipal constellation lifted the developmental point of view into a fundamental orienting perspective. Among other things, this orientation emphasized the complex interaction between internal readiness and external events. The apparently narrow focus of the treatment may have provided the very conditions necessary to discover a new therapeutic approach for disorders in childhood along with a new concept of psychological growth.

THESE PAPERS ON LITTLE HANS DOCUMENT THE VARIOUS WAYS A CASE may be explored. The papers have yielded a complex meta-psychological profile reflecting multiple determinants—explored *retroactively.*

Many papers about "A Phobia of a Five-Year-Old Boy" (S. Freud, 1908) follow this retroactive re-evaluation. I will choose a different approach. I intend to raise the question, How did Freud analyze the *emerging* oedipal conflicts? Does his approach imply a different method of therapeutic intervention other than the conventional views?

In reading Freud's commentary about the case provided by Hans's father, one cannot help but be awed by Freud's capacity to create the first child psychoanalysis. After all, nothing in the history of the

Clinical Professor, The Psychoanalytic Institute at New York University Medical Center; Editor, *The Psychoanalytic Study of the Child.*

Presented as part of a panel on "Little Hans" at the American Psychoanalytic Association, January 21, 2006.

The Psychoanalytic Study of the Child 62, ed. Robert A. King, Peter B. Neubauer, Samuel Abrams, and A. Scott Dowling (Yale University Press, copyright © 2007 by Robert A. King, Peter B. Neubauer, Samuel Abrams, and A. Scott Dowling).

young science had prepared him to apply his discoveries to the treatment of children. He accomplished this by advising the father to stay close to Hans's inner life, where libidinal and aggressive strivings were interacting with conditions in the environment. It is likely that focusing upon mother's pathology, or the potential trauma of the birth of a sibling, or various forms of seductive behavior and even the threats of castration would have led him astray from following the developmental unfolding of the little boy's inner conflicts.

On his part, Little Hans was a very good patient. He was curious about exploring the causes of his discomforts; he was ready to offer associations; he willingly recovered memories that allowed Freud to reconstruct the castration anxiety as well as the dynamics that gave rise to his fear that later materialized as a phobia. Hans, thereby, helped Freud find the resolution to the oedipal conflicts while tracing the path to the neurosis. It also provided the conditions for Freud to intervene as he maintained his focus on preconscious and unconscious psychological components, resulting in the first child analysis in history. What may seem upon the revelation of new data to have been an overly narrow view of the mind of Hans may have been exactly the necessary laboratory conditions for Freud to initiate a new method of exploration into the inner life of children.

The treatment differs in some respects from many of its present day counterparts. There is the absence of transference interpretations for one and the unusual absence of playing that might otherwise be anticipated in a five year old. Yet this did not limit Freud from gaining insight into Hans's conflicts or from engaging him in the psychoanalytic process. Little Hans gave Freud a clear view of his oedipal struggle and this confirmed Freud's insight about the dynamic complex that he had hypothesized from his analyses of adults. While Hans's phallic struggle was most pronounced, there were transformations from oral through anal conflicts and then onto the oedipal phobic symptoms. This confirmed Freud's insight about antecedent genetic factors undergoing changes in the course of growth. By recognizing the manifestations in the clinical situation, Freud offered us the development point of view, with its implication for transformations, thereby adding to the components of regression and fixation further understanding on how the mind grows.

In her paper, Elisabeth Young-Bruehl (2007) proposes that "*Der Kleine Hans* is . . . a founding text with all the authority that belongs to a beginning. It was the first extended statement by Freud of his ideas about child development . . . Little Hans's story, as it appears in

the case study, is not a reconstruction. It is a narrative of development in progress and an infantile neurosis in *statu nascendi.*" To examine this case history is to recognize Freud's creative ability to
formulate a theory of child development and child analysis. Dispositional factors, the blueprint of the developmental change, supported
by the developmental pull, also surfaces as a biological focus for
Freud. Speculating about other dispositional features, Freud wonders if there may have been some limitation in the child's somatic capacity for achieving satisfaction from his frequent masturbatory activities. The resulting persistence of sexual excitement at such a high
pitch of intensity was bound to bring about revulsion, quite aside
from the external prohibitions he might have encountered. Freud
cautions, however, that such speculations about somatic factors
might best be left aside until fresh experiences can come to our assistance.

It is impossible to attach too much importance to chronological
events alone for precipitating the outbreak of Hans's illness. He had
shown signs of apprehensiveness long before he saw the "bus-horse"
fall down in the street. Nevertheless, the neurosis attached itself
directly upon this chance event. This outcome is consistent with
Freud's conceptualization of trauma, which is not defined by the external event but rather by the internal reaction to it. This highlights
the psychoanalytic perspective of internal readiness rather than external circumstances.

This important proposal—that inner psychic conflicts utilize external events—emphasizes the primary role of the inner preparedness
rather than the potentially disruptive power of the external events
alone. This principle guided Freud when he considered the pathogenic role of the birth of Little Hans's sister, the maternal physical aggression or the falling of the horse. Perhaps, it is never possible to
clearly distinguish the role of fear as a reaction to specific outer dangers from the influence of a pre-existing state of anxiety in the con-
struction of phobic states, but Freud offers some heuristic advantages
for leaning one way rather than the other.

The case of Little Hans is also remarkable in its frequent references to day residues that provide the reality-related components for
Hans's anxieties. Examples include the observation of the falling of a
horse, the biting by a horse, and open castration threats imparted by
the mother. When emerging fantasies become connected to actual
occurrences, each is less isolated so that the product of the two can
be more effectively addressed much in the manner of comprehend-

ing screen memories. Perhaps it is this feature of the fantasy-driven component upon reality that contributes to the ready resolution of such a phobic condition.

When a therapist witnesses an infantile neurosis in *statu nascendi*, he is forced to make a choice whether to intervene and how to do so. Should he proceed to analyze the expectable conflicts with their concomitant anxieties? Under what circumstances can the clinical findings be designated as pathological? Freud suggested some criteria in the naming of his paper "A Phobia in a Five-Year-Old Boy." This implies that, however transient, he conceptualized the situation as a clinical change from a fear to a phobia. This was sufficient reason to intervene and analyze Little Hans. Nevertheless, he states "that no sharp line can be drawn between 'neurotic' and 'normal' people— whether children or adults—that our conception of disease is purely a practical one and a matter of degree, that predisposition and the eventualities of life must combine before the requisite degree can be reached, and that consequently a number of individuals are constantly passing from the class of healthy people into that of neurotic patients, while a far smaller number also make the journey in the opposite direction" (1908, p. 286).

Freud's statement that no sharp line can be drawn between "neurotic" and "normal" people implies that the infantile neurosis is both a part of normal development and a part of pathology. This poses a problem in terminology. What differentiates normal from pathology? The presence of an infantile neurosis itself does not provide us with the necessary criteria for making a clear diagnostic assessment between a pathological disorder and the presence of an expected developmental achievement.

There are differences between Freud and his daughter with respect to conceptualizing genetic and developmental propositions. Freud claims it is possible to understand the diverse expressions of the neuroses in childhood as a result of the "multiplicity of the phenomena of repression exhibited by neuroses and the abundance of their pathogenic material do not prevent their being derived from a very limited number of processes concerned with identical ideational complexes" (Ibid, p. 287). Anna Freud, however, proposes a developmental point of view. (A. Freud, 1965, p. 153) She suggests that "the field of mental disorders in childhood is more extensive than expected from adult psychopathology . . . [t]here is, of course, a nucleus of all the typical forms of compulsions, ceremonials, rituals. Anxiety attacks, phobias, traumatically caused and psychosomatic disorders, inhibitions, and character deformations . . . or the severe withdrawals from the object world . . . But these are by no means the majority." For Sigmund Freud the infantile neurosis is the model for the adult neurosis. For Anna Freud, however, the infantile neurosis may undergo continuous transformations so that a direct linkage to adult disorders may no longer be evident.

All theories of human development share the view that growth proceeds from the simple to the more differentiated complex mental functions. This implies that the earlier times reflect a simpler, less differentiated mental organization, still a considerable distance from what will become a diverse and more adaptive repertoire. Consequently, all theories that take the first years of life as an approach for understanding normality or pathology rely on a limited developmental model. This applies, for example, to the attachment theories, to Melanie Klein's propositions, and Margaret Mahler's core model (encompassing the first three years of life). Such theories lend themselves to criticism because they are flawed conceptually and also because they reduce the range of strategies available for effective therapeutic intervention.

Sigmund Freud came upon a developmental point of view while examining Hans's conflicts. He reconstructs the past and then shows how he follows Hans's re-experiencing of the past within an ongoing present developmental process in preparation for a new hierarchically more complex developmental organization. This establishes a fundamental sequence: mental functions become transformed into new psychological organizations. By studying how developmental processes re-organize the past and prepare for the future our psychoanalytic theory of development is more precisely refined. Sam Abrams[1] actively pursues this view.

This way of conceptualizing development expands our clinical perspective. We can now add to our focus upon the reconstruction of the past and its re-enactment in the transference ways of searching for and supporting new choices that become available as mental functions transform into new developmental organizations.

A few words about Hans's father and Freud's method of therapy are in order. "We have already described the child's behavior at the beginning of his anxiety, as well as the first content which he assigned to it, namely, that a horse would bite him. It was at this point that the first piece of therapy was interposed. His parents represented to him that his anxiety was the result of masturbation, and encouraged him to break himself of the habit. I took care that when they spoke to

1. Personal communications.

him great stress was laid upon his affection for his mother, for that
was what he was trying to replay by his fear of horses" (Freud, 1908,
pp. 260–61). Freud's recommended interpretation is startlingly direct; apparently, he felt he had no need to address the role of resistances or to elicit free associations. And indeed, Hans was so open at
this point to face his conflict, so conscious of it, that the interpretation offered was not only accepted without signs of resistance but was
rewarded by Hans offering additional memories.

How fortunate that Freud's curiosity to confirm his developmental
theory was matched by Hans's curiosity to explore the emerging features of his own development. As already noted, the narrative of
Hans's therapy has some unusual features. This is a child analysis
without play; Hans and his father stay on a verbal level. Hans does
not enact his conflicts in his relationship with his father; he does not
use displacement through play as a useful mode of resolving the conflicts whenever they cannot be resolved in the relationship with the
primary objects. There is one reference by Hans about his playing.
His father responds to the content with the same directness as if it
were a verbal communication. Hans follows it without insisting that
he remain in the arena between fantasy and reality. Perhaps, the
treatment proceeded in this way because the primary objects were
present as targets for libidinal and aggressive aims in the service of
development. This is one of the special qualities of this particular
child psychoanalysis that may help explain its successful outcome.

This unusual feature of the therapeutic intervention deserves further exploration. It raises the general question of whether child analysts pay sufficient attention to the needs of development while approaching conflicts and to the nature of the phase within which the
conflicts appear.

The more we learn about the dynamics of the Graf family and the
pathological features of each member, the more surprising that Little
Hans's pre-oedipal and oedipal struggles do not reflect the variety
and severity of the family abnormalities. Equipped with the knowledge of such a family history most analysts would be prone to predict
that a child reared in such surroundings would have more severe and
long-lasting developmental deviations. On the contrary, Hans had a
productive life, free of psychopathology. This makes it even more imperative that we re-evaluate those basic propositions that inform our
empirical observations and clinical approaches. What mode of therapeutic action occurred within that first child psychoanalytic treatment conducted in such a short time and devoid of the customary
technical complexities? It would be most fruitful if we were to use this

period of re-evaluation of the first child psychoanalytic case history as an opportunity to expand and refine our views of normal and pathological development rather than simply try to affirm that they have been valid all along

Finally, it is worth underscoring that the support of patterns of on-going development readily allies itself with the correction of antecedent deviations. Thereby, the analysis of the past is linked to our therapeutic role of facilitating future development.

BIBLIOGRAPHY

FREUD, ANNA (1965) *Normality and pathology in childhood.* New York: International Universities Press.

FREUD, SIGMUND (1908) Analysis of a phobia in a five-year-old boy. *Collected papers: III* 149–289. London: The Hogarth Press.

YOUNG-BRUEHL, ELISABETH (2007) Little Hans in the History of Child Analysis. *The Psychoanalytic Study of the Child* 62 (this volume).

APPLIED PSYCHOANALYSIS

August Aichhorn

A Different Vision of Psychoanalysis, Children, and Society

ISAAC R. GALATZER-LEVY, M.A., and ROBERT M. GALATZER-LEVY, M.D.

Though August Aichhorn, in name, remains a significant figure in the history of psychoanalysis, his ideas have been all but abandoned in the modern clinical conception of the treatment of children and adolescents who act out. The current treatment of children and adolescents, so disturbed that their behavior demands treatment outside of their home environment, is currently rudderless and highly dependent on broad societal counter-transferential reactions to disturbed youth. We argue that not only does Aichhorn hold a distinguished position in the history of the treatment of youngsters, but that his ideas about the meaning of severely disruptive behavior as well as the techniques which align with those theories remain relevant and, if utilized, would improve the treatment of severely disturbed youth.

AUGUST AICHHORN FATHERED THE PSYCHOANALYTIC MILIEU THERAPY of adolescents. Over a period of fifty years, he developed ideas and methods that remain relevant to the treatment of delinquent youth and adolescents in general. Transformed through later developments, his concept of "induction" of a transference and its use as a therapeutic tool continues to inform treatment of youngsters and adults. His

Isaac R. Galatzer-Levy, Department of Clinical Psychology, Teachers College, Columbia University, New York. Robert M. Galatzer-Levy, Institute for Psychoanalysis, Chicago; Department of Psychiatry, University of Chicago.
The Psychoanalytic Study of the Child 62, ed. Robert A. King, Peter B. Neubauer, Samuel Abrams, and A. Scott Dowling (Yale University Press, copyright © 2007 by Robert A. King, Peter B. Neubauer, Samuel Abrams, and A. Scott Dowling).

ideas about the psychopathological character of delinquency, coun-
tortransference, and the nature of social responses to delinquents remain urgent and important.

Non-punitive treatment of delinquent adolescents had a long history before Aichhorn's attention to the subject. Aichhorn's goal was
not to posit a theory of delinquency. He viewed his main contribution to be in the treatment of adolescents, particularly those who had
to be removed from society because of their toxic effects on their surroundings.

Milieu Therapy and the Modern Treatment of Severely Ill Adolescents

The idea that schools could be most effective if based on an understanding of children's psychologies (A. Freud, 1927, 1966) found obvious extension in the idea that an environment built on psychoanalytic principles could be useful in treating disturbed youngsters.
Anna Freud used psychoanalytic understanding to design milieus for
youngsters during the London "blitz" (A. Freud, 1941–1945, 1944,
1966, 1973; A. Freud and Burlingham, 1944).

After World War II, a small group of institutions, infused with psychoanalytic method, were established to treat children and adolescents with a range of psychological disturbances. From the onset,
these were heavily influenced by August Aichhorn's work. Fritz Redl
built the Pioneer House in Detroit Michigan based on Aichhorn's
theories about children's aggression and Kurt Lewin's "field theory"
(Redl and Wineman, 1952). In 1944, Bruno Bettelheim took charge
of the Sonia Shankman Orthogenic School at the University of Chicago. Believing that a warm, healthy environment, with loving, consistent, and predictable care would often be sufficient to improve the
lives of severely ill children, Bettelhiem designed a school whose entire environment provided warmth and comfort. He believed that
meaning could be found and used therapeutically in all behavior, no
matter how seemingly deranged (Zimmerman and Cohler, 1997).
The children treated at the Orthogenic School suffered from a wide
range of conditions from autism to adjustment reactions. Their common feature was, in Bettelheim's opinion, that they needed an environment like the one provided by the school. Both Bettelheim and
Redl believed that many children who required institutional care
were in a "pre-ego" state, that is, events in the child's life produced a
failure to develop a psychic apparatus adequate to modulate emotions and affect. They held that if the child could be removed from

conflict and be placed in a warm, understanding environment, the ego would develop (Bettelheim, 1949; Redl and Wineman, 1951).

Many lauded the milieu system's perceived successes in treating profoundly ill children. But with changes in funding and the decreased popularity of psychoanalysis, psychiatry's general emphasis shifted toward more psychopharmacological, behavioral, community-based, and individual therapy models and away from psychodynamically informed milieu treatments (Luhrmann, 2001). Institutions that once boasted waiting lists began to have trouble maintaining an adequate census. Although some institutions, for example the Orthogenic School, still use milieu therapy to treat adolescents, the treatments for adolescents with oppositional-defiant disorder and conduct disorders have grown ever more pharmacological and behavioral (American Academy of Child and Adolescent Psychiatry, 1997; Barkley and Benton, 1998).

AICHHORN'S USE OF TRANSFERENCE

More than any other analyst, August Aichhorn provided a systematic vision of ways to help delinquents. His approach grew from attempting to understand delinquents' psychology and, even more important, understanding the psychology of social responses to them. Writing between 1925 and 1950, he often used psychoanalytic terms differently from how they are used today, so we will begin by clarifying some of his language.

Like his contemporaries, Aichhorn used the term *transference* broadly to refer to emotional attitudes toward important people, institutions, and the analyst. He included the "unobjectionable positive transference," which Freud believed promoted analysis and should not be disturbed. The term neither implied a repetition of early conflicted experiences nor repressed wishes toward the transference object. Aichhorn wrote before the emergence of alliance concepts (Greenson, 1965; Zetzel, 1970; Meissner, 1992). Nor did he conceptualize the transferences that he observed and/or "induced" as related to the narcissistic object relations described by Freud (1911, 1914), and, of course, he did not recognize that, contrary to Freud's belief that these are unanalyzable transferences (Freud, 1911), their analysis could lead to the healing of narcissistic pathology (Kohut, 1971).

Aichhorn believed that a positive transference toward the therapist, the institution, and the group is central and necessary for the treatment of adolescents. He assumed that youngsters initially saw the therapist and the institution as colluding with their parents and society against the adolescent's interests, so that the adolescent resisted therapeutic influence. Aichhorn underlined that the adolescent's attitude is *not* a misconception. The youngster often presents for therapy after a long, intense family struggle, often involving police, schools, and courts. Many youngsters have been threatened with therapeutic placement if they do not function acceptably and, so, think the school is a punishment (Bettelheim, 1950). They therefore are likely to perceive the school as dangerous (Aichhorn, 1925). Any therapy introduced to control the child's "bad" behaviors or as part of a continuum of aversive measures designed to make the child conform to social expectations is likely to be seen by the child as punishment and/or against the child's interests. In addition to their reasonable mistrust of schools and therapists Aichhorn observed that delinquent adolescents have difficulty forming positive transferences because of their impaired abilities to develop meaningful, caring relationships with other people and because ordinary adolescent-adult relationships are often problematic. By emphasizing the realistic elements of the child's perception of the therapist, Aichhorn built a foundation upon which other elements, such as the impact of the child's earlier experiences, the child's conflicts about drives, regressive longing, and demanding superego, could be addressed and a trusting working alliance could be furthered.

How did Aichhorn proceed? First, consistent with his own view of his role, he tried to show the child that he was not an agent of the court or parents. (Emulating him in this regard requires careful self-exploration to recognize true allegiances. Much harm results when therapists who function as social control agents present themselves as the delinquent's ally.) Aichhorn taught that in the initial interview treaters should make it clear that they are not punitive agents of society. The treater's job is not to resolve society's frustrations but to assist the child toward his own goals. Aichhorn discouraged an overly eager or overly friendly attitude, since the youngster, already wary of strangers, will read it as a weakness or a trick. Aichhorn believed that with youngsters who could not develop real friendships (termed "asocial" at the time), it was a mistake to approach them as a friend, or to even use that word. However, such asocial youngsters do form instrumental alliances and may be reached through them (Aichhorn, 1925). Aichhorn tried to show youngsters that the school was a safe place, free from retaliation. He tried to demonstrate his understanding of the adolescent's behavior as something that had developed in response to their life and family experience and that it was something they sometimes felt necessary.

Aichhorn was aware that it is impossible to form a therapeutic relationship on these rational bases alone. The patient must be emotionally engaged with the therapist and the institution. He believed the therapist should seek to actively induce a positive transference: "[the therapist] must take the child's part, be in agreement with his behavior, and in the severest cases even give the child to understand that in his place he would behave just the same way" (Aichhorn, 1925, p. 123). He believed that the child needed to become dependent on the therapist, the institution, and counselors, and that this could only be achieved after they had demonstrated a capacity to understand the child's "true nature" (Aichhorn, 1936).This "induction" could be accomplished only through an appreciation of the patient's specific form of adaptation in combination with what Aichhorn regarded as typical adolescent modes of relating.

AICHHORN'S TYPOLOGY OF DELINQUENTS

Out of his vast experience working with adolescent delinquents, Aichhorn gave vivid descriptions of several types of particularly challenging youngsters. These included, among others, the pseudo-independent delinquent, the youngster lacking a developmental experience of idealizable authority figures, and the narcissistic delinquent. This typology, however, was not developed into an explicit, systematic typology or etiological framework.

THE "PSEUDO-INDEPENDENT" TYPE OF DELINQUENT

A first type of delinquent consisted of adolescents whom Aichhorn described as superficially agreeing to treatment and showing little manifest resistance. Such youngsters easily settle into environments, establish superficial bonds with other students, and do what is asked of them, but vigorously resist establishing real closeness. They do not believe that they need the institution or its help.

Aichhorn held that it was important to make such youngsters uncomfortable with this stance. In *Wayward Youth* he describes subtly encouraging such a youngster to run away from the institution. He believed the boy labored under a fantasy of himself as an independent, worldly man held back by being at the school and imagining that if only he were free of it all his problems would vanish. The youngster eventually ran away, only to return ten days later, distraught and in desperate need of support and nurturing. When the child returned to the school, Aichhorn avoided reproaching him but showed concern for his situation. "How long has it been since you've had something to eat?" (p. 141). The youth, having had his defensive delusion that he could function independently shattered, was ready to form a dependent transference to the school and therapist. "The next morning the transference was in effect." Aichhorn underlines that this is an example of the manipulation of the transference, not a general formula for dealing with delinquent youth or even this sort of youth. Each youngster must be understood individually and therapeutic interventions custom tailored.

The full implications of Aichhorn's therapeutic use of the transference would not be appreciated for decades. Before Aichhorn, transference was used primarily to help become aware of how past experience is relived in the present and to rework that influence. Aichhorn saw transference as a means to induce closeness to the youngster, so that the child could pick up where his development has been arrested (Aichhorn, 1936).

DELINQUENTS LACKING A DEVELOPMENTAL EXPERIENCE OF IDEALIZABLE AUTHORITY FIGURES; THE INDUCTION OF A POSITIVE TRANSFERENCE THROUGH IDEALIZATION AND ITS VICISSITUDES

Aichhorn is famous for dramatically "inducing" idealization in delinquents. He believed only certain types of children needed to develop an idealizing transference toward authority figures. The most important group of this type was those children deprived of significant benign relationships with authority figures; these youngsters, as a result, needed to be brought to be able to identify with such a figure as a step towards transcending delinquency. Idealization, a common element in adolescents' relationships to adults, often centers on qualities of the adult that the young person consciously admires and wishes to emulate. Idealizations of teachers, athletes, musicians, political and military heroes, thinkers, writers, and, sometimes, "outlaws" that are central to adolescent cultures go beyond selecting figures to emulate in the development toward maturity. These idealizations (and the non-traumatic de-idealizations that commonly follow them) form the basis of identifications that contribute to the experience of self (Galatzer-Levy and Cohler, 1993a). The experience of self may change either as the adolescent comes to view himself as like the admired figure, either by taking on qualities of that figure and integrating them in a useful way with the rest of the personality, or by the adolescent coming to see himself as part of the community and establishing an identity as a member of the group following the idealized figure. In either case, the idealization centers on an actual attribute of the idealized figure.

Aichhorn recognized the need for such realistic attributes but saw that they are not the core emotional experience of idealization. The attributes must allow the adolescent to experience idealization in an ego syntonic way. A youngster committed to antisocial behavior is unlikely to admire an adult for thoroughgoing compliance with legality. Furthermore, the admiration must be consistent with a realistic picture of the adult. For the idealization to be sustained, the idealized figure must be at ease with being admired and idealized, at least sufficiently so as not to interfere with the idealization (Galatzer-Levy and Cohler, 1993b). Kohut (1971) observed that analysts are often overstimulated by idealization and, as a result, interfere with them through premature or inaccurate interpretations. Similarly, teachers commonly feel over-stimulated by adolescent idealizations and react against what could have been a developmentally valuable experience for the student (Cohler and Galatzer-Levy, 1992). Aichhorn understood that, even more than having abilities that the adolescent can admire, treaters of adolescents must be at ease with and realistic about idealization and able to refrain from either interfering with it or being swept up in unrealistic beliefs about themselves and, of course, not be seduced into exploiting it.

Aichhorn described no general way to induce idealization. Many of his examples—besting the youngster at pool or planning a bank robbery far better than the youngster could on his own—require skills and talents that are irrelevant to many youngsters and beyond the capacities of many treaters. The arena of idealization must be jointly shaped by the delinquent's needs and the treater's capacities. No formula can work. Aichhorn wrote, "this much can be said: the child should experience within the shortest possible time that the personality which now impinges on his life is absolutely competent to make decisions, is self-assured, and proceeds toward the goal with a firm will" (Aichhorn, 1936, p. 170).

Clearly, Aichhorn would have found the emphasis of many of the skills-based interventions currently widely touted in the United States (e.g., athletic participation and wilderness experiences) profoundly misplaced. They try either to create idealizations in a one-size-fits-all way likely to be unsuitable for many youngsters and treaters or they attempt to instill moral values through direct education. Because they are not based on these adolescents' central psychological needs for an experience of idealizing an adult whose qualities coincide with the youngster's vision of a truly admirable figure, Aichhorn recognized they are unlikely to succeed. He would also have been aware of the sadism inherent in many of these programs, as well as the dangers of a problematic countertransference response to idealization—believing the idealization represents material reality.

Aichhorn believed idealization must be actively induced by exhibiting some admirable feature of the treater. His examples almost always refer to a talent associated with delinquency, such as the ability to effectively plan criminal acts. Some potential treaters of delinquents misunderstand these examples as indicating that they must have athletic or mental talents that they do not have, and so are discouraged from using Aichhorn's model. Indeed, for some youngsters the treater's impressive skills and charismatic personality may be essential to engage the youngster in the brief time available. But our experience is that, given a chance, youngsters who need to idealize a therapist will do so provided the therapist does not interfere with the process. Commonly, anxieties stimulated in the therapist in response to idealization lead the therapist to inappropriately confront the adolescent with the realities of the therapist's abilities, unrealistic features of the idealization, or, worst, to respond to the idealization with contempt for or exploitation of the adolescent.

Aichhorn taught that therapists could not induce positive transferences while actively identifying with society and its rules because he believed that therapists must identify with the delinquent youngster and his motivations. He states, "Whoever wants to work successfully with young delinquents has to be capable of stepping out of his own secure position in the social community, to identify himself with the offender, and thereby to become receptive to and understanding of the intricacies of the delinquent's character structure" (1948, p. 229). The delinquent sees himself as embattled with society. To identify with him, the treater must not see him as arbitrarily attacking his surroundings, but as a child defending his life. "Of crucial importance is the need to learn how the wayward youth himself experiences society. Often he fights a single-handed battle against society as a rebel who resents all demands for conformity as an unnatural deprivation of his freedom." (p. 230).

THE "NARCISSISTIC" DELINQUENT
AND THE NARCISSISTIC TRANSFERENCE

Aichhorn described yet another group of delinquents whose interests in others only extends to how the other contributes to the delinquent's sense of self. These youngsters use the therapist and other, people primarily either as figures to whom they can attach, thereby achieving a more integrated sense of self, or as sources of admiration for the youngster, which he uses to bolster a weak sense of self. Freud (1911, 1914) was pessimistic about analytic work with such patients because the major tool of analysis, the analysis of object-libidinal transferences, is unavailable. In recent decades, half a century after Aichhorn explored the topic, Kernberg (1974) and Kohut (1971), among others, have systematically explored the narcissistic forms of the relationships he described.

Describing a patient with a "narcissistic transference," in which the therapist is not seen as a separate object, Aichhorn posits, "he has failed to develop any object-libidinal relationship to our person" (1936, p. 175). In effect, the patient's attraction to the therapist is an attraction to his own self. The patient experiences an overflow of positive feelings toward the therapist.[1] As with idealization, Aichhorn believed these transferences did not emerge spontaneously but resulted from the therapist's active promotion. The therapist not only makes clear that he understands the delinquent behavior by identifying the youngster's conscious intentions manifest in his behavior but also makes it clear that he would be more successful at the same crimes. Thus, the client becomes attached to an ideal image of himself.

Aichhorn gives an example of this technique in the case of an 18-year-old boy brought to him for stealing and selling his mother's jewelry. Aichhorn asked the boy if he would return the money. The boy said he would not. Aichhorn then told him to give him the money, which he did. Aichhorn wrote him a receipt and then asked him what he was thinking. The boy responded that he did not know why he gave the money to Aichhorn and that he was angry that he did because he had promised to take two friends to the movies. Aichhorn then asked whether there was anything else the boy could steal to get money. Surprised, the boy said that his sister had a bracelet he could

---

1. Kohut (1971) described the same phenomena, but conceptualized the patient's attitude toward the therapist not as a product of overflowing narcissistic libido, but as resulting from the patient's need for the therapist's enthusiasm to compensate for the patient's inadequate experience of a vigorous coherent self.

steal, and described how he would do it. Aichhorn suggested several ways he steal it more successfully. He then gave the boy enough money from the envelope for the movies. Aichhorn deliberately left the boy confused about how to understand Aichhorn and the relationship between them, but had set him up to admire Aichhorn as a more able version of the boy.

TRANSFERENCE AND GROUP COHESION

Aichhorn worked with delinquents primarily in groups and institutions. He recognized the power of the adolescent group to shape development and socialization. Aichhorn held that the therapeutic group is maintained not through internal coercion, but through the positive transference of the children toward the agents of the institution. "In agreement with Freud's conclusions in *Group Psychology and the Analysis of the Ego* (1921), we conceive of these processes in the following way: after a period of increasing aggressiveness, the boys developed a strong emotional attachment to the women counselors, to myself, and later to our psychologist. This intensive object attachment resulted in due course in a mutual identification of all the pupils, and therefore a mutual emotional relationship. This kept the group together. No other force could possibly account for such a result. As we have stressed already, no external pressure was applied to prevent the group from falling apart" (Aichhorn, 1922, p. 37).

RESPONSES TO DELINQUENTS

Aichhorn explored individual and societal response to the "delinquent" youngster. Although his primary interest was to provide better care for delinquents, he saw deeply into the dynamics of the hostility and anxiety that these children stimulate. Reviewing historical approaches to delinquents he observed, "When the educator tries to persuade the delinquent gently and benevolently to give up his subjective personality voluntarily, he sees his efforts fail, and then he often gives up this approach and resorts to violence" (Aichhorn, 1948, p. 230). Delinquent children commonly precipitate rage, sadism, and contempt in their caretakers and society. They are often seen as dangerous, out of proportion to the actual harm they do. These perceptions are often used to rationalize harsh treatment and inattention to delinquents' psychology. They stimulate anxieties that result in extraordinarily cruel treatment (Kernberg, 1965). Historically, societies have responded to antisocial conduct through means designed to sharply differentiate good and bad individuals, to demonstrate that good individuals differ fundamentally from bad ones, and to expel bad individuals and the "scandal" associated with them from the community (Foucault, 1965, 1975).

Heated debate continues about appropriate social responses to antisocial behavior by adolescents. Should they be punished, rehabilitated, restrained, or ignored? These debates do not move forward but the passions with which positions are held and the strong feelings delinquent adolescents arouse in the adults who debate about them are clear. Adversaries label one another with hostile epithets—"bleeding heart," "something out of Dickens." Little serious attention is given to the debater's psychology even though impassioned positions are supported by reference to personal experience. For example, a local African-American juvenile court judge was famous for the harshness with which he treated young offenders and his rage at defense attorneys who suggested that the impoverished backgrounds and experiences of abuse reduced youngsters' responsibility. He angrily told attorneys who brought forward these excuses and even spontaneously lectured youngsters who did not offer such excuses that he himself came from an abusive impoverished background. Since he had grown up to be a responsible citizen, the harsh circumstances of the defendants' lives in no way excused their conduct. The judge was unaware that his identification with the youngsters before him influenced his harshness with them.

Analysts commonly become angry and frustrated when treating patients with disorders of the self (Kohut, 1971). Kohut argues that these feelings arise because these patients commonly treat the analyst as if he were not a person with a will of his own. Angry responses (often disguised as a need to educate or socialize the patient) or boredom that commonly arises in the analysis of these patients results from the patients' implicit demand that the analyst function, not as an independent person with an independent sense of initiative, but as a part of the patient's psychological structure. These demands threaten the analyst's self-cohesion. We believe rageful responses against delinquents have a similar origin. Their "disrespect" of authorities is particularly likely to precipitate hostile responses. Translated into psychological terms "disrespect" means that the adolescent fails to provide the affirmation of the authority's self and, as a result, precipitates states of rage in the adult. Aichhorn, of course, did not have a conceptual framework within which he could encompass this observation, but he did observe that those who wanted to work successfully with delinquents need a firm sense of personal integrity.

A variant on this theme occurs when treaters are enraged by narcissistic demands and at the same time stimulated by them. Treating the
child sadistically simultaneously enacts both sides of the ambivalence. For example, the treater who is both anxious and stimulated
in response to idealization may push the child away, simultaneously
disrupting the painful transference and enacting it by demonstrating
his power.

From another point of view, Kernberg (1965), observing similar responses in treaters, believed that these phenomena arise from res-
onating processes of projective identification in which aggression is
expelled from each party into the other. Treaters who are unable to
absorb and live with the delinquent's hostility respond by attacking
the delinquent (often stimulating further attacks from the delinquent). In the process the delinquent becomes the target of aggression that has origins in the treater.

Another source of hostility toward delinquents centers on the
treater's fear of being like the patients and unconsciously seeking distance from them. Punitive attitudes may be part of an effort to repu-
diate the patient's world view and demonstrate that the treater does
not share it. The youngster is seen as a totally alien creature. Diagnostic labels and neurological theories may be used to suggest that the
child is essentially different from the treater and to show the distance
between therapist and patient. These labels may be rationalized by
the belief that clear diagnoses contribute to good patient care. Having told the therapist private and difficult things, the child whose experience is summarized as "borderline," "schizophrenic," or "psychopathic," that is, essentially different from the treater, is left more
alienated and rejected.

Whatever their source, hostile acts are almost always rationalized as
justice, attempts to educate or reform, necessary to protect society, or
the result of rules imposed on the treater. Currently in the United
States, sadistic treatment is commonly rationalized by reference to
behavioral psychology. However, these highly punitive approaches
are usually inconsistent with dominant behavioral paradigms. Moreover, although punishment may disrupt ongoing behaviors, it is not
effective in shaping more adaptive or positive behaviors (Benjet and
Kazdin, 2003; Skinner, 1971).

Aichhorn made clear that the problem of hatred toward the delinquent was not limited to those who treat them. He asserted that psychoanalytic clinicians should address the wider social problem of
hostility toward these youngsters. He explored unconsciously motivated hostility toward delinquent children on the individual, institu-

tional, and societal level. He believed that the intense feeling of lack of control over the individual who refuses to conform to the basic rules of society stimulates sadism toward the rule breaker, justified as discipline to help the youngster conform to society's demands. Aichhorn asserted that this hostile position is the opposite of what the youngster needs. As the object of hostility a child cannot feel safe or understood. The hostilely motivated intervention becomes a barrier to effective work with these children, the result of which, Aichhorn argued, is counter-therapeutic, "The juvenile delinquent whose plight induced us to approach them with mildness, kindness, and friendliness are the same who, in reformatories of the old type, compel the staff to take an attitude of stern opposition; life in such institutions is therefore toned down (or if you wish, toned up) to the well-known level of sadomasochism" (Aichhorn, 1925, p. 39).

Aichhorn applied his understanding of responses to delinquency to the classroom. Aichhorn observes that teachers quickly respond defensively as they try to maintain the order they believe essential for learning. This defensive position interferes with addressing children's psychological needs. Rather than seeing themselves as primarily concerned with children's welfare, such teachers see themselves as agents of repression. Their loyalty is to the school and to conceptions of what education should be. "If, in each case, if the teacher were able to observe his own behavior exactly and to submit to self-criticism, he would soon discover that an emotional reaction had set in well before any rational check, and that the check had not always sufficed to produce an objective attitude. If such self-criticism is sufficiently searching, the observer will also notice that it is not the type and seriousness of the offense itself which determine the way a delinquent pupil should be judged; our attitude toward the delinquent depends not on the gravity of the misdemeanor as such but on the effect which the transgression may have upon ourselves. However, this effect does not pertain to the delinquent alone. It is determined also by the momentary psychological conditions in which we happen to find ourselves, as well as by our libidinal reactions to the wayward child and to the rule which he has transgressed" (Aichhorn, 1925, pp. 50–51). The end result is that the child, already weakened by internal struggles, finds himself in opposition to those best placed to support positive change so he feels further depleted and less able to master the chaos of his internal and external life.

As the previous quotation suggests, Aichhorn saw self-inquiry as a major tool for overcoming counter-therapeutic responses to delinquents. This leads logically to the idea that analysis should be available to teachers and others who deal with delinquent youngsters. Aichhorn declared that no amount of abstract pedagogic or psychological theory can substitute for analytic or self-inquiry and its associated psychological working through. This is because adults' emotional response to a child is more important than any concrete detail of that response. Emotional attitudes cannot be faked or play-acted. They must originate in the adult's actual attitudes. If the person dealing with delinquents responds counter-therapeutically to delinquents, only self inquiry or analysis can alter these attitudes. Additionally, as Aichhorn suggests, these responses occur quickly, intensely, and cannot be controlled by reason alone.

Aichhorn did not have today's conceptualizations of countertransference available, so he did not consider the possibility that the enactments associated with the treater's authoritarian responses, based in his identification with society, and the delinquent's counter-responses could be used analytically. Opportunities to analyze transference-countertransference enactments in work with delinquents are more limited than with other patients because delinquents tend to have very low tolerance for therapists' failings. If the patient flees, interpretations of mutual enactments are useless. In addition, many delinquents who have been abused will have had the experience of being told, "You made me do it" by their abusers. Attempts to interpret enactments can come perilously close to repeating these experiences.

DELINQUENCY AS MENTAL ILLNESS AND SOCIETY'S RESPONSIBILITY TO THE DELINQUENT CHILD

Since antiquity, moral and legal responsibility for antisocial acts has been linked to the offender's mental state and his ability or inability to choose to act differently. This association has led to recurring debates about where to draw the line between acts for which the individual is fully responsible and acts for which there is diminished or no responsibility (Katz, 1987). The juvenile offender brings this debate into sharp focus. There is wide agreement that immaturity and psychological disturbance reduce culpability. Aichhorn not only confronted these issues directly; he believed addressing them is integral to the work of the psychoanalyst–youth worker. He held society, not the individual youth, responsible for youthful misconduct because antisocial behavior arises from society's failure to provide needed developmental experiences.

The idea that society should provide what individuals need to fulfill their unique potentials permeates thinking from philosophy (Putnam, 2002), to economics, (Sen, 1992, 2000) and to feminism (Nussbaum, 2000). Aichhorn asserted that society as a whole is responsible for misbehavior that results from mental illness and should be blamed if the child is not helped to live a productive, fulfilling life. Thus, Aichhorn viewed social reform of the treatment of young people as integral to his work. More than a mere opinion, he saw it as part of his professional identity to be a reformer. In this regard, he differed from most of today's mental health professionals, who despite believing that many delinquents' difficulties originate in social failures, do not see attempting to remedy those failures as part of their professional work.

Particularly in the United States, psychoanalysis is primarily regarded as a procedure for treating individual patients. To a significant extent, because of a wish for the safety afforded by acting within a medical model and, to a lesser extent, because its attempts to address major social issues have been met with little success, psychoanalysis has had ever less to say about social problems. Even though many analysts believe analysis has wide explanatory power and that its value extends beyond individual treatment, few articles appear in contemporary psychoanalytic journals on broad social issues (e.g., Kernberg, 2003a, b) and analysts rarely see intervening in social issues as part of their professional role except, possibly, when the issue directly affects practice. Goldstein, Freud and Solnit's (1975, 1979) work on child custody, Menninger's (1959) and Brown's (1986) advocacy of humane attitudes toward criminals and recent work on children exposed to urban and political violence (Sklarew et al., 2004) are among the rare exceptions. Radical works, like those of Fanon (1968) and Marcuse (1955), though based in psychoanalysis, are not generally regarded as part of the psychoanalytic canon. Aichhorn would have seen the flight from social issues as a failure to do the work of psychoanalysis.

The same psychological factors responsible for therapists' and educators' inability to see a suffering child rather than a destructive monster may explain why the idea of delinquency as a psychological symptom is so often negatively received by courts and legislatures. Aichhorn claimed that the judges, legislators, and policy makers adopt punitive anti-therapeutic attitudes toward delinquents because they unconsciously fear being themselves delinquent. Their responses are unconsciously designed to show that they were different from delinquents. They treat youngsters in the same harsh way they felt that they should be treated for their own antisocial wishes.

(Eissler [1949] developed this idea further in a *Festschrift* honoring
Aichhorn.)

Aichhorn saw it as part of his job to educate, persuade, and confront the psychologies of policy makers. Aichhorn believed that his
job did not end at the office door but extended to any situation
where delinquents might be helped. He did not think that psychoanalytic insight should be given only to those who define themselves as
patients, but also to those who shape patients' lives.

Aichhorn argued that the behavior classified as delinquent is symptomatic of disturbed development and should be treated as such. He
believed that everyone who interacts professionally with delinquents,
from the school teacher to the judge to the therapist, should understand this. He hoped society at large would come to understand this,
and that treatment rather than punishment would become normative. Even if a punitive approach does sometimes succeed in altering
the child's behavior, the disappearance of a symptom is not the cure
of the underlying illness. "When, for example, a young thief stops
stealing as the result of an appropriate punishment, society at large is
satisfied and pacified. But the question of whether he himself has
been cured falls outside the competence of applied penal law" (Aichhorn, 1925, p. 59). In particular, he observed that there are latent periods of delinquency during which the youngster does not act anti-
socially. This does not mean that he is no longer going to act in a
pathological manner, or that the internal deficiencies that caused
the behavior have been rectified. If Aichhorn was right, "that delinquency consisted fundamentally in a state of arrested—or regressed
—personality development" (quoted in A. Freud, 1951) and that
"the cure of delinquency fundamentally a problem of (redistribution
of) libido" (Aichhorn, 1925, p. 226), then the child's ability to conform his conduct to society's demands, however desirable, should
not be the endpoint or goal of treatment.

Aichhorn not only asserts that society is responsible for children's
delinquency but adds that society is responsible to care for these disturbed youngsters, and this responsibility goes beyond society's general commitment to children's well-being. He asserts that because society let the child become so distressed, "one must concede that the
juvenile delinquent is entitled to hold society responsible for letting
him grow up a law breaker" (Aichhorn, 1925, p. 77).

Aichhorn's observations in Vienna in the first and second decades
of the twentieth century apply equally well to the contemporary
United States. Current social structures and interventions often exacerbate the pathology that leads to antisocial conduct. One need

only look at the foster care system in which discontinuous and inadequate care is the norm for a large group of children most at risk of psychological disturbance. Similarly, many juvenile courts, despite their mandate to help children, fail dismally in this role. It is a common observation of juvenile court personnel that it is many of the children first seen by the court as victims of abuse and neglect who are subsequently seen by the same court as juvenile offenders.

Another important example concerns the different treatment of the genders. Girls, on average, are admitted to residential treatment facilities at a later age and in smaller numbers than boys (Nadelson, 1989). This is not because girls are less disturbed than boys but probably because boys are more likely to act on their surroundings with symptoms of conduct disorder and antisocial personality disorder, while girls more often act upon themselves, presenting with symptoms of depression (Nadelson, 1989). Though both antisocial and depressed behaviors signal distress and have serious prognoses, far more resources are expended on boys, whose symptoms are experienced by the community as more intolerable. However, because communities place a higher priority on managing disruption than assisting disturbed children, neither boys nor girls receive treatment based on their needs. But the boy's symptoms more often become so intolerable that he must be managed and treatment is initiated to do this.

THEORY OF DELINQUENCY

Aichhorn showed little interest in broad theories of delinquency, adolescence, or neurosis. His primary interest was the treatment of children cast out by society. Though several chapters of *Wayward Youth* have titles like "The Causes of Delinquency," they contain little general theory beyond a basic explanation of the conflict theory of neurosis. *Wayward Youth* contains little new by way of conceptualization of neurosis in children and adolescents, though, as previously discussed, it contains much that was new about practice.

Wayward Youth was written to be accessible to a broad range of professionals. Perhaps this is why Aichhorn provides so little theory explaining his practice. Aichhorn focused on his main point—delinquency results from neurosis, in the sense of poorly resolved psychological conflict, rather than wickedness. Furthermore, Aichhorn was intensely loyal to Freud, at a time when putting forward ideas different from Freud's was seen as disloyal. This may have led him to avoid positing theories that did not fit with Freud's. Concepts of self and object relations that best explain Aichhorn's technical innovations would not be formulated for another four decades and are not easily reconciled with classical libido theory. Insofar as he recognized them, Aichhorn may have suppressed these ideas. Most important, Aichhorn's native mode of thought involved an intimate engagement with concrete specific psychological situations not abstractions. Consider Aichhorn's response to Gina Bettelheim, who sought advice from him about assessing a seven-year-old girl who, despite few overt symptoms, seemed significantly disturbed. He wrote, "When you cannot decide whether a child is disturbed or not, just turn to other children for an opinion. They will know for sure" (Sutton, 1996, p. 96). The question of the appropriateness of analysis for a particular child was already an issue that Anna Freud was approaching from a sophisticated point of view that would ultimately result in *Normality and Pathology in Childhood* (1965). Gina Bettelheim's question would doubtless have evinced a thoughtful systematic answer from her. In contrast, Aichhorn's answer is brief, profound, concrete, and atheoretical. Aichhorn's reply suggests that he did not operate by applying theories to clinical situations but, instead, used his superb clinical judgment and treated theory as a secondary matter.

Aichhorn briefly discusses his own ideas about the genesis of delinquency in a number of his papers. He strongly believed that delinquency results from a combination of environmental stressors and a biological predisposition (Aichhorn, 1925). Aichhorn saw the "wayward" child as having not yet developed the reality principle. The child cannot reliably postpone pleasure in the moment in response to social or societal constraints.

Aichhorn (1948) also attributed delinquency to an imbalance of libidinal energy. This imbalance results from "the need for love satisfied either too little or too much; being shut out of the community or overly involved in it" (p. 231).

Aichhorn believed that delinquents' superego failures result from inability to identify with parents caused by the parents being emotionally absent. Ordinarily, according to Aichhorn, children glean "guiding principles" from adult caretakers. Aichhorn is not positing a simple model in which children fail to learn these principles because they are not exposed to them. Rather, he argues that because the relationship to the parent is emotionally empty the child cannot identify with the caretaker, and thus, fails to internalize the parent's beliefs about the world and how it works. Furthermore these failures of early object relations impair the child's ability to later identify with figures from whom they might acquire superego functions, "Children form the most tender relationships with their parents, and therefore the nucleus of the superego is formed in the nursery. All later identifications, with teachers, religious leaders, characters in literature, etc., form layers around this nucleus. The nucleus of the superego will not develop if children are deprived of needed love. This happens when parents pay little attention to their children, neglect them, or are indifferent to them. It happens when children are shuttled early in life from one foster home to another, as is the case with public dependents, where children do not have time to develop feelings of affection toward foster parents and to identify with them. Such children absorb all later identifications as loose structures that do not really take hold. Their superego is an unreliable guide; they consequently have a labile attitude toward all demands of society. Many wayward symptoms are thus explained, and they are amenable to cure through correct re-education" (Aichhorn 1948, pp. 231–232).

TREATMENT OF THE VIOLENT YOUNGSTER

As with many aspects of Aichhorn's work, his theory and practice of treating violent children developed together. "The Aggressive Group" at Oberhallabrunn, the school Aichhorn founded, emerged from the school's ordinary process. Aichhorn allowed the students to group themselves because he thought that group cohesion was of utmost importance. After the students had grouped themselves, twelve remained. They had been rejected by the rest because of their aggression and destructiveness. The staff debated how to treat these students. Despite their therapeutic orientation, many staff members thought the only way to approach these children was through aggressive punishment and manual labor. Aichhorn decided that, rather than meeting the students' behavior with counter-aggression (which, after all, had not worked with each of these youngsters on innumerable occasions), their treatment should be based on an understanding that the youngsters' aggressive behavior was a reaction to aggressive treatment in their upbringing and that continuing a pattern that began their aggression would not lead them away from it. "[The youngster's] aggression and hatred are only childish reactions resulting from the harshness which he experienced from the father or other persons in authority. If the educator employs even harsher discipline, he is using the same methods which brought the child into the original conflict. Thus he strengthens the antagonistic impulses which already existed and increases rather than mitigates the tendency to delinquency" (Aichhorn, 1925). Concretely, Aichhorn told the staff not to intervene in the group unless there was real danger of serious bodily harm. He also demanded the staff not take sides, no matter how strongly they felt. The staff was available for as much one-on-one time as students requested, but in the dorm, allowed students to act as they chose. "Our treatment of this group could be characterized thus: a consistently friendly attitude, wholesome occupation, plenty of play to prevent aggression, and repeated talks with individual members. No pressure that could be avoided was brought to bear on them" (Aichhorn, 1925, p. 172). If they chose not to participate in the group's activities, they were allowed to do so. If they chose not to eat at the group table, they could eat alone.

Aichhorn believed that aggressive children, most of whom had been abused, anticipated being treated hostilely. When Aichhorn and his staff did not behave this way the youngsters were forced to confront their self-fulfilling expectations about the world. At first the youngsters became even more frustrated and aggressive. The staff's kindness confused and infuriated them. They escalated their aggression to incur the expected response. Being able to push the counselor to violence and abuse would justify the child's hatred of the threatening and sadistic world. Aichhorn observed that it was after the child was most aggressive that he identified most with the counselor. "This intensive object relationship to the common leader paved the way for identification with him and in turn led to an emotional relationship to each other. Since no external pressure was exerted to hold them together, this tie was the only force which held them together. Libido, no matter what its source, can be used as aggression that finds its expression in dissocial behavior (Aichhorn, 1925, pp.177–178).

The group became so violent that the dormitory was destroyed. All of the children abandoned the table in favor of eating in protected corners or the play room. Slowly, periods of calm emerged and lasted longer. Aichhorn called this a "latent period." One by one, the students broke down into rageful tears often lasting entire days. This was followed by a period of intense sensitivity and then by appropriate behavior. This laid the ground work for a positive transference. "The normal tender feeling which had been repressed found easier outlet after each discharge and, thus freed, was gradually able to attach itself to an appropriate object, the worker" (Aichhorn, 1925, p. 178). In the resulting calm, Aichhorn saw an opportunity to increase the positive feelings the students were finally having towards the staff and to "heighten some strong pleasurable emotion"(p. 176).

The children were all given special presents for Christmas. A few days later they were moved into a brand new dorm Some of the staff resisted this move, asserting these students should not be given a new building to destroy. Aichhorn held firm. He believed the students had developed a level of group cohesion at least as strong at that of the other groups at the school and now posed no more problem then any other group. At this point, leadership of the dorm was handed over to the school's psychologist, who purposely acted frustrated and disapproving when the children were dissocial. Through this process, as Aichhorn describes it, they were slowly weaned to normal social expectations.

This is the most extreme example of Aichhorn's manipulations of transference. He deliberately unleashed enormously potent group processes, in effect, creating a primal horde. Doing so, he forged a situation in which the students finally could identify with powerful pro-social figures. This was possible because of the benign nature of these figures who had benign relationships to their own superegos and so could continue to be loving and professional despite the sadism stimulated in them by the delinquents' actions.

Contemporary analysts are likely to be discomforted by this vignette. Few contemporary analysts, even if they could, would feel at ease releasing the intense psychological forces Aichhorn describes. Contemporary analysts, focused on work in the analytic dyad, are unlikely to see group processes as a potent tool for change. We are also likely to be more aware of the potential dangers of emotional group processes. The experiences of the eight decades that separate us from the period when Aichhorn worked, especially the destruction of German civilization in the face of group processes fostered by the Nazis, leave us with a profound fear and mistrust of these processes. On a less dramatic level, systematic studies by social psychologists (Brown, 1986) and in popular fiction (Golding, 1954) lead many analysts to a strong awareness of the dangers of irrational group processes. We are also less sure of our theories than Aichhorn appears to have been. Few of us would have the confidence implicit in Aichhorn's sticking to a therapeutic approach that initially had such apparently negative impact and in the face of opposition from a school's staff. The current multiplicity of analytic viewpoints makes it difficult to believe any one of them to the extent necessary to support an Aichhorn-like certainty. On another level, the idea of manipulating individuals through the transference, even for therapeutic ends, seems morally repugnant to many contemporary analysts (Blass, 2003), who regard personal autonomy as a central value and are committed to an ideal that any analytic activity that promotes un-realistic thinking in the patient is inappropriate.[2]

CONCLUSION

Psychoanalysis at the beginning of the 21st century occupies a para-doxical place. Many of its ideas are so thoroughly intellectually tri-umphant that they have become the clichés of everyday discourse. On the other hand, psychoanalysis is in danger of becoming increas-ingly marginalized as a therapy, either as an intervention for the "worried well" (and hence the subject of derisive comedy) or as a treatment of last resort for those unaffected by less intensive thera-pies and medication. Often ideas from psychoanalysis are used in somewhat disguised form, without mention of their origins, by other therapeutic approaches, such as cognitive behavioral therapy.

Beginning with Anna Freud's work in the schools, analysts and their allies have been in the forefront of applying an understanding of persons based on empathy and the attention to personal meaning to a broad range of social problems, especially those related to chil-dren's development. Aichhorn was a major contributor to that work. Aichhorn's vision of psychoanalysis was that, far from being a therapy limited to the treatment of neurotic individuals or a general psychol-ogy, psychoanalysis was a broad world view that shapes the analytic thinker's picture of people in whatever context they are encoun-tered. The analytic approach, in his view, is equally applicable in five-times weekly treatments with patients on the couch, in working with institutionalized delinquents, in addressing policy makers, or in pre-senting information to judges with power over litigants' lives. In all of these contexts, an analytic approach is appropriate and necessary. Its core is the in-depth psychological understanding of all participants in the situation.

Far from seeing interpretation as the analyst's only tool, Aichhorn believed that analytic understanding suggests a wide range of thera-peutic methods, including creation of milieus that induce psycholog-ical change, manipulations of the transference, and education. For Aichhorn, far from being anti-analytic, these techniques grew from an analytic appreciation of the psychology of the individuals he was attempting to influence. This approach widened the scope of appli-

2. Promoting unrealistic transferences in the manner that Aichhorn describes should be differentiated from allowing transferences to emerge in the analytic setting by avoiding premature interpretations that may impede their clear manifestation.

cation of psychoanalysis decades before the era of "the widening scope" (A. Freud, 1954; Stone, 1954).

The attitude toward analysis implicit in Aichhorn's work has largely disappeared from organized psychoanalysis. For whatever reasons, technical innovation in psychoanalysis, especially innovations that build on or exploit the transference rather than focusing on its analysis, are now perceived as anti-analytic (see however, Gedo, 1979). To an even greater extent, analysts have progressively limited the fields they attempt to influence, leaving broad social issues to others and discouraging speculations about individuals whom they do not know with analytic depth. This attitude simultaneously reflects an increased appreciation of how hard it is to know people in depth and a timidity. This timidity limits analytic discourse about matters where analysts have much to contribute and leaves it to non-analysts who are more at ease using analytic concepts broadly.

Psychoanalysis may be viewed in many different ways—as a therapy for neurotic and personality disordered individuals, as a group of psychological theories that can inform a wide range of psychological phenomena and have wide applications, and as a world view. The ethical demands placed on analysts have been understood to range from providing a technical service competently to effective political action. In the United States, despite some exceptional efforts in the opposite direction, psychoanalysis has focused on ever narrower goals and its role as a treatment for a small, elite population. August Aichhorn provides a model of a different vision of psychoanalysis, engaged with the problems of the day and passionately committed to helping people in need through a wide range of means informed by psychoanalytic understanding.

BIBLIOGRAPHY

AICHHORN, A. (1922). On education in training schools. In O. Fleischmann, P. Kramer, and H. Ross, ed., *Delinquency and Child Guidance: Selected Papers* (pp. 15–48). New York: International Universities Press (1964).

AICHHORN, A. (1925). *Wayward Youth*. New York: Viking Press (1965).

AICHHORN, A. (1936). On the technique of child guidance: The process of transference. In O. Fleischmann, P. Kramer, and H. Ross, ed., *Delinquency and Child Guidance: Selected Papers* (pp. 101–192). New York: International Universities Press (1964).

AICHHORN, A. (1948). Delinquency in a new light. In O. Fleischmann, P. Kramer, and H. Ross, ed., *Delinquency and Child Guidance: Selected Papers* (pp. 218–235). New York: International Universities Press (1964).

176   *Isaac R. Galatzer-Levy and Robert M. Galatzer-Levy*

American Academy of Child and Adolescent Psychiatry (1997). Practice parameters for the assessment and treatment of children and adolescents with conduct disorder. *J Am Acad Child Adolesc Psychiatry*, 36 (10 suppl.).

BACHRACH, H. (1989). On specifying the scientific methodology of psychoanalysis. *Psychoanalytic Inquiry*, 9.

BARKLEY, R., and Benton, C. (1998). *Your Defiant Child*. New York: Guilford.

BENJET, C., & KAZDIN, A. E. (2003). Spanking children: The controversies, findings, and new directions. *Clinical Psychology Review*. 23 (2): 197–224.

BETTELHEIM, B. (1949). A psychiatric school. *Quarterly Journal of Child Behavior*, 1: 86–95.

BETTELHEIM, B. (1950). *Love Is Not Enough: The Treatment of Emotionally Disturbed Children*. Glencoe, Ill.: Free Press.

BION, W. (1977). *Seven Servants*. New York: Aronson.

BLASS, R. (2003). The ethical issues at the foundation of the debate over the goals of psychoanalysis. *International Journal of Psychoanalysis*, 84, 929–943.

BROWN, R. (1986). *Social Psychology the Second Edition*. New York: Free Press.

COHLER, B., & GALATZER-LEVY, R. (1992). Psychoanalysis and the classroom: Intent and meaning in learning and teaching. In N. Szajnberg, ed., *Educating the emotions: Bruno Bettelheim and psychoanalytic development* . New York: Plenum, pp. 41–91.

EISSLER, K. (1949). *Searchlights on Delinquency: New Psychoanalytic Perspectives*. New York: International Universities Press.

EISSLER, R. (1949). Scapegoats of society. In K. Eissler, ed., *Searchlights on Delinquency: New Psychoanalytic Perspectives*. New York: International Universities Press, pp. 288–305.

FANON, F. (1968). *The Wretched of the Earth*. C. Ferrington, trans., New York: Grove Paperback.

FOUCAULT, M. (1965). *Madness and Civilization: A History of Insanity in the Age of Reason*. R. Howard, trans., New York: Pantheon Books.

FOUCAULT, M. (1975). *Discipline and Punishment*. A. Sheridan, trans., New York: Pantheon Books.

FREUD, A. (1927). Four lectures on child analysis. *The Writings of Anna Freud* 1: 3–69. New York: International Universities Press.

FREUD, A. (1941–1945). Monthly reports. *The Writings of Anna Freud* 3: 3–540. New York: International Universities Press.

FREUD, A. (1944). *Infants Without Families*. New York: International Universities Press.

FREUD, A. (1951). Obituary of August Aichhorn. *International Journal of Psychoanalysis*. 32: 51–56.

FREUD, A. (1951). Observations on child development. *The Psychoanalytic Study of the Child*. 6: 18–30.

FREUD, A. (1966). A short history of child analysis. *The Psychoanalytic Study of the Child* 21: 7–14.

FREUD, A. (1965) *Normality and Pathology in Childhood: Assessments of Development*. New York: International Universities Press.

FREUD, A. (1973). *Infants without Families—Reports of the Hampstead Nursery 1939–1945. The Writings of Anna Freud.* Vol. 3. New York: International Universities Press.

FREUD, A., & BINGHAM, D. (1944). *War and Children.* New York: International Universities Press.

FREUD, A., & BURLINGHAM, D. (1944). Infants without families. In *The Writings of Anna Freud* 3: 543–669. New York: International Universities Press.

FREUD, S. (1911). Psycho-analytic notes on an autobiographical account of a case of paranoia (dementia paranoides). J. Strachey, trans., *Standard Edition of the Complete Psychological Works of Sigmund Freud* 12: 3–82. London: Hogarth Press and the Institute of Psycho-Analysis.

FREUD, S. (1914). On narcissism: An introduction. J. Strachey, trans. and ed., *The Standard Edition of the Complete Psychological Works of Sigmund Freud.* 14: 73–102. London: Hogarth Press.

GALATZER-LEVY, R., & COHLER, B. (1993a). *The Essential Other: A Developmental Psychology of the Self.* New York: Basic Books.

GALATZER-LEVY, R., & COHLER, B. (1993b). The psychological significance of others in adolescence: Issues for study and intervention. In B. Cohler and P. Tolan, eds., *Handbook of Clincial Research and Practice with Adolescents.* New York: Wiley.

GEDO, J. (1979). *Beyond Interpretation.* New York: International Universities Press.

GOLDING, W. (1954). *Lord of the Flies.* London: Faber and Faber.

GOLDSTEIN, J., FREUD, A., & SOLNIT, A. (1975). *Beyond the Best Interests of the Child.* New Edition. New York: McMillan.

GOLDSTEIN, J., FREUD, A., & SOLNIT, A. (1979). *Before the Best Interest of the Child.* New York: Free Press.

GREENSON, R. (1965). The working alliance and the transference neurosis. *Psychoanalytic Quarterly, 34,* 155–181.

JACOBY, R. (1993). *The Repression of Psychoanalysis.* New York: Basic Books.

KATZ, L. (1987). *Bad Acts and Guilty Minds.* Chicago: University of Chicago Press.

KAZDIN, A. (1987) Treatment of antisocial behavior in children: Current status and future directions. *Psychological Bulletin,* 102: 187–203.

KERNBERG, O. (1965). Notes on countertransference. *Journal of the American Psychoanalytic Association,* 13 (1), 38–56.

KERNBERG, O. (1974). Further contributions to the treatment of narcissistic personalities. *International Journal of Psychoanalysis,* 55: 215–243.

KERNBERG, O. (2003a). Sanctioned social violence: A psychoanalytic view Part I. *International Journal of Psychoanalysis,* 84: 953–968.

KERNBERG, O. (2003b). Sanctioned social violence: A psychoanalytic view Part II. *International Journal of Psychoanalysis,* 84 953–968.

KOHUT, H. (1959). Introspection, empathy, and psychoanalysis: An examination of the relationship between mode of observation and theory. In P.

Ornstein (ed.), *The Search for the Self* 1: 205–232. New York: International Universities Press.

KOHUT, H. (1971). *The Analysis of the Self.* New York: International Universities Press.

LONG, P., FOREHAND, R., WIERSON, M., & MORGAN A. (1994). Moving into adulthood: Does parent training with young noncompliant children have long term effects? *Behaviour Research and Therapy,* 32: 101–107.

LUHRMANN, T. (2001). *Two Minds.* New York: Knopf.

MARCUSE, H. (1955). *Eros and Civilization.* New York: Vintage.

MEISSNER, W. (1992). The concept of the therapeutic alliance. *Journal of the American Psychoanalytic Association,* 40(4), 1059–1088.

MENNINGER, K. (1959). *A Psychiatrist's World: Selected Papers.* New York: Viking Press.

MOHR, G. (1995). August Aichhorn, 1878–1949: Friend of the wayward youth. In F. Alexander, S. Eisenstein, and M. Grotjahn, eds., *Psychoanalytic Pioneers,* pp. 348–359.

NADELSON, CAROL C. (1989). Teenagers in distress. Feinstein, Sherman C., Esman, Aaron H., Looney, John G., Orvin, George H., Schimel, John L., eds., *Adolescent Psychiatry: Developmental and Clinical Studies,* Vol. 16. (pp. 53-69). Chicago: University of Chicago Press.

NUSSBAUM, M. (2000). *Women and Human Development: The Capabilities Approach.* Cambridge, Mass.: Cambridge University Press.

PLOMIN, R., & DANIELS, D. (1987). Why are children in the same family so different from one another? *Behavioral and Brain Science,* 10: 1–60.

PUTNAM, H. (2002). *The Collapse of the Fact/Value Dichotomy and Other Essays.* Cambridge, Mass.: Harvard University Press.

REDL, F., & WINEMAN, D. (1951). *Children Who Hate.* New York: Free Press.

REDL, F., & WINEMAN, W. (1952). *Controls from Within: Techniques for Treatment of the Aggressive Child.* New York: Free Press.

SEARLE, J. (1980). Minds, brains and programs. *Behavioral and Brain Sciences,* 3: 417–457.

SEGAL, H. (1988). Silence is the real crime. H. Levine, D. Jacobs, and L. Rubin (eds.), *Psychoanalysis and the Nuclear Threat: Clinical and Theoretical Studies.* Hillsdale, N.J.: Analytic Press.

SEN, A. (1992). *Inequality Reexamined.* Cambridge, Mass.: Harvard University Press.

SEN, A. (2000). *Development as Freedom.* New York: Anchor Books.

SHAPIRO, D. (1976). The analyst's own analysis, *J. Amer. Psychoanal. Assn.,* 24: 5–42.

SKINNER, B. F. (1971). *Beyond Freedom and Dignity.* New York: Knopf.

SKLAREW, B., TWEMLOW, S. W., & WILKINSON, S. M. (eds.) (2004). *Analysts in the Trenches: Streets, Schools, War Zones.* Hillsdale, N.J.: Analytic Press.

SQUIRE, L. (1982). The neuropsychology of human memory. *Ann. Rev Neurosci.,* 5: 241–273.

STONE, L. (1954). The Widening Scope of Indications for Psychoanalysis. *Journal of the American Psychoanalytic Association,* 2: 567–594.

SUTTON, N. (1996). *Bettelheim: A Life and a Legacy.* New York: Basic Books.
ZETZEL, E. (1970). *The Capacity for Emotional Growth.* New York: International
    Universities Press.
ZIMMERMAN, P, & COHLER, B. (1997). Youth in residential care. *Psychoana-
    lytic Study of the Child,* 52, 339–385.

Interdisciplinary Psychoanalysis and the Education of Children

Psychoanalytic and Educational Partnerships

JONATHAN COHEN, Ph.D.

Since the original "Wednesday night" meetings Sigmund Freud and ensuing generations of psychoanalysts have been interested in applying psychoanalytic discoveries to the education of children and adolescents. Child analysts and educators are potentially natural allies: both are concerned with promoting children's healthy development and capacity to learn. This paper traces and critiques the inter-generational history of the four major ways that analysts have worked with educators: directing psychoanalytically informed schools; consultations; developing replicable programmatic school-based efforts; and working with colleges of education and/or continuing education for practicing school personnel. Finally, I describe similarities and differences between clinical and applied work as well as how the following three steps will further fruitful interdisciplinary work and learning: including and valuing applied analysis within psychoanalytic institute curriculum; creating more forums where analysts and non-analysts can

President, Center for Social and Emotional Education; adjunct professor in Psychology and Education, Teachers College, Columbia University; member, International Psychoanalytic Association and American Psychoanalytic Association.

The Psychoanalytic Study of the Child 62, ed. Robert A. King, Peter B. Neubauer, Samuel Abrams, and A. Scott Dowling (Yale University Press, copyright © 2007 by Robert A. King, Peter B. Neubauer, Samuel Abrams, and A. Scott Dowling).

*learn from one another; and, most importantly, supporting the system-
atic study of applied analytic efforts.*

INTRODUCTION

CHILD PSYCHOANALYSTS AND EDUCATORS OF YOUNG CHILDREN ARE
potentially natural allies. Both are primarily concerned with promoting children's healthy development and capacity to learn. These mutual interests were apparent from the first hours of psychoanalysis as
Sigmund Freud and his "Wednesday night" colleagues wondered
how they could apply analytic ideas to the education of children, including their own. These meetings opened an evolving dialogue
about the application of psychoanalytically informed thinking and
work to the education of young children. Freud came to consider
such an application as "perhaps the most important activity of psychoanalysis" (Freud, 1933, p. 146).

In this paper, I will review the multi-generational history of how
psychoanalysts and pre-kindergarten through 12th grade educators
have worked and learned together.[1] Building on this history, I will
consider current psychoanalytic-educator partnerships. Finally, I will
comment on the growing recognition within psychoanalysis that we
can and need to consider how to build on this history of multi-disci-
plinary work.

ANALYSTS AND EDUCATORS LEARNING AND WORKING TOGETHER: HISTORICAL AND CURRENT DEVELOPMENTS

Hermine Hug-Hellmuth (1914) was the first of many child analysts to
recognize how mental health professionals need to work collaboratively with educators—as well as parents—to promote children's
learning and development. Anna Freud, building—in part—on
Hug-Hellmuth's work, created a framework for educators and child
analysts to learn and teach together. Beginning her professional life
as a teacher, Anna Freud came to psychoanalysis not only as Sigmund
Freud's daughter but as someone deeply involved with teaching and
learning with young children. From her early study group meetings
with Bernfeld, Hoffer, and Aichhorn in the 1920s, Anna Freud
sought to systematically discover how analytic understanding might

---

1. In this paper, I will focus on 4- to 18-year-old children and adolescents or kinder-
garten through 12th grade in the American educational system.

illuminate the developmental experience of children and promote psychosocial capacities in and outside of the classroom (Young-Bruehl, 1988).

Drawing on earlier and contemporary experiences of psychoanalysts' involvement in the world of childhood education, I propose that there are four major modes of work or, ways in which educators and psychoanalysts have worked together. First, analysts and educators have worked together to organize and direct psychoanalytically informed schools. Second, there is another long-standing tradition of analysts' providing consultative assistance to educators about a given child, school, and/or larger educational system. Third, they have worked together to develop replicable analytically informed programmatic school-based efforts. And, finally, analysts and educators have worked together with departments and colleges of education and/or continuing education for practicing school personnel.

In this paper, I will summarize these four overlapping areas or approaches to collaborative work. I will then address the following three questions: What it is about this applied analytic work that makes it "psychoanalytic"? To what extent does the work actually produce the desired results? And, is the work described "generalizable" and/or is it largely a function of the one individual who is practicing it?[2]

PSYCHOANALYTICALLY INFORMED SCHOOLS FOR NORMAL AND/OR TROUBLED STUDENTS

The longest-standing analytic-educational tradition involves psychoanalysts organizing and directing psychoanalytically informed schools for normal and/or troubled children. Willie Hoffer and Siegfried Bernfeld's educational programs in the Baumgarten Institute in Vienna initiated this work during the early 1920s to provide care for war orphans and abandoned Jewish children (Geissmann and Geissmann, 1998). August Aichhorn also developed the Oberhollabrünn Institute for delinquent adolescents around the same time. He detailed how an analytically informed understanding of the developmental experience of the child, parent-child experiences, transference-counter transference dynamics and the internalization of a "new" relationship with the teacher fostered learning and healthy development (Aichhorn, 1935).

2. These questions have been an organizing framework in my study and writings about applied work. I am indebted to Sam Abrams, M.D., for suggesting them to me many years ago.

At roughly the same time, a children's school affiliated with the Psychoanalytic Institute of the Soviet Union was established for chil dren, age 1–5, who were cared for by specially trained educators. In the late 1920s the school was closed by Stalin (Miller, 1998).

Anna Freud helped to form a school that was directed by Eva Rosenfeld (for one year) in the late 1920s. This work created the foundation for the Vienna Jackson Nursery for deprived infants that Anna Freud co-founded with Dorothy Burlingham in 1937. When they moved to England, they founded the Hampstead Nurseries in 1940 that included three nurseries for vulnerable children and one home for older children displaced and in need of institutional care as a result of the war (A. Freud and Burlingham, 1973). Each of these early opportunities was based on naturally occurring opportunities and settings for educators and analysts to learn and work together. This work became the first sustained child psychoanalytic center for observational research as well as teaching and learning for young children. The work of the Hampstead Clinic (now the Anna Freud Centre) was one of the first not only to initiate an analytically in- formed school, but to work in the three other areas of analytic-educa- tional collaboration: consultation, developing analytically informed programmatic school-based efforts, and teacher education. Virtually all of Anna Freud's and her colleagues' work was grounded in natu- ralistic in-depth observation and anchored in a collaborative ap- proach to child-rearing and education.

In the United States, there has been a wide range of ways that ana- lysts applied psychoanalytically informed thinking, including hospi- tal care, working with delinquent youth, legal work, law enforce- ment, and considerations about what is in the best interest of the child. Educator-analysts partnerships were one important part of in- terdisciplinary and applied work. Anny Katan founded the first psy- choanalytic early childhood program in America, which later be- came a part of the Hanna Perkins Center (Furman and Katan, 1969). This work, as well as an evolving dialogue between Anna Freud, Peter Neubauer, and Albert Solnit and their colleagues in London, New York, and New Haven spawned a number of additional psychoanalyti- cally informed school programs. Most of the early educational work focused on early childhood. Bruno Bettelheim's work at the Ortho- genic School—a coeducational residential treatment program for children and adolescents in need of support for behavioral or emo- tional issues—was another important example of analytic school- work. Over the years, many of these schools closed or moved away from an analytic focus.

Today, there are a number of vital, analytically informed early childhood schools: the Allen Creek Preschool, Ann Arbor, Michigan; the Hanna Perkins Center, Cleveland, Ohio (Furman and Katan, 1969); Harris School, Houston/Galveston, Texas (Farley and Manning, 2002); the Cornerstone Project in San Francisco (Kliman, 1975, 1979); and Lucy Daniels Center for Early Childhood, Cary, North Carolina (Rosenblitt, 2004). In fact, these schools are founding members of the recently formed Alliance of Psychoanalytic Schools (Rosenblitt, 2003). I will comment on two of these schools.

The Cornerstone method provides interdisciplinary education and treatment for emotionally disturbed or developmentally disordered children ages 3 to 6 years. Within a therapeutic or special education classroom group setting (Kliman, 1975; Lopez and Kliman 1979), a therapist works 6 or more hours per week. During that time he provides psychotherapy individually right in the classroom to each of the five to eight children in the group, each child for 15 to 20 minutes a day. During each child's in-classroom psychotherapy session a full range of play therapy and analytic techniques are often used, including interpretations of transference, dynamic and genetic interpretations. The interpersonal and educational setting allows a "here and now" focus on resistance to successful socializing and learning. Since sessions occur almost daily and take place in a real life space, there is little need to delay talking to a child whose attention span might not allow discussion of an event a few days later.

Two early childhood educators are in charge of the classroom educational activities, which proceed with all the other children throughout any one child's in-classroom psychotherapy sessions. Teachers and therapist brief each other with the child's help before and after each child's classroom psychotherapy session. The team meets weekly to share communications from parents, as well as to view videotapes and hear the material gathered during treatment that may not have been overheard in the class session. Parents are interviewed and guided by the teacher each week and by the therapist once a month. Most of the children have existing emotional disturbances, but are also accepted for preventive reasons such as death of a parent, or placement in foster care. Kliman's, Zelman's, and Hope's data (summarized in Kliman, 2006) show considerable rapid emotional growth measured by Children's Global Assessment Scale (DSM IV, Axis V) scores and intellectual growth measured by Wechsler Preschool Scale of Intelligence (Revised version) "I.Q." scores.

Kliman and his colleagues were the first group of analysts to operationalize, manualize, and make both retrospective and prospective psychoeducational studies of their efforts. Statistically significant findings include educationally and clinically impressive results of the interdisciplinary treatment (Hope, 1999; Zelman et al., 1985; Zelman, 1996; Kliman, 2006). I.Q. gains average one to two standard deviations among 52 twice-studied children, while 60 comparison and control children show no such gains. Among foster children an additional measure has been used for Cornerstone patients: Transfer rates among homes. In a study of 30 foster children in the program transfer rates were reduced to zero over the course of a year, compared to 25 percent a year in comparison populations (Kliman, 2006; Kliman and Schaeffer 1983). Replication and training for others to carry out the method is now occurring in two sites (Cornerstone Buenos Aires and the Ann Martin Center, Piedmont, California). A manual and illustrative videos are available without charge from Kliman at gil.kliman@cphc-sf.org.

Another important example of a psychoanalytically informed educational setting is the Lucy Daniels Center program. This program resembles the Cornerstone Project with one exception: the former works clinically with children outside the classroom, while Cornerstone treats children clinically within the classroom. Like Cornerstone, the Lucy Daniels Center for Early Childhood Intervention Program (EIP) is an intervention program for children at high risk for emotional and social difficulties. Extensive clinical evaluations, for example, revealed that all of the children were significantly "off" their appropriate developmental course, and the vast majority met criteria for DSM diagnoses (Rosenblitt, 2006). In a 10-year follow-up study, the parents of 32 out of the 47 graduates of the program (68 percent) reported the EIP approach positively changed the school course of children who were at the highest risk of school failure. The vast majority of these children were able to remain in standard (non-special education) classrooms and were promoted at each grade. Ten years later, parent satisfaction is reportedly extremely high (Rosenblitt, 2001).

The application of psychoanalytic thinking to the creation of schools is one of the most common forms of applied analytic work in education. Historically and to a great extent currently, most of these efforts have focused on early childhood. These programmatic efforts are psychoanalytically informed in four major ways: (1) each tends to emphasize the intra-psychic meanings of behavior; (2) they are each profoundly focused on the mother-child dyad (e.g. the fundamental importance of the real as well as the internalized maternal figure as protector, nurturer, and facilitator of development); (3) each pays close attention to and fosters the child's attempts to master both internal and external demands while increasing adaptive functioning over the course of development; and (4) each program appreciates how relationships (interpersonal and intrapsychic) shape learning and development (Rosenblitt, 2004).

The vast majority of information or data that we have about these educational efforts are anecdotal reports: the literature is filled with ethnographic and case study reports about how successful these schools are. However, it is rare that analysts and/or educators in these schools have delineated goals and methods in a way that allow us to evaluate to what extent these goals are reached, and which components of their programs are actually helpful. The Cornerstone and the Lucy Daniels programs are the only two that have begun to systematically evaluate these efforts. With these two exceptions, it is difficult to know to what extent reported positive gains have been the function of one or more individuals and/or whether this work can be generalized. In fact, the lack of systematic study has also—inadvertently—undermined analysts' ability to be learners in general.

Most psychoanalytic school efforts are not grounded in any kind of ongoing systematic research. This dearth, in turn, has dramatically reduced the interest of educators, school systems, and philanthropic foundations in these projects. Echoing the evolution and debate within the clinical world (e.g. Kernberg, 2006) there has been a major shift in education over the past 25 years to systematically study goals, methods, and outcomes (Cohen, 2006). Public school systems and foundations are now encouraged, if not mandated, to consider *only* programmatic efforts—psychoanalytic or otherwise—that have been empirically evaluated (U.S. Department of Education, 2005).

Psychoanalytic approaches to research have generally been clinically based, with almost exclusive attention to the details of individual experience. Case studies and anecdotal reports certainly do provide rich data from which we can learn and generate hypotheses. The Cornerstone and the Lucy Daniels Center projects have gone a step further and have translated these clinically generated hypotheses into systematic efforts of research and evaluation. These efforts have also created a model that others may use to further empirical study of process and outcome of programmatic efforts. This has the potential for broader application and dissemination of psychoanalytically informed observations and innovations that benefit the health, education, and well-being of children.

CONSULTATIONS WITH EDUCATORS, SCHOOLS
AND/OR LARGER EDUCATIONAL SYSTEMS

Consulting with educators, schools, and occasionally larger educational systems is another common way that analysts have worked with educators to further children's learning and development. There are countless instances of psychoanalytically informed clinicians—around the world—who consult at schools about given children and, sometimes the school as a system.

There are scores of reports describing this kind of work stemming from Anna Freud's early consultative work. Growing out of the Committee on Psychoanalytic Education (COPE) group[3] is a developing program titled a *Curriculum to Teach Courses on Psychoanalytic Thinking Applied to Community and Social Problems;* Wilkinson (2004) has summarized and annotated these reports. The vast majority are case studies that focus on the *inner* lives of children over time: the historically dominant psychoanalytic focus.

One of the many ways that Anna Freud was such an extraordinary leader and learner was her exploration and writings about how the culture and climate of the environment that children live within powerfully shapes social-emotional growth (Freud and Dann, 1951). In the 2001 volume of the *Psychoanalytic Study of the Child* a series of papers re-examine this important and neglected topic. This work was a precursor to current educational research and practice that focuses on how the "climate" of the school, as well as the home, creates—or undermines—a climate for learning and for discovering how internal and external reality are always shaping one another. Although this is a truism, it has not been a consistent focus for applied—or clinical—analytic work in the education and/or treatment of young children until recent years (Cohen, 1997a).

There has been little psychoanalytic consultation work with larger K–12 systems: school districts, state and/or national Departments of Education, or educational ministries. Interestingly, this has not been the case with younger children (zero to four years). As described in more detail below, The National Center for Infants, Children and Families/Zero to Three was founded by a group of analysts and nonanalysts. Its work has shaped American and to some extent, interna-

3. Group members include: Phyllis Jean Cath, M.D., Jonathan Cohen, Ph.D., Nancy Kulish, Ph.D. (co-chair), Steven Marans, Ph.D., Henri Parens, M.D., Moisy Shopper, M.D., Bruce H. Sklarew, M.D., Stuart W. Twemlow, M.D. (co-chair), and Sallye M. Wilkinson, Ph.D.

tional research, as well as practice and policy in programs that involve infants, toddlers, and their families.

There have been some analysts consulting in larger educational
systems. Berkovitz (1999), for example, has been involved with and
contributed to an important movement within American education
to make the school a community center: a base for a range of health
and mental health services (Blank and Berg, 2006; Dryfoos and
Quinn, 2005). James Comer's early thinking and work with schools
was shaped—in part—by Anna Freud's and Al Solnit's analytically
informed narratives about child development (Comer, 1988, 1995).
Comer's important consultative work with two inner-city low-income
elementary schools became the foundation for the School Development Program, which has been utilized in more than 1000 schools
over the last 25 years (Comer, Joyner, and Ben-Avie, 2004). The organizing foundation for this substantive school reform effort is understanding how child development shapes learning. Twemlow and colleagues
have worked with the Jamaican government to further analytically informed violence prevention efforts (Twemlow and Sacco, 1996).

Over the last ten years, a number of my colleagues at the Center
for Social and Emotional Education (CSEE) and I have worked with
a growing number of school districts, county Departments of Education (New York; El Paso, California), State Departments of Education
(New York, Ohio, Rhode Island), and foreign educational ministries
(Australia, Israel, Switzerland, Singapore, Sweden, Norway). This
work has ranged from developing social emotional educational/vio-
lence prevention/school safety guidelines for a state (Fuchs-Nadeau
et al., 2002) to working directly with school leaders about how they
can and need to become reflective social emotional learners themselves to educate students most effectively and create coordinated
and effective educational-mental health partnerships (Cohen, 1999a;
Marans and Cohen, 1999). All of our work is grounded in two processes: educating and supporting parents and educators to purposively promote K–12 students' social, emotional and cognitive com-
petencies and ethical dispositions as well as working to create safe,
caring, participatory and responsive schools and homes (Cohen, 2001
and 2006).

In each consultation the following ingredients have been central
psychoanalytically informed elements: (1) promoting reflective capacities and deeper understandings of intrapsychic meanings attributed to learning, teaching, youth development and the purpose of
K–12 education; (2) appreciating unrecognized aspects of school
life; (3) being keenly attuned to children's developmental experi-

ence; and (4) appreciating how inherently anxiety-provoking learning, teaching, and school life can be on the one hand and how (adaptive or maladaptive) defensive strategies color the process of development and learning on the other hand (Cohen, 1999a, 2006). In an overlapping manner, our consultation work with schools builds on a long-standing analytic tradition of listening, observing, collaboratively identifying realistic and helpful goals and working on them together.

Our appreciation of empirical and systematic research—its strengths as well as its limitations—has been an additional factor contributing to invitations to confer with these larger educational systems. Interestingly, after research-related findings are established, I have consistently discovered an often paradoxical response to empirical research findings as they are introduced into our consultation work. As much as educational leaders want and need to believe that our work is "research based," most educators also recognize that the process of teaching and learning can never be reduced to measurable or simply observable, operationally defined variables. These leaders and other educators have a deep appreciation that teaching and learning is "grounded' in human relationships. Like many clinicians and clinical researchers, these education professionals also recognize that fundamentally important aspects of relationships, often those unconscious and pre-conscious contributing elements, are extraordinarily challenging to measure and study empirically.

Educational systems request our assistance because we have expertise that they imagine they don't. And, typically this is the case. But, just as it is unhelpful to simply tell a patient what they need to do, the history of school reform is filled with unsuccessful instances where "outside experts" told school leaders what to do. It never works. We position ourselves as "co-discovers" with educational leaders. What is working and not working? What are the meanings that they attribute to their strengths, challenges, and problems? What is clear and not clear about how accurate these narratives are? To what extent do other school staff, parents, and students share these perceptions? How ready is the system to embark on a process of substantive learning, goal setting, and hard work that is virtually always an integral part of change? Establishing an alliance or a trusting relationship is an essential part of this initial process of co-discovery, community building, and goal setting. This is a process that typically entails months of work to establish.

There are now almost 300 empirical studies from school-based mental health, risk prevention, health promotion, character, and so-

cial emotional education programs that support the notion that
when we purposively teach students to become more socially and
emotionally competent and simultaneously work systemically to create a safe, caring, participatory, and responsive school, academic
achievement increases and school violence decreases (Weissberg,
Kumpfer, and Seligman, 2003; Weissberg, Durlak, Taylor, and Dymnicki, submitted for publication; Zins, Weissberg, Wang, and Walberg, 2004).[4]

We help schools to develop goals that are aligned with research
and best practices. I have asked educators and parents across America and abroad what they hope their sons, daughters and/or students
will have learned and "be" when they graduate from high school.
Their answers have been very consistent: they want their children/
students to be life-long learners, to be responsible, caring members
of the community who can work and love and participate in a democracy. Although they do occasionally mention wanting their child to
get into a "good college" this is always secondary to the social, emotional, and ethical goals that are in the forefront of the adults'
dreams and wishes for their children. What I have described above
begins to outline the first and to some extent a second "stage" in a
five-stage school climate improvement process that I will describe below. Transforming a school—like working with an individual—is
necessarily a process that occurs over years. We have begun to systematically study schools that are using this model (Cohen, Shapiro, and
Fisher, 2006).

There are scores of anecdotal reports about analytic consultative
work. My impression is that there is a much larger number of works
in this area that have not been documented. And virtually none of
it has been studied in a systematic manner: ethnographically, experimentally, or otherwise. Hence, it is difficult to make thoughtful
generalizations about work in this area. Based on my review of the literature (Wilkinson, 2004), as well as talking with clinicians and educators in America and Europe, and to a much lesser extent, Scandinavia and Japan, my impression is that there are two overlapping

4. Although none of these studies are psychoanalytic in nature, many of them grew
out of early psychoanalytic work and writings (Cohen, 2006). These researchers have,
for the most part, been cognitive-behavioral/primary prevention specialists who, in
important ways, built on analytic ideas and practices, empirically studying those ideas,
simplifying them, but rarely honoring or crediting the analytic roots of their findings.
This is another instance where the psychoanalytic "anti-research" culture has inadvertently undermined credibility and reputation and retarded learning within the analytic community (Cohen, 1997a).

themes that make this kind of consultative work psychoanalytic in nature: a focus on developmentally informed unconscious as well as conscious experience and the meanings attributed to experience.

We know little about whether this work actually produces desired results. More often than not, goals are so general (e.g. "conferring to be helpful") that it is not possible to understand what has and has not been helpful on the one hand and to what extent positive results are due to a gifted clinician and/or are grounded in analytic insight that is larger than one clinician's gifts.

There is another trend that has colored too much of our consultation work with educators that is worth noting. Psychoanalysts and educators could be natural partners. However, too often analysts have positioned themselves as the "expert" in ways that inadvertently undermine collaboration and learning. In a penetrating analysis of three analytic efforts in schools by Sklarew, Manning and Farley, and Kusché (see Cohen 2002), Shepherd (2002) describes how the analytic interventions, "at least as described in the articles, are either imposed on the work of teachers and students or isolated from that work. Either circumstance ultimately limits the impact of the intervention. I claim that analysts and teachers are natural allies despite lack of evidence for alliance in these articles." More often than not, educators expect that analysts will assume a somewhat imperious and uncollaborative stance. Unfortunately, this assumption has undermined educators' interest in learning from and with analysts and about analytically informed thinking.

DEVELOPING ANALYTICALLY INFORMED REPLICABLE EDUCATIONAL PROGRAMMATIC EFFORTS

Creating analytically informed replicable programmatic efforts overlaps with the development of schools like the Cornerstone and the Lucy Daniels Center programs described above. Many of these school efforts, for example, have included programmatic efforts to work with children and sometimes parents. There are scores of reports describing short-term and, typically, short-lived analytic-educational programmatic efforts (Wilkinson, 2004).

Here I will focus on another—less common—analytic-educational tradition: the development of programs that create replicable guidelines, curriculum and/or learning activities. In the United States, there has been a dramatic educational movement to ground educational and psychoeducational programmatic efforts in behaviorally based terms that can be operationally defined and evaluated. This trend is also growing in Europe, Scandinavia and Asia (Japan, Malaysia, and Singapore).

Perhaps the largest and most validated programmatic effort is the Life Space Crisis Intervention (LSCI) model for working with children in crisis (Long, Wood, and Fecser, 2001). The LSCI model grew out of Aichhorn's work (1935). One of Aichhorn's students was Fritz Redl. Trained by Anna Freud and committed to working with delinquent youth, Redl moved to America in the late 1930s. The boys he worked with had extremely poor self-regulatory capacities, and their lives were a series of crises. Redl and his colleagues described how adults can and need to focus on creating an emotionally healthy milieu as well as recognizing the importance of a positive peer group as an essential foundation for healthy development. He created the notion of the "Life Space Interview" that focuses on how adults can engage the youngster in crisis (Redl and Wineman, 1957). They detailed how analytic principles need to shape understanding and the management of the youngster's crisis as it is occurring to maximize social and emotional learning and therapeutic work. For example, the overlapping notion that students usually are "doing their best" (an appreciative attitude), as well as the idea that behavior typically signals unrecognized internal experience, are simple, but profound examples of analytically informed thinking. When Redl became the chief of the Child Research Branch of the NIMH, he continued his systematic studies of LSI, group process, psychotherapy and remedial interventions. One of the Redl's younger colleagues—Nicholas Long —added to this work in important ways.

In a series of studies and linked manuals, Long and his colleagues translated, concretized, and added to Redl's work in developing a series of specific, operationally based steps (Long and Newman, 1963). They delineated, for example, the specific skills, knowledge, and conceptual frameworks adults need to understand what various "crises" may be signaling. Explicitly building on Aichhorn's and Redl's work, Long and colleagues stated that the goal is to transform problems into opportunities for social emotional learning. The emphasis is to discover the underlying causes and patterns of self-defeating behaviors. They specified a series of intervention strategies in the actual milieu that clinical and research work had shown to support adults making a student crisis an opportunity to learn (Long, Wood, and Fecser, 2001). This work has been independently evaluated in a series of studies—-nationally and internationally—and is now recognized as a powerful framework and strategy for professional staff to teach youngsters engaged in destructive behavior to act more responsibly. It is now an integral facet of many special education school systems and some regular education systems, and it is taught in a growing number of colleges of education.

Another project that focuses on troubled children is the School-Based Mourning Project. This program has been designed to help high-risk inner-city elementary school children deal with multiple losses and trauma. This model is based—in part—on the notion that grieving is especially difficult for inner city children living in a chaotic environment of poverty and often traumatized by violence. The program is designed to enable these children to deal with the feelings of hopelessness, the pain of grief, violent fantasies, and guilt. Preliminary clinical pre- and post-testing indicate the effectiveness of the intervention (Sklarew et al., 2002).

The PATHS Curriculum (*P*romoting *A*lternative *TH*inking *S*trategies) is an analytically informed social emotional learning program that can be taught to K–5 children (Kusché and Greenberg, 2001). Initially developed for special education students, it is now being used within a growing number of regular education settings as well. In a series of controlled studies with randomized control versus experimental groups, psychoanalyst Carol Kusché and developmental psychologist Mark Greenberg have demonstrated that this program increases children's ability to recognize emotions, understand social problems, develop effective alternative solutions to problems, and, decreases the frequency of aggressive/violent solutions. Teachers reported significant improvements in a variety of student prosocial behaviors. This work also had a positive effect on children's cognitive testing. One-year teacher follow-up study indicated impressive reductions in behavioral difficulties (Kusché andGreenberg, 2001). The PATHS curriculum is included in most national registries of "research-based" and "approved" programs, a designation that is increasingly required if American school systems are to receive state and/or federal funding to support educational, risk prevention, and/or health promotion efforts.

Since 1969 Henri Parens and his colleagues have been involved in parenting education (Parens, 1988). They have developed the Curriculum for Students in Grades K–12, as well as Workshops for Child Caregivers (Parens et al., 1997; Parens and Rose-Itkoff, 1997). These parenting materials and strategies grew out of their Early Child Development Program, a longitudinal observation project that lasted 7 years, the effects of which, based on a 19-year follow-up study, revealed significantly improved adaptive functioning in the areas of legal difficulties, drug and alcohol use, and education, improved aggression profiles in the children, and a dramatic positive change in self-esteem and parenting style in the mothers (Parens, 1993; Parens et al., 2006). The thrust of the Curriculum for Students in Grades K–12 is that children will learn about child and adolescent development in ways that will support their becoming thoughtful and caring parents. Many of these students will become parents within years of graduating from high school.

Parens' work has been used in a number of American sites as well as in Israel. It has also provided the foundation for *Educating Children for Parenting* (ECP), an effort that has educated more than 125,000 young people (K–12) by helping them to understand and develop skills linked to parenting. ECP provides a school-based parenting education curriculum and trains teachers to integrate that curriculum across all academic subjects. ECP has conducted several independent evaluations that show it helps young people to alter defensive strategies and fosters learning and interpersonal problem solving (Puriefoy-Brinkley et al., 2004).

Twemlow, Sacco, Fonagy and their colleagues have a programmatic effort that is organized around the bully-victim-bystander cycle that has two aims: to reduce bully-victim behavior and to promote responsible, caring communities. This effort teaches students—and school personnel—skills and linked sets of understanding about the toxicity of being a passive bystander and sets in motion a community-wide effort to promote "upstander" behavior (Twemlow et al., 2001). This is an important and ongoing educational and research effort that has experimentally demonstrated that it reduces violence in schools and increases academic achievement (Fonagy et al., 2005). In addition, this group of analysts and educators is looking at a variety of individual student as well as teacher characteristics. For example, a recent study of educators showed that teachers who experienced bullying themselves when young are more likely to both bully students and experience bullying by students both in and outside the classroom (Twemlow, Fonagy, Sacco, and Brethour, 2006). Although this finding will not surprise analysts, it is important in two ways. Bullying by teachers has been an overlooked—but common—problem. It also applies a psychoanalytically informed perspective about personality development to a fundamentally important school problem. Twemlow, Fonagy, and their colleagues have developed the notion of "mentalizing communities" and are studying its application to three arenas: (1) reducing bullying and creating a peaceful climate in schools; (2) promoting compassion in cities by a focus on end-of-life care; and (3) a mentalization-based intervention to modify the parenting styles of borderline and substance abusing parents (Twemlow, Fonagy, and Sacco, 2005).

As noted above, the Center for Social and Emotional Education has developed a five-stage school improvement process that builds on our Comprehensive School Climate Inventory (CSCI) that assesses how K–12 students, parents, and school personnel experience the school. School climate refers to the quality and character of school life. School climate is based on patterns of people's experience of school life and reflects norms, goals, values, interpersonal relationships, teaching, learning and leadership practices, and organizational structures. A sustainable, positive school climate fosters youth development and learning necessary for a productive, contributing and satisfying life in a democratic society. This climate includes norms, values and expectations that support people feeling socially, emotionally and physically safe. People are engaged and respected. Students, families, and educators work together to develop, live, and contribute to a shared school vision. Educators model and nurture an attitude that emphasizes the benefits and satisfaction from learning. Each person contributes to the operations of the school and the care of the physical environment.

School climate trends are very strongly associated with and/or predictive of students' self-concept, absenteeism, high school graduation rates, behavioral problems, effective risk prevention, and academic achievement as well as teacher satisfaction and retention (Cohen, 2006; Cohen, McCabe, Mitchelli, and Pickeral, in press; Freiberg, 1999). The CSCI is garnering a great deal of attention from U.S. State Departments of Education and several foreign educational ministries. Although there are literally hundreds of school climate measures, there is only one other measure that has been developed in a scientifically sound manner and is comprehensive in two important ways: assessing all three of the major school groups (K–12 students, parents, and school personnel) and evaluating all of the dimensions that researchers and practitioners understand, color, and shape our subjective experience of school life. Surveys are—necessarily—thin: they reveal conscious and delimited accounts of experience. Nonetheless, they are potentially very meaningful in education because what is measured "counts." Today, what is measured and what counts are two dimensions of student life: reading and math achievement. In America and abroad, there is a growing awareness that this represents only "one leg" of the proverbial elephant and that we need to recognize and promote the social, emotional, and ethical capacities of K–12 students. To the extent that school systems and State Departments of Education use comprehensive school climate measures, we will influence educational policy and practice.

"Test results" are often not understood and fail to be used as a springboard for learning and change. This is true for an individual child's comprehensive psychoeducational test findings (Cohen, 1997b) as well as school climate measures. As a result, our Center has developed a "road map" that helps school leaders appreciate that the CSCI is simply a springboard for community-wide learning, goal setting, and implementation efforts.

We have developed a series of detailed guidelines, resources, and web-based learning communities to support the following five phases of school climate improvement: (1) recognizing past efforts and planning for evaluation and change; (2) evaluating the social, emotional, and ethical as well as academic aspects of school life; (3) understanding and "digging deeper" into evaluation findings and creating an action plan; (4) implementation; and (5) reevaluation and planning for the next phase of school improvement. In a number of ways, the third stage is particuarly important and analytically relevant. To begin with, school personnel are too often in a continually "reactive mode" and anything but reflective. This third stage of "unpacking evaluation findings and creating an action plan" provides a wealth of opportunities to support school leaders—as well as the whole community—to become more reflective. For example, parents and educators in a recent 12-school study reported that bullying was a "minor" or "moderately severe" problem. On the other hand, students in all of the schools report bullying to be a "severe" problem (Cohen, 2006). From an analytic-large group perspective, this student-based experience has been split off. Recognizing that all or a given sub group of students are experiencing a significant problem presents opportunities to not only think together about why this is the case and what can be done. It also raises larger questions about why this experience has been unrecognized.

Although there have been many school-based analytically informed programmatic efforts, it is only in recent years that analysts have developed programmatic efforts that include replicable guidelines, curricula, and/or learning activities. These efforts are important as they are garnering attention—for good reason—outside of the analytic community. Too often in clinical and applied analytic work we have just talked to each other and not created a platform for an inter-disciplinary dialogue and scientific discovery.

Echoing what I have described above, there is no single answer to the question of what makes these applied analytic programs psychoanalytic. Their work is analytically grounded in appreciating (1) unconscious life; (2) the central role of emotional development; (3) the importance of understanding the inter-relatedness of social, emotional, ethical and cognitive growth; and (4) the essential importance of creating safe, caring, and responsive environments for children to grow up within.

For many years in America and abroad, risk prevention and health promotion efforts were characteristically "stand alone" programmatic efforts split off from the rest of school life. Sklarew's and Paren's programs are examples of this: they are added on to the students' schedule and not integrated into the life of the classroom and/or school. A series of meta-analytic studies have revealed that risk prevention and health promotion efforts for children in general and disadvantaged and/or troubled children in particular are dramatically more effective when they are a part of a wide, coordinated, and comprehensive school effort (Catalano et al., 2002). Long's work with special education students and Kusché's, Twemlow's and our Center's work with special as well as general education students are examples of programmatic efforts that have been successfully integrated into the day-to-day fabric of student life. It is not surprising that they have garnered national and international attention.

EDUCATING EDUCATORS

Another significant area of work has to do with educating educators. When analysts teach and learn with educators during their formative training, we potentially shape how they understand and work with generations of colleagues, students, and their parents. Psychoanalysts have lectured and led workshops at colleges of education on many occasions. However, there have been few sustained efforts that have focused on the education of teachers. Most of these efforts have focused on early childhood educators (Furman, 1987, 1995; Manning, et al., 1996; Cath, 2004) who have, historically, been most appreciative of an analytically informed perspective.

Anna Freud initiated the tradition of educating educators in an ongoing manner when her study group contributed to a psychoanalytic pedagogy magazine and developed the first course on the application of psychoanalytically informed thinking to teaching young children in the early 1920s. This work gave rise to her 1920/30's lectures to teachers (Freud, 1930/1974). There have been a number of other individual efforts to influence teacher education (Ekstein and

Motto, 1969; Shane and Shane, 1974), but these efforts have not become an ongoing facet of teacher education in America or abroad.

The Bank Street College of Education is the first and one of the
very few examples of a psychoanalytic/educational partnership that
shaped the curriculum and educational process within a college of
education. A group of European analysts and American educators
constituted the college's original leadership team. From its inception
in 1931, Bank Street has been committed to promoting children's
developing social and emotional as well as traditionally "academic"
competences and underscoring the fundamental importance of being a *reflective* educator. Promoting reflective capacities has always
been *the* organizing center for this teacher education program (Lewis,
1991).

In the 1960s a teacher education program began under the aus-
pices of the Chicago Institute for Psychoanalysis and evolved into the
Human Development and Learning Program when a partnership
was formed with DePaul University's School of Education. This program operated for 34 years and created a forum to bridge educational-mental health-analytic perspectives. Case studies and the role
of children's developing emotional as well as cognitive life were an
organizing focus for teaching and learning (Cox, 1980).

The single most important analytic-educational/multidisciplinary
effort affecting teacher education is the National Center for Infants,
Children and Families: Zero to Three. Although their primary emphasis is on the first three years of life, their inclusion of four and even
five year olds warrants including the group in the 4 to 18 year old
scope of this paper. From its inception, the founders created an interdisciplinary forum where research and practice informed one another in an ongoing manner. This effort has dramatically influenced
the education of early childhood teachers as well as having a major
impact on diagnostic, educational practice, treatment, and policy.

James Comer's focus on the fundamental importance of understanding children's development (Comer, 2004) to support learning
and health is beginning to have a national impact on K–12 teacher
education. Under Comer's and others' leadership the National Institute of Child Health and Human Development and the National
Council for Accreditation of Teacher Education (NCATE) have just
issued an important report on the gap between children development research on the one hand and teacher education on the other
hand (National Institute of Child Health and Human Development/
NIH/DHHS, and the National Council for the Accreditation of
Teacher Education, 2007). This educator–mental health partnership

has the potential to actually influence practice when it is endorsed and supported by major national educational organizations like NCATE.

The Center for Social and Emotional Education has also been involved with teacher education in a number of ways. Our Teachers College Press *Social Emotional Learning* series has become an award winning series of edited and authored volumes for academics as well as practicing school personnel. Several books in the series (Cohen, 1999b, 2001; Devine and Cohen, 2007) have been organized around cases written by analysts. These narratives of students' lives over time are a "red thread" that runs through each volume. There have also been many chapters written by analysts about analytically informed efforts. In 2004, in response to a request from the City University of New York, our Center developed a new four course, graduate level sequence in *Social, Emotional and Academic Education* (for details see, www.csee.net); we are hopeful that this certificate bearing sequence will be recognized by the New York State Department of Education as a new area of teacher expertise in the near future.

Although there have been few examples of sustained efforts at teacher education, several common denominators make this applied work "psychoanalytic." These efforts have all included the explicit goal of promoting the adults' reflective capacity in general and an appreciation that conscious and unrecognized emotional, social, and cognitive life are inter-related and shape mental life and behavior. Case based learning tends to be a core method used to achieve these goals.

Unfortunately, we know very little as to whether this work is significantly more helpful than non-analytically informed efforts that have been carried out along similar lines. With the exception of Zero to Three, there have been few attempts to systematically study the impact of these efforts over time. As a result it is difficult to know to what extent the work is "generalizable" and/or is largely a function of the one individual who is implementing it.

CLINICAL AND INTERDISCIPLINARY WORK

Clinical work and applied work with an educational system differ in many important ways. The intimacy and depth of clinical work is, naturally, unique. Before I suggest three steps that will further interdisciplinary work, I want to briefly note several interesting similarities as well as differences in the theory, goals, and methods that define clinical and applied or interdisciplinary work. Our theory always—consciously and not—shapes our goals, which in turn, ideally suggests particular methods designed to actualize given goals.

Many levels of theory guide our work (e.g. about psychosocial functioning and development; therapeutic action; role definition and more). There is not one psychoanalytic theory of mental functioning that clinicians adhere to. Although some clinicians think systemically, more commonly analysts who work with educators also use systems theory to understand how facets of school life color and shape behavior. Another critical theoretical dimension is related to how we conceptualize modes of therapeutic action and our role. Most analysts consider transference analysis or the process of discovering unrecognized meanings and structures to be an essential mode of therapeutic action in child and adult analysis. Unlike clinical work, this framework is typically in the background rather than the foreground of our interdisciplinary conversations. In the clinical situation, we conceptualize and position ourselves as the expert and "provider" of treatment. As I described above this stance has deleteriously colored and inadvertently undermined much of our consultative work with educators. I suggest that a more helpful applied/interdisciplinary role definition is that we are and need to be true "learners as well as teachers." We are not "healers." However, this distinction is not a neat one. I believe many, if not most, clinicians would say that they are co-discovers or learners as well as having expertise that leads us to provide or create a "platform" for co-discovery.

Clinical and applied goals are similar and importantly different. Both have an overall goal of "improving functioning." Clinically, our goal is to understand and help an individual child and to a greater or typically lesser extent, the family. In applied consultative work our goals are often broader. Even if we are in the role of consultant focusing on a given child, we tend to necessarily be attuned to peers in the classroom, the family, and the overall climate of the school. And, often, our goals are to influence larger groups of students, parents, or school personnel. Often our goal is to promote learning rather than to heal or address conflict and the range of ways that children's development has become stymied. Methodologically, there are few similarities between clinical and interdisciplinary work. Although we may think in very similar ways (e.g. about unrecognized experience and developmentally informed psychosocial functioning) and work toward similar goals (e.g. discovering together what is and is not working as well as learning together how this came to be), few analysts today work with educators in the way we work with patients.

FUTURE DIRECTIONS IN INTERDISCIPLINARY
PSYCHOANALYTIC WORK

Applied and Interdisciplinary psychoanalysis has been a subject for discussion within the field from its inception. It has been an area of sustained work and learning for child analysts since its inauguration. In recent years, there has been a growing appreciation that the future of analysis will to an important extent rest on this type of work. There is growing interest in this work in national and international psychoanalytic organizations (Ramzy, Twemlow, and Maher, 2004). At the same time, there continues to be another analytic tradition that defines anything save intrapsychically focused clinical work as "not analysis." Applied analysis tends to be devalued by many clinical analysts. I have been surprised and at times disheartened to discover how few analysts are interested in work outside of the consulting room.

To further effective applied analytic work in the educational arena, there are three important areas to consider. First, we need to include courses on applied analytic work in the curriculum of our institutes. That it is not an integral facet of training is but one manifestation that this work is institutionally devalued. In fact, there is a growing range of creative applied analytic work in schools and the community (e.g. Rosenblitt, 2004; Sklarew, Twemlow, and Wilkinson, 2004). As noted above, a COPE group has developed curricular guidelines for institutes that want to consider adding this course of study (Twemlow and Parens, 2006).

Secondly, I suggest that we need to create more forums where analysts and non-analysts learn from one another. Too often our efforts have been focused on "applying" analytic ideas to education, rather than being part of an interdisciplinary process of being learners as well as teachers together. To the extent that we position ourselves as "the experts" who are not also "learners," we undermine our capacity to be effective teachers as well as learners. The American Psychoanalytic Association's *Committee on Schools*, The International Society for Adolescent Psychiatry and Psychology, and the newly formed International Association for Applied Psychoanalytic Studies are committed to these efforts.

Finally, we need to support the systematic study of applied analytic efforts. How can we operationally define what is psychoanalytic about a given form of applied work? How can we discover what the power and limitations of these factors are? It is well known that clinical psychoanalytic work has suffered because we only recently began to systematically study process and outcome. The same is true for applied analytic work in schools and the larger community. Encouraging the systematic study (serial case study, ethnographic, empirical, or otherwise) of these efforts is the single most important step we can now take.

Research efforts can and should overlap with policy-related considerations. Too often, in our applied efforts—like our clinical ones—we have operated in splendid isolation. In fact, state and national policy powerfully shapes funding, dissemination efforts, and educational practice.

Freud's original vision was that psychoanalysis had the potential to be a healing force in society generally and in the education of young children in particular. It has been. We have ample opportunities and a responsibility to continue and deepen this tradition.

Acknowledgments

I am pleased to thank Phyllis Cath, M.D., Barbara Eisold, Ph.D., Gil Kliman, M.D., Donald Rosenblitt, M.D., and William Solodow, Ph.D., for their very helpful comments and suggestions about this text. I am particularly grateful to Steven Marans, Ph.D., for his detailed and very helpful comments, suggestions, and support.

BIBLIOGRAPHY

AICHHORN, A. (1925). *Wayward Youth.* New York: Viking Press.
BERKOVITZ, I. H. (1999). School-based mental health services: The future of child and adolescent psychiatry. *Adolescent Psychiatry: Developmental and Clinical Studies,* 24, Hillsdale, N.J.: Analytic Press.
BLANK, M. J., & BERG, A. (2006). *All Together Now: Sharing Responsibility for the Whole Child.* Alexandria, Va.: Association for Supervision and Curriculum Development.
CATALANO, R. F., BERGLUND, M. L., RYAN, J. A. M., LONCZAK, H. S., & HAWKINS, J. D. (2002). Positive youth development in the United States: Research findings on evaluations of positive youth development programs, *Prevention & Treatment,* 5, Article 15.
CATH, P. (2004). Personal communication, December 15, 2004.
COHEN, J. (1997a). Child and adolescent psychoanalysis: Research, practice and theory, *Int. J. Psychoanal.* 78, 3: 499–520.
COHEN, J. (1997b). On the uses and misuses of psychoeducational evaluations, *Adolescent Psychiatry: Developmental and Clinical Studies,* 21: 253–268.
COHEN, J. (1999a). The first "R": Reflective capacities, *Educational Leadership,* Vol. 57 (1): 70–75.

COHEN, J. (ED.) (1999b), *Educating Minds and Hearts: Social Emotional Learning and the Passage into Adolescence*. New York: Teachers College Press

COHEN, J. (2001) Social emotional education: Core principles and practices. In J. Cohen (ed.), *Caring Classrooms /Intelligent Schools: The Social Emotional Education of Young Children*. New York: Teachers College Press.

COHEN, J. (2002). Guest Editor: *Psychoanalysis and Education*, published in the *J. Applied Psychoanal. Studies (Special Issue)* 4, 3.

COHEN, J. (2006). Social, emotional, ethical and academic education: Creating a climate for learning, participation in democracy and well-being, *Harvard Educational Review*, 76 (2): Summer, 201–237.

COHEN, J., SHAPIRO, L. & FISHER, M. (2006). Finding the heart of your school: Using school climate data to create a climate for learning, *Principal Leadership* (journal of the National Association of Secondary School Principals), 7 (4): 26–32.

COHEN, J., McCABE, L., MITCHELLI, N. M., & PICKERAL, T. (in press). School Climate: Research, Policy, Teacher Education and Practice. *Teachers College Record*.

COMER, J. P. (1988). *Maggie's American Dream: The Life and Times of a Black Family*. New York: Penguin Books.

COMER, J. P. (1995). *School Power*. New York: Free Press.

COMER, J. P., JOYNER, E. T., & BEN-AVIE, M. (2004). *Six Pathways to Healthy Child Development and Academic Success: The Field Guide to Comer Schools in Action* (Comer Schools in Action). Thousand Oaks, Calif.: Corwin Press.

COX, C. H. (1980). Between teacher and child: An interview with Kay Field, *Curriculum-Review*, 19 (5): 390–394.

DEVINE, J., & COHEN, J. (2007). *Making Your School Safe: Strategies to Protect Children and Promote Learning*. New York: Teachers College Press.

DRYFOOS, J., & QUINN, J. (2005). *Community Schools: A Strategy for Integrating Youth Development and School Reform: New Directions for Youth Development*. San Francisco: Jossey-Bass.

EKSTEIN, R., & MOTTO, R. L. (1969). *From Learning for Love to Love of Learning: Essays on Psychoanalysis and Education*. New York : Brunner Mazel.

ERIKSON, E. H. (1979). *Identify: Youth and Crisis*. New York: Norton.

FARLEY, A. J., & MANNING, D. (2002) A three-tiered, applied psychoanalytic intervention to support young children's emotional development. *J. Applied Psychoanal. Studies*, 4, #3.

FONAGY, P., TWEMLOW, S. W., VERNBERG, E., SACCO, F. C., & LITTLE, T. (2005). Creating a peaceful school learning environment: The impact of an anti-bullying program on educational attainment in elementary schools, *Medical Science Monitor*, 11 (7): 317–325.

FREIBERG, H. J. (ED.). (1999). *School Climate: Measuring, Improving and Sustaining Healthy Learning Environments*. Philadelphia: Falmer Press.

FREUD, A. (1974). 1922–1935 Lectures on psychoanalysis for teachers and parents. In *The Writings of Anna Freud*, 1: 73–136. New York: International Universities Press (Original work published 1930).

204   *Jonathan Cohen*

FREUD, A., & BURLINGHAM, D. (1973). *Infants without Families. Reports on the Hampstead Nurseries 1939–1949.* New York: International Universities Press.

FREUD, A., & DANN, S. (1951). An experiment in group upbringing, *Psychoanalytic Study of the Child*, 6: 127–168.

FREUD, S. (1933) (1964). New introductory lectures on psychoanalysis. *SE* 22: 146.

FUCHS-NADEAU, D., LaRUE, C. M., ALLEN, J., COHEN, J., & HYMAN, L. (2002). *The New York State Interpersonal Violence Prevention Resource Guide: Stopping Youth Violence Before It Begins.* New York State Center for School Safety, New York State Office of the Governor and the New York State Education Department, Albany.

FURMAN, E. (1987). *The Teacher's Guide to Helping Young Children Grow.* Madison, Conn.: International Universities Press.

FURMAN, E. (ED.) (1995). *Psychoanalytic Consultations with Parents, Teachers, and Caregivers.* Madison, Conn.: International Universities Press.

FURMAN, R. A., & KATAN, A. (1969). *The Therapeutic Nursery School.* New York: International Universities Press.

GEISSMANN, C., & GEISSMANN, P. (1998). *A History of Child Psychoanalysis.* London: Routledge.

HOPE, M. (1999). Outcomes of Cornerstone treatment: A controlled assessment. Doctoral dissertation, Wright Institute, Berkeley, Calif.

HUG-HELLMUTH, H. (1914). Kinderpsychologie, Padadogik, *Jahrbuch fur Psycho-analytische und psychopathologische Forschungen*, 6: 393–404.

KERNBERG, O. (2006). The pressing need to increase research in and on psychoanalysis, *Int. J. of Psychoanal.*, 87: 4.

KLIMAN, G. (1975). Analyst in the nursery: Application of child analytic techniques in a therapeutic nursery, *Psychoanalytic Study of the Child*, 30.

KLIMAN, G. (1997) The Cornerstone project: Analysis in special ed classes, *The Am. Psychoanalyst*, 31, (2): 27–28.

KLIMAN, G. (2006). Methods for maximizing the good outcomes of foster care: Evidence-based strategies for reducing transfers among homes and raising I.Q.'s *Int. J. Applied Psychoanal.* 3 (1): 4–16.

KLIMAN, G. & SHAEFFER, M. (1983) Summary of two psychoanalytically based service and research projects: Preventive treatments for foster children. *J. Prev. Psychiat.* 2:1.

KUSCHÉ, C. A., & GREENBERG, M. T. (2001). PATHS in your classroom: Promoting emotional literacy and alleviating emotional distress. In Cohen, J. (ed.), *Caring Classrooms / Intelligent Schools: The Social Emotional Education of Young Children.* New York: Teachers College Press.

LEWIS, C. (1991). The early years of the advisement program at Bank Street College, *Thought and Practice*, 3 (1): 29–32.

LONG, M. L., & NEWMAN, R. G. (1963). The teacher's handling of children in conflict, *Bulletin of the School of Education, Indiana University*, 37 (4).

LONG, N. L., WOOD, M. M., & FECSER, F. A. (2001). *Life Space Crisis Intervention: Talking with Students in Crisis.* (Second edition). Austin: Pro-ed.

LOPEZ, T., & KLIMAN, G. (1979). The Cornerstone treatment of a preschool boy from an extremely impoverished environment, *Psychoanalytic Study of the Child*, Vol. 35, New York Times Press,

MANNING, D., RUBIN, S. E., GUNTHER, P., GONZALES, R. G., & SCHINDLER, P. (1996). A "worry doctor" for preschool directors and teachers: A collaborative model, *Young Children*, July, 68–73.

MARANS, S., & COHEN, J. (1999). Social-emotional learning: A psychoanalytically informed perspective. (Chapter 7) In J. Cohen (ed.) *Educating Minds and Hearts: Social Emotional Learning and the Passage into Adolescence*. New York: Teachers College Press and the Association for Supervision and Curriculum Development.

MILLER, M. A. (1998). *Freud and the Bolsheviks*. New Haven: Yale University Press.

National Institute of Child Health and Human Development/NIH/DHHS, & the National Council for the Accreditation of Teacher Education. (2007). Child and Adolescent Development Research and Teacher Education: Evidence-Based Pedagogy, Policy, and Practice. Washington, DC: U.S. Government Printing Office (Available on: www.nichd.nih.gov/about/org/crmc/cdb/_).

PARENS, H. (1988). A psychoanalytic contribution toward rearing emotionally healthy children: Education for parenting. In *New Concepts in Psychoanalytic Psychotherapy*, J. M. Ross and W. A. Myers (ed.), pp. 120–138. Washington, DC: American Psychiatric Press.

PARENS, H. (1993). Toward preventing experience-derived emotional disorders: Education for Parenting. In: *Prevention in Mental Health*, H. Parens and S. Kramer (ed.), pp. 121–148. Northvale, N.J.: Aronson.

PARENS, H., & ROSE-ITKOFF, C. (1997). *Parenting for Emotional Growth: The Workshops Series. (1) On The Development of Self & Human Relationships; (2) On Aggression; (3) Conscience Formation; (4) Sexual Development in Children.* Philadelphia: Parenting for Emotional Growth, Inc. © TXu 842–316 & 317.

PARENS, H., SCATTERGOOD, E., DUFF, S., & SINGLETARY, W. (1997). *Parenting for Emotional Growth: A Curriculum for Students in Grades K Thru 12. Vol. 1, The Textbook; Vol. 2, The Lesson Plans.* Philadelphia: Parenting for Emotional Growth, Inc. © TXu 680–613.

PURIEFOY-BRINKLEY, J., & BARDIGE, B. (2004). Learning from babies: Vital lessons for school children. *Journal of Zero to Three: National Center for Infants, Toddlers and Families*, 24, (3): 22–287.

RAMZY, N., TWEMLOW, S. W., and MAHER, A. (2004). Psychoanalysis in the larger world: The International Association for Applied Psychoanalytic Studies, *The Am. Psychoanalyst*, 38, (2): 12–13.

REDL, F., & WINEMAN, D. (1957). *The Aggressive Child*. Glencoe, Ill.: Free Press.

ROSENBLITT, D. L. (2001). Lucy Daniels Center for Early Childhood Early Intervention Program 10 year Follow-up Study Interim Data. Unpublished paper.

206   *Jonathan Cohen*

ROSENBLITT, D. L. (2003). The Alliance of Psychoanalytic Schools, *Association for Child Psychoanalytic Newsletter*, Winter, 11.

ROSENBLITT, D. L. (2004). Translating psychoanalysis from the playroom to the classroom: Opportunities and choices. *J. Am. Psychoanal. Assn.*, 53 (1): 181–211.

ROSENBLITT, D. L. (2006). Personal communication, September 25, 2006.

SHANE, E., & SHANE, M. (1974). An exceptional child in the normal classroom: A psychoanalytic-developmental approach to teacher education, *Califor. J. Teacher Education*, 2 (2): 86–101.

SHEPHERD, M. J. (2002). Consultant or comrade: Comments about analysts' working relationships in schools. *J. Applied Psychoanal. Studies*, 4 (3): 331–345.

SKLAREW, B., KRUPNICK J., WARD-WIMMER D., & NAPOLI C. (2002). The school-based mourning project: A preventive intervention in the cycle of inner-city violence, *J. Applied Psychoanal. Studies* 4 (3): 317–330.

SKLAREW, B., TWEMLOW, S. W., & WILKINSON, S. M. (2004). *Analysts in the Trenches: Streets, Schools, War Zones*. Mahwah, N.J.: Analytic Press.

TWEMLOW, S., FONAGY, P., SACCO, F. C., GIES, M., & HESS, D. (2001). Improving the social and intellectual climate in elementary schools by addressing bully-victim-bystander relationship power struggles. In Cohen, J. (ed.), *Caring Classrooms / Intelligent Schools: The Social Emotional Education of Young Children*. New York: Teachers College Press.

TWEMLOW, S. W., FONAGY, P., & SACCO, F. C. (2005). A developmental approach to mentalizing communities: I. A model for social change. *Bull. Menninger Clin.* 2005 Fall 69(4): 265–81.

TWEMLOW, S. W., FONAGY, P., SACCO, F. C., & BRETHOUR, J. R. (2006). Teachers who bully students: A hidden trauma. *International Journal of Social Psychiatry*, 52 (3): 187–198.

TWEMLOW, S. W., & PARENS, H. (2006). Might Freud's legacy lie beyond the couch? *Psychoanalytic Psychology*, 23 (2): 430–451.

TWEMLOW, S., & SACCO, F. (1996). Peacekeeping and peacemaking: The conceptual foundations of a plan to reduce violence and improve the quality of life in a midsized community in Jamaica. *Psychiatry*, 59: 156–174.

U.S. Department of Education (2005). *No Child Left Behind Act of 2001*. Retrieved November 25, 2005, from www.ed.gov/nclb/.

WEISSBERG, R. P., DURLAK, J. A., TAYLOR, R. D., & DYMNICKI, A. B. (submitted for publication). Promoting social and emotional learning enhances school success: Results and implications of a meta-analysis.

WEISSBERG, R. P., KUMPFER, K. L., & SELIGMAN, M. E. P. (2003). Prevention that works for children and youth: An introduction. *American Psychologist*, 58 (6–7): 425–432.

WILKINSON, S. (2004). COPE: *Curriculum for applied psychoanalysis in the community* Bibliography—With Some Annotation. Unpublished manuscript.

YOUNG-BRUEHL, E. (1988). *Anna Freud: A Biography*. New York: Norton.

ZELMAN, A., SAMUELS, S., & ABRAMS, D. (1985). IQ changes of young children following intensive long-term psychotherapy. *Journal of Psychology*, 34: 215–217.

ZELMAN, A., & SAMUELS, S. (1996) Children's IQ changes and long-term psychotherapy: A follow up study. Chapter in Zelman, A. (ed.) *Early Intervention with High-Risk Children: Freeing Prisoners of Circumstance*. Northvale, N.J.: Aronson.

ZINS, J., WEISSBERG, R. W., WANG, M. C., & WALBERG, H. W. (2004). *Building School Success on Social Emotional Learning: What Does the Research Say?* New York: Teachers College Press.

TREATMENT OF
CHILDREN OF TRAUMA
AND DISRUPTION

Still Searching for the Best Interests of the Child

Trauma Treatment in Infancy and Early Childhood*

ALICIA F. LIEBERMAN, Ph.D., and WILLIAM W. HARRIS, Ph.D.

*Winner of the Albert J. Solnit Award, 2007

This article describes recent developments in theory and clinical practice with traumatized children in the birth to five age range. It revisits the treatment of an abused two-year-old girl and her mother from the perspective of the child's reappearance in the clinic twenty years later to ask about her past. The early treatment of the child and the mother is re-examined from the perspective of the advances in theory and practice about early childhood trauma in the intervening decades. These advances are contrasted with the persistent gap between the urgent needs of maltreated children and their families and the availability of services designed to support their mental health.

Alicia F. Lieberman is Irving B. Harris Endowed Chair of Infant Mental Health and Professor in the Department of Psychiatry, University of California San Francisco and Director, Child Trauma Research Project, San Francisco General Hospital. William W. Harris is Chairman of Children's Research and Education Institute, Inc.

Support for this article was provided by a generous donation from the Coydog Foundation.

The Psychoanalytic Study of the Child 62, ed. Robert A. King, Peter B. Neubauer, Samuel Abrams, and A. Scott Dowling (Yale University Press, copyright © 2007 by Robert A. King, Peter B. Neubauer, Samuel Abrams, and A. Scott Dowling).

Dedication
To Al, with love and appreciation for his wisdom, humor,
guidance, and friendship

THIS ARTICLE IS THE PUBLISHED VERSION OF THE ALBERT J. SOLNIT
Second Memorial Lecture, which took place at the Yale Child Study
Center in April, 2006. That lecture and the ensuing article trace an
arc that began 23 years ago, when Dr. Solnit, in his then role as editor
of *The Psychoanalytic Study of the Child,* invited the publication of
"Searching for the best interests of the child: Intervention with an
abusive mother and her toddler" (Lieberman and Pawl, 1983), a clinical study of a 2-year-old girl, who in the course of treatment was removed from her mother's care and subsequently adopted. The present paper returns to focus on the same clinical case, with the goal of
elucidating what has changed and what has remained the same in
the intervening decades in theory, clinical practice, and the realities
facing abused children and their families and the clinicians who treat
them.

Our thinking is profoundly influenced by the views articulated in
Beyond the Best Interests of the Child (Goldstein, Freud, and Solnit,
1973), a seminal contribution to the problem of child placement
when parents are unable to provide for the physical and psychological well-being of their child. Goldstein, Freud, and Solnit were pioneers in advancing the still controversial position that the law must
give first priority to the child's needs for continuity and quality of
care, placing these needs above parental rights and institutional effi-
ciency when necessary. Balancing their unambiguous preference for
upholding the child's needs, these authors also assert the importance of parental privacy and freedom to raise the child with minimum state intervention except in cases of maltreatment and abandonment. They assert, moreover, that adult rights are also protected
when the law upholds the best interests of the child: "To say that a
child's ongoing relationship with a specific adult, the psychological
parent, must not be interrupted, is also to say that this adult's rights
are protected against intrusion by the state on behalf of other adults"
(p. 106). Their statement summarizing the import of their position
is still a clarion call for attending to the social implications of every
decision made on behalf of an individual child: "Each time the cycle
of grossly inadequate parent-child relationships is broken, society
stands to gain a person capable of becoming an adequate parent for
children of the future" (p. 7). The overriding message is that every
effort must be made to prevent inadequate parenting. Only by im-

proving parenting can we hope to break the cycle of intergenerational transmission of maltreatment from parent to child.

Associating ourselves with the contributions of this groundbreaking book, we will explore some aspects of continuity and change during the past two decades in the clinical approaches to young children experiencing parental maltreatment. Treatment will be framed in the context of the exogenous factors in the family's environment. We will argue that the social and economic circumstances of many maltreated children and their families continue to restrict the potential effectiveness of clinical practice alone because the prevalent poverty and racial/ethnic disparities of families in the child welfare system substantially *increase* the likelihood of chronic traumatization for the child and the parents while drastically *decreasing* their access to the quantity and quality of the services they need. We will use the case study of the maltreated 2-year-old girl as a lens to examine the interface as well as the disjunctions between social realities and the limits of clinical practice. We will then re-examine the case study retrospectively from three separate viewpoints: theory (i.e., what explicit and implicit theories guided the treatment plan?), clinical practice (how were the theories implemented in the treatment?), and reality (what constraints were imposed on the intervention by the circumstances of the family?). We will then discuss some of the factors that have remained the same and those that have changed in each of these domains. Finally, we will offer recommendations for future action to improve the chances of recovery for young children and their families.

We hope that our simultaneous focus on child maltreatment, its ecological matrix, and its association to larger socioeconomic and political forces will constitute a fitting tribute to the memory of Al Solnit, who pursued social justice as a fundamental component of his mission as a psychoanalyst, teacher and commissioner of mental health for the state of Connecticut.

THE CASE PRESENTATION

"Searching for the best interests of the child" described the treatment of Tanya, a European-American 2-year-old girl who was referred to treatment by the court following the severe physical abuse of her 5-year-old brother by their 23-year-old mother, Jody. At the time of the abuse, Tanya's brother was placed in a long-term foster home without reunification services for his parents because they had abused him repeatedly and were deemed unable to benefit from intervention on his behalf. Tanya and her mother were referred for treatment by the judge, who reasoned that Jody might turn her anger against her daughter once her son was out of the home. The judge also ordered Jody's partner of six years and the father of her two children to leave the home because he believed that the domestic violence he perpetrated on Jody had become a chronic trigger for Jody's abusive parenting. Jody responded to these court orders with clear-eyed directness. She said: "I got to keep Tanya, but at what price. I lost my old man and I lost my son." She readily acknowledged her ambivalence about keeping Tanya at the expense of losing her boyfriend, a long-time crack addict who disappeared from her life soon after the court decision was issued. This situation is an example of the paradox that the law is both indispensable and ill-fitted as an instrument to address child abuse and other family problems.

Tanya and her mother were treated jointly using infant-parent psychotherapy, consisting of joint child-parent sessions supplemented with individual sessions with the mother, with the goal of improving the mother's ability to provide safe care for her child through increased understanding of the emotional obstacles that interfered with adequate parenting (Fraiberg, 1980; Lieberman, Silverman and Pawl, 2000). In traditional infant-parent psychotherapy with non-maltreating parents and their children, the "client" is neither the child nor the parent but the relationship between them. This therapeutic stance is only possible when there is no danger to the child's safety. When a clinical choice must be made because the best interests of the child collide with the parents' wishes or psychological needs, the child's well-being must always come first.

The treatment of Tanya and her mother must be placed in the context of some general considerations about what is involved in conducting psychotherapy with parents who have a legal mandate to participate in treatment as a condition for keeping or regaining custody of their child. In these conditions, psychotherapy is missing two pillars of successful intervention: client motivation and the assurance of complete confidentiality. Providing psychotherapy under these circumstances becomes for the clinician a balancing act that demands full engagement with the parents while simultaneously watching with a fourth eye and listening with a fourth ear to scan for the legal and ethical responsibility to report abusive behavior. The inherent tension between serving two masters—the clinical needs of the client and the legal and institutional mandates of the state—gives rise to recurrent clinical dilemmas that may give rise to complex counter-transference reactions, including punitive impulses toward the maltreating parent that may coexist with rescue fantasies toward the child and may alternate with guilt and identification with the parent's plight and with an internal polarization of feelings toward the parent, the child, and the representatives of the legal system.

To cope adaptively with these inevitable stresses, the clinician must create a therapeutic framework where the objective obstacles to clinical work are explicitly addressed. The parents need to receive a clear explanation about the domains of the work that the therapist will keep confidential as well as the limits of confidentiality, including possible expectations from the legal system for a report or court testimony and the clinician's legal duty to report abuse or neglect of the child. It is not only the parents, however, who should be told about the role of confidentiality in the clinical process. Judges, attorneys, and child welfare workers also need to understand that confidentiality is essential in promoting the parents' collaboration in the treatment, and they must accept that the clinician will report only information that is relevant to the well-being of the child.

We alluded to the use of a fourth eye and a fourth ear to scan for reportable parental maltreatment. What about the third eye and the third ear? Those are reserved for the special demands of the parent-child relationship. Everything the child does and says is filtered in the clinician's mind through its implications for how the child perceives the parent. Reciprocally, everything the parent says and does is viewed not only as an individual experience but also as a reflection of where the child fits in the inner world of the parent. To paraphrase the sage Hillel, the essence of a child-parent relationship treatment is to help the parents see the world through their child's eyes and to respond to the child accordingly. Everything else is commentary.

THE GHOSTS IN THE NURSERY

Accurate assessment is a prerequisite to good treatment. In the case of Tanya and Jody, the clinician[1] (AFL) conducted a comprehensive evaluation of the child, the mother, and their relationship with each other. It emerged in this process that Jody's mother had had repeated psychotic breakdowns throughout Jody's childhood, and often was either absent from the home or violently abusive with her son and daughter. Jody did not remember ever having met her father, but her brother once told her that their father had been violent

---

1. The terms "clinician" and "therapist" are used interchangeably to reflect the different roles that AFL played as assessor, therapist, and child advocate.

against their mother. From early childhood through adolescence, Jody and her brother lived in about ten different foster homes, where they were often physically abused and sexually harassed. By her report, Jody was raped at age three by neighborhood children; at age six, she tried to choke herself to death in order to escape a foster mother's punishment. Whether or not these memories were factually accurate, they had become an integral part of Jody's sense of self as damaged beyond repair. This self-perception was reinforced by the fact that Jody developed a seizure disorder at age 12 and was put on medication. The seizures were largely under control, but Jody still had occasional grand mal episodes whenever she forgot to take her medication, perhaps with the hope that she no longer needed it.

The pattern of abuse and disruptions of care continued until Jody turned 18 and was on her own. She became involved with a series of abusive men, several of whom were her pimps. At 25 she met the children's father, a European immigrant who spoke little English and responded with violence when Jody did not understand him or failed to do what he wanted. Their son was born soon afterward, followed by Tanya two years later. The relationship between Jody and her boyfriend, although often violent, was remarkably stable, and they lived together until the court ordered him to leave the home. The pattern during these years was one of continuous intervention by community agencies: the boyfriend was jailed for theft twice; Jody was also jailed twice, once for prostitution and once for leaving bruises on her son. These events had a severe impact on the stability of her children's lives. Tanya and her brother were placed three times in a respite shelter and once in a foster care home for three months in the two years before the current referral.

Al Solnit would have shouted: "Enough! What are the child welfare workers waiting for? When will they attend to the best interests of these children, remove them from these unfit parents, and place them in adoptive homes?" This praiseworthy impatience with institutional guidelines and regulations that conspire against the well-being of children was supported then (and has become increasingly justified by the empirical evidence of the intervening decades) by emerging research evidence showing the cumulative negative effect of multiple risk factors on children's developmental outcome (see, for example, Rutter, 1979, and Sameroff, Seifer and Zax, 1982). At the age of two, Tanya had been a witness to domestic violence between her parents, had been exposed to her parents' substance abuse and their abuse of her brother, had been subjected to chaotic and neglecting patterns of caregiving, and had suffered repeated and prolonged separation from her mother and placement in foster care. Jody's history of chronic and unrelieved traumatization and her per vasive antisocial behavior suggested that her prognosis for improve-ment was guarded at best. The child welfare worker, who was a kindly but clear-eyed advocate for Tanya's welfare, wanted to place the child for adoption as the most straightforward way of meeting the best interests of the child. Instead, the court mandated treatment for Jody and Tanya but agreed with the clinician's stipulation that she could agree to provide treatment only if warranted by the results of the assessment.

TO TREAT OR NOT TO TREAT?

Jody's behavior during the assessment did not give much reason for hope. She consistently blamed others for her situation, and she had sharp mood fluctuations that could change in one session from convulsive crying to intense anger and then to a tough, devil-may-care attitude punctuated by shrill laughter. When she became angry at the clinician, she cursed coarsely and once threatened to hit her. On the other hand, and to make things more ambiguous, she faithfully attended the assessment sessions as well as her monthly sessions with her psychiatrist, who had been monitoring her medication for many years. Her outbursts of anger were invariably followed by apologies and expressions of remorse. She also had a searching wish to know why she felt compelled to abuse her son in spite of loving him deeply. In an emotional session at the end of the assessment, she hugged herself while crying convulsively and asked whether the clinician thought of her as a child abuser, and whether there was a chance she could change. She then said: "I want so much to be a good mother. I don't understand why when I start hitting my son I can't stop."

Precisely what is so difficult about work with maltreated children and their parents is that the best interests of the child may clash with the best interests of the parent, and once the parents have revealed the sources of their pain it is impossible to categorize them only as abusive and unfit. However, neither the parents' self awareness, nor their wish to change, and certainly not the clinician's feelings of compassion for their suffering are sufficient reasons in themselves to recommend that they retain legal custody of their children in the presence of danger for the child. In the case of Jody, two factors led to the offer of treatment. The first consideration was Tanya's obvious adoration of her mother and Jody's centrality in her emotional life. It was clearly too late in this child's developmental course to pretend that she would not be damaged by losing her beloved mother. In every assessment session, Tanya turned to her mother for comfort and reassurance in situations of uncertainty and stress, in a clear demonstration of secure base behavior (Ainsworth et al., 1979) that was all the more astounding given the external and emotional upheavals in the child-mother relationship. The cost for Tanya of maintaining this attachment was high: she was precociously attuned to her mother's moods and concerned about her well-being, in a role reversal where she often became her mother's caregiver (Lieberman and Zeanah, 1995). The second consideration, clearly related to the child's love for her mother, was the exquisite sensitivity of Jody's behavior toward Tanya, which she showed consistently although by no means exclusively. It was stunning to observe this abused and abusive mother's attunement with her child's moods and her sensitivity to Tanya's bids for attention and care, which alternated with her matter-of-fact expectation that Tanya would minister to her whenever she was sad or upset. Jody had spoken relentlessly about the "ghosts" that crowded her nursery. Her empathic responsiveness to her daughter, although distorted by her own narcissistic needs in many ways, made the clinician wonder about the hidden presence of "angels," which she had perhaps consciously forgotten but which might be evoked in the course of treatment to help Jody become less impulsive when her strong negative feelings were aroused (Fraiberg, Adelson and Shapiro, 1975; Lieberman et al., 2005). These considerations highlight the multifaceted nature of the best interests of the child. Abstract descriptions of what this ideal condition entails consistently use similar general terms in outlining the desirable conditions for the child's current circumstances and long-term developmental outcome. When considering the case of an individual child, however, it is not always clear how to best achieve these goals. Is it more promising to choose the direct, shorter road (presumably, in Tanya's case, adoption by competent and loving parents) or the long, circuitous road (in this case, the uncertain outcome of treatment involving Jody to improve her competence as a mother and her own mental health)? The unintended consequences that are often a byproduct of different decisions are also difficult to anticipate. In Tanya's case, the sources of uncertainty were multiple. Would the ideal adoptive parents actually materialize, as fantasized by the child welfare worker? How long would Tanya need to wait for their appearance, what would happen to her in the meantime, and how would the adoptive parents respond to the day-to-day stresses of caring for a maltreated child who was mourning the loss of an ambivalently loved mother after having also lost her father and her brother? How high was the risk of a failed adoption? Ambiguity is the most prevailing state of affairs in many clinical situations involving the best placement options for maltreated children.

A powerful authority—the letter of the law—was also on Jody's side, at least for the time being. She had not abused Tanya, and she had never before been offered services to help her improve her parenting. There was no legal justification to terminate parental rights, and even if there had been, she had a right to services before her parental rights were terminated. The central question faced by the clinician was whether Jody could change, as she had so disarmingly asked at the end of the assessment. The tentative conclusion was that, in the best interests of the child, it was less damaging to attempt the change than to sever the child-mother relationship without trying.

THE COURSE OF TREATMENT AND ITS AFTERMATH

The beginning of treatment was promising. Jody and Tanya consistently attended their weekly sessions and Jody seemed to make good use of opportunities to observe Tanya's behaviors and reflect on their meaning, to talk about her own emotional experiences, and to explore links between her perceptions, moods, and states of mind and her past and present experiences of relationships. After about three months of sustained improvement in the individual functioning of mother and child and in their interaction, Jody started becoming erratic in attending sessions, evasive in responding to therapeutic interventions, and easily irritated both with Tanya and with the clinician. In a dramatic and unexpected development about five months into treatment, Jody revealed in an individual session that she was a "junkie," and pulled up her sleeves to show the fresh purple tracks in an incredibly thin and fragile-looking arm. The clinician explained that she needed to make a report to the child welfare worker because Jody's drug abuse constituted a major risk to Tanya's welfare. Although Jody protested at first, she finally made the call herself during the session, explaining to the child welfare worker in the clinician's presence that she was using drugs and wanted to enter a treatment program. The course of treatment from then on illustrates both the destructive power of entrenched psychopathology and the failure of the system of care to respond in a timely and therapeutic manner to the multiple needs and crises facing maltreated children and their families. Against all odds given the scarcity of openings both in substance abuse programs and in childcare programs, the difficulty of accessing these services was quickly surmounted through an almost optimal collaboration among the child welfare worker, Tanya's and Jody's respective attorneys, and the clinician. However, access to services was not enough. Neither the substance abuse treatment counselors nor the childcare providers had an understanding of Jody's and Tanya's emotional needs. The substance abuse counselors enforced a "tough love" policy that mobilized the most primitive of Jody's defenses and made her aggressive and defiant. Jody's planned involvement in a job training program to help her pursue her dream of becoming a beautician could not happen because of funding cuts that eliminated the program. The childcare center could not tolerate Tanya's incessant crying for her mother, to which they responded by giving her "time out" in spite of the clinician's efforts to help the childcare providers understand that this strategy compounded Tanya's separation anxiety. "Tanya is old enough to learn that she is safe by watching the other children," they maintained. By the time Jody came to pick her up at the end of the day, Tanya was defiant, sullen and rejecting, and Jody interpreted her behavior not as an expression of the child's difficulty separating from her but rather as confirmation of her conviction, internalized during her abusive childhood, that she was not worthy of being loved. Eventually, the intrapsychic obstacles and exogenous forces conspiring against Jody's efforts to change were too strong. She quickly relapsed in her substance abuse, and Tanya was removed from her care and placed in a foster home. Tanya's removal was extremely painful for Jody, who screamed that she had now lost both of her children. She agreed, however, to individual treatment and to resume her substance abuse treatment. Her responsiveness to institutional efforts to help her was impressive indeed.

The therapist continued to see mother and child for reunification efforts after Tanya was removed from Jody's care, and added weekly individual sessions with Tanya to the treatment format. Two episodes from Tanya's treatment stand out as examples of her internal disruption and her efforts to keep her feelings of loss at bay. In one session, she spent the hour carefully placing the baby doll on the crib and then abruptly tipping the crib so that the doll fell on the floor. Tanya then picked her up, cuddled her, and ceremoniously put her back in the crib and covered her with a blanket, only to tip the crib and have the doll land on the floor once again. This sequence was repeated numerous times in a self-absorbed manner, with Tanya paying no attention to the therapist's narration of what was happening. In the subsequent session, Tanya carefully removed the contents of her bag, which included a photograph of her parents, a comb, a hair pin, her doll and its bottle, and her diapers, and then she equally carefully put them back in the bag, asking the clinician to tie the bag tightly. The therapist commented that everything was where it needed to be, and Tanya nodded solemnly. The therapist added: "Tanya wants to be where she needs to be, with her mommy." Tanya replied: "Be quiet, Alicia. This is my life!" She was not yet 3 years old, but she already knew that there was no point in pining for what she could not have. She was precociously prescient. Three months later Jody suddenly stopped attending her substance abuse program, stopped attending treatment, and stopped visiting her child. By then, a couple who was willing to adopt Tanya had been identified and had been visiting Tanya in her foster home. Soon afterward Tanya was permanently placed in their home.

Jody did not resurface again. The therapist continued to provide treatment for Tanya, with a focus on helping her grieve the loss of her mother and to make an attachment to her adoptive parents. After approximately six months of treatment, she was ostensibly doing well and her new parents were eager to terminate treatment as a way of leaving Tanya's past behind. Over the years, Tanya's adoptive mother called the clinician periodically for telephone check-ups, including advice regarding how to help Tanya adjust to her adoptive parents' impending divorce when she was 9 years old. The mother promised to follow up on the recommendation for individual psychotherapy for Tanya to help her through this transition, which would reawaken the experiences of the loss of her mother, father, and brother when she was a little girl.

One year ago, Tanya's adoptive mother called again after a hiatus of many years to say that she was at her wit's end because Tanya, at age 23, had become "just like her birth mother," using drugs and being sexually reckless. A few weeks later, by coincidence, the therapist received an envelope from the child welfare worker in the case. It contained a note saying that she was retiring and was entrusting to the therapist the contents of the envelope: photographs of Jody as a beautiful young woman. The child welfare worker wrote that Jody had given her the photos at the time of the adoption to give to Tanya, but she thought that doing so would disrupt Tanya's incipient attachment to her adoptive parents and she kept the photos in Tanya's file waiting for the right time to give them to her, which had never come.

The "right time" did eventually come, but perhaps too late. Six months later the therapist's phone rang and a young woman's voice said: "I am Tanya. My mom told me that you were my therapist when

I was little. Do you remember me?" Yes, the therapist did remember her, and Tanya asked if she could come to talk about her birth mother. When the therapist gave her the photos, Tanya looked at them tenderly and asked: "Do you think that I look like her?" She then asked about her mother. The therapist told her how much her mother had loved her and how much she struggled with a drug habit that she could not break in an effort to keep Tanya. She listened quietly but did not volunteer any information about herself; she wanted only to hear about scenes from her childhood with her mother. Then she left, taking the photos with her, and has not called again.

REFLECTIONS ON A TREATMENT THAT DID NOT SUCCEED: WHAT HAVE WE LEARNED?

Tanya's life history demands a re-examination of the premises that guided the conceptualization and implementation of her treatment. At the time, infant mental health was an emerging new field that held the promise, with appropriate intervention, of preventing individual psychopathology by addressing early risk factors before they become internalized into chronic maladaptive states of mind and behavioral patterns. The first three years of life were identified as the cornerstone of the child's healthy developmental course, and some of the most distinguished child psychoanalysts of the time, including in alphabetical order Selma Fraiberg, Stanley Greenspan, Reginald Lurie, Peter Neubauer, Sally Provence, and Al Solnit, founded Zero to Three: National Center for Clinical Infant Programs (currently renamed Zero to Three: National Center for Infants, Toddlers and Families) in order to propagate the importance of early clinical intervention. Psychoanalysts were also instrumental in applying developmental research to the study of the origins of psychopathology, with the infant-parent relationship, and particularly the quality of maternal care, identified as a focal point for intervention and treatment (e.g., Ainsworth et al., 1979; Bowlby, 1969/72, 1973, 1980; Fraiberg, 1980; Mahler, Pine, and Bergman, 1975; Provence and Lipton, 1962; Stern, 1977, 1985). Infant-parent psychotherapy (Fraiberg, 1980) emerged in this context as the most systematically elucidated treatment of infant mental health disturbances. The hallmark of this approach was the therapeutic focus on the relationship between the infant and the primary caregiver (usually the mother), with the goal of extricating the child from engulfment in parental intrapsychic conflicts by helping the parent acquire insight into the infant's role as a negative transference object taking the place of early figures from the parent's childhood. Infant-parent psychotherapy combined sophisticated psychoanalytic understanding with an awareness of the toll that environmental stresses exacted from parents who were burdened by poverty, limited education, lack of access to resources, and social disenfranchisements such as racism and marginalization. An integral component of the infant-parent psychotherapist's work is the mandate of attempting to ameliorate environmental stresses through active intervention with the social systems impinging on the parent and the child. Practical interventions, including crisis management and assistance with problems of living, are implemented in tandem with insight-oriented clinical strategies. The infant-parent psychotherapist integrates a sense of social justice into the therapeutic work, an inner stance that makes this approach particularly well suited for intervention with maltreated infants and their families. In creating what she called "psychoanalysis in the kitchen," Fraiberg (1980) implicitly blended psychoanalysis with the ecological theory developed by Bronfenbrenner (1979, 1986), which urged an examination of individual functioning in the context of the family, neighborhood, and broader society.

And yet, the clinician's effort to remain flexibly attuned and responsive to the internal and external needs of the child was not sufficient to prevent Tanya from behaving very much like her self-destructive mother when she became a young adult. What have we learned in theory and clinical practice since Tanya was a toddler, and would this new knowledge have allowed for a different outcome if it had been available at the time?

There have been important advances in theory and clinical practice that could have improved the treatment process for Tanya and her mother. The concept of trauma, rarely used 20 years ago to refer to child abuse and exposure to violence in infancy and early childhood, now occupies center stage in efforts to conceptualize the emotional impact of these experiences and to develop effective treatments. The definition of a traumatic event in infancy and early childhood has acquired an operational definition restricting it to events that involve actual or threatened death or serious injury or threat to the physical or psychological integrity of the child or another person (Zero to Three, 2004), rather than encompassing intrapsychic processes as well. There have been major advances in the past 20 years in the diagnosis and treatment of child traumatic stress, including a new emphasis on the diagnosis and treatment of post-traumatic stress disorders in infancy and early childhood (American Academy of Child and Adolescent Psychiatry, 1998; DC-R: Zero to

Three, 2004; Gaensbauer and Siegel, 1995; Scheeringa et al., 2003; Osofsky, 2004), The interplay between trauma and attachment processes has become a focus of theory, clinical practice, and research, with efforts to frame the mental representation of trauma in the context of children's memory and interpersonal relationships (Fivush, 1998; Lynch and Cicchetti, 1998; Lieberman, 2004).

Traumatic triggers and traumatic expectations are increasingly understood as often hidden underpinnings of traumatic stress and anxiety responses, and systematic efforts to identify and address them directly help to guide the course of treatment (Pynoos, 1993; Pynoos, Steinberg and Piacentini, 1999). This insight has important implications for the treatment of traumatic stress in infancy and early childhood. In the past ten years, Trauma-focused Child-Parent Psychotherapy (Lieberman and Van Horn, 2005) was developed as an elaboration of infant-parent psychotherapy to treat children in the birth-five age range exposed to violence. While preserving its roots in psychoanalysis and attachment theory, Child-Parent Psychotherapy also makes use of intervention strategies derived from developmental psychopathology (Pynoos et al., 1999), Trauma-Focused Cognitive-Behavioral Therapy (Cohen, Mannarino, and Deblinger, 2006) and learning theory (Patterson, 1982; Reid and Eddy, 1998). Interventions are tailored to the child's developmental stage and to the family's culturally influenced childrearing values and practices. The integration of different theoretical contributions within an overarching psychodynamic orientation is consistent with the approach advocated by Horowitz (2003) for the treatment of traumatic stress syndromes in adults.

If Tanya and Jody were in treatment now, the clinician would take the initiative to name systematically the specific traumatic stressors that she had experienced, including witnessing domestic violence and her brother's abuse, while using judicious timing to avoid overwhelming the child. At the time, the primary modalities of infant-parent psychotherapy were free association and free play to let the parent and the child tell their stories at their own rhythm and in their own time. Clinicians working with traumatized young children and their parents have learned in the intervening years that if the therapist does not ask, the children don't tell—or at least, they don't tell for a long time, and during all that time the unspoken trauma and the child's fantasies, distorted cognitions, and related affects may be derailing the course of healthy development. The children may also be saying to themselves: "Why doesn't the therapist talk about what happened to me? Isn't that her job? Maybe it's too terrible to talk about. Maybe it's my fault." This is no idle speculation. A well-known child psychoanalyst tells of a 9-year-old boy who was in treatment with her when she was still in training. This boy had found his father dead of a heart attack in the family garage when he was 6 years old, but the topic had not been brought up in treatment at the recommendation of the supervisor. The analyst eventually decided to say to the child that she knew the child had found his father dead when he was a young boy. The child immediately proceeded to enact the scene, and at the end of the session he asked shyly: "Why didn't we do this before?" Another psychiatrist tells of a 10-year-old who was brutally physically abused by his father. The psychiatrist felt himself unable to bring up the topic because of strong countertransference responses to speaking about the abuse. When he finally was able to do so, the child asked him: "What took you so long?" Many similar anecdotes, told in the course of informal exchanges, support empirical findings attesting to the clinical value of addressing the trauma directly, with the appropriate considerations for timing and tactfulness.

Preverbal children may not be able to speak about the traumatic event they endured but may be asking for the clinician to address it through their play, rigidly repeating traumatic themes over and over again until they elicit the desired response. For example, a non-verbal 2-year-old girl pretended for weeks to cut her mother's face with a toy knife until the clinician found the courage to ask: "Are you showing me something that you saw?" When the child nodded, the therapist asked the mother what the child was referring to. The mother revealed that the child's grandmother, who suffered from an organic psychosis, routinely lifted a knife and threatened to cut the mother's face. Until this exchange, the mother had ignored the child's witnessing of this threat and her re-enactment of it during the sessions. This session marked a turning point in the mother's ability to understand her child's experience and to create a safer framework for her everyday life. The child's ability to symbolize, in turn, became increasingly freer following the clinician's permission to tell.

Proactive clinical interventions in the treatment of child trauma have become a clinical responsibility because they normalize the traumatic stress response and instill hope by conveying that the traumatized person is not an outcast, that the therapist understands the situation because other people have gone through similar things, and that traumatic stress responses are a universal reaction to events that threaten our safety or the safety of others, particularly those one loves. While free association continues to have a uniquely important place as a road to the unconscious, a different therapeutic approach needs to apply when it comes to the client's experience of a traumatic event that is consciously remembered but "dares not speak its name" due to shame, fear of rejection, and fear of being overcome by dysregulated emotions. This approach involves modeling a way of articulating viscerally rending experiences so that the parent and the child can differentiate between remembering and reliving the trauma and can learn to anticipate and modulate overwhelming responses to the memories.

Theoretical and clinical advances have been reflected in the accumulation of empirical evidence in support of psychodynamic child trauma treatment approaches (Lieberman, Ghosh Ippen and Marans, in press). Specifically, the therapeutic focus on the child-parent relationship advocated by Fraiberg thirty years ago has been confirmed as an effective treatment approach. Four randomized studies have demonstrated that this relationship-based treatment approach shows efficacy with preschoolers exposed to domestic violence (Lieberman, Van Horn and Ghosh Ippen, 2005; Lieberman, Ghosh Ippen and Van Horn, 2006), maltreated preschoolers (Cicchetti, Rogosh and Toth, 2006; Toth et al., 2002), anxiously attached infants (Lieberman, Weston, and Pawl, 1991) and toddlers of mothers with major depression (Cicchetti, Toth, and Rogosch, 1999; Toth, Rogosch, and Cicchetti, in press).

An unexpected and promising treatment outcome finding suggests that the focus on the child-parent relationship is beneficial not only for the child's recovery from traumatic stress but for the mother's mental health as well (Lieberman et al., 2005, 2006). Battered women who participated in Child-Parent Psychotherapy with their preschoolers had significantly lower frequency and intensity of PTSD symptoms of avoidance, and a trend toward lower global distress symptoms of anxiety, depression, and other mental health problems at the termination of treatment than the comparison group mothers, 70 percent of whom had attended individual psychotherapy. The significant decrease in avoidance associated with CPP treatment was particularly noteworthy because the treatment focused on helping the child and the mother process the domestic violence they had endured and on dispelling the taboo often associated with speaking about the trauma. The findings from the follow-up assessment, conducted six months after the termination of treatment, are even more persuasive. The children in the CPP condition were still performing significantly better than the control group. In addition, their mothers continued to improve in their global distress symptoms while the mothers in the control group remained the same, with the result that by now there was a significant statistical difference favoring the mothers in the CPP group. We believe that these findings reflect the longer term benefits of decreased maternal avoidance of trauma that we saw at the end of treatment, which led mothers to feel increasingly less anxious, angry and depressed as time went on. We also interpret the findings as suggesting that mothers' sense of self is so intricately connected with their feelings of competence as mothers and with their satisfaction with their children's well-being that their individual mental health improves when their children are doing well and when their self-perception as mothers improves.

To use the counterbalancing metaphors of "ghosts" and "angels," these empirical findings indicate the therapeutic value of exploring in treatment how parent and child may serve as mutually reinforcing traumatic triggers that elicit self-reinforcing and overwhelmingly unmodulated traumatic responses. In asking whether she was an abusive mother, Jody was also asking whether she was embodying the ghosts of her traumatic past. Her abusive behavior toward her son represented her identification with the aggressor as personified by her violent although consciously forgotten lost father and her abusive boyfriend, while Tanya represented the neglected and victimized parts of herself. The goal of treatment was to enable Jody to achieve a psychological stance where she could say: "I see the ghost, but I am not the ghost; I can act like an angel who creates benevolent triggers that balance out the traumatic triggers in myself and my child." This could not be achieved. It is noteworthy that throughout the year of treatment, Jody could never remember a loving caregiving figure in her past or identify a loving figure in her present life. Perhaps these figures did not exist for her; perhaps they were buried in her unconscious because conscious remembrance would force her to re-experience the pain of having lost them (Lieberman et al., 2005).

The direct focus on eliciting a narrative of the traumatic event experienced by the children applies also to work with maltreating parents, who as a rule have long-standing histories of abuse, neglect, and exposure to societal violence. Traumatized mothers and fathers often thank their therapist for asking specifically about their traumas, saying: "Nobody asked me about it before. I thought I was crazy for feeling that way." The effort to identify and promote desensitization to traumatic triggers is now an integral component of individual treatment with traumatized adults. In the treatment of Tanya and Jody, the clinician would now search for the triggers that set off Jody's abusive behavior toward her son and her self-destructive use of sex and drugs, and bring her attention to these triggers as a way of understanding and forgiving herself and as an incentive for behavioral change. For example, for a long time Jody refused to enroll Tanya in childcare in spite of relentless pressure from the child welfare worker, who believed—with reason—that Tanya would be exposed to a more developmentally appropriate environment in a good day care center than spending all day with her mother. Jody's refusal might have been prompted by the fact that her son's preschool teacher had noticed his bruises and made a report to Child Protective Services. The social worker who came to investigate took the child straight from preschool to shelter, so that when Jody went to pick him up at school, he was not there and she started screaming in anguish and rage. It stands to reason that Jody was afraid the same thing would happen again if Tanya was enrolled in childcare.

There is no guarantee that the theoretical and clinical advances of the past 20 years would have led to a different outcome for Jody. Efforts to explore the link between Jody's experience of not finding her son at preschool and her later reluctance to allow Tanya to attend childcare were not productive. Perhaps this was because Jody's difficulty of putting Tanya in childcare was multidetermined. She was afraid of being alone, and she used Tanya for company and protection. She also associated school with her own social and academic failures. Finally, the idea of getting up early to take Tanya to school was simply more than she could handle in light of her partying and drug use, which were not revealed until much later. In the context of all these overlapping and mutually reinforcing motives, identifying and addressing traumatic triggers can present major clinical challenges. Given the multiple adversities in Jody's childhood and in her present circumstances, each traumatic trigger would have taken a long time to identify and address well enough to lead to meaningful change. Once Jody revealed her drug addiction, she had no choice, regardless of her motivation, but to enroll Tanya in childcare while attending her drug treatment program, and the child blossomed. This was short lived, however, due to Jody's quick relapse. This set of circumstances is a sobering reminder of the limitations of treatment even when new and promising modalities are added to the clinician's therapeutic repertoire. While necessary, psychotherapy is insufficient when external circumstances constitute unsurmountable obstacles against improvement (Harris, Lieberman and Marans, 2007). Would the theoretical and clinical advances of the past 20 years have changed the course of Tanya's life if she had received the kind of treatment we now consider optimal? It is difficult to know.

There is a paradoxical divergence between the steadily accumulating knowledge about the mental health needs of traumatized children and their families and the increasing popularity of brief, time limited approaches to treatment. Administrators in the public health system service are pressured by an unholy alliance between insufficient funding and the allure of tightly structured, evidence-based treatments into advocating for always more streamlined, short-term, supposedly cost-effective treatments for pathologies that are long-term and severe. Treatment modalities that were developed to address acute disorders are routinely used for chronic conditions (Harris et al., in press). It is an open secret that the traditional weekly or twice-weekly 50-minute hour in the clinic is simply not enough for children and parents with complex and overlapping sources of trauma and resulting co-morbidities. Although treatment sessions with Jody and Tanya lasted about 90 minutes and involved home visits whenever they missed a session as a way of monitoring safety and maintaining continuity, they needed more frequent sessions than we were able to offer at the time given the clinic's funding and staff resources.

The constraints on resources are often compounded by the limits of parental availability and motivation for treatment. Parents who work long hours often have difficulty adjusting their schedules to meet clinician availability. The objective obstacles to accessing treatment are often compounded by motivational issues both for the parent and the clinician. For the parent, avoidance of reminders of the trauma is one of the manifestations of traumatic stress, and resistance to treatment is often one of the manifestations of avoidance even when treatment is mandated by the legal system. For the clinician, countertransference reactions are a risk factor for the success of treatment because these responses reinforce this parental resistance. Conducting therapy with severely and chronically traumatized children and their parents can be emotionally draining and may become vicariously traumatizing, particularly when the clinician does not have ongoing access to consultation and reflective supervision. Even in optimal workplace conditions, however, countertransference reactions can crowd into therapists' personal lives and undermine clinical effectiveness when they feel so identified with the child's plight that they respond to the parent with anger or dismissal, or conversely, when their empathy for the parent's suffering clouds their awareness of the children's experience, or the danger, they face. For these reasons, additional handicaps to adequate treatment, such as the scarcity of funding resources and agency support, often become a tipping point that drains the clinician's commitment to a difficult-to-treat family and undermines the treatment's chances for success.

The lack of integration between child and adult mental health services is another major obstacle to effective treatment with traumatized young children. Just as they did 20 years ago, adult psychologists and psychiatrists continue to live in a world that is essentially separate from that of their child counterparts. When adult mental health providers are asked about their patients' children, the most frequent response is some version of "I don't know." Conversely, child therapists do not routinely incorporate the parents as integral participants and collaborators in the individual treatment of the child. Mental health services for children and adults are usually offered by different institutions, in separate locations, and often with different reimbursement schemes.

This professional split reflects the primacy of individualism as a cultural value in the United States. However, separating adult and child mental health services is becoming increasingly unhelpful as more immigrants arrive from countries with a collectivistic approach to family and community life. One vignette illustrates this cultural divide. A child therapist asked a 5-year-old Mexican-American child to draw a picture of his family, and the child drew a detailed picture of his mother, his father, his two brothers, and himself. The therapist said, "Now I want you to draw a picture only of yourself." The boy replied: "But I don't want to." The therapist saw this as a classic example of enmeshment and told the parents during the feedback session that their child had not developed age-appropriate autonomy and self-esteem. The parents interpreted the therapist's stance as an example of American-style narcissism. They said: "What's wrong with our son seeing himself as part of the family? We don't want therapy to make him selfish." For them, the child's sense of family belonging was a virtue that needed to be protected against the dangers of self-centeredness. This is an example of how different cultural groups may look down on the other's prevailing cultural values, missing a chance to enrich each other by recognizing the extent to which different perspectives provide a richer tapestry of possibilities. Perhaps one of the contributions of immigrant groups may be to increase the demand for changes in service delivery systems to make them more responsive to the interconnections among family members while acknowledging the importance of the individual.

Is Clinical Treatment Enough?

Although there is substantial evidence of effective treatments for child trauma, even treatment modalities that are generally successful cannot promise to serve the best interests of every individual child. The case of Tanya raises the question: How is it possible that, after being adopted at age three by reasonably loving and competent adults, after early efforts to intervene to help her grieve the loss of her mother and form sound attachments to her new parents, and after having been raised from then on in safe and comfortable surroundings, she is in her early 20s engaging in the same behaviors that were so destructive to her mother? The answer is unequivocally multilayered, and individual theoretical preferences will undoubtedly lead different clinicians to weigh some predictive factors more heavily than others. Nevertheless, after meeting Tanya again at age 23, the clinician carries a sense of missed opportunities when thinking of Tanya as a little girl. If only treatment had continued for longer after adoption, could Tanya have resolved her grief at losing her mother sufficiently so that she could relinquish a self-destructive identification with her? If only treatment had been more trauma-focused, could Tanya have learned to understand and modulate her strong negative feelings rather than using sex and drugs to avoid them, as her mother had? If only Tanya had received her mother's photos when she was supposed to, could those pictures have provided an anchor that reassured her of her mother's love and permitted a greater sense of continuity in her sense of self?

What about the environment in which Tanya and Jody lived? Visits to their apartment left the clinician feeling overwhelmed and hopeless by the enormity of the stresses they lived with. Drug trafficking took place in daylight on the street corner leading to their apartment. Drive-by shootings were common. There were no parks, playgrounds, community centers or grocery stores within 20 blocks of where they lived.

The elevator to their sixth floor apartment often broke down, and the stairs were dark and filthy. Their apartment was dark and almost empty except for some mattresses on the floor. Magical thinking about the ideal therapeutic interventions that could serve as a "silver bullet" in promoting psychological change is tempered by the sober realization that changing these toxic conditions is beyond the therapist's power and control.

THE POWER OF REALITY

Tanya stands for the millions of children for whom opportunities continue to be missed. Our theories have become more comprehensive, we have improved diagnostic capabilities for systematic identification of co-morbid conditions including depression, PTSD and anxiety disorders, there is an accumulation of rigorous empirical data about the impact of trauma on the brain and on cognitive, social and emotional development, and there is an increasing number of reasonably successful, evidence-based approaches to treatment. What has not improved is the toxicity of the environment in which a growing number of children are raised. The statistics show a growing gap in income between the rich and the poor, with a corresponding increase in the percentage of children living in poverty, which is now 1 in 4 for the population as a whole but disproportionately higher among ethnic minorities, who are over-represented in foster care and the juvenile justice system as a result of family and community violence. There is a stark overlap between poverty and domestic violence: a federal report shows that the incidence of domestic violence is two percent in homes with an income of more than $75,000, but 20 percent in homes where the income is less that $7,500. This is not surprising. The Reverend William Sloan Coffin enlarged and completed the dictum that power corrupts and absolute power corrupts absolutely by pointing out that powerlessness also corrupts, and absolute powerlessness does so absolutely, in the form of bitterness, cynicism, and failure to recognize and respect the experience of others—internal experiences that often find expression through violence in intimate relationships and in the public domain. Research findings continue to confirm the long-term health and mental health costs of cumulative traumatic stressors and early adversity. The ACE (Adverse Childhood Experiences) study by Vincent Felitti and his colleagues at Kaiser Permanente (Felitti et al., 1998) found that nine categories of traumatic childhood events—psychological, physical, and sexual abuse; violence against the mother; living as a child with a household member who abused substances, was suicidal, or mentally ill, or was ever imprisoned; absence of one or both parents; and physical or emotional neglect—exhibit a highly statistically significant graded relationship to ten leading causes of adult death and disability, including ischemic heart disease, liver and lung disease, cancer, and fractures. In the realm of mental health, respondents who had experienced four or more of these adversities had a 4- to 12-fold increased likelihood of alcoholism, drug abuse, depression and suicide attempts when compared to individuals who had not experienced any of these stressors.

The primacy of ACEs in predicting later negative outcomes has been well established across multiple domains. It is important to note, however, that in the statistical analyses each ACE is counted only once, although each ACE could have occurred repeatedly during an extended period of development. Furthermore, the interaction between or among two or more ACEs is not factored into the statistical results even though there may be multiplicative effects in the interactions among risk factors. Finally, even if one or more ACEs is persistently present, the chronicity of the adverse experiences is not factored into the statistical analyses. Therefore, the ACEs accounting system, while extremely illuminating, is likely to be a conservative index of the extent to which childhood adversity predicts later disease and psychopathology (Draft report of the Presidential Commission of the American Psychiatric Association).

These considerations have direct applications to the case of Tanya and Jody. Not only had Jody experienced all 9 of these adversities—they had happened to her again and again, in a chronic and unrelieved pattern that victimized her and degraded her in her own eyes and the eyes of others. In addition, the intergenerational pattern of transmission of psychopathology was evident in Tanya's experience as well: at age two, she had already been exposed to eight out of the nine adverse events. While there was no evidence that she had been sexually abused, there was the likelihood that she had been exposed to overstimulating and frightening sexual behavior both between her parents and between her mother and Jody's sexual clients. The authors of the ACE study show that the relationship between adverse childhood events and the onset of adult disease years later is mediated by health-risk behaviors such as smoking, drug or alcohol use, and reckless sexual behavior, which are used to cope with anxiety, depression and anger (Felitti et al., 1998). This was graphically illustrated in both Jody's behavior and in Tanya's behavior when she reached her mother's age at the time of the treatment.

A LOOK TO THE PRESENT AND THE FUTURE

What is our responsibility as clinicians and as citizens toward traumatized children? We know that most of these children are not found in mental health settings but in the everyday environments of their homes, childcare centers and schools, as well as in foster care and the juvenile justice system, where, according to a federal report, most of those are found to need mental health services but are not even screened for mental health services, and about 75 percent of those identified as needing services do not receive them. This is an inevitable result of the fact that the service providers most likely to come in contact with traumatized children receive no training on screening for exposure to trauma and no training on recognizing the behavioral manifestations of traumatic stress. Among the professionals and paraprofessionals with little or no training in child trauma we can count pediatric care providers, childcare teachers, police officers, child welfare workers, juvenile justice and probation officers, child attorneys and judges, and only too often, mental health providers as well. As a result, these providers routinely misinterpret child trauma symptoms as evidence of antisocial, manipulative, or oppositional behavior and are likely to respond in ways that reinforce and perpetuate rather than alleviate the child's fears. It is imperative to adopt a "supraclinical" approach to intervention with traumatized children, where clinicians see themselves as partners with service providers within and across systems of care that include the continuum from normative to emergency services—among them, pediatric care, childcare, schools, law enforcement, child protective services and the courts. Disseminating knowledge about the manifestations of child trauma and adapting therapeutic modalities to the non-clinical settings that serve the vast majority of traumatized children and their families need to become an integral part of the professional identities and responsibilities of therapists working with this population. There are sterling national examples of programs that meet traumatized children where they are and engage in model collaborations with key relevant agencies and service providers. The SAMHSA-funded National Child Traumatic Stress Network, for example, represents an important effort to increase access to care and enhance the standard of care for traumatized children throughout the country. There is, however, an immense divide between what we offer and the scope of what traumatized children need. Mental health services are not brought up to the scale of the need, and neither are services that might prevent many children from needing mental health services, such as home visiting programs and good quality child care. These programs need to be part of a concerted national effort to stem child poverty and to coordinate dispersed resources around the recognition that child trauma resulting from violence drains the talent and productivity of millions of children.

CONCLUSION

As we look back on the developments of the past two decades, we can point with pride to significant advances in theory, diagnosis and clinical practice. However, this satisfaction with academic and clinical progress must be counterbalanced by a clear-headed assessment of the living conditions and systemic deficiencies that prevent these advances from being successfully applied to children and families at risk, including the toxic environments, complex payment schemes, and insufficient funds to address the burdens carried by these families. What we learned from research about the negative health sequelae and financial costs of early trauma demonstrates unmistakably that any approach for prevention and long-term treatment success requires us to address the toxic environments and inequalities experienced by the poor, and particularly by disenfranchised racial and ethnic minorities. No real progress in alleviating child maltreatment through the discovery and application of new theories and through the training of more accomplished clinicians can be made without addressing the supraclinical environmental realities faced by children and families at risk. Attention to the intrapsychic realm needs to incorporate a concerted effort to defuse the pathogenic exogenous factors that become internalized and transmitted from generation to generation. Psychoanalysis and the ecological theory pioneered by Bronfenbrenner must become seamlessly integrated into a "unified theory of the mind" that demands social change as a necessary vehicle for internal change. Doing so will demand a fundamental change in public policy and resource allocation strategies extant today. Twenty years from now, psychoanalytically oriented therapists will be most successful when they are also devoted to improving the living conditions and systems of care for children and their families.

So where do we stand? A saying from *Pirkey Avot* states: "You are not expected to complete the work, but neither are you allowed to refrain from it." We must always remain hopeful, even in the face of overwhelmingly negative and toxic environments and even when our resources are blatantly inadequate. We have seen "miracles," greatly stressed and compromised clients from the most difficult circumstances, emerge as whole, productive people and achieve adequacy as parents. At the same time, however, we can ill afford to sit back and wait for more miracles. Our tasks are to work diligently, provide hope and care, and recommit ourselves to improving the environments in which these children and their parents exist.

As one survivor of Hurricane Katrina quoted by Dr. Russell Jones put it: "There is a hole in my roof but there is a bigger hole in my heart because no one is looking out for the kids." Al Solnit looked out for the kids. The opportunity to honor his memory is also the right time to re-dedicate ourselves to the example he set for us.

BIBLIOGRAPHY

American Academy of Child and Adolescent Psychiatry (1998). Practice parameters for the diagnosis and treatment of posttraumatic stress disorders in children and adolescents. *Journal of the American Academy of Child and Adolescent Psychiatry*, 36 (10, Suppl.), 4S-26S.

AINSWORTH, M. D. S., BLEHAR, M. C., WATERS, E., & WALL, S. (1978). *Patterns of Attachment: A Psychological Study of the Strange Situation.* Hillsdale, N.J.: Erlbaum.

BOWLBY, J. (1969). Disruption of Affectional Bonds and Its Effects on Behavior. Canada's *Mental Health Supplement*, 59, 12.

BOWLBY, J. (1969/80). *Attachment and Loss, Vol. I: Attachment.* New York: Basic Books.

BOWLBY, J. (1973). *Attachment and Loss, Vol. II: Separation: Anxiety And Anger.* New York: Basic Books

BOWLBY, J. (1980). *Attachment and Loss, Vol. III: Loss: Sadness and Despair.* New York: Basic Books.

BOWLBY, J. (1980). By ethology out of psycho-analysis: An experiment in interbreeding. *Animal Behaviour,* 28(3), 649–56.

BRONFENBRENNER, U. (1979). *The ecology of human development: Experiments by nature and design.* Cambridge: Harvard University Press.

BRONFENBRENNER, U. (1986). Ecology of the family as a context for human development: Research perspectives, *Developmental Psychology,* 22, 723–42.

CICCHETTI, D., ROGOSCH, F. A., & TOTH, S. L. (2006). Fostering secure attachment in infants in maltreating families through preventive interventions. *Development and Psychopathology,* 18, 623–60.

CICCHETTI D., TOTH S. L., & ROGOSCH F. A. (1999). The efficacy of toddler-parent psychotherapy to increase attachment security in offspring of depressed mothers. *Attachment and Human Development* 1, 34–66.

COHEN, J. A., MANNARINO, A. P., & DEBLINGER, E. (2006). *Treatment trauma and traumatic grief in children and adolescents.* New York: Guilford Press.

FIVUSH, R. (1998). Children's recollections of traumatic and nontraumatic events. *Development and Psychopathology,* 10 (4), 699–716.

FRAIBERG, S. (1980). *Clinical studies in infant mental health.* New York: Basic Books.

FRAIBERG, S., ADELSON, E., & SHAPIRO, V. (1975). Ghosts in the nursery. *Journal of the American Academy of Child and Adolescent Psychiatry,* 14, 387–421.

GAENSBAUER, T. J. (1995). Trauma in the preverbal period: Symptoms, memories, and developmental impact. *The Psychoanalytic Study of the Child,* 50, 122–49.

GAENSBAUER, T. J., & SITE AL, C. II. (1995). Therapeutic approaches to post-traumatic stress disorder in infants and toddlers. *Infant Mental Health Journal,* 16 (4), 292–305.

HARRIS, W., LIEBERMAN, A. F., & MARANS, S. (2007). In the best interests of society. *Journal of Child Psychology and Psychiatry,* 48 (3-4), 392-411.

HOROWITZ, M. (2003). *Treatment of stress response syndromes.* Washington, D. C.: American Psychiatric Association.

LIEBERMAN, A. F. (2004). Traumatic stress and quality of attachment: Reality and internalization in disorders of infant mental health. *Infant Mental Health Journal,* 25 (4), 336–51.

LIEBERMAN, A. F., GHOSH IPPEN, C., & MARANS, S. Psychodynamic treatment of child trauma. In: E. Foa, J. Cohen, et al. (Eds.) (in press). *Effective treatments for PTSD: Practice guidelines from the ISTSS.* New York: International Society for the Study of Traumatic Stress.

LIEBERMAN, A. F., GHOSH IPPEN, C., & VAN HORN, P. (2006). Child-Parent Psychotherapy: 6-month follow-up of a randomized controlled trial. *Journal of the American Academy of Child and Adolescent Psychiatry,* 45, 913–18.

LIEBERMAN, A. F., PADRON, E., VAN HORN, P., & HARRIS, W. W. (2005). Angels in the nursery: Intergenerational transmission of benevolent parental influences. *Infant Mental Health Journal,* 26(6), 504–20.

LIEBERMAN, A. F., & PAWL, J. H. (1984). Searching for the best interests of the child: Intervention with an abusive mother and her toddler. Psychoanalytic Study of the Child. 39: 527–548.

LIEBERMAN, A. F., SILVERMAN, R., and PAWL, J. H. (2000). Infant-parent psychotherapy: Core concepts and current approaches. In C. H. Zeanah, Jr. (ed.), *Handbook of infant mental health,* 2nd ed. (pp. 472–84). New York: Guilford Press.

LIEBERMAN, A. F., & VAN HORN, P. (2005). *Don't hit my mommy: A manual for child parent psychotherapy with young witnesses of family violence.* Washington, D.C.: Zero to Three Press.

LIEBERMAN, A. F., VAN HORN, P. J., & GHOSH IPPEN, C. (2005). Toward evidence-based treatment: Child-Parent Psychotherapy with preschoolers exposed to marital violence. *Journal of the American Academy of Child and Adolescent Psychiatry,* 44, 1241–248.

LIEBERMAN, A. F., WESTON, D., & PAWL, J. H. (1991). Preventive intervention and outcome with anxiously attached dyads. *Child Development,* 62, 199–209.

LIEBERMAN, A. F., & ZEANAH, C. H. (1995). Disorders of attachment in infancy. *Child and Adolescent Psychiatric Clinics of North America,* 4 (3), 571–87.

LYNCH, M., & CICCHETTI, D. (1998). Trauma, mental representation, and the organization of memory for mother-referent material. *Development and Psychopathology,* 10 (4), 739–59.

MAHLER, M. S., PINE, F., & BERGMAN, A. (1975). *The psychological birth of the human infant.* New York: Basic Books.

OSOFSKY, J. D. (2004). *Young children and trauma: Intervention and treatment.* New York: Guilford Press.

PATTERSON, G. R. (1982). Coercive family process. Eugene, Oregon: Castalia.

PROVENCE, S., & LIPTON, R. (1962). *Infants in institutions.* New York: International Universities Press.

PYNOOS, R. S. (1993). Traumatic stress and developmental psychopathology in children and adolescents. In J. M. Oldham, Riba, M.B., and Tasman, A. (ed.), *American Psychiatric Press Review of Psychiatry* (Vol. 12, pp. 205–38).

PYNOOS, R. S., STEINBERG, A. M., & PIACENTINI, J. C. (1999). A developmental psychopathology model of childhood traumatic stress and intersection with anxiety disorders. *Biological Psychiatry,* 46 (1), 1542–1554.

REID, J. B., & EDDY, J. M. (1998). The prevention of antisocial behavior: Some considerations in the search for effective interventions. In: D. M. Stoff, J. Breiling, J. D. Maser (eds.), *Handbook of Antisocial Behavior.* New York: Wiley, 343–56.

RUTTER, M. (1979). Protective factors in children's responses to stress and disadvantage. In M. W. Kent and J. E. Rolf (Eds.), *Primary prevention of psychopathology, Vol. 3: Social competence in children* (pp. 231–256). Hanover, N.H.: University Press of New England.

SAMEROFF, A. J., SEIFER, R., & ZAX, M. (1982). Early development of children at risk for emotional disorder. *Monographs of the Society for Research in Child Development,* 47 (7), Serial No. 199.

SCHEERINGA, M. S., ZEANAH, C. H., MYERS, L., & PUTNAM, F. W. (2003). New findings on alternative criteria for PTSD in preschool children. *Journal of the American Academy of Child and Adolescent Psychiatry,* 42 (5), 561–70.

STERN, D. N. (1977). *The first relationship.* Cambridge: Harvard University Press.

STERN, D. N. (1985). *The interpersonal world of the infant.* New York: Basic Books.

TOTH, S. L., MAUGHAN, A., MANLY, J. T., SPAGNOLA, M., & CICCHETTI, D. (2002). The relative efficacy of two interventions in altering maltreated preschool children's representational models: Implications for attachment theory. *Developmental Psychopathology,* 14, 877–908.

TOTH, S. L., ROGOSCH, F. A., & CICCHETTI, D. (in press). Toddler-parent psychotherapy reorganizes attachment in the young offspring of mothers with major depressive disorder. *Journal of Consulting and Clinical Psychology.*

Zero to Three/National Center for Infants, Toddlers, and Families (2004). *Diagnostic Classification of mental health and developmental disorders of infancy and early childhood,* Revised. Washington, D.C.: Author.

Repeating and Recalling Preverbal Memories Through Play

The Psychoanalysis of a Six-year-old Boy Who Suffered Trauma as an Infant

INGE-MARTINE PRETORIUS, Ph.D.

This paper explores the impact of trauma on the later development of a 6-year-old boy. The trauma disturbed his development and psychic functioning in almost every area, including his attainment of object constancy, capacity to regulate affects and tolerate frustration, his sense of self and self-protective functioning, as well as his capacity to symbolize. Three phases can be distinguished in his analysis based on his capacity to deal with memories of his traumatic past: initially attempting to forget but expressing them through persistent increased arousal and re-enactment behavior, followed by recalling and re-enacting salient incidences, and finally, remembering and playing through early memories in displacement. Each phase was characterized by an increasing level of affect regulation, symbolic play, and capacity to tolerate and think about the unbearable. The paper explores the different

The Anna Freud Centre, London.

Tessa Baradon, who supervises the case, is gratefully acknowledged for her insightful comments on this paper. Ben's analysis could not have been maintained without Mary Donovan and Duncan McLean's work with his parents. The first two years of Ben's analysis were financially supported by a grant from the Association for Child Psychoanalysis in the USA.

The Psychoanalytic Study of the Child 62, ed. Robert A. King, Peter B. Neubauer, Samuel Abrams, and A. Scott Dowling (Yale University Press, copyright © 2007 by Robert A. King, Peter B. Neubauer, Samuel Abrams, and A. Scott Dowling).

ways in which chronic trauma and the salient traumatic event, experienced in infancy are repeated, recalled, and expressed verbally and through behavior.

INTRODUCTION

THIS PAPER DESCRIBES MY WORK WITH A BOY WHOM I WILL CALL BEN, who witnessed murder, suffered chronic trauma and repeated abandonment before the age of three. Soon after he turned 6, he began psychoanalysis with me (4 sessions weekly), which continues 4 years later.

While it is widely recognized that trauma occurring in the pre-verbal period can have significant effects on the child's physiological, behavioral and psychic organization (Perry, Pollard, Blakley, and Vigilante, 1995; Schore, 2001a, 2001b), whether and how the trauma is internally represented and remembered, remains unclear. In addition, chronic trauma and the salient traumatic event are likely to be represented, remembered and expressed in different ways from each other.

Clinical studies, as well as research suggest that chronic (or cumulative or repeated) trauma and the salient traumatic event experienced in early childhood, influence the brain's development differently, and are stored, recalled and expressed differently. Since the maturation of the infant's brain is experience-dependent, chronic trauma can impact negatively on the brain's developing capacity for affect and impulse regulation, leading to a predisposition to act in an aggressive, impulsive and behavioral reactive fashion (Perry, 1995; Balbernie, 2001; Edelman, 1992; Damasio, 1994). The consequences are most deleterious if the chronic trauma occurs during the first two years of life; the period of optimal neuroplasticity of the orbitofrontal cortex, involved in homeostatic regulation and attachment functions (Schore, 2001a, 2001b). With repeated exposure, these states can become more readily activated such that they become characteristic traits of the individual (Perry, Pollard, Blakley, Baker, and Vigilante, 1995), so-called state-dependent storage and state-dependent recall of cumulative trauma (Ungerleider, 1995).

Clinical and research data suggests increasingly that infants register and remember salient aspects of observed and experienced traumatic events. The availability of language at the time of experiencing an event is not necessary for that event to be remembered over a long time, or for a memory of the event to be expressed verbally

(Bauer and Wewerka, 1995; Gaensbauer, 1995, 2002, 2004). Because these retained internal representations create distorted perceptual prisms through which the child interprets environmental stimuli, they significantly alter the child's subsequent responses to his surroundings.

Ben suffered chronic trauma as well as witnessing a salient traumatic event. While recognizing that a child's play in analysis can have many meanings and functions (Marans, Mayes, and Colonna, 1993), this paper considers the different ways in which he used play to recall and express his memories of these two forms of trauma. Ben entered analysis unable to regulate his affects, think about loss or his early experiences. I hope to show that as the therapeutic setting became an increasingly safe (Sandler, 1987) and predictable environment and this therapist a dependable, non-retaliating object, he was able to recall, think about, and work through his early experiences.

Three phases can be distinguished in his analysis based on his capacity to deal with memories of his traumatic past; initially attempting to forget, but expressing them through persistent increased arousal and re-enactment behavior, followed by recalling and re-enacting salient incidences and finally, remembering and playing through early memories in displacement. Each phase was characterized by an increasing level of affect regulation, symbolic play, and capacity to tolerate and think about the unbearable.

Ben initially expressed his anxieties through his body in the form of hypervigilance, hyperactivity, risk-taking behavior, and violent outburst of aggression. During this first phase he seemed to be attempting to ignore and forget his memories. My role seemed primarily to contain and survive his attacks without retaliating, and to provide him with the experience of a new way of relating. After 18 months of analysis, Ben seemed to perceive the setting and his therapist as sufficiently reliable and to begin to recall aspects of his trauma. This ushered in the second phase of analysis, during which he started re-enacting his reconstructed memories of his early traumatic experiences. He began to speak about events that were "known" all along, but had remained unsaid until then. During this phase, my role seemed to be a container for his powerful projections and tremendously painful feelings aroused in the counter-transference. In the third phase, Ben moved from re-enacting to playing through the past in displacement. In this phase, it seemed important for me to accept and adhere to the tightly scripted role he gave me, in order to afford him a sense of control as he began to investigate his past.

Ben, aged 5 years 2 months, was referred by his adoptive mother for his aggressive and oppositional behavior that threatened a breakdown in the adoption. His adoptive parents described him as angry, stubborn, and incapable of expressing affection. The referral was prompted by an exacerbation in his long-standing symptoms when he moved from the protected nursery school environment to primary school at the age of 4 years 10 months. His concentration was poor and he showed little concern for safety.

FAMILY CONSTELLATION

BIRTH FAMILY

Ben's birth mother was described as "sensitive, reflective and intelligent, gifted and artistic," but she seems to have been a fragile and dependent woman. His birth father was described as "violent, unstable and irrational, with no formal qualifications." Following much marital violence, mother fled with 1-year-old Ben and obtained a court order that precluded father from having access to his son. However, father found their address, entered through a window and strangled mother. Ben—aged 18 months—witnessed the murder from the sofa in which he sat. After killing mother, father blacked out for an unknown period of time. When he woke, Ben was still sitting in exactly the same position, apparently babbling to himself. Father fled with Ben for 4 days, until he surrendered to the police. It is anticipated that Ben will be 16 years old when his father is released from prison.

I have included the brutal details of the murder for two reasons. Their shocking impact has reverberated in the therapy sessions, at times, making me feel momentarily suffocated and unable to speak and leaving me profoundly shocked and saddened. Secondly, although Ben has only been told that his father "pushed the air" out of his mother, his play in analysis suggests he registered and remembered many details of the events.

FOSTER PARENTS

Following his father's imprisonment, Ben lived with a foster family for 1 year (between 1½ and 2½ years of age). Initially, Ben screamed if foster father or other men approached him, and he became extremely distressed if foster mother left his sight. However, he became strongly attached to this family that included 4 children. Such an ongoing fear response to adult males has been documented in infants who witnessed or were subjected to violence by their fathers (Goenj-bauer, 1982, 2002).

ADOPTIVE PARENTS

Ben's transition to his adoptive parents when he was 2½ years old, was characterized by temporary regression in toilet training, sleeping and eating. He settled well, but remained prone to violent outbursts, tantrums, and minor accidents. His play was very repetitive and the Social Worker described him as "emotionally numb." Ben's adoptive mother was adopted herself as a baby. From a previous marriage, adoptive father has two grown-up sons who have a good relationship with Ben. After failed IVF treatment, the couple adopted Ben, who is their only child. A series of au pairs have lived with the family. These remained nameless and unmentioned in analysis until the third year, when Ben named and spoke about one of his au pairs, suggesting he had—for the first time—allowed himself to become attached to her.

WORK WITH BEN'S PARENTS

Ben's analysis was preceded by a year of preparative work with his parents, conducted by an Adult Therapist (not Ben's analyst). These meetings continued throughout Ben's analysis, approximately every month; a frequency manageable by his parents. Initially, there seemed to be some repetition in the parenting patterns of Ben's birth and adoptive parents in adoptive mother's greater sensitivity to his needs and her difficulty in setting limits, and adoptive father's explosive and authoritative tendencies. The parent work focused initially on helping them unite as a couple, set appropriate boundaries, and develop more realistic expectations of Ben. His mistrust of adults and reticence to demonstrate affection—particularly to his adoptive mother—was a recurring theme of discussion until Ben started giving her quick hugs and buying her little gifts, in the third year of his analysis. Ben's excellent attendance at his sessions evidenced his parents' dedication to his analysis.

INITIAL CONTACT

Ben is a very attractive boy with a mop of curly hair. His playfulness and humor elicited warm feelings in me and other adults at the clinic. However, his capacity to switch very rapidly from being playful to being extremely violent made it very difficult to be with him.

In the initial sessions, Ben revealed his overriding preoccupation with keeping animal "babies" and "mommies" together and safe. He seemed to intuit his need for a safe place where he could begin to process his traumatic past and build a coherent sense of self. He frequently evoked the omnipotent and omniscient power of God, suggesting that his objects had failed him. In the fourth session, he surprised me by taking a camera from his pocket and photographing me! Ben invariably brought objects from home to his sessions during the first weeks of therapy, such as mother's notebook and father's aftershave lotion. The photo and "transitional objects" (Winnicott, 1951, p 4) pointed to his need for concrete representations of his objects and his precarious object constancy (A. Freud, 1965).

While very verbal, Ben's play was disorganized and frequently threatened to overwhelm him, revealing his difficulty in regulating his affects. His play often depicted terrifying and violent, yet exciting objects. Within weeks, most of the toy animals were maimed and damaged. Ben kept—and continues to keep—all the broken toys and pens, bits of paper and empty cellophane tape rolls, assuring me "we need everything" and revealing his fear of loss. His activity easily escalated into uncontrolled lashing out and risk-taking behavior (such as leaning over banisters, jumping down stairs, and leaping on furniture) that precluded him from thinking or hearing my words. I had to be vigilant and agile to ensure his and my physical safety and to contain these outbursts for him to regain some equilibrium.

The function of self-preservation is very gradually taken over by the child from the mother who initially fulfills this function for the child (A. Freud, 1949). It develops within a "good enough environmental provision" (Winnicott, 1956, p 304) as the toddler gradually separates and individuates (Mahler, Pine, and Bergman, 1975). Failure to develop self-preservation is associated with relative deprivation of object love and inadequate cathexis of the child's body (Frankl, 1963), both of which probably occurred to Ben.

Ben repeatedly attempted to test and engage me in negativistic power battles. Limits and frustrations that I imposed, unleashed uncontrolled outbursts of narcissistic rage (Kohut, 1972) in which he tried to attack me or damage the room. I struggled against my tendency to become authoritarian and didactic in the face of his provocations and aggression. I understood his behavior to be a maladaptive attempt to keep me engaged. His rage suggested his fragile self-esteem and ego functioning. Ben seemed to be repeatedly expressing and actualizing in the transference, his enduring patterns of thought, feeling, motivation that were internalized in the course of his traumatic early relationships. Consequently, I seldom interpreted and avoided power struggles by using play and humour, which allowed him to save face. I merely tried to survive and contain his attacks to afford him a "new object" (A. Freud, 1965, p 38; Hurry, 1998) and a different form of a relationship that was potentially reparative and healing (Westen and Gabbard, 2002a, 2002b).

At the end of sessions, Ben invariably tried to trash the room and refused to leave, revealing his difficulty with endings and separations. Playfulness on my part helped make these less painful for him. For instance in the first month, when he feigned falling asleep at the end of one session, I spoke aloud of my hope that he would not sleepwalk to the waiting room. This comment incited him to get up, hold both arms outstretched and "sleepwalk" downstairs. This became our mode of ending sessions for 8 months. While it enabled him to end the session without losing face, I was aware that this collusion did not help him face the reality of the separation.

IMAGINARY COMPANIONS AND GREATER SYMBOLIC PLAY

By the third month of analysis, Ben brought things to therapy less often. His play became more creative and his narratives more coherent. Ben introduced three imaginary companions who sometimes "attended" analysis with him, or instead of him. These included "Okra," his naughty imaginary companion; "Genie," a powerful but sensitive magician; and "the robot of Ben," an automaton devoid of feelings. These imaginary companions—that apparently did not communicate with each other—seemed to reflect Ben's fragmented self. Although Ben used these characters defensively to split off and disown his actions (Fraiberg, 1959; Nagera, 1969), they enabled us to talk in displacement about his feelings and behavior. For instance, if I alluded to something in a previous session that Ben did not want to talk about, he often claimed that not he, but one of his imaginary companions had been present. I could then recount the events and encourage us to reflect on them. These imaginary companions attended his analysis regularly for 10 months and then disappeared mysteriously, suggesting that he was beginning to integrate these split-off parts of himself. They still reappear occasionally when he needs to distance himself from his feelings and actions.

In the eighth month of analysis, Ben began to use words or symbolic actions, instead of violent actions, suggesting a growing capacity to regulate himself. In the following vignette Ben managed—for the first time—to express himself symbolically, in a playful and creative manner, rather than attack me physically.

> Ben shouted orders at me repeatedly to line up the toy animals. After a while, I made the little toy panda complain that "Shouting Ben is frightening." Ben snatched the panda and threw him in a box, which he called the dungeon. He held his hand like a walkie-talkie and said to me: "Assistant, assistant, can you hear me?" I answered, speaking into my hand as if it were a walkie-talkie "I can hear you loud and clear, Ben." Ben said that I should punish panda severely, because he had been very naughty. I said that panda had only said that he was afraid of the shouting and that expressing feelings was allowed. Ben repeated that I should punish panda and then walked to where I sat, smiled slightly and said "click" pretending to turn off my walkie-talkie.

Ben's growing capacity to regulate himself allowed me to lower my vigilance of his physical safety and set greater limits. For instance, 9 months into analysis, instead of indulging his desire to play a game at the end of a session, I opened the door and said, "We have run out of time and must go downstairs." Ben walked downstairs with me, suggesting that he was ready to make the developmental step encouraged by my "failure" in adaptation (Winnicott, 1958, p 7). Thereafter, he mostly walked downstairs with me, although his behavior continued to fluctuate dramatically, particularly around breaks in analysis.

BREAK IN ANALYSIS AND "BROKEN BONES"

Ben's parents reported that he had regressed considerably during the first long holiday; he had numerous aggressive outbursts and would not be left alone. While playing on a climbing frame, he fell and broke his left forearm. Periods in which the object world proved disappointing have been linked to an increased tendency to self-destructive acts and accidental injuries (Frankl, 1963). Ben returned to therapy with a plaster cast, unsettled, angry, and needing to control me. When I fetched him from the waiting room for the first session, he denied his return, claiming he was not Ben but "Inge's dreams and her *imaginovation.*"

After a session in which he became so violent that I had to restrain him physically from trashing another therapy room, he claimed I had hurt his wrists. Aware of the anger he engendered in me, I felt guilty for apparently restraining him too tightly, so soon after his plaster-cast was removed. It became apparent that he perceived my restraining him in order to keep him safe, as willfully hurting him. Similarly, he seemed to perceive interpretations as deliberate attempts to hurt him. Thus, when I frustrated him, I rapidly became a hurtful object in his mind (Klein, 1975). When I later spoke about that violent session, he claimed his imaginary companion Genie had attended instead of Ben and he said to me, "You hurt his (Genie's) feelings and even broke his bones." Ben linked breaking his arm to his feeling of being abandoned and hurt by me during the summer holiday. This pivotal session, which Ben called "that fateful day," ushered in many sessions during which Ben cellophane taped furniture together, suggestive of a wish to repair our relationship, damaged by the summer break in analysis. Ben easily used an entire tape roll per session and would have used more, had it been available!

After "that fateful day" I became aware that Ben was particularly averse to physical restraint. He showed fear and some panic when restrained. I began to wonder whether being restrained while feeling dysregulated triggered a stress response that had become instrumentally or classically conditioned through rough handling as an infant (Arnand and Hickey, 1987; Blass, Ganchrow, and Steiner, 1984; Little, Lipsitt, and Rovee-Collier, 1984). This hypothesis seemed supported when Ben spoke months later about his memory of being squeezed too tightly by his birth father, described below.

THE LOSS OF THE AU PAIR AND LOSING TOY ANIMALS

In the eleventh month of his analysis, the unexpected departure of his au pair precipitated a dramatic regression in most areas of behavior. Ben had difficulty going to the therapy room with me, staying there, and leaving at the end. His tremendously controlling behavior suggested the extent of his lack of safety and mistrust in the "unreliable and abandoning" au pair. During a session in which he would not leave the waiting room, I spoke to him and his father about the au pair's departure.

> Father said, "Ben was not always nice to her" (au pair), and I said that Ben was maybe worried that he made her leave. Ben got up and headed for the therapy room and I followed. In the course of our play, Ben said that the little toy panda liked being small because it got treats. I acknowledged this and added, "But the grown-ups also tell him what to do and sometimes they leave without telling him they are going." Ben became silent and looked straight ahead. He remained pensive and then said "She [au pair] said she didn't care

about me." There was a pause and I said "How hurtful." He looked at the panda. I said that he was maybe worried that if he was horrid to me, I would not care about him and would leave. Ben said, "Shuuuut uuuup," prolonging the words emphatically.

Ben did not lash out but told me to shut up in a tone that was more impatient than aggressive. In this session, in which he managed to talk about the unexpected loss of his au pair and his corresponding fear that I or his parents might also abandon him, Ben initiated a new theme of play that consisted of tying toy animals to string and lowering them from the (second-floor) window. The animals frequently dropped out of the window and were declared "dead." Rescuing them from amongst the plants at the end of the session was important to Ben who invariably brought them back to life again, suggesting his wishful universe in which there is no death or permanent loss. In general, this game which was reminiscent of the "fort-da" play (Freud, 1920), suggested his intense preoccupation with loss, absence, and the permanence of death as well as his helplessness and need to turn passive into active and identify with the aggressor (Ferenczi, 1933; A. Freud, 1936; Sandler and A. Freud, 1985).

Reminders of a traumatic event are potentially re-traumatizing, but can also desensitize and modify the child's negative expectations (Gaensbauer, 2002a). Ben's play suggested that the au pair's departure had rekindled his earlier trauma of abandonment by his parents and foster parents, but also suggested that the analysis was becoming a sufficiently trustworthy setting in which to process his numerous losses experienced as an infant. Whereas he previously defended against feelings elicited by loss and tended to act out his distress (for instance by breaking his arm), he now seemed more ready and able to allow himself to experience—to some extent—the memories of loss and the concomitant feelings.

At the end of the first year of analysis, his teachers reported that following the unsettled period precipitated by the au pair's departure, Ben entered a very good phase of learning and co-operation. He mastered the alphabet and became interested in learning. With great pride, Ben sang the alphabet correctly to me in the waiting room and his omnipotent and controlling behavior receded. It seemed that learning the alphabet gave Ben a sense of mastery that enabled him to relinquish some of his need to control and denigrate me. His play became more co-operative, and he tolerated more interpretations.

SECOND MAJOR BREAK IN ANALYSIS AND MORE "BROKEN BONES"

During the December holiday, Ben broke his right elbow after falling from a climbing apparatus. He began the second year of analysis wearing a plaster cast and feeling unsettled. He denied the break in therapy, claiming "The animals did not miss me, I saw them every day, even Saturdays and Sundays!" He accused me of neglecting the toy animals saying "You did not give elephant enough air or oxygen in the holidays," suggesting that his own sense of "going on being" had been disrupted by the break (Winnicott, 1956, p 303).

After breaking his elbow, Ben became the rescuer and protector in games. The "fort-da" theme was modified so that animals no longer "died" but "broke bones" when they fell. In particular, the little panda—with which Ben identified increasingly—frequently "broke bones" and needed a "plaster cast." In becoming the protector, Ben turned passive into active in his attempts to process the accident. He showed that he understood that the cast fulfilled two functions: healing his arm and keeping him safe, as it restrained impulsive actions. He said, "Panda is still small and needs someone to look after him," suggesting his awareness of his ongoing need of external help to manage his feelings and body. Ben slowly abandoned the "fort-da" game as the term progressed. He began to comb his hair like his father and claimed to be "good at fixing things," suggesting a growing identification with his adoptive father.

PHASE 2: RECALLING THE PAST AND SPEAKING THE UNSPOKEN "KNOWN"

Ben's mastering his falls and "broken bones" through play seemed to give him a sufficient sense of control and safety to allow memories of very early sensations and experiences to begin to emerge. He began to verbalize things that were "known" all along, but had remained unspoken. My role during this phase of analysis seemed primarily to acknowledge his memories and bear the tremendously strong counter-transference feelings of sadness and pain, elicited by his re-enactments of reconstructed memories.

Eighteen months after starting analysis, Ben's parents reported that he began to mention events from his past. These memories emerged unexpectedly, apparently triggered by some cue in the environment (Gaensbauer, 2002). For instance, while taking a bath, he told his adoptive mother that when his biological father held him, he "squeezed so hard that it hurt." Interestingly, he began talking about his birth parents after 18 months of analysis, which concurs with his age when he witnessed the murder. In the following vignette, Ben spoke about his birth parents for the first time in analysis.

> Ben said that the toy "baby elephant" would grow bigger to be like the "daddy elephant." I said, "Just like you're growing to be like your dad." Ben said, "He is not my dad, he is my fake dad. My real dad is in prison. My mom is not my mom, she is my fake mom, because my mom is in heaven." After a pause he continued, "My dad killed my mom and so she went to heaven." Ben turned to me and said, "You know all that, Inge. Why didn't you ever talk about it?" I said, "I didn't know *you* wanted to talk about it."

His words shocked me greatly, perhaps because his tone was devoid of affect. In a subsequent session, Ben clarified "fake means I was not born to her." Concerned that his adoptive parents might feel hurt if he used this terminology, I began to speak about "mommy A" and "mommy B" to distinguish his birth and adoptive mothers. Sessions followed in which Ben played games of rescuing and resuscitating his mother. Ben brought a wilted lily to a therapy session.

> Ben held the wilted lily under the running water, saying he would "make it come alive." I said, "It is so horrid that some things cannot come alive again, even if we wish it." Using chairs and the couch cover, he constructed a tent-like structure, which he said was a "night-train." He crawled inside, taking the lily. He said he was going to heaven to take his mother the lily "Because lilies make oxygen that make things come alive." He made snoring sounds. After a while, I said that he wanted so much to make his mommy A alive again. Ben said in an impatient voice, "You're disturbing the night-train to heaven, could you please shut up?" I remained silent. Ben snored for a while longer and then said he had arrived. He said he had a walkie-talkie and spoke, "Can you read me? Over." I said, "I can read you loud and clear Ben. Where are you?" He said, "I'm in heaven. Do you think God's here?" I said I thought he was, but I did not think that people could see him. Ben confirmed, "God is here, but he's unvisible." I asked what else he saw and he said, "lots of stuff," but did not elaborate. He said he would return to earth by train.

These sessions were extremely moving and evoked strong counter-transference; my breathing became labored, I gasped for breath and felt immobilized, while Ben was in the "night-train to heaven." While he wished desperately to resuscitate his birth mother, I seemed to mirror her immobility and breathlessness. Having spoken about his birth parents for some sessions, Ben retreated into wordless actions and organized the sessions to preclude me from talking. For instance, he brought a noisy toy airplane, or spent a session on the stairs. I respected this as his need to regulate the pace at which he confronted his past.

In a subsequent session, Ben told me his reconstructed memories of the murder he witnessed at 18 months. He said, "My dad said he would give her a necklace and he went behind her and he strangled her. I remember that part because I saw it." Sessions followed in which he enacted murder scenes and did not tolerate any interpretations or comments. In these games, someone—often me—was violently "murdered." The police arrived always too late. These sessions were perturbing and draining; my counter-transference feelings included having difficulty speaking, feeling restrained, helpless, and bewildered.

Ben's agitated state culminated in his refusal to enter the building one day. Exasperated, his mother called me on her mobile phone. I went outside to find a very angry Ben, sitting on the sidewalk. It seemed that even the therapy room had become unsafe and frightening for him. I said that the toy animals would wonder where Ben was. This seemed to remind him about a familiar aspect of analysis and enable him to enter the therapy room with me, for the last 5 minutes of the session:

> After "greeting" the toy animals and spending 5 minutes in the therapy room, we returned downstairs. Mother stood at the main entrance, speaking on her mobile phone. Ben ran past her, into the garden and I followed, concerned about his safety. Mother continued to talk, turning her back so as not to be disturbed. He started yanking at the locks, cables, and dials of the motorbikes and bicycles parked outside the building. I spoke about his strong feelings that made him want to damage the bikes. Ben then turned—unbeknown to him—to my bicycle and tried to pick the lock violently, using a little stick. He persisted in an agitated state before starting to tear at the cables and lights. Fifteen minutes after the end of our session, mother stopped talking and I left Ben in her care.

Anxious not to reveal that it was my bike, because I feared it would intensify his attacks, I became helplessly unable to protect it. I seemed to be experiencing one aspect of Ben's trauma: the sudden paralysis and inability to do anything, except witness a destructive attack. My mounting anger at mother's ignoring us and at Ben's destructiveness, gave me a strong urge to retaliate violently. In my mind, Ben had become his murderous birth father, and I, his birth mother, who was unable to protect myself or my bicycle from his attacks. I felt tremendous anger toward his adoptive mother who left

me to experience and deal with his provocations. That evening, I had
to painstakingly extract the splinters jammed in my lock, before I
could cycle home feeling shaken and angry!

Break from Analysis Without "Broken Bones"

Ben returned after the long summer holiday without "broken bones,"
but berating me: "You are useless at your job; you did not look after
panda in the holidays!" Ben resumed his games of robberies and
murders. The police always arrived too late and the reinforcements
were never able to prevent the crime. These sessions were very poi-
gnant.

> I said that I thought that his play about a murder and the policemen
> coming was telling us that he wished that the police had come to stop
> his dad. Ben paused, looked at me and said, "They did, he is in jail." I
> said, "I know, they did come, eventually." Ben asked "what do you
> mean, eventually?" I answered, "I mean they did not come in time to
> stop him." Ben looked at me intently and said, "Yes they did!" There
> was a silence and he said softly, "No they didn't." I said, "Maybe you
> wish the reinforcements had come in time to stop him from killing
> mommy A." There was another silence and Ben said, "They got into a
> fight, because he wanted to hold me. He got the death penalty, but
> they changed the law, so he is in jail forever."

Draining sessions in which we played out his early experiences
were interspersed with ones that precluded broaching difficult issues. We spent some sessions sitting on the stairs, talking about
school. He said he sometimes lost at games. This concession, which
would have been impossible at the beginning of analysis, suggested
his growing sense of self. Being together in an ordinary way seemed
the most important feature of those sessions.

He told me how happy his dog and he were when his current au
pair returned from a holiday. After a succession of au pairs who had
remained unmentioned and nameless—yet whose departures had
unsettled him hugely—he told me her name and spoke about her.
For the first time, he allowed himself to become openly attached to
an au pair. Once, he called me by her name, before rapidly correct-
ing himself and adding, "I hate you, remember? I just come here,
'cause my dad brings me."

Phase 3: Playing Through the Past

After a half-term break in analysis, Ben returned and—predictably—
berated me for neglecting the toy panda and elephant that, Ben said,

ran into the snow and caught an "antibiotic." Panda caught "panda-monia" and died in hospital. This initiated a new theme of play—2 years and 3 months into analysis—which Ben continues to elaborate. In this third phase of analysis, Ben seemed to leap from re-enacting to playing through the past, in displacement, using the toy animals. Ben's confidence that I was dependable and could be relied on to maintain the realm of displacement seemed to facilitate this phase. Characteristic of this phase was that Ben needed me to adhere to the precise role he assigned me.

Panda—with whom Ben identified—became his vehicle for play-ing out his personal themes. He scripted wonderfully inventive and complicated plots, whispering to me what I—cast as panda's adoptive mother—had to say and do, and becoming angry at my slightest devi-ation in tone, word, or action. When I ventured an interpretation that linked our game to his experience, Ben retorted furiously, "Shut up. We're *not* talking about me, we're talking about panda!" I allowed the play to remain in displacement thereafter. I was initially irritated by his tight control over me, but as his scenes began to approximate his experiences more closely, I came to believe that he needed ab-solute control and the confidence that I would maintain the illusion of play, in order to venture into his past. Consequently, my irritation diminished substantially and I played my part faithfully. If I ventured an occasional comment or deviated from my prescribed words, Ben typically excluded these from our game by temporarily moving out of the realm of play (Winnicott, 1971), saying "Stop the game. Panda's mother doesn't say that, you're spoiling the game. Now start again!"

In Ben's game, after my "birth" panda died from "pandamonia," I bought and "adopted forever" a new panda. Ben said that the two pandas were so similar that I was not aware of having a new panda. Ben made me elaborately sign and stamp "identity and adoption pa-pers" and threatened to put me in prison if I lost them. Many adven-tures befell panda that mirrored Ben's current or past experiences. Ben expressed his anger when I would not allow him to take my "identity paper" home from analysis by making panda write me an angry letter. Ben read it aloud: "Dear mom, I hate you but I really miss you. I wish you would get out of my life. I am going to Africa for-ever. Your son, Panda." Ben then instructed me to pretend to rush to the airport to prevent panda from leaving!

Ben seemed to be grappling with the meaning and permanence of adoption and the strength of relationships: would the mother re-claim her adoptive son, despite his angry letter? If a panda (or mother) died could one buy and adopt a new one without noticing the difference or mourning the loss?

Inge-Martine Pretorius

In one game, Ben said that I had murdered someone and he threw me in prison. When I anguished over my adopted son panda, Ben said "Panda will be adopted away from you. He'll go to the fosters. There are lots of children at the fosters." Indeed, there were 4 other children in the foster family that cared for Ben (when he was 18 months to 2½ years). In another session, Ben made panda die to punish me for deviating from my script:

> Ben said: "We are gathered here to remember our beloved panda." He whispered, "You make polar bear talk." (Polar bear was cast as panda's birth father.) I spoke for polar bear: "Panda was my beloved son and I have many happy memories of him. He sometimes did not think and then got into trouble or hurt himself. When it snowed one winter and he did not think, he ran into the snow and caught an antibiotic." Increasingly impatient with my lengthy speech, Ben interrupted me, "You need to say that you murdered!" Ben explained the story to me: "Polar bear is his real dad (birth dad), he's on the run. After he murdered, he took panda and ran away from the police and they looked for him, for days. Then they gave up and that is how he could come to the funeral." Ben explained: "Panda was only a little baby. He couldn't talk or walk, so he doesn't remember." I asked what happened after that, and Ben said, "His dad gave panda for adoption and he kept running. The police got tired and stopped looking." Ben hummed a tune and said, "Amen." He told me to sing panda's favorite song. I asked what it was and he said indignantly, "*You* should know, you're his mother!" I hummed a tune and Ben said, "Amen." Ben said that panda could write us a letter from heaven. He said, "His address is 869@heaven.com. There are so many of them up there that they can't keep the password secret."

His play revealed his preoccupations with uncovering the truth and what could be remembered. I felt tightness in my chest as Ben spoke about panda's abduction. Ben had not been told that after the murder, his birth father fled with him for 4 days before surrendering to the police. His play seemed to belie his claim that panda was too little to remember. His yearning for contact with his mother, suggested by panda's e-mail address, moved me greatly.

In another session, Ben imprisoned me for having the wrong adoption papers and proceeded to replay his mother's strangulation:

> Ben put me in "prison" saying sternly: "You will be a very old girl when you come out!" Ben instructed me to escape to try to find panda. He caught me and threw me back in prison and said, "You will be punished for escaping." He continued, "Pretend your necklace is getting tighter and tighter and all the air comes out." Ben whispered, "Now you almost die," and so I dropped my head. Ben

said I was not dead, only dazed, and made us repeat this sequence three times; trying to escape and being partially strangled as a pun ishment. Ben then pretended to be a different policeman who carried a photo of the perpetrator He compared me to this photo and called out in alarm: "The wrong mommy has been killed!" Ben rushed me to hospital and called to the doctors: "Quick bring oxygen." Ben reassured me: "Don't lose hope, this is oxygen coming in," as he pretended to administer a life-saving infusion.

Although panda and his adoptive mother were often on the brink of death, they always survived. Four years after starting analysis, Ben continues to explore themes of loss, adoption and attachment through scripting the adventures of panda and his adoptive mother.

CONCLUSION

Psychoanalysis has been interested in the impact of trauma occurring in the preverbal period and the nature of its representation in memory, since the "Wolf Man" (Freud, 1918), whom Freud hypothesized, was traumatized at 18 months by witnessing the primal scene. More recently, advances in cognitive neuroscience have revolutionized our understanding of memory, the nature of representations and the interaction of cognition and affect. The advances include the conceptualization of parallel processing (instead of serial processing), memory systems (instead of memory stores) and differentiating implicit from explicit memory (Westen and Gabbard, 2002a). Furthermore, research has recently documented that memories of early experiences can become altered over the course of development (Terr, 1988), something that psychoanalysts have long understood (Freud, 1899).

All three phases of Ben's analysis illustrate Freud's idea (1920) that compulsive repetition in children's play is a means of mastering the trauma. The compulsion to repeat encompasses a repetitive aspect related to Freud's notion of transference (Freud, 1912). It also contains a reparative aspect in that the individual seeks to repeat an old object relationship while hoping that the new version could be different and healing. Ben's representation of the self as unprotected, rejected and abandoned, supported not only by childhood experiences, but also by subsequent experiences to which he contributed, remained a live dynamic that he repeated compulsively. For instance his rejecting and aggressive behavior threatened a breakdown in the adoption that prompted the referral. This tendency made his past more likely to be recapitulated in the present, and not least in his relationship with his therapist (Westen and Gabbard, 2002b).

According to Perry (1995), a child who has been the victim of un-predictable violence learns (consciously or unconsciously) that violence will occur and it is preferable to control when it happens. Consequently, such children frequently engage in provocative, aggressive behavior in an attempt to elicit a predictable response. If this behavior is punished severely, it reinforces the child's view of the world that adults are aggressive and solve problems using force. Instead, the child needs the experience to be contained by someone else who can stand it better than he can. This may go on for some time, months of even years, until the experience is less overwhelming and less indigestible (Alvarez, 1992).

In the first phase, Ben's hypervigilance, hyperactivity, risk-taking behavior, and aggression suggested the state-dependent recall of state-dependent storage of cumulative trauma (Ungerleider, 1995). Ben's chaotic play, vacillations and fluctuations suggested the expression of implicit memories that were encoded automatically and expressed through behaviors and emotions, without conscious awareness. During this phase, my attempts at verbalizing or interpreting Ben's states seemed unhelpful and even harmful. He seemed to experience my offering insights into his conflicts and omnipotence as attacks that disorganized and frightened him further. Such insights could even represent a further trauma (Edgcumbe and Gavshon, 1985). While in a state of hyperarousal—a persisting fear state—a child is unable to process and understand complex cognitive information, such as a verbal interpretation of his behavior. Instead the child focuses on nonverbal cues like body movement, facial expression, and voice intonation. Only when sufficiently "calmed" can such children benefit from words. Consequently, my role was primarily to contain his strong unwanted affects and through this, show that the unbearable was knowable and bearable. In addition, I began to provide him with a set of consistent alternative memories based upon trail after trail of neutral or positive interaction. Rather than enhancing Ben's awareness during this phase, my role was to activate networks of associations that were different to his chronically activated and dysfunctional ones (Westen and Gabbard, 2002b). This was facilitated by me by offering him a "corrective object relationship" (Segal, 1973, p 123), a process that has been termed "developmental help" (Hurry, 1998, p 37).

Separations seemed to trigger Ben's state-dependent recall during this phase; separation from analysis and me during weekends and holidays that lead to "broken bones," and most notably the unexpected loss of his au pair. Once Ben managed to verbalize his fear that his "horrid" behavior had driven his au pair away, he moved into symbolic play of loss and recovery in the "fort-da" games During the beginning of the first phase, I colluded to some extent with his wish to deny separations, in the "sleepwalking" game at the end of sessions. However, this seemed part of my containing function: to bear his unwanted and unbearable feelings until he became more confident in the safety and dependability of the setting, to begin to process them himself. According to Alvarez (1992) the therapist may have to contain the child's unwanted feelings for long periods of time, as well as respect the child's need to keep out the past, while the child builds confidence in the setting.

After 18 months of analysis, Ben seemed to rely sufficiently on our way of being together, to allow himself to remember salient traumatic events. This ushered in the second phase of analysis, during which he talked about the unspoken "known" memories of his early traumatic experiences. It seems that he no longer needed to defensively repress memories to such an extent, and could begin to allow their expression. The first early memory that he expressed was that his biological father "squeezed so hard that it hurt." This was a verbal expression of a somatic memory. Ben's very moving re-enactments of the murder and retelling of the events he witnessed were not veridical replicas of the events. This would be expected, given his immature perceptive capacities at the time of their occurrence, and the current understanding that memory is not fixed, but a reflection of a dynamic process that is continuously modified by internal and external influences (Loftus, 1979).

During this second phase, Ben showed a growing capacity to symbolize and reflect and concomitantly, to regulate himself and tolerate frustration. The reflective function that is usually acquired within the intersubjective process between infant and parent is critically important for affect and impulse control, self-monitoring and the experience of self-agency (Gropnik, 1993; Fonagy and Target, 1997, 1998). Consequently, I no longer needed to be so vigilant of his or my safety, which created more space for me to think and reflect. Although Ben still required me to participate physically in his re-enactments, my actions were proportionately more determined and scripted by his play than reactions to his dysregulated states. Ben sometimes tolerated my words and interpretations of his re-enactments. Containing his powerful projections and tremendously painful feelings aroused in the counter-transference seemed crucial in this phase. I frequently felt that I carried all Ben's despair, anger, and yearning about his past. I had difficulty breathing when he played out the "night-train to heaven" to rescue his mother. When he attacked my bicycle, I felt my-self powerfully drawn into playing a role scripted by his internal world. In his actualization of an internal scenario, he tried to elicit what he feared: violent retaliation.

A long break from analysis that did not lead to "broken bones" en-abled a third phase to begin, in which Ben moved from re-enacting to playing through the past in displacement. Symbolization and dis-placement created sufficient distance from the actual event, for him to work through them. Ben's scripts did not replicate his early experi-ences, suggesting that his internal representations had been ex-panded and modified, toward increased organization and narrative coherence, but also toward distortion. For instance, he thought—and probably wished—that the police had arrived in time to prevent the murder. However, Ben remembered and talked about his abduc-tion by his birth father with remarkable accuracy. He experienced this at 18 months and has never been told about it. The relationship between nonverbal memory capacity and language development is of particular interest during the second year of life and has received considerable research attention. Evidence suggests that the availabil-ity of a verbal code at the time of the trauma is not necessary for it to be remembered or expressed verbally later (Bauer and Wewerka, 1995, Gaensbauer, 2002). Ben remembered accurately, despite his claim that "Panda was only a little baby. He couldn't talk or walk, so he doesn't remember."

Ben's capacity to play was apparent from the beginning of his analysis and suggests some very good and creative experiences with his birth mother (Winnicott, 1968). Furthermore, he soon showed a sophisticated capacity to move in and out of the shared illusion of play, in statements like "Inge, stop the game. Panda's mother doesn't say that, you're spoiling the game. Now start again!" His creative use of play to express and represent his experiences, to learn, to experi-ence pleasure, and to engage his therapist is beyond the scope of this paper which focuses on his use of play to process his early experi-ences. The repetitive nature of some of his games suggests his at-tempts to master high anxiety (Winnicott, 1945) like the re-enacting of a murder or robbery where the police always arrived too late. In this third phase, it seemed important for me to accept and adhere to the tightly scripted role he gave me, to afford him a sense of control and agency, as he began to investigate and integrate his past. Accord-ing to Pines (1993), if psychic change is to be effected in psycho-analysis, the traumatic factors in the patient's life must enter the psychoanalytic space in the patient's own way and within his omnipotence (Winnicott, 1956). Experiencing the horror present in Ben's analysis, I have come to appreciate the necessity of play in making it bearable.

I believe that the longevity and consistency of the setting as well as the dependability of the meaningful therapeutic relationship has enabled Ben—very bravely—to confront and begin to process his past. His aggressive outbursts have diminished significantly with a concomitant increase in his capacity for regulation and symbolization. However, anxieties—particularly related to the threat of loss—continue to overwhelm him easily. Greenacre (1953) maintains that no truly traumatic event is ever wholly assimilated and an increased vulnerability inevitably remains. It is conceivable that he may need help at later developmental stages.

BIBLIOGRAPHY

ALVAREZ, A. (1992) Child sexual abuse: The need to remember and the need to forget. In Alvarez, *Live company.* pp 151–162. London and New York: Routledge.

ARNAND, K. S. & HICKEY, P. R. (1987) Pain and its effects in the human neonate and fetus. *New England Journal of Medicine,* 317: 1321–1329.

BALBERNIE, R. (2001) Circuits and circumstance; the neurobiological consequences of early relationship experiences and how they shape later behaviour. *Journal of Child Psychotherapy,* 27(3): 237–255.

BAUER, P. J. & WEWERKA, S. S. (1995) One-to-two-year-olds' recall of event: The more expressed the more impressed. *Journal of Experimental Child Psychology,* 59: 475–496.

BLASS, E. M., GANCHROW, J. R., & STEINER, J. E. (1984) Classical conditioning in newborn humans 2–48 hours of age. *Infant Behaviour and Development,* 7: 223–235.

DAMASIO, A. R. (1994) *Descartes' Error.* New York: Grosset Putnam.

EDELMAN, G. M. (1992) *Bright Air: Brilliant Fire.* New York: Basic Books.

EDGCUMBE, R. & GAVSHON, A. (1985) Clinical comparison of traumatic events and reactions. *Bulletin of the Anna Freud Centre,* 8(1): 3–21.

FERENCZI, S. (1933) Confusion of tongues between adult and child. In *Final Contributions* (1995) pp 156–167, London: Hogarth Press.

FONAGY, P. & TARGET, M. (1997) Attachment and reflective function: Their role in self-organisation. *Development and Psychopathology,* 9: 679–700.

FONAGY, P. & TARGET, M. (1998) An interpersonal view of the infant. In A. Hurry (Ed.) *Psychoanalysis and Developmental Therapy,* pp 3–31. Monograph Series of the Psychoanalysis Unit of University College London and the Anna Freud Centre. London: Karnac Books.

260 *Inge-Martine Pretorius*

FRAIBERG, S. H. (1959) *The Magic Years.* New York: Charles Scribner's Sons.
FRANKL, L. (1963) Self-preservation and the development of accident prone-ness in children and adolescents. *The Psychoanalytic Study of the Child,* 18: 464–483.
FREUD, A. (1936) *The Ego and Mechanisms of Defence.* London: Karnac Books.
FREUD, A. (1949) Aggression in relations to emotional development: Normal and pathological. *The Psychoanalytic Study of the Child,* 3: 37–42.
FREUD, A. (1965) *Normality and Pathology in Childhood.* London: Hogarth Press.
FREUD, S. (1899) *Screen memories.* Standard Edition, III: 301–322.
FREUD, S. (1918) *Aus der Geschichte einer Infantilen Neurose.* Gesammelte Werke, XII: 27–157.
FREUD, S. (1920) *Jenseits des Lustprinzips.* Gesammelte Werke, XIII: 3–69.
GAENSBAUER, T. J. (1982) The differentiation of discrete affects: A case report. *The Psychoanalytic Study of the Child,* 37: 29–66.
GAENSBAUER, T. J. (1995) Trauma in the preverbal period, symptoms, memories and developmental impact. *The Psychoanalytic Study of the Child,* 50: 122–149.
GAENSBAUER, T. J. (2002) Representations of trauma in infancy: Clinical and theoretical implications for the understanding of early memory. *Infant Mental Health Journal,* 27: 259–277.
GAENSBAUER, T. J. (2004) Telling their stories: Representation and re-enactment of traumatic experiences occurring in the first year of life. *Zero to Three,* May 2004: 25–30.
GREENACRE, P. (1953) *Trauma, Growth and Personality.* London: Hogarth.
GROPNICK, A. (1993) How we know our minds: The illusion of first person knowledge of intentionality. *Behaviour and Brain Sciences,* 16: 1–14, 29–113.
HURRY, A. (1998) Psychoanalysis and developmental therapy. In A. Hurry (Ed.) *Psychoanalysis and Developmental Therapy,* p 32–73. Monograph Series of the Psychoanalysis Unit of University College London and the Anna Freud Centre. London: Karnac Books.
KOHUT, H. (1972) Thoughts on narcissism and narcissistic rage. *Psychoanalytic Study of the Child,* 22: 360–400.
KLEIN, M. (1975) *Envy and gratitude and other works 1946–1963.* London: Karnac books.
LITTLE, A. H., LIPSITT, L. P., & ROVEE-COLLIER, C. (1984) Classical conditioning and retention of the infant's eyelid response: Effects of age and interstimulus interval. *Journal of Experimental Child Psychology,* 37: 512–524.
LOFTUS, E. (1979) *Eyewitness testimony.* Cambridge, Mass.: Harvard University Press.
MAHLER, M., PINE, F., & BERGMAN, A. (1975) *The Psychological Birth of the Human Infant: Symbiosis and Individuation.* New York: Basic Books.
MARANS, S., MAYES, L. C., & COLONNA, A. B. (1993) Psychoanalytic views of children's play. In A. J. Solnit, D. J. Cohen, and P. B. Neubauer (Eds) *The*

Many Meanings of Play: A Psychoanalytic Perspective. New Haven: Yale University Press.

NAGERA, H. (1969) The imaginary companion: Its significance for ego development and conflict resolution *Psychoanalytic Study of the Child*, 24: 89–99

PERRY, B. D. (1995) Incubated in terror: Neurodevelopmental factors in the cycle of violence. In: J. D. Osofsky (Ed) *Children in a Violent Society*. New York: Guilford Press.

PERRY, B. D., POLLARD, R. A., BLAKLEY, T. L., BAKER, W. L., & VIGILANTE, D. (1995) Childhood trauma, the neurobiology of adaptation and "use-dependent" development of the brain: How "states" become "traits." *Infant Mental Health Journal*, 16(4): 271–291.

PINES, D. (1993) *A Woman's Unconscious Use of Her Body: A Psychoanalytical Perspective*. London: Virago Press.

SANDLER, J. (1987) *From Safety to Superego: Selected Papers of Joseph Sandler*. New York: Guilford Press.

SANDLER, J. and Freud, A. (1985) *The Analysis of Defence: The Ego and the Mechanisms of Defence Revisited*. New York: International Universities Press.

SCHORE, A. N. (2001a) Effects of a secure attachment relationship on right brain development, affect regulation and infant mental health. *Infant Mental Health Journal*, 22 (1–2): 7–66.

SCHORE, A. N. (2001b) Effects of early relational trauma on right brain development, affect regulation and infant mental health. *Infant Mental Health Journal*, 22 (1–2): 201–269.

SEGAL, H. (1973) *Introduction to the Work of Melanie Klein*. London: Hogarth and the Institute of Psycho-Analysis.

TERR, L. (1988) What happens to early memories of trauma: A study of twenty children under the age five at the time of documented traumatic events. *Journal of the American Academy of Child and Adolescent Psychiatry*, 27: 96–104.

UNGERLEIDER, L. G. (1995) Functional brain imaging studies for cortical mechanisms for memory. *Science*, 270: 769–765.

WESTEN, D. & GABBARD, G. O. (2002a) Developments in cognitive neuroscience: I. conflict, compromise and connectionism. *Journal of the American Psychoanalytic Association*, 50(1) 53–98.

WESTEN, D. & GABBARD, G. O. (2002b) Developments in cognitive neuroscience: II. implications for theories of transference. *Journal of the American Psychoanalytic Association*, 50(1) 99–134.

WINNICOTT, D. W. (1945) Why children play. In *The Child, the Family and the Outside World* (1964) pp 143–146. London: Penguin.

WINNICOTT, D. W. (1951) Transitional objects and transitional phenomena. In: *Playing and Reality* (1971), pp 1–25. Hove: Brunner-Routledge.

WINNICOTT D. W. (1956) Primary maternal pre-occupation. In: *Through Paediatrics to Psychoanalysis*, pp 300–306. London: Hogarth Press.

WINNICOTT, D. W. (1958) The first year of life: Modern views on emotional life. In *The Family and Individual Development*, (1965) pp 3–14. London: Tavistock.

WINNICOTT, D. W. (1968) Playing, Its theoretical status in the clinical situation. *International Journal of Psycho-analysis.* 49; 591–599.

WINNICOTT D. W. (1971) *Playing and Reality.* Hove: Brunner-Routledge.

From Loss to H.O.P.E.S.

Safeguarding the Analysis of an Eight-year-old Boy with Multiple Diagnoses in Foster Care

EKATERINI STRATI, BSc (Hons), MSc

This paper traces the unfolding of the therapeutic relationship in the analysis of a boy with marked presenting difficulties in Foster Care and attempts to address the technical issues regarding psychoanalytic work with looked-after children but also with children who have experienced early deprivation and neglect. The patient's disrupted attachment history of early loss called for a gradual building of interpretative work in the context of his growing trust and sense of safety within the therapeutic relation. It will be shown how the differential use of the therapist as a transference, developmental and contemporary object enabled him to resume his "arrested" development, as it helped him reconnect with disowned feelings of rage, helplessness, as well as despair and longing for his lost objects. Emphasis will be particularly placed on the use of Countertransference, as at times the only means to be in touch with the patient's predicament and affective experiences which have been preverbal and possibly unverbalizable.

What is believed to be essential for mental health is that the infant and young child should experience a warm, intimate and continuous relationship with his

At the time of treatment, Ekaterini Strati was in training at the Anna Freud Centre, London, and in a training post at a Child and Adolescent Mental Health Service. She is currently in private practice in Athens, Greece.

The Psychoanalytic Study of the Child 62, ed. Robert A. King, Peter B. Neubauer, Samuel Abrams, and A. Scott Dowling (Yale University Press, copyright © 2007 by Robert A. King, Peter B. Neubauer, Samuel Abrams, and A. Scott Dowling).

mother (or permanent mother-substitute) in which
both find satisfaction and enjoyment.
—Bowlby, 1952

INTRODUCTION

SIMON IS AN ATTRACTIVE, WELL-BUILT, BLACK-AFRICAN CARIBBEAN
boy known to Social Services (in the U.K.) since his birth in 1993,
when he was under the care of his birth mother (age 13), who herself
was in the custody of Social Services at the time.

Simon shows the detrimental effects of "double deprivation"
(Henry, 1988), the first being the primary impingement of his traumatic early life, full of losses and disruptions in his attachment history (the combined effect of maternal mental illness, and the inadequate protective provisions from those in subsequent parental
capacity, including Social Services), and the second, through his maladaptive (adaptive) defensive system, which prevented closeness with
subsequent caregivers, through intensely hostile, and rejecting behavior, handicapping him in regards to receiving help and breaking
the cycle of abandonment and neglect, resulting in nine failed placements by the age of 8.

At the time of referral, Simon had already been diagnosed with Attention Deficit Hyperactivity Disorder with associated features of Oppositional Defiant Disorder and Anxiety Disorder, and was taking
Ritalin since age seven, with no significant improvements. His long-
standing difficulties stemming from infancy included uncontrollable
aggressive outbursts, and self-harming behavior as well as soiling and
smearing feces, urinating in his room, eating poorly, and stealing
food. He had been excluded from previous schools due to the disturbing effect he had on both the teachers and the children and was
currently classified as having special educational needs, including
one to one learning support.

This dismal picture raised the question: What could therapy hope
to achieve in the context of such developmental arrest, and environmental failure?

The nature and level of his emotional deprivation meant that a lot
of our initial interactions belonged to a much earlier developmental
level, and it was necessary that my technique would adapt, in order to
meet these particular needs. Hence, features of the early mother-infant mode of communication and interrelating (Stern, 1985), such
as gaze-turn taking, matching my intonation (Trevarthen, 1993), and
mirroring colored our contact, so that interpretative work in order to

ascribe meaning and give affective content to his experiences that have been preverbal could only be gradually introduced,

This paper aims to trace how the analytic process brought Simon's intense, albeit disowned, feelings of rage, helplessness, and unsafety to the fore. Working in the unfolding transference particularly around separations, in the context of his stable home placement, enabled Simon to emerge from the "frozen failed situation" (Winnicott, 1954), and to resume some of his latency development, with a more integrated sense of self, capacity to relate, a more adaptive affect regulation and a growing insight, which have helped him to begin mourning some of his losses.

The technical issues regarding psychoanalytic work with looked-after children, but also children who have experienced early deprivation and neglect, will also be raised.

FAMILY BACKGROUND

Simon's mother, whose early experience was in many ways similar to her son's, had experienced instability and trauma since the first year of her life. She was removed from her natural family at the age of two months following physical abuse by her mother, who suffered from schizophrenia. She was returned to her mother, who further abused her, and was finally removed at the age of one, having then a series of unsuccessful placements.

Simon at 5 months was placed on the Social Services Register of Children at Risk under the category of Neglect. An independent assessment in a mother-baby unit in which they spent two months confirmed mother's inability to care for her son, as she ran away and left him on a few occasions and he was found to have burn marks on his legs. It seems that Simon had become the unconscious target of mother's projection of her abused and abandoned child-self.

Simon was temporarily placed with another foster family before he was returned to his mother's last foster family. Mother, described as "autistic-like," was quite frozen in her responses and is thought to have had very little interaction with him to the point of ignoring him. She was at sea in terms of knowing how to handle him: She would allegedly not respond to his cries when he needed changing or feeding, and she would often yell at him for not being clean. Simon's adoptive mother (biological mother's half-sister) has recently described how "Simon used to hopelessly cry, and cry with no expectation that his needs would ever be met." This may be connected with the development of Simon's markedly avoidant pattern and his rejection of closeness, reflecting his concerns about mother's mental health and her inability to parent him.

We can imagine the detrimental effects this environment had on Simon. According to Shore "a relational growth-inhibiting early environment, in which the abusive caregiver not only shows less play with her infant, but also induces traumatic states of enduring negative affect in the child. . . . This caregiver is inaccessible and reacts to the infant's expressions of emotions and stress inappropriately and/or rejectingly, and therefore shows minimal or unpredictable participation in the various types of arousal regulating processes. Instead of modulating she induces extreme levels of stimulation and arousal, very high in abuse and/or very low in neglect. And because she provides no interactive repair the infant's intense negative states last for long periods of time" (Shore, 2002).

Those "states" had become "traits" (Perry et al., 1995) for Simon, who as early as two, showed marked affect-regulation difficulties, being described as "hyperactive like his mother," aggressive and difficult to contain. It should be emphasized that Simon had been placed in seven foster homes between the ages of one and three, and during this time, mother had repeatedly failed to attend contacts with Social Services, which affected Simon immensely. It is noteworthy that Simon used to call everyone "mummy," including children slightly taller than he.

Social Services refused contact between mother and son when Simon was two and a half years of age. Eventually, he was placed with his mother's half sister and her mother when he was four years old, and adoption was completed just short of his sixth birthday. Every day Simon proved a handful for his new family: smearing feces, urinating in his toy box, eating poorly, stealing food, and attacking other children. He reportedly cut himself with a knife to stop himself from stealing, and there were other incidents of self-harming.

His uncontrollable aggressive outbursts, with frequent kicking, spitting, screaming, extended to his nursery teacher and classmates. He would alternatively resort to head-banging. Teachers were at a loss with his extremely disruptive behavior. He was diagnosed as having a "Reactive Detachment Disorder."

In infant school, he was expelled after a few days, as he had such a negative impact on the other children in the class, to the point that some of them appeared quite depressed in his presence. His level of dysfunction put such strain on the teacher that she needed to be sent home.

An analogous, if not more uncontainable scenario at home, made his adoptive mother quite desperate for respite care and to move Simon into a residential setting. Simon was placed on an emergency foster placement with Mr. and Mrs. C in November 1999

At the same time the school had also contacted Social Services convinced that "Simon was physically and emotionally at risk from himself and home." This instigated a referral for a psychiatric assessment of his complex mental health issues. He was diagnosed as suffering from Attention Deficit Hyperactivity Disorder with associated features of Oppositional Defiant Disorder and Anxiety Disorder. At age seven, Simon was prescribed Ritalin.

His challenging behavior at the new foster home appeared to be exacerbated by erratic contact with his adoptive mother. Simon had a period of play therapy but it seemed to make no difference.

At the time of his referral to our Child and Adolescent Mental Health Services (a National Health Services clinic), Simon had already been classified for Special Educational needs, including having a one-to-one learning support at his new school because of his significant emotional and behavioral difficulties.

Nevertheless, there were increased concerns that no improvements were seen with the current increased Ritalin dosage, which was further not being monitored. The foster mother reported more self-harming incidents like breaking a double glazed window and using the broken glass to cut his fingers. Enuresis and encopresis still dominated his mode of communicating and relating, driving the foster placement to a breaking point.

Trapped in his predicament, Simon aroused feelings of hostility, despair, and rejection in his caretakers, perhaps projections of his own overwhelming feelings of hopelessness, sense of rejection and abandonment.

At this time, Simon's birth mother seems to have had a schizophrenic breakdown, fueling the anxieties in adoptive mother that he was "brain damaged, crazy like his mother."

The consultant psychiatrist in CAMHS recommended that Ritalin be discontinued and referred him for psychoanalytic psychotherapy on the basis that his behavior was connected to emotional issues stemming from his disrupted attachment history of early loss and neglect. In addition to his severely compromised emotional development, Simon was severely underperforming at school, although thought to be an intellectually able child. Simon started four times a week individual psychotherapy, while his foster caretaker received parent work by a colleague every fortnight.

SIMON'S FATHER

There is minimum information about father. He was in his early thir-
ties when he impregnated Simon's mother, claiming that he thought
she was older. Despite this, he impregnated her again before her six-
teenth birthday, but the pregnancy was terminated. He saw Simon on
a few occasions during his first year. He was invited to discuss Simon's
adoption and the care plan. He stayed for one minute of this meeting and left without saying a single word. Simon had another half
brother from his mother, of whom he was aware and who was also in
foster care, as well as numerous half-siblings from his father.

FIRST IMPRESSIONS

When I first saw Simon I was struck by two contrasting presentations:
he was demure and polite when he greeted me, and then detached,
independent, and self-important moments after. He followed me
rather defeatedly up to my room, yet soon confidently led the way. At
the second floor, obviously disoriented and looking at a loss, he became stuck in an agonizing squirm, unable to move or to ask for
help. When I gently pointed out our direction, he quickly muttered,
"oh yeah," as if he really knew.

Toward the end of our chaotic first meeting, and having earlier described my role, I wondered whether he would like to come to see me
again. His response was clear: "I don't want to come and live with
you; I want to live with auntie C" (his current foster mother).

When I explained what I meant and articulated what had been the
confusion, he soberly yet heartbreakingly said: "But this has been my
life."

In the second session, he asked to bring a copy of *Winnie-the-Pooh*
from the reception area. In the room he told me he found this a nice
book. When I asked about it, he spoke of Winnie and Tigger, the
main characters, "being in this place, where there was a lot of water
around, like a flooding." With more probing he spoke of the two
characters "not knowing what to do, water being everywhere, maybe
in the streets, maybe in the house." He did not know how they would
feel; his face looked frozen, as I suggested they could be scared. His
fleeting communication of his own helplessness in the face of the cataclysmic early losses was quickly reversed when in a composed manner he told me that he had not finished the story yet; I would have to
wait.

EARLY PHASE OF ANALYSIS: FINDING THE LOST CHILD

From the onset, Simon brought to his therapy his anxieties and con cerns about himself and the future in a very powerful manner. He explained to me that he needed help for a thousand things; there was something wrong with him, and he did things that got him into trouble. He had bad habits and was stuck in a pattern.

Despite the obvious fact that he was reiterating what he must have heard numerous times from the adults around him, I felt that on some level, he was aware of his difficulties, and further troubled by their conflictual nature as he volunteered that he did not mean to upset his foster mother. The seeds of treatment alliance were in place when I suggested that he and I together, like detectives, could try to figure out what it was that made him worry and behave in this way. His face lit up as he thoughtfully said, "I'd like that."

His profound sense of being damaged and the anxieties it evoked also surfaced. In the third session, while fiddling with the plasticine making some food for the dolls figures, he sneezed and saliva droplets covered the table. He became extremely agitated, started shaking, and then he apologized. I calmly said that it was okay. He was still terribly distressed and said, "Now my germs will be all over this place, and it will be my fault." I wiped the table, and repeated that it was okay, acknowledging his worry that something inside was really bad and should not come out. He looked at me bewildered, but calmed down.

In these early days, he would habitually draw on the blackboard or on paper robots with dark shades, "so you could not see their eyes." He would not tell me more about them other than he has been drawing them since he was little. He spoke of an invisible shield so that if bombs came it meant that the robot would not get hurt. One could easily understand Simon's identification with the robots, strong and devoid of emotions and in full control of their bodies. I wondered whether this was how Simon protected himself, making sure that he did not get hurt by having a sort of protective shield, a "dissociative" protection.

My curiosity about the robots led him to give me a "clue." He drew a shotgun next to them, and in a very serious tone told me "it can blow your brain." I was aware of Simon's deep-seated anxiety (as it was directly reinforced by his adoptive mother that "there was something wrong with his brain"). However, this imagery served as a very powerful, albeit disturbing, communication of Simon's traumatic early experiences, which had a crippling impact, feeling like or actually being a "blow to his mind."

Under the facade of the "omnipotent clever" boy, lay a narcissistically vulnerable ego, which would not dare play or experiment with toys, and paint, out of fear of destroying them or proving his inadequacy.

In the fourth session, he demonstrated this fear by struggling to sketch a dinosaur, erasing and discarding his futile attempts as rubbish, "rubbish as my brain." This effort brought an almost bodily collapse, which had a powerful countertransference effect. A very conscious shift in me helped me to recognize that Simon needed an experience with someone who would not treat him as damaged, and I feel this created an important "background" to the unfolding of the total therapeutic relationship.

In the third week, Simon offered another clue for our detective work: he told me he was sad, always has been sad, because his mum [biological mother] is sad. I wondered about his hopeless self-fulfilling prophecy. Mother could not but be sad for not being with him (total denial of being rejected, and unwanted), and he, in identification with her, kept the contact alive through this unresolved mourning, an everlasting sadness.

His ability to share all this was not matched with any insight regarding his feelings. In fact, as I came to realize, his precocious intellectual development masked his severely impaired emotional development. This was often demonstrated when confronted with the possibility of losing in a game, when he felt insecure and unsafe in my presence, or when unpleasant feelings surfaced, particularly around separations. Observing his typically restless presentation, his fidgeting and frequent rocking motion, I understood how Simon still relied on bodily means in an attempt to regulate, self-soothe, and discharge painful affects (reminiscent of infantile functioning and suggestive of the absence of a containing/reliable mother figure).

I suspected that this was also pivotal in his symptomatic enuresis and encopresis, which had also acquired a secondary meaning/significance in his ongoing relationships with new caretakers. He repelled them thus jeopardizing his placement, leading to the all-too-familiar rejection and abandonment.

A central aspect of the therapeutic work was the sustained attention on the minutiae of his communications—verbal, but mostly nonverbal, as well as naming and differentiating affects.

STRUGGLE FOR CONTROL; CREATING A SENSE OF SAFETY

Simon for the first few weeks would bring to his session various books from the reception area, typically the *Big Book of Knowledge,* or the *World History Encyclopedia.* His thirst for knowledge was a hopeful sign, but it was mainly used defensively, to gain control over others or me (by "knowing the facts, the answers") and to maintain the illusion of narcissistic superiority, and thus independence; he did not need anyone, he could find answers and solutions himself.

His concrete belief that the more he learned the less he would have to rely on others is illustrated in the following. He took apart a pocket calculator in order to see how it worked; he would then automatically know all his sums. His intelligence was used to master an impossible solution, and I suspect this is why his learning was severely compromised. As reality proved more complex, his shaky self-esteem was repeatedly injured, leaving him with a deeply felt blow: adults always won.

In a defensive denial of feeling needy and humiliated, Simon imposed a clear routine in his sessions that enabled him to have control in creating continuity, and thus, a relative sense of safety in his new encounters with me. As it became part of the "beginnings ritual," we spent a few minutes reading through these books, him "teaching [me] facts, about dinosaurs, the Earth, Europe." During those times, it felt necessary that he was allowed to feel powerful in my presence.

His ritual further involved checking that everything in his box was okay, sometimes muttering "I knew it," when he could not immediately find something, signifying his disappointment and basic expectation that safety was precarious, replacement was unavoidable. Characteristically, after the very first Wednesday break, he started by painting aliens on the blackboard and looking around for "clues," as he was convinced that somebody had been fiddling with his things.

The underlying issue of trust was consistently addressed by me as I would verbalize how important it was for us to get to know each other at his own pace, acknowledging the difficulty in meeting yet another "person who wants to help him," and also how hard it was to trust, when every time his trust was broken. He would sometimes deny this was a problem, and other times nod, somehow in disbelief that I would really understand his experience. One day, he asked me whether I was German, clarifying that he could never trust me if I were German: they started the World War II, didn't I know?

His striking ability to remember what we had been doing in the previous sessions (despite the Wednesday or weekend break) pro-

vided partial positive evidence that he was beginning to be engaged
in our therapeutic relationship, but it mainly demonstrated his defensive need to avoid acknowledgment of the gap between sessions,
thus denying our separation and the existence of rivals. As his anxieties came alive with each goodbye, my verbalizations of the difficulty
of the endings were naturally dismissed, as he tried to shut me up,
talk over my voice: bla, bla, he knew it all.

It was often the case that insightful interpretations were rejected,
as they pierced too quickly his vulnerable internal world and defenses. The dire effects of Simon's early deprivation called for a
modification of technique, in line with what Alvarez (1992) describes
as the "grammar" of interpretation, the gradual building of interpretative work in the context of the growing trust and sense of safety
within the therapeutic relation.

This required simple and carefully timed interpretations, with
close observation of his responses and capacity to take them in.
Once, when I commented only that "it is as if we never say goodbye,"
he sighed with relief and began more readily to express his distaste
about the short duration of the session and the worries it evoked. For
a few weeks, each time he entered the room, he would immediately
ask, "Is it time to finish now?" "Is it time to tidy up, time to go?" "How
much time we have left?" (all with a playful, cheeky smile).

In my protests, "but we have not even started," I was left to experience the frustration, and the worry about time not being enough,
which he now allowed me to verbalize. Perhaps more importantly, it
provided the opportunity to show a different way of managing such
concerns, as it laid the foundations for the use of me as a safe object.
In response he introduced the making of a cake, which he coined the
"never ending cake" (in contrast to the sessions that did end), and we
busily engaged in long preparations that occupied a portion of the
session and involved coming up with the "right flavor" and texture
for this over-determined creation.

Simon was expectedly sensitive about sudden changes in his therapy and was constantly preoccupied with the possibility of breaks, a
reflection of the unpredictable nature of his life so far. It was striking
that in January, a few months into treatment, he wanted to know
about the summer break, as "surely, you are going to leave for a while,
Katerina." Feelings aroused by my leaving him, even for planned holidays, were hard to get to, as he denied any distress, anger, or worry
about my going or my not returning. His profound sense of being rejected and infinitely abandoned was the basic organizer of his defensive make-up, and feeling humiliated and unwanted were too disturbing to confront and own up to.

Early in his treatment, I had to cancel one session because I was going to a conference. He was deeply surprised and perplexed with this: "he thought I know everything already." In the last session before this long weekend, "the 8-year-old scorpion" (a character he had clearly identified with in previous play) gathered all the animals, lined them up, and addressed a personal goodbye to each of them (he was going to live alone in the desert), in a language that was unintelligible to me, but meaningful to them.

During this long goodbye, my attempts to articulate the relevance to our separation were ignored. As I was cut-off from the possibility of sharing and understanding what was now painfully denied, I felt that "words" with Simon had lost or never acquired their proper meaning, in his experience of all the sudden, unthinkable losses and the shattering of false hopes. Maybe part of the therapeutic endeavor would also be to "invent" a language together with Simon.

Following this first longer separation he would typically leave something to be linked with me: a question, a task. Before the first Christmas break, he drew a compass on the blackboard so I could find my way back.

ENACTMENTS OF FEELINGS OF UNSAFETY

Simon would jump in terror if he heard footsteps outside our door; the telephone ringing by mistake would leave him frozen, despite being immersed in animated play. In the counter-transference, I experienced a strong sense of generalized danger and diffuse anxiety, which I took as evidence of Simon being a very frightened little boy, who resorted to manic omnipotence to deal with underlying feelings of paralyzing helplessness. In fact his ego suffered from a marked limitation in reality testing faculty exacerbated by his unmodulated affects.

Simon's profound lack of an internal sense of safety was repeatedly enacted in our sessions, where despite my efforts to keep him safe, he would either consciously get into risky play, like jumping from the top of the stairs, or more typically, he would suddenly trip and fall, seemingly unable to keep himself together, usually at the beginning and ending of sessions, marking in that way his fragile and uncontained predicament. I also had to become watchful, and often I was able to prevent an accident from happening. He was always surprised if I did, attributing omnipotent powers to me and feeling very persecuted as a result. In the times when I was not able to protect him, his primary belief that he was alone and no one can protect him was sadly confirmed.

It became clear that part of this behavior was a direct testing of whether I would fulfill his transference expectations. However, I confined myself to acknowledging his wish that I keep him safe, before I could interpret his fear that I, like his caretakers, could not protect him and would reject him.

This also brought a flow of material that revolved around the precarious nature of safety, which we were able to work through, initially in displacement. For the first months, in the wild-animals' play, carnivorous and herbivorous animals were living right next to each other, "risking their lives," as Simon would tell me, but "they had no choice." Repeatedly, the plant-eaters would be ambushed and fiercely attacked and oddly "they would be the only ones to blame."

His sadistic, harsh superego was transparent in his oscillation between identification with the aggressor and identification with the victim (the first were hungry, the others were silly, and should be punished), leaving him in an enraged state, as I questioned the motives and circumstances of this endless violent bloodbath.

In a denigratory manner he accused me of "not getting it," "that is the way the wildlife works." Obviously this was the way Simon's internal world operated too, as it was shaped from his real encounters. I suspected that my questioning was evidence of my condemning such aggressive activity (and indirectly Simon), and eventually accepted the finality of the situation, and repeatedly emphasized my wish to understand this.

Simon was in response intrigued, and as the analytic process unfolded, it opened up the possibility of a "new way of being" for our wild animals when he suggested "things can be different" and moved the giraffe and the elephants across the lake, giving them one of the herbivorous dinosaurs for protection. As his superego lessened in severity and acquired more benign aspects, together with his internalizing a protective object, his self-harming behavior (which had a punishing quality) also ceased.

After a mid-term break a year into treatment, he made elaborate games with two turtles I had in his box. He explained how they "carry their home." He showed me various scenarios where the turtles were exposed to danger, but they could always retreat inside their shell. I commented that "they carry their protection." Simon movingly added "I wish I had one." His vulnerability was momentarily exposed, but he habitually hid under his defensive shield, his robot armor, behind which his fragile ego was struggling to keep overwhelming feelings at bay.

During the first year of treatment, there were often times when he would shout at me "do not look at me," in the middle of other activities, often when something painful had been re-evoked. He would order me to keep my eyes shut, a necessary stage it felt before he could feel less persecuted and safer with me.

I wondered whether his paranoid anxiety about my "persecutory" gaze was not just a projection of his overwhelming aggression, but maybe represented a fragment of his experience with a frightening state of mind in his mother or other caregivers.

Gradually, he allowed me, through the transference, to talk to him about how he wanted me to experience what it was like to have to trust someone, one who could potentially be scary and dangerous to me (as his throwing things at me clearly demonstrated). Of course my persecutory eyes were also used to read his face and to try to understand his emotional experiences, thus exposing his vulnerability, upsetting his internal equilibrium. Surviving his aggression, allowing the process of "destroying the object," promoted his eventual capacity to "use" the object, as we will later see.

Pre-Oedipal Longings/Aggressive Claims

Throughout his treatment, Simon presented extremely aggressive behavior (which subsided in his external life). "A child's persistent longing for his mother is often suffused with intense, generalized hostility . . . In its origin much of the anger of separated children is directed towards the missing mother-figure" (Bowlby, 1980; A. Freud and Burlingham, 1974, p.13).

The longing for a mother-figure, which is never gratified but is rather perpetually frustrated by the series of separations and losses, aggravates the unconsciously felt hostility. One can speculate that this has a distorting effect on the internal representation of the loved object, which now becomes an abandoning, cruel, rejecting object (which was often experienced in the transference and in his relationships with the multiple caretakers).

Despite his compliance and his eager running up the stairs, Simon would often enter the room in a violent mode, kicking at the box with bricks that is next to my desk and then banging at my chair. Any attempts to take up his anger or disappointment with me (it became noticeable that this mood was more prevalent after the Wednesday break or the weekend) inflamed him further.

During one session at six months of treatment, he sat playfully at my desk chair but soon began to dangerously bash himself on the desk, on the door, at the radiator. I verbalized how difficult it was to keep himself safe. "It's your office, your chair," he spitefully replied. I spoke of how sometimes it felt unsafe being here close to me, how I felt dangerous. I also had to put a firm stop to his behavior, by placing my hand on the chair. Simon closed his eyes and asked me to move him in the room. I spoke of how it was as if he were my baby in his buggy and I took him for a stroll. With a satisfied smile he made cooing sounds in agreement. I felt that Simon was letting me know about the inherently unsafe intimacy of his infancy, and perhaps it was through re-creating and reliving the danger that he could be in touch with his infantile longings and experience closeness.

Early mother-child games were introduced, particularly around breaks. Interestingly, hide-and-seek was too anxiety-provoking. He found the solution in peek-a-boo through the open windows in the doll's house. The pleasure in discovery of each other somehow played down my sense of his fear that he would really lose me, but I persisted with articulating the difficulty in believing that we could meet again, and that I would remember him. After the first Easter break and a relentless hide-and-seek sequel, he admitted "it was hard not to see each other."

Often, when the material was chaotic and Simon was in a regressed state, emotionally overwhelmed and physically challenging, the technical emphasis was more on the experiential side of the therapeutic contact. Hence, containment was possible, invariably through the experience of "being with him," (informed by my reverie) in a sensitive manner, which relied less on words, and more on my presence and the tone of voice, resembling the soothing nature of an attuned mother-baby dyad.

TRANSITIONAL SPACE, CAPACITY TO PLAY

From early on in Simon's treatment, and from the useful feedback from the parent work, it emerged that one of the most distressing difficulties he had was his inability to play, by himself or with others. He was in constant need of stimuli, protesting he was bored, but would never properly engage, or show pleasure in the interaction. Adults complained that he did not behave like a child. I also observed how his play was often rather automatic, devoid of creativity and serving defensively his need to keep order and control in his unpredictable external reality and chaotic internal world.

It is hardly surprising that this has been the case for Simon. His severe early emotional deprivation, compounded by the series of losses, prevented the unfolding of transitional phenomena, which require a facilitating environment that now for the first time, through therapy and in the context of his stable new home life, could be envisaged.

Winnicott has suggested that "psychotherapy takes place in the overlap of two areas of playing, that of the patient, and that of the therapist" (1971, p. 44). But what happens when the patient can not play?

I often found myself sometimes doing what is expected of a maternal object like ". . . pulling the child, drawing the child, . . . or *interesting the child*" (Alvarez, 1992, p. 77, personal emphasis).

Decorating the doll's house, cooking meals, and playing "ordinary life" scenarios became a feature of the sessions. The first time we played this, I spontaneously gave the baby a bath, as he needed changing. Simon got engrossed in my handling and caring for the baby and would always ask after this: "can you please be the mummy changing the baby?"

Latency interests like football and Cluedo slowly emerged and similarly provided the arena to explore, mostly through the transference, his internal dilemmas and feelings of rage about "not knowing," not having control, feeling inadequate.

Making plasticine models and painting became another favorite activity, and Simon discovered his artistic talent, which offered a great opportunity for sublimation. Once I pointed out how in our sessions we discovered not only clues about worrying feelings but also nice things about himself, and Simon sincerely thanked me for helping him discover something good about him (maybe for the first time).

With hindsight, I believe that my showing an active interest in his thoughts and ideas, and lending faith in his capacity to create and entertain them, provided the emotional scaffolding for him to feel safe and confident to experiment and play. A few months into treatment, he claimed, full of joy, that his ideas in therapy worked.

Nurturing his creative potential lessened his clinging onto omnipotent thinking. In positive identification with me, he slowly developed a mentalizing faculty, strengthening his ego with direct effects on his capacity to relate to peers, thus reinforcing a more positive sense of self.

Ten months in therapy, Simon read in class the following poem:

Under the Dinner Table
When I feel sad (When I want to be quiet), or I have nothing to do,
I go under the dinner table, I like it there . . .
Because the dinner-table is right beside my wonderful garden;

When I sit under the dinner table I hear the practice purring
of our next door neighbor's skinny cat, and the tweeting and
chirping of the sparrows in the weedy pear tree.
I also like the sound of the refreshing wind . . .

ENURESIS / SUBSTITUTE FOR TEARS

Simon's presenting symptom of enuresis slowly began to fade in the early months of treatment. As it surfaced only at crisis points (after fights with foster mother, loss of a social worker), I understood it as an extreme attempt, via the body, to evacuate unbearable feelings of rage and fear of loss, linked with fragments of his original trauma.

Throughout his sessions, however, Simon would bring in the "wetting" by water play in the sink that was out of control, leaving the room in "almost" flooded states. In the countertransference, I had a powerful feeling of disconnectedness but also a primitive "drowning" element, which prevented my thinking and left me numb. I wondered about the cataclysmic nature of Simon's early object relations, as well as the overwhelming impact of their loss.

Simon was able to act out these feelings, but the question remained whether he could really feel them. I meticulously tried to link particular triggers (usually separations) with this behavior, verbalizing the relevant affect.

One day in the seventh month, I informed him about a short break. Despite being in touch with his anger, Simon relentlessly wet the room. I said it felt like a storm. I wondered about his stormy feelings. He said: "It was like a storm when I was a baby and they took me away from my mum, she was too young to have me . . . I was only one month old, just a baby."

Understanding and working through the underlying feelings of sadness and abandonment were crucial. His enuresis stopped, and foster mother reported how Simon cried for the first time since he moved in with them after watching the Lion King.

ENCOPRESIS; IDEALIZED UNION WITH MOTHER

Simon's other distressing multilayered symptom was his soiling, which he never "brought in the room." I observed, however, that once he felt more secure in the therapeutic space, he enjoyed messy play with paint and sand. Anality "felt safe," while also he had strong reaction formations (he always cleaned up). I've already indicated how I was assigned the role of "changing the baby" in the play. I also noticed how he would always ask to go to the toilet after a very re-warding interaction between us, in restored moments of companion ship after "stormy" feelings.

One day toward the end of the first year during a play in the doll's house, he had to rush to the toilet. In displacement, I spoke on be-half of little George (the baby boy in our doll play) and said how young toddlers offer their mummies their pooh as a gift. He told me, somehow embarrassed, that he used to think that he had to be in nappies for his mum to realize it is him, as that's how she left him.

It seems that with his soiling Simon attempted to maintain the hope of an idealized union with his mother. As his early history de-scribed his being left unchanged for questionable lengths of time, one can speculate whether the soiling brought him "closeness" with his (now lost) mother by compulsively repeating a fragment of the trauma.

Winnicott describes how the "self may defend against specific envi-ronmental failure, by a freezing of the failure situation." Along with this goes an "unconscious assumption, that opportunity will occur at a later date for a renewed experience in which the failure situation will be able to be unfrozen . . . in an environment that is making ade-quate though belated adaptation" (1954, p. 281). Simon's encopresis disappeared after the first year of treatment.

Positive Transference/Idealization of the Analyst

Simon was able to experience intense moments of negative transfer-ence (treating me as a depriving, rejecting object), while also build-ing on positive transference experiences. These incorporated times of idealized transference, which I viewed as a development, belong-ing to the realm of early mother-infant relationship. When he lost one of his milk teeth, a few months into treatment, he brought it in to show me, explaining about the "tooth fairy" and how "they are re-ally the mothers" and placing his tooth on my palm.

Technically, it was important to distinguish the significance of al-lowing these moments to surface by not interpreting them too quickly, as I felt Simon needed ". . . to create a benign atmosphere" (Rosenfeld, 1987, in Alvarez, 1992). In order to reach the normal stage of disillusionment, the infant must experience what stems from his "partly creating, partly finding" the object he needs. Further-more, it is in the context of a shared experience of positive affection which a separate and authentic sense of self can be developed (Hurry, 1988).

Mourning of Earlier Losses

THE LAST SOUP

Fifteen months into treatment, during "cooking" play, Simon told me, with a broken voice, how he came back from school one day (when he was 7), and was greeted by his grandmother, who told him that he would have his last soup. "I saw a small suitcase by the staircase, and there was this lady there, but I did not understand, Katerina, what was this last soup about? Were we running out of soup? And then I realized. I was so scared, and confused . . . what had I done?"

He continued molding the plasticine but paused as I spoke, merely acknowledging how sad and scary this must have been for him. "Nobody could hear my cries," he painfully added. I stayed with him in silence for a few moments, the sadness filling the atmosphere and mirrored in our faces and my tone of voice when I later said he must have felt very lonely and frightened when no one was able to hear his cries.

"How come you do, Katerina?" he said, this time not with the panicky threatened feel of somebody who's been discovered or exposed, but with the sense of relief of someone who is understood.

It is interesting to note that in the last care review meeting before the summer holidays, school reports and particularly his learning support worker's feedback were highly positive. "Simon has done exceptionally well at school (he is at the top group for English, Maths, and Science). Overall he is a polite and pleasant little boy. There have been no major behavioral incidents. Simon is an active boy who excels in sport. He loves playing football, and he's now able to contribute to the team, and be part of a team. He is well coordinated, and very competitive. In PE and at play he is now one of the first to be picked, and his team will say 'Yay, we have got Simon.' This puts a smile on his face, and is good for his growing self-esteem. He has also been enjoying strategic games like chess, and Connect Four."

In his sessions during the second summer term (at this point two years into treatment), he continued with latency play (Cluedo, chess) and football, in which we were able to experience genuine moments of togetherness, with appropriate doses of competitive drive. I was allowed to score a goal and be skillful; his ego strength made "losing" in games more tolerable, and Simon, with his growing insight, pointed that "this was a change."

As permanency plans were securely in place by May of that term,

Simon increasingly felt safe in his home-environment and in his therapy. He brought for me to see pictures of himself and his birth mother. I noticed that they were all taken on the same day.

He stressed that it was hard "not knowing how [his] mother's face looked." He pointed out that he was a toddler, still in nappies when these photos were taken. His longing to have more proof of his lost moments with mum, now preciously held in fantasy and the disappointing evidence I was now holding in my hands, made me empathize with him. Simon's affect changed to a deeply felt anguish, as he said: "Everyone says I should be happy, but you get it, I can now remember only *this day*."

In the sessions that followed, Simon, turning passive into active, suggested we do "[his] life history" book (edited by Simon and Katerina). The life history book is something typically done by the Social Service social worker and foster child and it includes information and photos of the child's life; these were also missing in Simon's case. Simon bravely attempted to reconstruct his early life and come to terms with the realization of having little information about his birth parents, his milestones, and the so far unthinkable circumstances surrounding his being "looked after." His insight and growing feelings of safety allowed him to have these memories.

As we explored his overwhelming feelings and I verbalized his sense of not being cared for, of being unlovable, he poignantly agreed: "the problem of being a 'looked after' child is that you don't feel looked after."

THE IMPACT OF A NEW LOSS

Two years and two months into the treatment, when Simon was 10 years old, I returned from our second summer break to find a number of messages from Simon's Social Worker, informing me about the impending disruption of his placement, which naturally left me in shock. This removal was instigated on unreasonable grounds by Social Services and was triggered by a communication failure during the summer break between foster mother and social worker. (The topic of how such miscommunications and splitting between agencies, caretakers, and clinicians occur in the case of children like Simon lies beyond the scope of this paper (see Discussion). Social Services insisted on implementing their unilateral decision in a high-handed and arbitrary way, despite the strenuous joint efforts on the part of the parent worker and myself to prevent this unnecessary and hurtful loss for Simon. These efforts were rebuffed by Social Ser-

vices, and, on the Friday of the first week back, I was told about the ir-
reversible nature of Simon's move to his tenth foster placement, the
timing of which was still uncertain.

In the midst of this upheaval, Simon came to his session with his
foster parents, extremely distressed, looking at another loss and unable to keep himself together. Quite shaken and in tears, he told me
that he was afraid "something bad was happening to his family." In
that short session, as he could not manage the uncertainty and his
apparent fragility, he further spoke of his sense of "losing his family."
I acknowledged the sadness and confusion he was experiencing and
became myself tearful as I shared his sadness, despair and helplessness for this unjustified loss.

In the following weeks, his affective state fluctuated between depressed, hopeless and vulnerable to an angry and fighting mode. He
retreated to more defensive card games and earlier modes of being
and relating (or surviving) by controlling the outcome of the game.
His triumphant pleasure in beating me in the games was short lived.
His inner despair and the frightening element of his feeling abandoned and helpless were palpable and powerfully experienced by me
in the countertransference.

At times where actions had failed us and words could merely touch
the violent awakening of the recurrent trauma, the strong treatment
alliance and his positive transference to me enabled the therapeutic
space to be an emotional anchor for Simon's distress.

During this stressful time, while talking about school, he tells me
that he is part of H.O.P.E.S. (an acronym coined by his school standing for Help Other People Enjoy School). He gave me a coherent account of his role during play time and breaks of helping other children: "I keep an eye on other children to see whether they are happy,
sad, or angry. If they are happy, I don't do anything!" We laugh. "But
if they are sad, or sitting by themselves, I go and try to help them, try
to understand what it is that troubles them, and maybe put a smile
back on their face."

I say that this reminds me of something. "Therapy," he volunteers,
with a glee in his voice. "But, you know, sometimes it is hard to talk,
sometimes when you are sad inside, you don't want to talk." As I nodded smiling, he added, "you know, as I am like this sometimes." He
then spoke of a little girl who would not tell him what was wrong (she
barely knew him), and he thought of calling over her older sister,
who was his classmate, and that helped!

In the midst of the recent traumatic loss of his foster family, I was
moved to see how Simon had internalized the caring aspects from

our therapeutic relationship, had developed a capacity for concern, but was also able to use his newly acquired ego achievements of emotional language and understanding, the observing faculty and the ability to relate to the mind of another. It was also reassuring that there was not an upsurge of his earlier maladaptive patterns of managing the disturbing effects of trauma. At my urging, his therapy continued for another half year, in face of the reluctance of Social Services, who did not see the need in light of his marked symptomatic improvement. Termination coincided with his transition to an academically selective grammar school (for students age 11–18) to which he had won admission.

DISCUSSION

As Simon's therapist, I felt that it was of paramount importance that I work closely with the system—that is, the foster family, as well as the social worker and the school. This included regular feedbacks with the various strands of the network as well as attending the periodic "Child in Care" reviews conducted by Social Services. My aim was to manage to keep Simon in the system's collective mind and to safeguard the permanency of the placement, as it was vital in offering some continuity in his chaotic world, while providing the necessary precondition for the therapeutic endeavor to develop.

It is often the case that once psychotherapy is offered, the child's need for a secure, stable family and social environment can lose its priority because the child's pathological means of managing his helplessness and distress are often mirrored in the network, placing a strain on the multi-agency working partnership and frequently resulting in splitting between the agencies, with distorted communication and powerful enactments of split roles (the rescuing good parent vs. the punitive rejecting bad one).

Hoxter (1983) argues that "emotional reactions to severely deprived children are likely to be very strong and whether we be therapists or substitute parents, we are liable to find aroused in ourselves defenses which are not dissimilar to those of the . . . children. Full awareness of the child's loss and suffering is often nearly as intolerable to us as it is to the child, and, like the child, we are tempted to use many ways of distancing ourselves . . . or to diminish the significance of the loss . . . We require to be vigilant that we are not drawn into playing a part in the 'cycle of deprivation'" (p. 126).

Working closely with the parent worker who was also the case manager, we put all our efforts to avoid repetitions and acting out of past traumatic separations and losses. This additional external role, which would traditionally be perceived as interfering with the protected analytic frame, is a reality that child psychotherapists working in the National Health Service have to confront. Despite the inherent difficulty in managing these multiple roles without compromising the undistracted unfolding of the therapeutic relationship, I felt it was essential to voice my patient's best interests and needs in a climate where often these were overlooked or dismissed.

Simon's capacity to survive in the face of adversity has been remarkable. He engaged in the therapeutic work with impressive results. The clinical material, I believe, delineates how the reliable setting and the transference relationship enabled Simon to resume his "arrested" development, as it helped him reconnect with feelings of anger, despair, and longing for his lost objects through the naming of affects, and linking them to his traumatic original losses. Hence, developmental therapy was integral and inseparable from the more classical means of interpretation of conflicts and defenses.

When faced with such chaotic and traumatic early history (and this extends to all patients who have suffered emotional deprivation and neglect), the attempt at reconstruction can easily seem to be a therapeutic priority. In our work, however, reconstruction was never a distinct aim in itself, as pursued in isolation it held the danger of defensive pseudo-intellectualization.

Although not a goal in itself, much reconstruction occurred as product of the dynamic nature of the analytic process, evident in Simon's recollection of particular traumatic episodes like "the last soup," his remembering of his mother, and his attempts to confront and write down his "life history." Without minimizing the value of a coherent narrative of past experiences, I felt that what was most urgent in Simon's case was the co-construction, not simply of a "story" but of a relationship.

Simon's "search for a particular object relation that is associated with ego transformation and repair" (Bollas, 1979, p. 99) was embodied in the development of the analytic relationship and the differential use of me as transference, developmental, and contemporary (real) object (Hurry, 1998).

Simon's strengthened ego was able to integrate some of the previously split-off needy aspects, and was in a position to use his intellect to further consolidate a more benign self-representation with feelings of safety and self-worth. Latency development was the fortunate "push" in this healthier trajectory.

Also instrumental was the stability of his foster family for the last almost four years and the opportunity to identify with positive male role figures like his foster father and his one-to-one learning support worker. Simon remains at risk, however, especially in his adolescence and in his interpersonal relationships as negotiating intimacy and ambivalence and regulating a safe distance with a potentially rejecting other may evoke painful associations and destructive coping mechanisms.

In this paper, I also described some "moments of meeting" (Stern et al., 1998) with Simon which had a pivotal effect on both the development of the analytic process, as well as the therapeutic outcome. Stern and colleagues suggest that such moments can have a powerful effect in reorganizing the patient's "implicit relational knowing that extend beyond the confines of the analytic encounter. This procedural knowledge of relationships, integrating affect, cognition and interactive dimensions, is thought to be a derivative of 'the primordial process of affective communication,' rooted in the earliest mother-infant relationship" (p. 918).

In those authentic, emotional exchanges, I became a companion in Simon's "explorations of himself, and his experiences" (Bowlby, 1988, p. 151). These moments of contact were often beyond the symbolic realm, as they emerged out of the "freedom and spontaneity" (Winnicott, 1951) of the transitional space, powerful unconscious communications via projective identification, and finally the use of the countertransference. My own countertransference feelings and sometimes responses were meticulously noted and employed, as at times the sole means of being in touch with Simon's predicament and of linking with those of his experiences that were preverbal and possibly unverbalizable.

It is now widely thought that young infants are likely to have an implicit memory of a past traumatic event in the form of somatic memory (Gaensbauer, 2002), experienced as bodily symptoms. Thinking about Simon's disturbing symptoms of enuresis and encopresis we may speculate as to how, in the presence of a reliable "thinking other" (his therapist), Simon was able to integrate the previously unconnected physical symptoms to his painful feelings of loss, abandonment and longing for closeness and reunion with his mother, thereby allowing for reflective thinking processes (Fonagy and Target, 1997) to emerge in the therapeutic dialogue.

Hunter (2001) emphasizes the "distinct role of therapists working with looked-after children, as they have extra responsibility for gathering up and integrating the child's experiences." For some children, this aspect of therapy alone is of enormous significance. "Being re-

86 *Ekaterini Strati*

membered," "being known," "being enjoyed," "being important" (Hunter, 2001, p. 26) may well constitute prototypes of experiences for lost children like Simon, all contributing to ultimately "being found."

ALVAREZ, A. (1992). *Live Company*. Routledge: London.
BOLLAS, C. (1979). The transformational object. In: G. Kohon (ed.), *The British School of Psychoanalysis: The Independent Tradition*. London: Free Association Books, 1986.
BOWLBY, J. (1952). *Maternal Care and Mental Health*. Geneva: World Health Organisation.
BOWLBY, J. (1980). *Attachment and Loss. Vol III. Loss, Sadness, and Depression*. London: Hogarth Press.
BOWLBY, J. (1988). *A Secure Base: Clinical Applications of Attachment Theory*. London: Routledge.
FONAGY, P. & TARGET, M. (1997) Attachment and reflective function: Their role in self-organisation. *Development and Psychopathology*, 9: 679–700.
GAENSBAUER, T. H. (2002) Representations of trauma in infancy: Clinical and theoretical implications for the understanding of early memory. *Infant Mental Health Journal*, 23(3), 259–277.
HENRY, G. (1988). Doubly deprived, in D. Daws and M. Boston (eds.) *The Child Psychotherapist*, Maresfield Library, London: Karnac.
HOXTER, S. (1983). Feelings aroused in working with severely deprived children, in M. Boston and R. Szur (eds.) *Psychotherapy with Severely Deprived Children*, London: Karnac.
HUNTER, M. (2001). *Psychotherapy with Young People in Care. Lost and Found*. East Sussex: Brunner-Routledge.
HURRY, A. (ED.) (1998). *Psychoanalysis and Developmental Therapy*. London: Karnac.
FREUD, A. & BURLINGHAM, D. (1974). *Infants without Families and Reports on the Hampstead Nurseries 1939–1945*. London: Hogarth Press.
PERRY, B. D., POLLARD, R., BLAKLEY, T., BAKER, W., & VIGILANT, D. (1995). Childhood trauma, the neurobiology of adaptation and "user dependent" development of the brain: How "states" become "traits," *Infant Mental Health Journal* 16(4):271–91.
SHORE, A. N. (2002). Dysregulation of the right brain: A fundamental mechanism of traumatic attachment and the psychogenesis of post-traumatic stress disorder. *Australian and New Zealand Journal of Psychiatry. 36(1):9-30.*
STERN, D. (1985). *The Interpersonal World of the Infant: A View from Psychoanalysis and Developmental Psychology*. New York: Basic Books.
STERN, D., SANDER, L. W., NAHUM, J. P., ET AL. (1998). Non-interpreting mechanisms in psychoanalytic therapy. The "Something More" than Interpretation. *International Journal of Psychoanalysis* 79, 903–921.

TREVARTHEN, C. (1993). The self born in intersubjectivity: The psychology of an infant communicating, in Neisser U. (ed.) *The Perceived Self: Ecological and Interpersonal Sources of Self Knowledge*. New York: Cambridge University Press.

WINNICOTT, D. W. (1951). Transitional objects and transitional phenomena, in D. W. Winnicot (1971) *Playing and Reality*. London: Tavistock.

WINNICOTT, D. W. (1954). Metapsychological and clinical aspects of regression within the psycho-analytic set-up, in *Through Paediatrics to Psycho-Analysis*. London: Karnac.

WINNICOTT, D. W. (1958). The capacity to be alone, in D. W. Winnicott (1965). *The Maturational Process and the Facilitating Environment*. London: Hogarth.

CHILD PSYCHOANALYTIC
TECHNIQUE

Do Children Get Better When We Interpret Their Defenses Against Painful Feelings?

LEON HOFFMAN, M.D.

This paper represents a step toward trying to integrate clinical and research perspectives. To achieve this integration, analysts need to be clear about the clinical constructs and specific interventions they utilize as they try to unpack the concept of "therapeutic action." In trying to understand "how" interventions work, technical interventions need to be clinically formulated in a narrow fashion within the more global therapeutic approach in which the particular analyst practices. In this paper, I address one specific technical approach. I discuss the therapeutic importance of an intervention, especially during the beginning phases of an analytic or dynamic therapeutic process: interpretation of defenses against unwelcome affects, a technique in whose development Berta Bornstein was instrumental. This paper puts forward the hypothesis (which remains to be systematically empirically verified or refuted) that this approach is not only a core element of defense analyses but may very well be common to all good psychodynamic treatments, regardless of the manifest theoretical orientation of the therapist or analyst, and regardless of the analyst's or therapist's explicit consideration

---

Training and Supervising Analyst and Director, Pacella Parent Child Center, The New York Psychoanalytic Society and Institute.

Presented at the New York Psychoanalytic Institute and Society, May 9, 2006, and at the American Psychoanalytic Association, June 16, 2006. An earlier version was presented as the Gerald H. J. Pearson Memorial Lecture at the Psychoanalytic Center of Philadelphia, October 14, 2005. I am grateful for the careful readings and critiques by many colleagues too numerous to enumerate.

The Psychoanalytic Study of the Child 62, ed. Robert A. King, Peter B. Neubauer, Samuel Abrams, and A. Scott Dowling (Yale University Press, copyright © 2007 by Robert A. King, Peter B. Neubauer, Samuel Abrams, and A. Scott Dowling).

that he or she is utilizing this approach. Clinical material from the literature is discussed in order to illustrate the technique and to show how, when analysts are attempting to demonstrate the value of other or new interventions, analysts may ignore how they are, in fact, utilizing the technique of interpreting defenses against affects.

INTRODUCTION

CHILD AND ADOLESCENT PSYCHOANALYSIS HAS BEEN ENRICHED BY AN extensive clinical literature dating back to Hermine Hug-Hellmuth, who worked prior to both Melanie Klein and Anna Freud (Hoffman, 1995). Despite the limitations of mainly using clinical reports for the development of a scientific discipline (Fonagy, 1999), a systematic approach to this vast clinical literature is crucial in order to mine the clinical reports both for clinical generalizations about therapeutic action as well as for hypothesis generation to be then evaluated systematically.

This paper is a step toward a goal of trying to integrate clinical material with research methods (Bucci, 2005). To achieve such an integration, analysts need to clearly spell out the clinical constructs and specific interventions they utilize as they try to unpack the concept of "therapeutic action." In trying to understand how (or even if) various interventions work, technical interventions need to be clinically formulated and described in a specific fashion within the more global therapeutic approaches within which the particular analyst practices. In this paper, I address one such specific technical approach. I discuss what I consider to be the therapeutic importance of a specific intervention, interpretation of defenses against unwelcome affects, first delineated by Berta Bornstein who was instrumental in the development of this technique. It is a technique especially useful during the beginning phases of an analytic or dynamic therapeutic process, but applicable throughout the treatment process.

I will first provide a brief example from my work to illustrate how "interpretation of defenses against unwelcome affects" may appear in a therapeutic context.

A nine-and-a-half-year-old boy who entered treatment because of aggressive problems was in the middle of a four-time-a-week analysis (Hoffman, 1989) when he "circumspectly alluded to fights between his parents when they were alone in their bedroom. He told me that he wet less when he built a fort around his bed (he shared a room with his sister), and he showed me a model of the fort. He wanted to play 'hit the donkey on the butt,' showed me his butt, and asked that I throw the nerf ball at him. Before I could respond or we could begin the game he said that he was tired. I said that he became tired because his feelings were uncomfortable. He did not respond to this, but told me that his half brother could beat anyone because he was not afraid. When he started to act tough with me, I said that he acted tough in order to make believe that he didn't worry about being hurt but that he was really trying to provoke me to hurt him, as in his asking to be hit in the butt. Discussion of his masochistic wishes and the defenses against them allowed his aggression to subside even though he continued to deny his wish to be hurt (page 70).

In this brief vignette, I illustrate how I demonstrated to the patient how he warded off uncomfortable feelings: by becoming tired to avoid both the danger that I might gratify his masochistic wishes and hit him in the butt, as well as by avoiding talking about those feelings. I also said that he avoided his unpleasant affects when he acted tough with me to prevent awareness that he was worried that he would be hurt by me as a result of his provocations.

The hypothesis put forward in this paper (which, of course, I cannot prove with the few examples I provide but has to be systematically verified or refuted) is that this approach is not only a core element of defense analyses (where the adage is "interpret defense before drive") but may be common to all good psychodynamic treatments, regardless of the nature of the child's pathology, regardless of the manifest theoretical orientation of the therapist or analyst, and regardless of whether or not the analyst or therapist consciously identifies his or her utilization of this approach. I would go so far as to say that this approach is so fundamental and ubiquitous that some authors, who are understandably more interested in explicating novel approaches or theoretical or therapeutic innovations, may lose track of the fact that they are effectively utilizing the technique of interpreting defenses against unwelcome affects. Unfortunately, this technique may be considered to be an "old" technique and thus omitted from contemporary discussions about the nature of the therapeutic action in any particular treatment or treatment in general. Although many of the ideas discussed in this paper have been discussed in a variety of contexts by too many authors to enumerate (dating back to Anna Freud, 1936), the novelty in this paper lies in highlighting in an organized way the therapeutic power of this systematic approach to defenses against unwelcome affects in children (and adults for that matter).

THERAPEUTIC ACTION

Understanding the nature of therapeutic action, that is, trying to understand how interventions are specifically effective (or ineffective, for that matter), has been an enterprise that has occupied psychoanalysts from the beginning of the field, dating back to the evolution of psychoanalytic technique by Freud. As is well known, Freud's central change in psychoanalytic technique involved the analytic approach to the inevitable resistances (that is, defensive responses) that arise in treatment. At first, Freud maintained that in order to bring about therapeutic change, the analyst's job was to attempt to overcome the patient's resistances in order to allow for free awareness and expression of unconscious libidinal wishes; the clear-cut problems which occurred with this technique led to the development of the structural theory. Freud understood that the resistances (defensive approaches), which were unconscious themselves, needed to be respected and analyzed rather than overcome. As Bush (1992) states, with the structural theory "a psychoanalytic working through of these resistances could truly be undertaken which would center on an understanding of the danger to the ego underlying the resistance" (page 1093).

In an early review in "The Nature of the Therapeutic Action of Psycho-Analysis," Strachey (1934) contended that the essence of psychoanalytic technique involved the "mutative interpretation" (that is, a series of transference interpretations which lead to modifications in the patient's harsh superego). However, Strachey also concluded that "the fact that the mutative interpretation is the ultimate operative factor in the therapeutic action of psycho-analysis does not imply the exclusion of many other procedures (such as suggestion, reassurance, abreaction, etc.) as elements in the treatment of any particular patient" (page 159).

Unfortunately, during its first century, psychoanalysis became weighed down by the seemingly endless and unnecessarily rift-promoting debates, often personality-driven rather than theory-driven. These debates have been essentially a result of the tension between two very broad conceptions of technique: interpretation and interpersonal relationship (Jones, 2000, page 3). On the one hand, some have been convinced that interpretation leading to insight, particularly focusing on the unconscious and the past, is the only mutative psychoanalytic technique; on the other hand, others have maintained that participating in and/or exploring the relationship between patient and analyst is the most critical therapeutic agent in psychoanalytic treatments, whether with adults or with children (see for example, Blatt and Behrends, 1987, and Chused, 2000). Clearly, both of these broad theoretical and therapeutic approaches are important in all analytic treatments, particularly with children. However, with some patients, relationship issues predominate, while in others, interpretative techniques are most prominent. With children, the consideration of developmental capacities and organization and the developmental process constitutes an added challenge when trying to uncover the therapeutic agent in any particular treatment (Abrams, 2001, 2003; Neubauer, 2003). For example, when trying to understand the nature of a child's capacity for insight, one has to take into consideration the child's developmental capacities (for example, Hoffman, 1989; Kennedy, 1979; Neubauer, 1979; and Schmukler, 1999).

In the contemporary child analytic and developmental literature, many stress the centrality (in treatment as well as in development) of the gradual enhancement of children's capacities for self-regulation of affects for their social, emotional, and cognitive development (Fonagy, Gergely, et al., 2002; Tyson, 1996, 2005). Certainly, an important aim of a psychoanalytic treatment is to help children develop their "capacity to make use of the signal function of affect" (Tyson, 2005, page 169) in order to further their adaptive resources in real life. Schmukler (1999), for example, maintains that before insight can occur, the child needs to be able to tolerate unpleasant affects, among other factors (page 340). In fact, many children (if not most) who are brought for treatment do have difficulty tolerating and modulating unpleasant affect states.

In the contemporary arena, there are a variety of conceptualizations of analytic and therapeutic techniques which are utilized to help children modulate their affects more effectively. One such example is the "mentalizing approach," which involves helping children discover their intentional stance or mentalizing capacity (Fonagy and Target, 1998; Slade, 1999). Fonagy and Target (1998) suggest that the development of a mentalizing capacity (finding meaning in one's own and others' psychic experiences) "underlies affect regulation, impulse control, self-monitoring, and the experience of self-agency" (page 92).

The question that needs to be asked is how does one differentiate the therapeutic impact of the "mentalizing approach" from other approaches such as "defense analysis," "developmental help," or a "supportive approach"? How similar and how different are the specific technical interventions that analysts use, when they assert that they

utilize one approach rather than another one? For example, Jones
and Pulos (1993) and Jones and Ablon (1998) have empirically
demonstrated that the specific therapeutic interventions utilized by a
clinician in an individual situation do not necessarily conform to the
clinician's avowed theoretical stance.

It is my contention that it is important for the progression of the
field that analysts specify in a narrow fashion the specific intervention they utilize so one can evaluate the value of such an intervention
as an agent for change regardless of the clinician's avowed theoretical stance. In fact, many contemporary psychotherapy investigators
stress the importance of trying to identify the active ingredients of
the therapeutic process of a particular treatment strategy (Kazdin
and Nock, 2003). A basic pre-requisite for such empirical investigation is that putatively therapeutic interventions be described with sufficient clarity that independent observers or raters can reliably agree
as to whether and when that intervention has been used at a given
point in the treatment. The theoretical "Tower of Babel" described
above often obscures the actuality of a given analytic intervention, as
very disparate interventions may sometimes be described under a
single theoretical rubric, while fundamentally similar interventions
may be described by adherents of different theoretical persuasions
under a plethora of different labels.

INTERPRETATION OF DEFENSES AGAINST UNWELCOME AFFECTS

The first step in any therapeutic endeavor, of course, is engaging the
patient. Without such an engagement treatment is not possible. I am
suggesting that there is a fundamental technical approach to a
child's *introduction* to treatment (or, any patient's, for that matter):
understanding, addressing, and interpreting the patient's defenses
against unwelcome affects. Only by evaluating the child's response to
such early interventions can the analyst determine to what degree
the child is amenable to further interpretive work and whether a
deepening of the analytic process can occur. In fact, *to me,* a sine qua
non of an analytic attitude is having an appreciation of and respect
for the child's defenses against unwelcome affects.

With regard to terminology, Samuel Abrams (personal communication) has said, "I prefer protection instead of defense (it's a different
implied metaphor) and I use explain rather than interpret—partly
because it diminishes the authoritative position of the therapist and
shifts the relationship toward one of co-operative partner." Although
Abrams's language is certainly more descriptive, a-theoretical, and

closer to the language one uses with patients, I continue to use the terms "defense" and "interpret" because they are ingrained words in the lexicon not only of psychoanalysis and psychology, but also of the general intellectual community. Abrams is certainly correct that all interpretive communications to patients should not be made as if *ex cathedra*, but within the context of the relationship between analyst and patient.

The psychoanalytic literature on the nature of interpretation—via verbal as well as non-verbal communication—is vast. To me, it is most clinically relevant to consider an interpretation to be a communication from analyst to patient in which the analyst tries to explain something about the patient to the patient that the latter is not fully aware of (Brenner, 1996, page 29). In that sense, the analyst's communication is a hypothesis or a conjecture about the meaning of some aspect of the patient's verbal or non-verbal activity (Bibring, 1954, page 758; Spence, 1984, page 594; Brenner, 1996, page 29).

Historically analysts have made a distinction between clarification and interpretation. Bibring (1954) states that in therapy, clarification (a term he cites as originating with Carl Rogers) addresses "those vague and obscure factors (frequently below the level of verbalization) which are relevant from the viewpoint of treatment; it refers to those techniques and therapeutic processes which assist the patient to reach a higher degree of self-awareness, clarity and differentiation of self-observation which makes adequate verbalization possible" (page 755). "In contrast to clarification, interpretation by its very nature transgresses the clinical data, the phenomenological-descriptive level. On the basis of their derivatives, the analyst tries to 'guess' and to communicate (to explain) to the patient in form of (hypothetical) constructions and reconstructions those unconscious processes which are assumed to determine his manifest behavior. In general, interpretation consists not in a single act but in a prolonged process. A period of 'preparation' (e.g., in form of clarification) precedes it" (pages 757–758).

In other words, from Bibring's classical analytic perspective, clarifications refer to experience-near interventions, whereas interpretation refers to both an evolving process as well as to a more experience-distant. From the perspective of this paper, I need to affirm that the term, "interpretation of the defenses against painful affects," refers to an experience-near intervention which is an amalgamation of the concepts, clarification and interpretation. I will discuss how, when addressing a child's defenses against awareness of unpleasant affects, the analyst must not stray very far from the surface and

should *not* "transgress the clinical data" (Bibring's idea of an interpretation), but rather stay as experience-near as possible. In the
opening vignette, I demonstrated how I tried to stay close to the
child's experience when I communicated to him that he was avoiding
disturbing affects.

It is also important to bear in mind that as an analytic process
evolves, one always analyzes and interprets all aspects of a compromise formation—wishes, defenses, unpleasurable affects, and self-
punitive trends, as discussed by Brenner (2002). In the context of
this communication, however, I focus on those interpretative communications which mainly address helping the child understand how
feelings are avoided or expressed (compare the discussion by Jones,
2000, pages 7–8). This preferential focus on the process of defense
against disturbing affects includes the caution not to focus prematurely on a patient's unconscious libidinal or aggressive wishes or, in
fact, defenses about which the patient has no awareness at all. The
analyst should try to avoid "guessing" what's on the patient's mind,
although inevitably a certain amount of guessing always takes place.
The ideas in this paper are consistent with Sugarman's (1994, 2003)
application with children of Paul Gray's (2005) technique. In Sugarman's (1994) words, the child is helped to expand "the control of the
conscious ego over other structures of the psyche" (page 329).

With this approach, from the very beginning of the therapeutic
work, the analyst or therapist first tries to understand, then judi-
ciously explore, and eventually describe the child's current mental
state—in terms of the defenses against a conscious awareness of the
emotional pain that the child seems to be experiencing. As the analyst understands how the child is hiding the emotional pain from
him- or herself (consciously or unconsciously keeping bad feelings
out of awareness, avoiding direct verbalization, or disavowing the
painful feeling states), the analyst needs to discern ways of addressing such defenses. When the analyst understands how the child is
protecting him- or herself from painful feelings, the analyst can try to
communicate this understanding verbally or non-verbally to the
child. The child feels understood by the other person and as a result
the therapeutic alliance and the analytic process can unfold.

The child's defensive maneuvers are explored and eventually interpreted to the child in a careful, respectful, and developmentally appropriate way. Exploration of the defenses which the child utilizes to
mask the emotional pain, ideally, leads to a situation where the child
feels less threatened by the painful feeling states. This allows the

child to share the feelings with the other person in a more direct or more elaborated though disguised way. The child then feels in greater control of him- or herself, leading to greater mastery of affects and more adaptive interactions with the environment. In some children, over time, there may be greater verbal elaboration of his or her feelings and fantasies and exploration of the origins of the painful feelings. However, for many children the analyst's interpretation of the child's defensive avoidance of painful affects allows the child ONLY to discuss the painful feelings more openly. In other words, there is evidence of greater mastery of feelings and diminishment of maladaptive defenses without direct verbal exploration of the origins of the overwhelming states.

HISTORICAL DEVELOPMENT OF THE TECHNIQUE OF INTERPRETATION OF DEFENSES AGAINST UNWELCOME AFFECTS

In the 1920s, Anna Freud (1926) observed that children generally did not develop a transference neurosis. Melanie Klein (1927) maintained that this failure to demonstrate a transference neurosis was a result of the preparatory phase (where the analyst acted in an exaggeratedly benign and giving way). Anna Freud (1945) argued that "even if one part of the child's neurosis is transformed into a transference neurosis as it happens in adult analysis, another part of the child's neurotic behavior remains grouped around the parents who are the original objects of his pathogenic past" (page 130). In contrast, Klein (1927) espoused the idea that in analytic work with children, the analyst should not be concerned with the child's relationship to the outside world and that reality issues and work with the parents were unnecessary and corrupting factors in a child's analysis because they interfered with the development of a transference neurosis.

Anna Freud (1926) continued to stress that, as superego and auxiliary ego figures for the child, parents were crucial to the child's life and therefore were needed to maintain the treatment. She recommended that the analyst needed to form an alliance with the child, so the child could trust the analyst, and as well as with the parents, in order to help them support the analysis both emotionally and realistically.

One resolution to the conflicting approaches between the Kleinian view and the Anna Freudian view was accomplished with the development of defense analysis with children. This technique may be

an unacknowledged forerunner of Paul Gray's (2005) conceptualizations about the lag in the utilization of defense analysis with adults
(Hoffman, 2000).[1]

Anna Freud (1966) explained, "So far as we were concerned, we
explored above all the alterations in the classical technique as they
seemed to us necessitated by the child's inability to use free association, by the immaturity of his ego, the dependency of his superego,
and by his resultant incapacity to deal unaided with pressures from
the id. We were impressed by the strength of the child's defenses and
resistances and by the difficulty of interpreting transference, the im-
purity of which we ascribed to the use of a nonanalytic introductory
period. This latter difficulty was removed later by Berta Bornstein's[2]
ingenious use of defense interpretation for creating a treatment alliance with the child patient."

BERTA BORNSTEIN'S CONTRIBUTION
TO CHILD ANALYTIC TECHNIQUE

Berta Bornstein (1945, 1949) spelled out the technique of defense
analysis in children in papers that are still clinically and theoretically
applicable, yet rarely referenced. The development of the technique
of defense interpretation with children (whether the child partici-
pates in a four-time-a-week analysis or not), allows the analyst or therapist to observe, understand, and appreciate the value of the de-

1. In a personal communication, Paul Gray (2000) wrote, "As I suspect you anticipated I'm very pleased by your 'Exclusion of Child Psychoanalysis' contribution
[Hoffman, 2000]. You are quite right about this neglect. Your drawing attention to a
'virtual exclusion' of child analysis in my writings prompts me to reexamine my own
position. As a non-child psychoanalyst I've consciously resisted publishing my ideas
about this area. In my various activities with a series of child analysts I try to engage
their minds toward a greater sense of inclusion. My explicit, and consistent gratitude
toward Anna Freud has allowed me to experience a degree of 'inclusion' of adult and
child work that probably is not apparent except to those analysts with both adult and
child training with whom I regularly exchange ideas. . . . as I look in detail at my own
papers I am impressed with your noting my 'virtual exclusion'. Although I found that
I 'exclude' it from my references, I firmly espouse the idea[s] in Anna Freud's 'Normality and Pathology in Childhood' . . . which recognizes what I feel is the important
reference to transferences that derive from attachments to authority that are not primarily for purposes of gratification, but are for defense. As you know I regard this as a
central issue that is emphasized in close process attention for purposes of conflict and
defense analysis."

2. Bornstein was part of the original group of child analysts who worked with Anna
Freud (1945, page 7) in the 1920s.

fenses to the child and to point out (interpret) the defenses against unwelcome affects[3] (Becker, 1974).

In her analysis of Frankie, Bornstein (1949) describes the play of a boy who was reacting dramatically to the birth of a sister. In his play "a lonely boy of 4 was seated all by himself, on a chair placed in an elevated position. The child's father was upstairs visiting 'a lady' who, he informed us, when questioned, 'is sick or maybe she's got a baby, maybe—I don't know, never mind.' He made the point that newborn babies and mothers were separated in this hospital. Casting himself in the roles of a doctor and a nurse, he attended to the babies in a loving way, fed and cleaned them. However, toward the end of the play, a fire broke out. All the babies were burnt to death and the boy in the lobby was also in danger. He wanted to run home, but remembered that nobody would be there. Subsequently he joined the fire department, but it was not quite clear as to whether the firemen had started the fire or put it out. Frankie announced: 'Ladies, the babies are dead; maybe we can save you!' Actually only those lady patients who had no babies were rescued by him. The one whom he several times—by a slip of the tongue—had addressed as 'Mommy,' however, was killed in the fire" (page 185). Bornstein describes how this game was repeated for many weeks and it was clear that Frankie lived in continual fear of retaliation, developing a phobia, having to stay near his mother all the time.

Bornstein explains that she chose not to interpret the child's unconscious wishes to hurt his mother because that would force the child to face unbearable impulses of retaliating against the mother for bringing a rival to this world. Nor did she simply allow for cathartic expression, nor did she just reassure him, nor condemn him for his "babyish" behavior. Rather, she states,

> **In order to bring about an ego change we chose for interpretation from the different themes revealed in the child's play that element in which the patient represented his ego. It was evident to us that he himself was the lonely 4-year-old boy in the hospital game, although feelings of sadness and loneliness had not been mentioned by him in his play. On the contrary, in his game he demonstrated only the *defense against* loneliness and sadness.**

By placing the little boy's chair in an elevated position he had reversed the reality situation, presenting himself as omnipotent and successful. Thus he became a person who actually knew what went on

3. During a discussion, Betram Ruttenberg reported that during supervision with Bornstein, when a supervisee would say what he thought during a session, she would say, *"No, but what did you feel?"*

in the hospital, who directed the events, and who had no reason whatever to feel excluded and unhappy. The omnipotence, as well as the destruction of mother and infant, were used as defenses by which he denied the affect of sadness (page 187),

Bornstein's first aim was to help the child become consciously aware of his sadness before addressing his conflicts and anxiety over his aggression. She notes that *"it is noteworthy that the uncovering of recent emotions is often extremely painful for the child, more painful than the direct interpretation of deep unconscious content, which is frequently easily accepted by children and taken as a permission to obtain instinctual gratification"* (page 187 fn).

It is important to stress Bornstein's choice of technique as well as the techniques which she avoided. Bornstein:

1. Did not interpret unconscious wishes—i.e., aggression against mother (and baby)
2. Did not simply allow for catharsis
3. Did not simply reassure the child
4. Did not promote superego injunctions against his symptoms—i.e., she did not attempt to make him feel ashamed, guilty, or humiliated.

Rather, she focused on the child's defenses against his unbearable affects (sadness and loneliness) (see discussion below). The introduction of the need to understand the child's current emotional state and then interpreting the child's defenses against such painful affects proved to be a nodal point in the evolution of child analytic technique and child dynamic technique.

CONTEMPORARY CHILD ANALYSIS

Certainly a most important technique utilized by analysts is helping the child verbalize his or her feelings, the importance of which was highlighted by Anny Katan (1961). Unfortunately, many still consider that in a "classical" analytic approach the analyst's interventions (verbalizations) are predominantly "translation" procedures. For example, Mitchell (1998) states that "traditional classical interpretations were regarded purely in semiotic terms, as a decoding, a translation of the manifest meanings of the patient's associations into latent unconscious meanings" (page 839). Many have written about the counter-therapeutic value of the translation procedure involved when providing direct id interpretations to children. In fact, Bornstein (1945) stated, "As we know, play is the first important step in the process of sublimation. Continuous interpretation of its symbolic meaning is likely to upset this process before it is well established. For the same reason it seems preferable not to interpret children's drawings, stories, or other forms of sublimation directly, but instead to use them as a valuable source of information about the child. At a later stage we may employ the knowledge gained from plays, stories, and drawings, just as we use the knowledge gained from the observation of his symptom-formation and his resistance" (page 156). Yet more than a half century later we still have not fully incorporated the risks associated with direct symbolic interpretations of analytic material.

Fonagy and Target (1997) describe the dangerous sequelae of what they describe as a "classical approach," as exemplified by a reported analytic interchange in which the analyst confronted the child's underlying unconscious wishes with remarks, such as talking to the child "about [the child's] his wish already to do what father and grown-up men (the big guns) do and explained about holes in women's bodies" (page 60).

They argue that the "classical model" "by which the patient is helped to recover threatening ideas and feelings that have been repudiated or distorted as a result of conflict and defense" is a technique for a limited number of neurotic children (1997, page 66). For certain children, they maintain that utilization of "developmental help" and what has come to be called the "mental process model" of treatment is more effective because the analyst engages the patient by "focusing on the thoughts and feelings of each person and how the child understands these" (1997, page 67).

Arietta Slade (1994) provides another example of the countertherapeutic value of a direct "id or content interpretation" (page 102). She discusses how play with the child should be allowed to unfold without needing to prematurely decode the "meaning" of the play. Slade addresses the importance of integrating the child's affect in the play (page 92).

In this communication I stress that in what has come to be called "modern conflict theory," a defense analysis with children follows Bornstein's lead and highlights the central therapeutic value of understanding and interpreting defenses against affects. I need to reiterate and stress that with such an approach, I refer to a process whereby the analyst addresses the child's defensive maneuvers while avoiding direct confrontation of id content (at least for a long period of time).

In a series of papers, Yanof (1996a, b, 2000) discusses the lack of appreciation of analysis of defense in children. She discusses the decreased weight that has been given to interpretative techniques (in-

terpretation of defense and transference interpretation) in contrast
to, for example, more recent emphasis on the child's play itself as a
helpful promotion for the child's development. Unquestionably, in
doing psychotherapeutic or psychoanalytic work with children, non-
interpretive techniques are ubiquitous. These techniques (under
the general rubric of "developmental help") include external management such as setting limits and education (see for example,
Abrams 2003; Anna Freud, 1974; Fonagy and Target, 1997, page 61;
Kennedy and Moran, 1991; Lament and Wineman, 1984; Miller,
1996). The younger or the "more" disturbed the child, the more often does one have to utilize non-interpretive techniques. Interestingly, Sugarman (2003) discusses how developmental interventions,
such as physically having to set limits, may, in fact, be examples of
"transference of defense interpretations at a concrete level" (page
189). In other words, the analyst communicates via his or her actions (not just with words).

Chused (1996) has also stressed the paramount importance with
children of the analyst's developmentally appropriate non-verbal
communication to the child, whether the child is "neurotic" or "developmentally delayed." Since children often have difficulties in
hearing the analyst, alternative ways have been devised in communicating interpretations to children, such as talking about other children rather than about the patient him- or herself.

In addressing the difficulties analysts encounter when they attempt
to directly and verbally address feelings with children, Yanof (1996)
adds that "verbal interpretations to children may fail not merely because they are verbal, but because we may tend to interpret drive derivative material. Despite this, the child has as much, if not more,
trouble than the adult in owning his own feelings and taking responsibility for them. **The child analyst may be tempted to call attention to
the unconscious wish or unacceptable affect and by so doing bypass
the child's defense.** This may increase the child's resistance and risk
cutting off further elaboration of material. In addition, bypassing the
defense restricts opportunities for the child to work on the maladaptive defense" (page 108).

In the final section of this paper I highlight two examples from the
literature (one by Judith Yanof and one by Peter Fonagy) which illustrate the hypothesis that often analysts do not explicitly highlight
how they address the affects against which the child is defending and
how they interpret those defenses, and instead focus on the potential
mutative aspects of other technical maneuvers. Without understand-

ing how children defend against an awareness of painful feelings, analysts will not be able to find ways of helping children achieve the "therapeutic benefit that can be gained when a child has an opportunity to express, verbalize, and understand intense feelings within the safety of an analytic situation" (Tyson, 2005, page 155). Certainly the data from these two cases do not prove the hypothesis (even inductively) that in all good psychodynamic treatments, interpretation of defenses against affects is critical. However, in these two representative cases (presented by two respected analysts to demonstrate two different techniques), the analysts, without expressly acknowledging the centrality of the intervention, interpreted the children's defenses against painful affects. It seems to me that this lends credence to my hypothesis.

ENGAGING A CHILD IN A THERAPEUTIC ENTERPRISE: ADDRESSING THE CHILD'S PAINFUL AFFECTS: TWO CONTEMPORARY VIGNETTES

AN ANALYTIC VIGNETTE BY JUDITH YANOF

In the most recent textbook of psychoanalysis in a chapter on "Technique in Child Analysis," Yanof (2005) does not refer to the use of interpretation of defenses against painful affects as an important technical intervention, even though, without naming it, she demonstrates how she utilizes this technique, which in fact, as I described above, she has discussed in detail in previous contributions (1996a, b, 2000).

In her most recent contribution, Yanof describes an analytic interaction with a 7 year old boy which she identifies as an example of "developmental assistance." This boy "lacked the perseverance and frustration tolerance necessary to stick to a task in order to overcome his learning disabilities . . . [Yanof goes on to describe how] during the analytic sessions, Robert began to use Legos for the first time . . . [The] objects were difficult to build . . . [And] he began to complain that he could not do it—that he was not smart enough to do it. He immediately demanded that I do it for him. I made a technical decision not to do it for him but to support his plan to build the object. I did not interpret conflict, but *I told him that learning how to do things was hard work and it made everyone feel like giving up*" (stress added) (page 276). Yanof reports that with continued encouragement, work, and support, Robert constructed increasingly difficult models.

In what way did Yanof's intervention help the boy? Yanof states that her work was an example of "development assistance." Was Robert's success a result of her encouragement and support? Was it a result of the comment in which she generalized (or universalized), that everyone who has difficulties feels like giving up? It is generally acknowledged that when an analyst or therapist universalizes problems, patients feel more at ease because of a diminishment in their sense of shame or sense of guilt. In this situation, as a result of Yanof's universalizing his feelings—*that everyone felt like giving up*— Robert could feel like he was not the only one with learning deficits who tended to give up.

However, is it accurate to say, as Yanof maintains, that she did not interpret conflict in this example? Certainly she did not infer unverbalized unconscious wishes and did not interpret conflicts over those inferred wishes. She did not make any symbolic translational comments. However, it seems to me that Yanof communicated to Robert that she understood his current and ongoing mental state—that giving up and failing (like in school) was much easier than allowing himself to experience unpleasant affects when something was very difficult for him to do.

Yanof understood the boy's defensive maneuvers (i.e., giving up in a myriad of ways) against very unpleasant affects (i.e., the affects associated with difficulty in doing his work) and communicated her understanding to him (that is, interpreted) the meaning of his "giving up" in an elegant, succinct way that utilized the common technique in child analysis of displacing the issue onto other people.

One could conjecture, although we do not have corroborating associations, that the experience of feeling understood allowed the boy to accept her continued encouragement and support. One would hope, of course, that with the ongoing analytic work he could tolerate the affects associated with his difficulties more easily and thus allow himself to try harder at his school-work (and allow himself to develop compensations for his learning disability).

If Yanof had not interpreted the defenses against his unpleasant affects, would Robert have accepted her support and her gentle rebuff when she did not help him do the project in the session? In other words, from the perspective of promoting the field of child analysis, one has to be very careful when one studies the impact of child analytic technique. One cannot rely on global judgments or descriptions when studying the effectiveness of a psychoanalytic or psychotherapeutic treatment. One cannot maintain that a child improved as a result of a "defense analysis," "developmental assistance," or a "mental process model" treatment. One has to examine the details of the interventions even as reported by the analyst in order to try to identify the nature of the supposedly mutative intervention.

AN ANALYTIC VIGNETTE BY PETER FONAGY

Fonagy describes a little 4-year-old girl's defensive exclusion of him during the beginning of their work together (Fonagy, Gergely, et al., 2002). Fonagy states that he "decided to tackle her anxiety directly, that a relationship with me would exclude her Mommy, which might make Mommy become angry and love her less. Although this allowed her to let her mother leave the room, her anxiety had not abated entirely. Being alone with me made her immensely anxious. She defended against the anxiety by taking command of the environment. She ordered me, in an agitated way, to rearrange the positions of the chairs, her play table, and even my big desk, and then she charged me with the task of controlling the lights, to help her to 'organize the show.' It was daylight, so it was clear that the lights stood for another aspect of the environment that she needed desperately to bring under her control. I felt that she was moving the external furniture, both to make the unfamiliar territory of the consulting-room as much hers as mine and to prevent us from moving forward in our dialogue about her state of mind. *I said that she felt worried she would be moved around by me, like she moved the furniture about. But while she moved the furniture, she didn't have to think about her worries.* Later, I added that it was terribly hard for her that our time together began and ended so abruptly, just as the light came on for such brief moments" (emphasis added) (page 271).

Fonagy says that the "refocusing on her psychic reality was helpful" and that she played cooperatively for the first time. He describes a process where he interpreted the meaning of various situations by communicating to the little girl that she was defending against anxiety. The analysis evolved to the point where he said, "I know some little girls who are very frightened of being so excited, because their thoughts make them feel hot and muddled and then everything goes wrong. She said, 'I think I am one of those girls'" (page 273).

Even though Fonagy utilizes other techniques, such as giving meaning to the girl's activities, he constantly focuses on the child's protection against thinking about her worries. One can see the similarities to Bornstein's technique in this opening of an analysis. Compare the brief interchange between Fonagy and his patient with

Bornstein's (1949) description of the evolution of the beginning of
her work with Frankie.

"In order to introduce this emotion into the child's consciousness
without arousing undue resistance, the loneliness of the little boy in
his game became the subject of our analytic work for several weeks.
The analyst expressed sympathy for the lonely child who is barred
from his mother's sickroom and who is too little to understand why
his father is admitted. Frankie responded to the analyst's sympathy
with growing sadness, which could be discerned only from his facial
expression. The analyst's sympathy made it possible for him to tolerate this affect.

Once he had been able to face his sadness, Frankie showed relatively little resistance when his specific situation was examined. We
asked whether by any chance he was a child who had been left alone
while his mother was in the hospital. Or had someone taken care of
him during that difficult period? He turned to his mother with the
question: 'Was I alone, Mommy?' and before she could answer, he
told about his father and his nurse's presence, adding that his nurse
would 'Never, never leave him alone'" (page 188).

CONCLUSION

Yanof's comment about how other people handle difficulties, Fonagy's comments about other little girls, and Bornstein's comment
about the boy in the game—all have the same aim *to help the child
address painful affects in order to master them more effectively.* As
Bornstein (1945) points out, "The child may lie about his daily experiences; but by observing his affects and their transformation we
make ourselves independent of his voluntary cooperation. If emotional reactions are distorted, as, for instance, when the child shows a
friendly smile instead of disappointment, or if he says, 'Who cares!'
or 'Skip it,' when we expect him to be unhappy, we know that the
normal course of affects and impulses has been upset. By minute observation we may gradually learn which situations in particular cause
the child to hide or to transform his affects, and—in favorable
cases—with whom the child identifies in his defense" (page 158).

There is a rich clinical literature in child analysis. It is important
that empirical investigators not jettison this literature as simply anecdotal data of no scientific value as some empirical researchers have
suggested. It may be possible to mine this literature to study systematically various aspects of treatment and technique, including thera-

peutic action. These systematic studies could be correlated with clinical studies and with findings from recorded treatments.

A few studies have provided evidence[4] that treatment notes bear some degree of systematic relationship to session material as documented through recordings. In an early study of this question, Knapp et al. (1966) compared treatment notes and transcripts for the first 10 minutes of two sessions; they concluded from qualitative examination that much of the essential clinical material was preserved. The gaps or biases in the notes primarily concerned the analyst's observations of his own expressions in the session.

Bailey et al. (in press) compared texts and notes for 20 consecutive 50 minute psychoanalytic sessions using computerized text analysis procedures. The analyst consistently wrote detailed process notes during sessions for all treatments; the tape recording was done for these 20 sessions only for purposes of the research. While the analyst felt the notes were quite complete, they in fact captured only 35 percent of the words on tape. The note coverage was essentially equivalent for analyst and patient, with the patient accounting for more than 85% of total contents of session and notes. The study also compared word categories measured using computer dictionaries: for the patient, the tape/note correlations exceeded .80 for all dictionaries, indicating considerable validity for these dimensions; for the analyst, the correlations ranged from .42 to .85, indicating, as in the Knapp study, somewhat lower, but still substantial validity with respect to the content and style of the analyst's productions.

It seems to me that child analysts can study micro-processes, including written case reports in the literature (such as the ones discussed in this paper) as well as process notes[5] in order to elucidate

4. At the New York Psychoanalytic Institute in collaboration with the Derner Institute in Psychology of Adelphi University, we have begun a Systematic Evaluation of 5 Decades of Treatment Notes from The New York Psychoanalytic Treatment Center of adult patients utilizing automated measures as developed by Wilma Bucci and Bernard Maskit (2005) and comparing them to clinical evaluations. This paragraph and the following one (in text, above) are excerpted from a detailed description of the project (Wilma Bucci and Leon Hoffman, Co-Principal Investigators).

5. In order to study narratives of detailed case reports of children and adolescents (including detailed case reports written for the literature), we will utilize a variety of automated language measures as developed by Wilma Bucci and Bernard Maskit. The language measures will enable us to identify nodal points in the treatment (e.g., points of valuable analytic work, points of potential disruptions in the treatment, interventions by the analyst to repair potential disruptions, points in the treatment where repair was not accomplished, etc.). Detailed process notes around such nodal

310   *Leon Hoffman*

particular interventions and their impact on the child. In other words, we need to better elucidate the "operative factor in the therapeutic action," to use Strachey's (1934) vocabulary or the "treatment mediator," in the contemporary research lexicon.

BIBLIOGRAPHY

ABRAMS, S. (2001). Summation-Unrealized Possibilities: Comments on Anna Freud's Normality and Pathology in Childhood. *Psychoanalytic Study of the Child* 56: 105–119.

ABRAMS, S. (2003). Looking forwards and backwards. *Psychoanalytic Study of the Child* 58:172–186.

BAILEY, E., BUCCI, W., MERGENTHALER, E., & GREER, J. (in press). What do process notes contain? An empirical test of data equivalence between transcribed tape recordings and psychoanalytic process notes using computerized text analysis procedures. *Psychotherapy Research.*

BECKER, T. E. (1974). On Latency. *Psychoanalytic Study of the Child* 29:3–11.

BIBRING, E. (1954). Psychoanalysis and the dynamic psychotherapies. *Journal of the American Psychoanalytic Association* 2: 745–770.

BLATT, S. J., & BEHRENDS, R. S. (1987). Internalization, separation-individuation, and the nature of therapeutic action. *The International Journal Psychoanalysis* 68: 279–298

BORNSTEIN, B. (1945). Clinical Notes on Child Analysis. *Psychoanalytic Study of the Child* 1: 151–166.

BORNSTEIN, B. (1949). The Analysis of a Phobic Child—Some Problems of Theory and Technique in Child Analysis. *Psychoanalytic Study of the Child* 3: 181–226.

BRENNER, C. (1996). The Nature of Knowledge and the Limits of Authority in Psychoanalysis. *Psychoanalytic Quarterly* 65: 21–31.

BRENNER, C. (2002). Conflict, Compromise Formation, and Structural Theory. *Psychoanalytic Quarterly* 71: 397–417.

BUCCI, W. (2005). "Process Research." In Person, E. S., Cooper, A. M., & Gabbard, G.O. (ed.) *The American Psychiatric Publishing Textbook of Psychoanalysis.* Washington: American Psychiatric Publishing, Inc., 317–333.

BUCCI, W., & MASKIT, B. (2005). Building a weighted dictionary for Referential Activity. In Y. Qu, J. G. Shanahan, J. Wiebe (ed.) *Computing Attitude and Affect in Text.* Dordrecht, The Netherlands: Springer.

BUSH, F. (1992). Recurring Thoughts on Unconscious Ego Resistances. *Journal of the American Psychoanalytic Association* 40: 1089–1115.

points will be examined with the automated measures. In addition, clinical evaluation of the material around the nodal points will be examined by experienced analysts blind to the study hypotheses in order to compare clinical evaluation with the conclusions of the automated measures. In future work, the process of psychotherapy and psychoanalysis will be compared using these measures.

CHUSED, J. F. (1996). The Therapeutic Action of Psychoanalysis: Abstinence and Informative Experiences. *Journal of the American Psychoanalytic Associa tion* 44:1047–1071.

CHUSED, J. F. (2000). Discussion: A Clinician's View of Attachment Theory. *Journal of the American Psychoanalytic Association* 48: 1175–1187.

FONAGY, P. (1999). Relation of theory and practice in psychodynamic therapy. *Journal of Clinical Psychology* 28(4): 513–519.

FONAGY, P., & TARGET, M. (1996). Predictors Of Outcome In Child Psychoanalysis: A Retrospective Study Of 763 Cases At The Anna Freud Centre. *Journal of the American Psychoanalytic Association* 44:27–77.

FONAGY, P., & TARGET, M. (1997). The Problem of Outcome in Child Psychoanalysis: Contributions from the Anna Freud Centre. *Psychoanalytic Inquiry* 17(S):58–73.

FONAGY, P., & TARGET, M. (1998). Mentalization and the Changing Aims of Child Psychoanalysis. *Psychoanalytic Dialogues* 8: 87–114.

FONAGY, P., & TARGET, M. (2002). The History and Current Status of Outcome Research at the Anna Freud Centre. *Psychoanalytic Study of the Child* 57:27–60.

FONAGY, P., GERGELY, G., JURIST, E. L., & TARGET, M. (2002). *Affect Regulation, Mentalization, and The Development Of The Self.* New York: Other Press.

FREUD, A. (1926). Introduction to the technique of the analysis of children. In *Writings Volume 1.* New York: International Universities Press, 1974, 3–69.

FREUD, A. (1936). *The Ego and the Mechanisms of Defense.* New York: International Universities Press, 1966.

FREUD, A. (1945). Indications for Child Analysis. *Psychoanalytic Study of the Child* 1: 127–149.

FREUD, A. (1966). A Short History of Child Analysis. *Psychoanalytic Study of the Child* 21:7–14.

FREUD, A. (1974). A psychoanalytic view of developmental psychopathology. *Writings Volume 8.* New York: International Universities Press, 1981, 57–74.

GRAY, P. (2000). Personal Communication.

GRAY, P. (2005). *The Ego and Analysis of Defense,* Second Edition, Northvale, NJ: Jason Aronson.

HOFFMAN, L. (1989). The Psychoanalytic Process and the Development of Insight in Child Analysis: A Case Study. *Psychoanalytic Quarterly* 58: 63–80.

HOFFMAN, L. (1995). Review of Hermine Hug-Hellmuth: Her Life And Work by George MacLean and Ulrich Rappen. New York/London: Routledge, 1991. *Psychoanalytic Quarterly* 64: 600–603.

HOFFMAN, L. (2000). The Exclusion of Child Psychoanalysis: Letters. *Journal of the American Psychoanalytic Association* 48: 1617–1618.

JONES, E. E., & ABLON, J. S. (1998). How expert clinicians' prototypes of an ideal treatment correlate with outcome in psychodynamic and cognitive-behavioral therapy. *Psychotherapy Research* 8:71–83.

JONES, E. E. (2000). *Therapeutic Action: A Guide to Psychoanalytic Therapy.* Northvale, NJ: Jason Aronson.

JONES, E., & PULOS, S. (1993). Comparing the process in psychodynamic and cognitive-behavioural therapies. *Journal of Consulting and Clinical Psychology* 61: 306–316.

KATAN, A. (1961). Some Thoughts about the Role of Verbalization In Early Childhood. *Psychoanalytic Study of the Child* 16: 184–188.

KAZDIN, A. E., & NOCK, M. K. (2003). Delineating mechanisms of change in child and adolescent therapy: methodological issues and research recommendations. *Journal of Child Psychology and Psychiatry* 44(8): 1116–1129.

KENNEDY, H. (1979). The Role Of Insight In Child Analysis: A Developmental Viewpoint. *Journal of the American Psychoanalic Association* 27(S):9–28.

KENNEDY, H., & MORAN, G. (1991). Reflections on the Aim of Child Analysis. *Psychoanalytic Study of the Child* 46: 181–198.

KLEIN, M. (1927). Symposium on Child-Analysis. *International Journal of Psycho-Analysis* 8:339–370.

KNAPP, P. H., MUSHATT, C., & NEMETZ, S. J. (1966) Collection and utilization of data in a psychoanalytic psychosomatic study. In L. A. Gottschalk and A. H. Auerbach (eds.), *Methods of Research in Psychotherapy*, New York: Appleton-Century-Crofts.

LAMENT, C., & WINEMAN, I. (1984). A Psychoanalytic Study of Nonidentical Twins—The Impact of Hemophilia on the Personality Development of the Affected Child and His Healthy Twin. *Psychoanalytic Study of the Child* 39: 331–370.

MILLER, J. M. (1996). Anna Freud: A Historical Look at Her Theory and Technique of Child Psychoanalysis. *Psychoanalytic Study of the Child* 51: 142–171.

MITCHELL, S. A. (1998). From Ghosts to Ancestors: The Psychoanalytic Vision of Hans Loewald. *Psychoanalytic Dialogues* 8: 825–855.

NEUBAUER, P. B. (1979). The Role of Insight in Psychoanalysis. *Journal of the American Psychoanalytic Association* 27(S): 29–40.

NEUBAUER, P. B. (2003). Some notes on the role of development in psychoanalytic assistance, differentiation, and regression. *Psychoanalytic Study of the Child* 58: 165–171.

SANDLER, J., KENNEDY, H., & TYSON, R. L. (1980). *The Technique of Child Psychoanalysis: Discussions with Anna Freud.* Cambridge, MA: Harvard Univ. Press.

SCHMUKLER, A. G. (1999). Use of Insight in Child Analysis. *Psychoanalytic Study of the Child* 54: 339–355.

SLADE, A. (1994). Making meaning and making believe: Their role in the clinical process. In: A. Slade and D. P. Wolf, *Children at Play: Clinical and Developmental Approaches to Meaning and Representation.* New York: Oxford University Press.

SLADE, A. (1999). Representation, Symbolization, and Affect Regulation in the Concomitant Treatment of a Mother and Child: Attachment Theory and Child Psychotherapy. *Psychoanalytic Inquiry* 19: 797–830.

SPENCE, D. P. (1984). Discussion. *Contemporary Psychoanalysis* 20: 589–594.

STRACHEY, J. (1934). The Nature of the Therapeutic Action of Psycho-Analysis. *International Journal of Psycho-Analysis* 15: 127–159.

SUGARMAN, A. (1991). Toward Helping Child Analysands Observe Mental Functioning. *Psychoanalytic Psychology* 11:329–339.

SUGARMAN, A. (2003). Dimensions of the Child Analyst's Role as a Developmental Object: Affect Regulation and Limit Setting. *Psychoanalytic Study of the Child* 58: 189–213.

TYSON, P. (1988). Psychic Structure Formation: The Complementary Roles of Affects, Drives, Object Relations, and Conflict. *Journal of the American Psychoanalytic Association* 36(S): 73–98.

TYSON, P. (1996). Object Relations, Affect Management, and Psychic Structure Formation. *Psychoanalytic Study of the Child,* 51:172–189.

TYSON, P. (2005a). Affects, agency, and self-regulation: Complexity theory in the treatment of children with anxiety and disruptive behavior disorders. *Journal of the American Psychoanalytic Association* 53: 159–187.

YANOF, J. A. (1996a). Language, Communication, and Transference in Child Analysis I. Selective Mutism: The Medium Is the Message II. Is Child Analysis Really Analysis? *Journal of the American Psychoanalytic Association* 44: 79–99.

YANOF, J. A. (1996b). Language, Communication, and Transference in Child Analysis I. Selective Mutism: The Medium Is the Message II. Is Child Analysis Really Analysis? *Journal of the American Psychoanalytic Association* 44: 100–116.

YANOF, J. A. (2000). Barbie and the Tree of Life. *Journal of the American Psychoanalytic Association* 48:1439–1465.

YANOF, J.A. (2005). Technique in Child Analysis. In Person, E. S., Cooper, A. M., and Gabbard, G. O. (ed.) *The American Psychiatric Publishing Textbook of Psychoanalysis.* Washington: American Psychiatric Publishing, Inc., 267–280.

ADULT DEVELOPMENT

Kafka's "Letter to His Father" and "The Judgment"

Creativity and Conflicts of Aggression

SAMUEL RITVO, M.D.

Kafka wrote "Letter to His Father" at the height of his conflict over marrying, which would be taking the parricidal step of equaling or surpassing his father. The conflicts of aggression took the form of self-blame and guilt while inflicting upon his father the behavior his father disliked and turning the aggression on himself in his guilt and victim-hood. Writing was his escape, and he could not risk it in the unpre-dictable vicissitudes of marriage. In "The Judgment" Kafka creates a total reversal of the father-son relationship but he cannot maintain it. The guilt prevails and the overthrow of the father is punished by death.

FRANZ KAFKA'S "LETTER TO HIS FATHER" (1954) AND "THE JUDGMENT" (1952) provide a unique opportunity to study the conflicts of aggression in coming of age as Kafka struggled with them and to examine the function of creativity in this struggle. Coming of age here refers to the biopsychosocial developmental steps to adulthood by which one chooses an occupation, finds a mate, and founds a family. In the Letter, Kafka explicitly identifies these as "the utmost" a man can achieve (at the time, the saying in Kafka's Prague was "A man is not a man without a wife"). Biologically, it is the preservation of the species; psychologically, it is coping with the conflicts that arise in the process by which the rising generation, challenging and overthrow-

Clinical Professor of Psychiatry, Child Study Center, Yale University School of Medi-cine; Training Analyst Emeritus, Western New England Institute for Psychoanalysis.
The Psychoanalytic Study of the Child 62, ed. Robert A. King, Peter B. Neubauer, Samuel Abrams, and A. Scott Dowling (Yale University Press, copyright © 2007 by Robert A. King, Peter B. Neubauer, Samuel Abrams, and A. Scott Dowling).

ing authority, displaces the ascendant one; socially, it is the succession of generations in the contemporary cultural mode. This is the
broader meaning of parricide as set forth by Loewald (1900). The
process is driven by murderous, aggressive impulses. When these are
directed at parental figures toward whom there are also affectionate,
caring ties, there is a need for atonement as reflected in Kafka's addressing the Letter to "Dearest Father."

Franz Kafka, born in 1883, grew up in a well-to-do middle class Jewish family under a domineering father whose approval he could
never win. He was educated in the German language schools in
Prague, took a law degree in the German language university and
had a bureaucratic position in a semi-governmental insurance association which closed at two o'clock, leaving time for his writing. Except
for the last two years of his life, he lived in the family apartment, writing in his room until late into the night. He was part of a literary
group which included Franz Werfel, Martin Buber, and his close
friend Max Brod who encouraged him to publish his early works.

In 1919, at the age of 36, still living in his parents' apartment,
Kafka, having broken two previous engagements, was once more unable to take the step of marrying. In this crisis he wrote the 58-page
history of the relationship with his father which lends itself to an exploration of that relationship from a psychoanalytic perspective. The
trigger for the letter was his father's asking why Kafka maintained he
was afraid of his father. He replies that his fear is so great that he
could not speak about it but could express it in writing. This suggests
that he did not trust himself to maintain control of his feelings in a
direct confrontation with his father; that even a speech action was
too dangerous for fear of the feelings and impulses that would be
aroused. In the quiet and solitude of his room at night he could
safely create a confrontation.

In the Letter, he cites his father's harshly critical, demeaning attitude and behavior and the effect it had on him. The Letter also provides insights into the ways he dealt with his own hostility toward his
father. One way was to accept the personality his father assigned to
him and in turn inflict it on his father as an expression of his hostility.
In this sense he is both victim and persecutor, roles that feature
prominently in his writings. He feels he is not charged with anything
improper or wicked except for his latest marriage plan. However, he
does feel that his father, who stresses how he worked hard all his life
and sacrificed everything for his ungrateful son, accuses him unfairly
of coldness, estrangement, and ingratitude. This is immediately followed by a gesture of atonement. He avers they are both blameless

and hopes this will diminish his father's unceasing reproaches. He would have been happy to have such a man as a friend, grandfather, uncle, or chief, but as a father he was much too strong for him and he was too weak to bear the brunt of it. In other words, he wished his father had been more of a mentor than a tyrant. In that case he would have had a strong, positive tie to a wise and faithful counselor and the assertive steps necessary to supersede the father would not have taken on such a hostile, guilt-producing significance. The mentor has an important maturational function, especially for the adolescent: he provides a safe, encouraging relationship with the ascendant generation at the time when the assault on the "King of the Hill" is being carried out (Ritvo 2003; Winnicott 1969).

Here Kafka introduces another theme of the conflict. He sees himself as a Lowy, his mother's family, with a certain basis of Kafka. He feels the Kafka is latently there but not set in motion by "the will to life, business and the will to conquest," implying an inhibition of the assertiveness necessary to match or surpass his father, an inhibition he assigns to the maternal side of his lineage. His father, the true Kafka, has all the qualities of strength and health, while he, the Lowyish spur, operates "more secretly, more diffidently and sometimes fails to work entirely." This characterization of himself, which can be viewed as a defense against the dangers of his aggressive impulses, goes in the direction of a feminine masochistic identification modeled on his mother's relationship to his father. He depicts his mother as utterly devoted to the father, tending to his needs at home, a dedicated worker in the business, dutifully devoted to the children, but apparently not shielding or supporting Franz against the abuse by his father.

The conflicts of aggression against his father appear again when he observes how different they are and in their difference so dangerous to each other. He would simply be trampled underfoot until nothing was left of him. In another gesture of atonement he asserts that he never believed any guilt to be on his father's side. His father could not help having that effect but should stop considering it some particular malice on Franz's part that he succumbed to that effect. This passage speaks strongly for the view that the behavior and demeanor that so irritated his father was a mode of expressing his hostility toward his father as well as a manifestation of his suffering. The conflict this generated can be heard in his repeated expressions of guilt as in the self-critical feelings of suffering, sadness, despair, and worthlessness he turned on himself.

At the point when he negates his malice he turns defensively to

memory. He recalls the only episode of his early years of which he
has a direct memory:

> Once in the night I kept whimpering for water, not, I am certain, be-
> cause I was thirsty, but probably partly to be annoying, partly to
> amuse myself. After several vigorous threats had failed to have any ef-
> fect, you took me out of bed, carried me out onto the pavlachek (bal-
> cony) and left me there alone for a while in my nightshirt, outside
> the shut door. I am not going to say that this was wrong—perhaps at
> that time there was no other way of getting peace and quiet that
> night—but I mention it as typical of your methods of bringing up a
> child and their effect on me. I dare say I was quite obedient after-
> wards at that time but it did me inner harm.

Condensed in this memory is the dreadful, frightening experience
of being overwhelmed, helpless and completely at the mercy of the
powerful father. But we must also bear in mind that the child can set
off and partake of this power by whimpering for water, as Kafka recognizes when he says "partly to be annoying."

The sense of nothingness that often dominates him, he says, comes
largely from his father's failure to encourage him, except when his father's sense of self-importance is at stake. Here Kafka has another
weapon—he can damage his father just as his father damages him.
He cites his father's rhetorical methods of upbringing: abuse,
threats, irony, spiteful laughter, and self-pity. Their profound effect
on him included a veiled hostile response—he became "a glum, inat-
tentive, disobedient child always trying to escape from something
and in the main to escape within oneself so you suffered and we suffered," in this way inflicting suffering on one another and on himself.
When his father showed signs of loving feelings as when his mother
was gravely ill or when he himself was ill, he would lie back and weep
for happiness. These moments of gratification of the wish to love and
be loved brought momentary relief from conflict although it suggests
that being ill or endangered, which raises the specter of loss, is a condition of that caring love.

To assert himself wittily and from a kind of vengefulness, he observed, collected, and exaggerated what he called "little ridiculous
things" about his father. He was happy about them. They were for
him an occasion for whispering and joking which his father sometimes noticed and was angry. Franz is quick to reassure him that it was
not malice but a means of attempted self-preservation not only compatible with the profoundest respect but part and parcel of it.

He likens his mother's role to that of a beater in a hunt. But he is
quick to add that she performed the role unconsciously. Her kind-

ness and good sense forestalled any likelihood that he might have responded with open hostility to his father's mode of upbringing with defiance, dislike, or hate, but inclined him again to his mode of provoking his father by being what his father disliked. Mother shielded him secretly from his father, by giving him something or allowing him to do something. This only made him feel guilty and worthless, one who could only get what was his right by underhanded methods. He could get protection from her but only in relation to father: she loved father too much and was too loyal and devoted to him "to constitute an independent and spiritual force in the child's struggle."

He devotes considerable thought to the place of Judaism in the relation to his father. He found little means of escape from his father in Judaism nor did it provide a shared intellectual and spiritual interest where they might have found each other and proceeded from there in harmony.

The only place of his own to which he could escape was his writing. That his father disliked his writing and all that, unknown to him, was connected with it, enhanced the escape value. With his writing he could get some distance away from his father. It was a treasured possession achieved by his own assertion. Writing provided a safe space, a mental distance. He could write in his room at night with his family around him. He likened himself to the worm that "as a foot tramples on the tail end of it, breaks loose with its top end and drags itself aside." Through his writing and the fantasy life from which it is derived, he defiantly survives his father's attack, secretly welcoming his father's immediate dislike of it. Though his vanity suffered from these attacks he was glad of them "not only out of rebellious malice, not only out of delight at a new confirmation of my view of our relationship, but quite spontaneously, because to me that sounded like 'Now you are free.'" Creativity, writing, and the fantasy out of which it is born is freedom. It is also a sublimated form of the hostile, rebellious impulses against his father. "My writing was all about you; all I did there, after all, was to bemoan what I could not bemoan upon your breast. It was an intentionally long drawn-out leave-taking from you. . . ." This enigmatic sentence can be read as the writing being a form of leave-taking, riddance or overthrowing of his father, a thought which ruled his life in childhood as a premonition, later as a hope, still later as despair—"dictating my few little decisions to me."

The parricidal conflict of aggression appears again when he tells how the difficulty in asserting himself affected the decisions involved in progressing in school and choosing a career. He suffered such anxieties of "the very deepest kind about asserting my spiritual existence that everything else was a matter of indifference to me." He declared that his sole defense against the destruction of his nerves by fear (of his father) and a sense of guilt was to be the "coldly indifferent, childishly helpless, brutally complacent child." Here the sense of guilt again opposes the hostile, malicious impulses toward his father, barely contained in the brutally complacent child.

In turning the aggression on himself he focused on the closest object, his own body. His hypochondriacal preoccupations included worries over his hair falling out, spinal curvature and "intensifying in innumerable gradations, finally ending with a real illness,"—the tuberculosis which ended his life only five years later. He was amazed by his good digestion. When that failed, "the way was open to every sort of hypochondria until finally under the strain of the superhuman effort of wanting to marry . . . blood came from the lung." He laid a share of the blame for this on the atmosphere in the apartment he took over for a while from his sister Ottla because he believed he needed it for his writing. This, too, was likely a hypochondriacal response to an assertive step because he viewed Ottla as an ally in the struggles with his father. She had no contact with the father and was determined to make her way alone.

Every progressive, successful step in school engendered expectations of the worst outcomes and evoked the image of his father's expression, indicating that success was a forbidden parricidal step. At the decisive moment of graduating from the Gymnasium, when the career decision could not be avoided, everything around him interested him "pretty much as a defaulting bank clerk, still holding his job and trembling at thought of discovery, is interested in the small current business of the bank, which he still has to deal with as a clerk." (Here we can see the model for K. in *The Trial*). Shunning ambition and satisfaction in mastery, he drifted into the law, a profession which allowed him to indulge his indifference without injuring his vanity. With foresight and premonition he had recognized his attitude of passivity and resignation as present since childhood—self-imposed constraints which both provoked the father and bowed to his criticisms.

However, he claims no foresight whatever about the significance and possibility of marriage, "up to now the greatest terror of my life that has come upon me unexpectedly" and loomed as a grimly bitter ordeal. Marriage became a hopeful attempt at escape and the failure was correspondingly great. On the one hand were concentrated all the "positive forces," that is, active, assertive forces which would serve his own best interests. On the other hand were gathered "with downright fury" all the negative forces which were the result of his father's upbringing—weakness, lack of self-confidence, and the sense of guilt which formed a barrier between himself and marriage. With this recognition of the negative forces which he attributes to his father's treatment of him and which he directs against himself, he comes close to realizing that he is not only the victim of his father's harsh treatment but that he is also the victim of his rage against his father which he turns upon himself.

With this preface he engages the crucial issue of marriage "that . . . high step which is impossible for him to climb even by exerting all his strength, that step which he cannot get up and which he cannot get past either." For him "marrying, founding a family, accepting all the children that come, supporting them in this insecure world, and even guiding them a little as well, is the utmost a human being can do at all." This is what he feels his father did not do for him; his father did not rear him to fulfill this role.

He asks himself why he did not marry. In response he describes the agonies he suffers when he faces that step: he can no longer sleep, his head burns day and night, life can no longer be called life, he staggers about in despair. It is not the worries that bring this about. The worries are "like worms completing the work on the corpse." The decisive blow comes from "the general pressure of anxiety, of weakness, of self-contempt." Trying to explain this more fully he brings the parricidal conflict closer to conscious awareness: marriage would be the most acute form of self-liberation and independence; he would achieve the highest thing and would be the equal of his father; shame and tyranny would be mere history. He likens himself to a prisoner who wants to escape and at the same time rebuilds the prison as a pleasurable place for himself. Marrying would be the greatest thing of all and would provide the most honorable independence but at the same time it is in the closest relation to father, so that getting out of the prison has a touch of madness about it.

The prospect of a close relation to his father lures him toward marrying. There would then be an equality between them, an equality his father would understand: "I could then be a free, guiltless, upright son and you could be an untroubled, untyrannical, sympathetic, contented father," what he always longed for and resented never having. It would make it easier to take the big step. He would feel empowered, entitled and no longer trapped by the conflicts of the past. Marriage is barred to him because it is his father's domain. Another reason to fear marriage is that if he were to have a son like himself—mute, glum, dry, doomed—he would find him unbearable. He seems to be aware that this is what, in his hurt and anger, he inflicted on his father.

He turns again to his writing. His greatest concern is about himself. His writing and all that is connected with it are his attempts at independence and escape. Typically, he is quick to add that nothing much will come of it. But he must watch over it and guard against dangers to it. Marriage presents the possibility of such a danger. He makes it quite clear that the greatest obstacle to marriage is the underlying parricidal conflict: he cannot see himself matching his father's strength that enabled him to support and in his own way guide a family. He adds the critical note that for all his strengths, his father failed where the children were concerned. He quickly turns on himself again; he, too, would find such a son unbearable.

Kafka closes the letter with an imagined rejoinder by his father in which he attacks himself in his father's voice. He justifies his father's reproaches, especially the charge of insincerity, obsequiousness and parasitism. In the end he feels that with the Letter they have come closer to the truth which will make their living and their dying easier. He anticipates his death, the ultimate aggression against his father and against himself.

The Letter was never sent.

The Judgment

In the midst of his struggle in 1912 over marrying, Kafka gave creative expression to the conflict in "The Judgment," a story he wrote in one night in his room in the family apartment. In the story the figure of a young man in search of mature identity is split into two characters—Georg Bendeman, who has taken over his aging father's business, and his anonymous friend who, dissatisfied with his prospects at home, has run away to Russia and, in poor health, is carrying on a failing business in St. Petersburg.

In a letter to his friend, Georg is considering advising him to return home but is concerned that his friend would feel humiliated as a failure. Georg, whose mother has died two years before, is sharing a household with his father and is engaged to be married. In this split identity, one figure is dealing concretely with the search for independence and safety in the parricidal struggle by putting physical distance between himself and the parent, an attempt that seems doomed to failure, while the other has dared to take over the father's position and is going to marry—the giant steps his friend cannot take. In creating these polar opposites Kafka gives expression to the internal struggle over his parricidal impulses and for the moment fantasies taking over the father's business and marrying, while simul taneously keeping in mind the self-punitive prospect of failure.

Here Kafka introduces the mother and marriage as a source of the father's power. During the mother's lifetime, the father insisted on having everything his own way, so Georg was hindered from developing any significant activity of his own. Since her death, the father has lost his strength and is much less assertive. The uneasiness with his own success is reflected in Georg's difficulty in letting his friend know about his flourishing business while his friend's business is failing. He can only write him about his engagement on the insistence of his fiancée, whose name is Frieda (peace) Brandenfeld (joy, revelry). Here we can note that Kafka dedicated "The Judgment" to F. and at the time he was engaged to Felice Bauer of Berlin, carrying on the relationship largely by correspondence, as Georg does with his friend in St. Petersburg.

Georg goes into his father's room to show him the letter. In one sentence he describes his father's failing vision. In the next, still awed by him, he remarks that his father "is still a giant of a man." He tells his father that, out of consideration for his friend, he had not wanted to tell him about the engagement, but finally decided to do so. The weakened father suddenly turns on him and accuses him of fabricating—he has no friend in Russia. He further accuses him of taking advantage of the father's infirmities to take over the business, infirmities aggravated by the death of "our dear mother," as though she were mother to both of them. Her death has struck the father harder than it has the son, again implying that the mother was a strong supporter of the father's power, a support she did not supply to Georg. This passage can be read as a variant of the oedipal conflict. Georg is accused of overthrowing the father who no longer enjoys the power-affirming effects of marriage, which Kafka cannot permit himself.

Stunned by his father's accusations, Georg begins to retreat from his dominant position. He responds with tenderness and concern for his father's frailty. He offers to close the business if it is undermining his father's health. He prescribes a detailed regimen for his father's care, much as a mother would in nursing an invalid child. Then, in a startling reversal of Kafka's early memory of his father carrying him onto the balcony at night and leaving him there alone, Georg picks up his father to carry him to his bed. He has a dreadful feeling when he notices that the "old man at his breast was playing with his watch chain. He could not lay him down for a moment, so firmly did he hold on to the chain." Kafka creates this surprising

scene which evokes a number of images: the roles of parent and child
are completely reversed; the dead mother returns with the infant at
her breast who could be father or son of both, father and son are in
atonement, literally, physically at one in a body metaphor.

The loving union is only momentary. As soon as he is covered up as
with a shroud, the father jumps up in full vigor and accuses Georg of
wanting to incapacitate and immobilize him, i.e. overthrow the father, so he could then marry. The strongest comment Georg can
make is "You comedian!," as though the father's voicing of this murderous thought is unbearable and must be denied by reducing the father to a comic figure. The father mocks Georg for being such an
easy prey to seductive feminine tricks and being ready to betray his
friend, disgrace his mother's memory, and stick his father into bed so
that he cannot move. Here Kafka has the father accusing Georg of
the hostile impulses toward his father that he himself is struggling
with. Father gloats that he is the stronger of the two because Georg's
mother has given him so much of her strength. This can be read as
implying that Kafka felt his mother did not support or value his male
assertiveness as she did the father's.

The father reveals that he has been in league with the friend and
ridicules Georg for taking so long to grow up, for being so self-cen-
tered, "an innocent child, yes, but still more truly a devilish human
being!—and therefore take note: I sentence you to death by drowning!" Again, in the father's voice, Kafka attacks himself as evil. As
Georg rushes down the staircase he runs into his charwoman who
cries out "Jesus" and covers her face. Driven toward the water he
rushes to the bridge and swings himself over the rail "like the distinguished gymnast he had once been, to his parents' pride"—a penul-
timate effort, as a Christ-like figure, to redeem himself and his parents.

In search of atonement, Kafka ends the story with an enigmatic expression of love for his parents which can be read as a love rooted in
the suffering they inflicted on one another. His last words are "Dear
parents, I have always loved you all the same."

Kafka's diary entry on the day following the long night of writing
gives us entrée to his state of mind while writing: " . . . The fearful
strain and joy, how the story developed before me, as if I were advancing over water. Several times during the night I heaved my entire
weight upon my back. How everything can be said. How for everything, for the strongest fancies, there waits a great fire in which they
perish and rise up again . . . Only in this way can writing be done,
only with such coherence, only with such a complete flinging open of

body and soul." (Glatzer, 1974, pp. 52–53). When asked by Gustav Janouch about the reality context in which the story was written, Kafka replied: "The Judgment is the ghost of a night." When Janouch says: "And yet you wrote it." Kafka responds: "That is only the verification and so the complete exorcism of the ghost" (p. 53). These comments indicate that the night of writing that produced "The Judgment" was a time of discharge in fantasy of the conflicted feelings toward his father in an effort to exorcise them—murderous impulses as well as tender, caring feelings. He exorcized the ghost only momentarily but created a lasting story, admired by the world, in which he turns the destructiveness against himself just as he did in life.

Juxtaposing "The Letter" and "The Judgment" lets us see that writing did provide an escape into fantasies of magical reversal of roles which he could present to himself and to the external world in that intermediate space of play, imagination and creativity. But in the end the tragic effects of the conflicts of aggression on Kafka's character and personality prevailed in the story as they did in life.

SUMMARY

Kafka wrote the "Letter" at the height of the conflict over marrying which, in his words, is to achieve the "utmost," the parricidal step of equaling or surpassing his father. The hostility toward his father is countered by his fear of him, by his expressions of guilt and the search for atonement. The expressions of guilt together with the acknowledgment and denial of malice towards his father warrant the hypothesis that inflicting upon his father the behavior his father disliked was one way of expressing his hostility and at the same time turning the aggression on himself in his victimhood. Writing was his escape and was so vitally necessary that he could not risk it in the unpredictable vicissitudes of marriage.

In "The Judgment" Kafka creates a total reversal of the father-son relationship but he cannot maintain it. The guilt prevails and the fantasied overthrow of the father is punished by death. The diary note on the morning after the long night of writing reveals his state of mind during the writing. His murderous and loving impulses gave rise to conscious fantasies in which the "ghosts" he created enacted the fantasies and were "exorcised" in the writing of the story. The story is then offered to an audience which is coping with myriad versions of these universal conflicts. The reader can then vicariously exorcize the ghosts stirred by his own fantasies or he might find them intolerable and put the book down. For Kafka writing was a necessary safe haven but, tragically, it did not alter his established mode of dealing with the conflicts of aggression in relation to his father by turning the aggression on himself. Five years after writing The Letter he died of tuberculosis at the age of 41.

BIBLIOGRAPHY

GLATZER, N. N. ED. (1974) *I Am a Memory Come Alive, Autobiographical Writings by Franz Kafka.* New York: Schocken Books.

KAFKA, F. (1952) "The Judgment," in: *The Selected Stories of Franz Kafka.* New York: Random House, pp. 3–18.

KAFKA, F. (1954) Letter to His Father. In *Dearest Father.* New York: Schocken Books, pp. 138–197.

LOEWALD, H. W. (1980) The waning of the Oedipus complex. In: *Papers on Psychoanalysis.* New Haven, Conn.: Yale University Press, pp. 384–404.

RITVO, S. (2003) Conflicts of aggression in coming of age: Developmental and analytic considerations; observations on reanalysis. *J. of Clinical Psychoanal.*, 12: 31–54.

WINNICOTT, D. W. (1969). Adolescent process and the need for personal confrontation. *Pediatrics*, 44: 752–756.

Transience During Midlife as an Adult Psychic Organizer

The Midlife Transition
and Crisis Continuum

CALVIN A. COLARUSSO, M.D., LIC.
and GUILLERMO JULIO MONTERO

The intent of this paper is to add to the psychoanalytic understanding of midlife by exploring the relationships among transience, uncertainty and time limitation; and their effect on intra-psychic conflict and change. After a presentation of definitions and relevant midlife development tasks, the focus shifts to a discussion of two of Freud's papers, "On Transience" (1916 [1915]) and "The Uncanny" (1919) in which Freud introduced important concepts that provide a foundation for psychoanalytic exploration of attitudes toward transience, uncertainty and death.

A major focus of the paper is a conceptualization of a developmental continuum from midlife transition to midlife crisis, rather than dichotomizing the midlife developmental process as either transition or crisis, followed by a discussion of three basic ways of processing the continuum and six common ways in which midlife pathology and/or more normative developmental progression are expressed.

Calvin A. Colarusso is Training and Supervising Analyst in Child and Adult Psychoanalysis, San Diego Psychoanalytic Institute; Clinical Professor of Psychiatry, University of California at San Diego. Guillermo Julio Montero is Training and Supervising Analyst, Argentine Psychoanalytic Association; President of the Travesia Foundation (Psychoanalysis for Midlife Transition and Crisis).

The Psychoanalytic Study of the Child 62, ed. Robert A. King, Peter B. Neubauer, Samuel Abrams, and A. Scott Dowling (Yale University Press, copyright © 2007 by Robert A. King, Peter B. Neubauer, Samuel Abrams, and A. Scott Dowling).

Two detailed, clinical examples illustrate the theoretical concepts and focus, in particular, on clinical presentation and transference and counter-transference. The intention is to link theory with clinical understanding and technique.

> "It is quite true what philosophy says: that life must be understood backwards. But that makes one forget the other saying: that it must be lived forwards."
> —Søren Kierkegaard

> "Maturity of the adult man: it means having found again the seriousness he had while playing when he was a child."
> —Friedrich Wilhelm Nietzsche

INTRODUCTION

THE FOCUS OF THIS PAPER IS THE PSYCHOANALYTIC UNDERSTANDING of midlife (ages 40–60) by exploring the relationships among transience, uncertainty, time limitation, and intra-psychic change, the effects of which may stimulate normative developmental growth and progression or psychopathology and developmental arrest.

After a presentation of relevant definitions, literature, midlife development tasks, and ideas from two of Freud's papers, we will discuss transience; the midlife continuum from transition to crisis; and the results of the successful, or unsuccessful engagement of these profound issues of midlife on normal and pathological development. This theoretical material will be illustrated by two detailed clinical vignettes.

It is our belief that the developmental process is life long and that midlife is a particularly dynamic and conflicted phase in human experience.

PSYCHOANALYTIC VIEWS OF DEVELOPMENT
AS APPLIED TO ADULTHOOD

Rene Spitz (1965) defined development as "the emergence of forms, of function and of behavior which are the outcome of exchanges between the organism on the one hand, the inner and outer environment on the other" (p. 5). The essence of this definition, with which we concur, is that development is always a result of the *interaction* among the biological organism, the environment and the psyche, as they exist at any point in the life cycle. One pole may exert greater influence at various times, but never to the exclusion of the others.

Agreeing with Shane (1977), we see development as a life-long process, not limited to childhood and the formation of psychic structure, but also including the dramatic changes in psychic structure that occur during adulthood as a result of the interaction between the adult body as it ages, the increasingly complex adult psyche, and an ever-changing environment which, for most, is centered on marriage, parenthood, work, and play. This interaction is particularly dynamic and conflicted in midlife.

Freud's (1905) ideas about psychosexual genesis were the beginning of a psychodynamic understanding of development. His description of the five developmental stages of childhood—oral, anal, oedipal, latency, and adolescence—are the basis of psychoanalytic developmental theory.

Unfortunately, Freud did not carry his complemental theory through to adulthood, but building on this work, Erik Erikson (1963) did. In "Childhood and Society" he described the eight stages of man, polarities and characteristics of psychodynamic developmental theory from birth until death. Although Erikson addressed the entire life cycle, a major contribution, he did not describe a complex theory of development in adulthood. Building on Erikson, many theoreticians have since focused on the midlife years.

Daniel Levinson and colleagues (1978), in their psychological, but non-psychoanalytic studies, divided all of adulthood into alternating periods of stable structure and transition. The early adult transition (ages 17–22), midlife transition (ages 40–45), and the late adult transition (60–65) are periods of dynamic, often dramatic, change which occur because the intra-psychic and environmental "structures" which existed prior to each period of transition are no longer adaptable to the developmental challenges at hand. Although we do not agree with the chronological markings of each transition, seeing them as too narrow in scope and in years, the concept of transition, in the sense described by Levinson, is very relevant to this paper.

Others, such as George Vaillant (1977) and Calvin Settlage et al. (1988) either did not focus on the concept of developmental stages or abandoned the idea entirely. Vaillant studied the evolution and increased sophistication of mechanisms of defense over time and Settlage focused on psychodynamic and developmental process. Although the notion of developmental stages in adulthood is not as precise as in childhood—for example, a man can become a father at 13 or 80—there is a clustering of developmental experiences for most individuals during certain chronological periods. Thus, following Erikson, we divide the adult years into the following phases: Young Adulthood (ages 20–40), Middle Adulthood (ages 40–60),

Late Adulthood (ages 60–80), and Late Late Adulthood (age 80 and beyond).

The developmental phases of adulthood differ from those of childhood and adolescence in that the central biological phenomenon is aging, not maturation, and quasi-universal experiences such as marriage, parenthood and work or career development occur across decades rather than months or a few years as is the case in childhood and adolescence. Despite these differences, the conceptualization of developmental phases to describe the adult years is useful clinically and theoretically.

Margaret Mahler's (1975) *Separation-Individuation theory* has proved to be a very useful theoretical framework for understanding the emergence of the sense of self and other in early childhood. Her ideas have stimulated considerable thinking about the nature of individuation throughout the life cycle. Blos (1979) described separation-individuation phenomena in adolescence, using the term *second individuation*.

Extending Mahler's and Blos's concepts of individuation to describe the continuous process of elaboration of the sense of self in adulthood, Colarusso (1990, 1997, 2000) described the continuous process of elaboration of the sense of self in adulthood, introducing the terms third, fourth and fifth individuations to describe the processes of individuation in young, middle, and late adulthood.

Finally, any contemporary understanding of development of midlife is based, in part, on the seminal work of Eliot Jaques (1965), the first to use the term *midlife crisis* and relate such behavior to coming to terms with personal mortality which he saw as a coming to terms with the depressive position and a renunciation of such manic defenses as the denial of aging and the refusal to mourn.

A Psychodynamic Developmental Definition of Adulthood and the Developmental Tasks of Middle Adulthood

A Definition of Adulthood

Within this framework an adult may be defined as a physically and sexually mature individual who has engaged and attempted to master the developmental challenges of childhood and adolescence and whose intra-psychic life and real involvements are centered on the developmental tasks and challenges of young, middle, and late adulthood.

It is the perspective of this paper that midlife may be defined as that moment in every individual's life when the transient nature of personal existence becomes a defining issue in the intra-psychic and real worlds.

DEVELOPMENTAL TASKS OF MIDDLE ADULTHOOD

DEVELOPMENTAL PHASES AND TASKS

Developmental phases in adulthood may have greater usefulness if they are augmented by the concept of adult developmental tasks. Building on Anna Freud's (1965) description of developmental lines for the childhood years, Colarusso and Nemiroff (1981) described phase-specific developmental tasks for adulthood. These may be thought of as quasi-universal issues that must be addressed as one progresses through the phases of adulthood.

The following is a brief discussion of some of the developmental tasks of Middle Adulthood (40–60), chosen for their relevance to the subject matter of this paper. All have in common the shocking awareness of the constancy of change in self and others, and the inevitability of these developmental events. The need to confront them simultaneously disturbs the psychic equilibrium and forces a major reworking of the psychic structures established earlier in life, leading to a new understanding of what it means to be human. A detailed elaboration of each of these tasks, for those who wish to consider them in more detail, may be found in "Child and Adult Development" (Colarusso, 1992).

THE ACCEPTANCE OF TIME LIMITATION
AND EVENTUAL PERSONAL DEATH

Stimulated by biology and environment, by the aging process in the body, the death of parents and contemporaries, the growth of children into adulthood, grandparenthood and the approach of retirement, individuals in midlife come face-to-face with their mortality with the painful unavoidable recognition that the future is limited and that he or she will die.

This increased preoccupation with aging and time limitation leads to what Jung (1933) called midlife introversion and Neugarten (1979) called interiority. This assessment of personal successes and failures, increased scrutiny of relationships and growing preoccupation with the meaning of life is the midlife equivalent of the life review which Butler and Lewis (1977) described as a central aspect of late life development.

Cohler and Lieberman (1979) and Lieberman and Tobin (1983) conducted studies which indicated that individuals in midlife become concerned with health and have increases in anxiety, depression and decreases in self esteem. These symptoms are indicative of the intense internal tension resulting from the engagement of the developmental task of confronting time limitation and eventual personal death. When the result of this universal conflict is positive, as described by Levinson et al. (1978, 1980, 1996), a midlife transition has occurred. When the work is unsuccessful, the result is the onset, sometimes for the first time, of psychiatric illness (Guttman, Griffin, and Grunes, 1982).

The result of the intra-psychic struggle was expressed as follows by Cohler and Galatzer-Levy: "As a consequence of increased awareness of the finitude of life, both men and women intensify concerns with self and display less patience for demands upon time and energy which are actively experienced as being in 'short supply' . . . Realization of goals and reworking the presently understood story of one's life course in order to maintain a sense of personal coherence become particularly important in late middle age and require time and energy which is then less available for other pursuits." (Cohler and Galatzer-Levy, 1990, p. 226).

For some, the mental work occurs primarily at an unconscious level. These individuals often deny that time limitation or eventual personal death play any place in their mental life, but they demonstrate the same changes, normative and pathological, as their more explicitly aware counterparts. Should the analyst, usually in middle or late adulthood, utilize similar defenses, the major dynamic conflicts of midlife may be totally avoided or dealt with as derivatives of infantile conflicts, rather than becoming the focus of significant analytic scrutiny.

The acceptance of time limitation and eventual personal death greatly enhances the quality of life for healthy individuals by stimulating a reassessment of goals, a reordering of priorities, and a greater appreciation of significant relationships and the value of time. How this dynamic process occurs is a central consideration of this paper.

ACCEPTING THE AGING PROCESS IN THE BODY

Physical decline begins to affect psychological development in the 20s and 30s. However, by midlife, because of the obvious evidence of aging, the increase in major illnesses and the death of contemporaries, thoughts and feelings about the aging body become a major mental preoccupation and stimulate engagement of the developmental task of the acceptance of time limitation and eventual personal death.

MAINTAINING INTIMACY

Whereas the young adult is involved in developing the capacity for intimacy, the middle-aged person is focused on maintaining it in the face of powerful psychological, physical, and environmental pressures, interferences, and distractions. These include changes in attitudes about sex and sexual functioning because of aging and psychological preoccupation with developmental pressures and realistic demands of family, elderly parents, and work. The establishment of an active sexual life during young adulthood is so essential to adult identity and self-esteem that changes in sexual functioning due to the aging process in midlife is experienced as a significant narcissistic injury (that healthy individuals master and continue active sexual lives) and another reminder of the loss of youthful vigor and physical decline.

CHILDREN: THEIR IMPACT ON TRANSIENCE

Young adult parental vigor and the unchallenged control of young children go hand in hand, but so do the middle-age awareness of physical decline and time limitation and the inevitable loss of control of adolescent and young adult offspring. As the parent moves into the later stages of middle adulthood and the son or daughter into the second half of young adulthood, all vestiges of the "child"—and the young parent—disappear. Physically, the youthful appearance of the adolescent and the adult of the early 20s is gradually replaced by the mature young adult who may already show signs of aging. Simultaneously, the parent is dealing with the strikingly obvious signs of aging and illness in self, spouse and contemporaries.

RELATIONSHIP TO PARENTS — REVERSAL OF ROLES, DEATH, AND INDIVIDUATION

Nothing brings home the awareness of transience and the constancy of change more than the relationship between middle-aged children and their parents. At some point, as elderly parents become less able to care for themselves, a reversal of the roles in their lifelong relationships occurs. The "child" becomes the "parent" of the parent, increasingly fulfilling the roles of physical and mental caretaker. Parental aging stimulates the ongoing intra-psychic process of psychological separation from them. The acute reversal of roles that occurs when parents are unable to take care of themselves, or die, forces the middle-aged child to anticipate their own demise.

WORK AND MENTORSHIP: GENERATIVITY VS. REPLACEMENT BY THE YOUNG

The recognition of the juxtaposition of maximum achievement and power in the work place and the acceptance of loss and eventual displacement by the next generation is at the core of the midlife worker's intra-psychic life. Passing on knowledge and power to the next generation, while recognizing that this process leads to one's eventual displacement, is the essence of generativity (Erikson, 1963). In the healthy individual, the anger at and envy of the subordinate is not acted on to any significant degree. It is recognized, processed mentally, and sublimated into generativity.

Most of these developmental experiences and tasks are experienced in adulthood regardless of culture or class. Of course, culture and class have a profound effect on how intimacy, parenthood, work and other aspects of adulthood are experienced, as well as what material and social resources are available to the individual in coping with these challenges. There are differences in the adult experiences of men and women, but a description of those is beyond the scope or intent of this paper. The interested reader is referred to *Adult Development* (Colarusso and Nemiroff, 1981).

TRANSIENCE AND UNCERTAINTY

In his paper "On Transience" (1916a [1915]), written during the First World War, Freud's attention was understandably drawn to thoughts about loss and impermanence. Speaking of a poet and a friend he noted: "The poet admired the beauty of the scene around us but felt no joy in it. He was disturbed by the thought that all this beauty was fated to extinction, that it would vanish when winter came, like all human beauty and all the beauty and splendour that men have created or may create. All that he would otherwise have loved and admired seemed to him to be shorn of its worth by the transience which was its doom" (p. 305). This is an eloquent statement of the essence of the midlife struggle with the developmental task of the acceptance of time limitation and personal death written long before psychoanalysis had conceptualized developmental tasks. Interestingly, Freud was 59 years of age when he wrote this paper.

It is precisely the midlife feeling that one is no longer "young and active," as Freud put it (p. 307), that forces the confrontation with the notion of transience, time limitation, and eventual personal death—or the frantic race away from the realization in the form of a true midlife crisis.

Freud's use of the concept of transience, directly or indirectly, stimulated psychoanalysts to use other words in their attempts to elaborate on the subject. Jacques (1965) used the term constructive resignation, without reference to Freud's paper on transience; Kernberg (1980) spoke of change in the perspective of time; Colarusso and Nemiroff (1981) defined the developmental task of the acceptance of time limitation and eventual personal death; and Montero (1989) used the phrase re-signation of a personal project.

In the remainder of this paper we will use the term transience to refer to the sense of uncertainty, dread, awareness of time limitation, and eventual personal death that becomes a central organizing factor in the intra-psychic life of the midlife individual.

UNCERTAINTY AND DREAD: FREUD'S PAPER ON "THE UNCANNY"

In his paper called "The Uncanny" (1919), Freud related the feeling of the uncanny to "what is frightening—to what arouses dread and horror . . . it tends to coincide with what excites fear in general" (p. 219). Although not the main subject of his focus, Freud has a great deal to say about the attempts of human beings to deal with the idea of death.

Unlike his comments in "On Transience," here Freud makes an eloquent statement of how humans struggle to avoid and rationalize the idea of a personal end.

"Two things account for our conservatism: the strength of our original emotional reaction to death and the insufficiency of our scientific knowledge about it. Biology has not yet been able to decide whether death is the inevitable fate of every living being or whether it is only a regular but yet perhaps avoidable event in life. It is true that the statement 'All men are mortal' is paraded in text-books of logic as an example of a general proposition; but no human being really grasps it, and our unconscious has as little use now as it ever had for the idea of its own mortality . . . since almost all of us still think as savages do on this topic, it is no matter for surprise that the primitive fear of the dead is still so strong within us and always ready to come to the surface on any provocation" (pp. 242–243). These two insightful, seminal papers of Freud's have been relatively neglected and, in particular, their relevance to adult development theory has not been sufficiently appreciated; hence, our focus on the ideas about adulthood that they contain.

TRANSIENCE AS AN ADULT PSYCHIC ORGANIZER

Rene Spitz (1965) defined the term *psychic organizer* suggesting that the emergence of the smile response, stranger anxiety, and negativism during the first two years of life indicated that quantum leaps had occurred intra-psychically, namely the formation of new psychic structure that allowed the infant and toddler to engage the world with increased capability and complexity. The authors suggest that evidence of the successful engagement and mastery of the midlife developmental task of accepting transience (discussed later in this paper) is just as significant developmentally to the adult as the emergence of the smile response, stranger anxiety, and negativism in the first three years of life were to the child and thus indicates the need for the use of the term adult psychic organizer.

Colarusso (1992) anticipated the concept of an adult psychic organizer more than a decade ago when he wrote: "Thoughts and feelings about having a limited amount of time left to live increase in frequency and intensity and become *an extremely powerful organizer* (italics ours), forcing a significant reexamination of all aspects of the life that has been lived in the past; its present positive and negative aspects, particularly in regard to marriage, family, and work; and a reassessment of how to use the time that is left" (p. 165).

The establishment of an adult psychic organizer such as the acceptance of transience in midlife always implies a process which encompasses, paraphrasing Freud (1937), terminable and interminable vicissitudes (Montero, 2000a). Thus, the acceptance of transience is a "living" process which occurs continually throughout life, but coalesces and achieves its highest level of integration in midlife, indicating that the ego and superego have been permanently altered by the acceptance of the transient nature of all existence, including the self.

THE MIDLIFE CONTINUUM: FROM TRANSITION TO CRISIS

The intra-psychic and behavioral changes that result from the engagement of the developmental tasks of midlife have been frequently described as midlife transition or crisis. In order to begin a discussion of these phenomena we offer the following definitions.

Midlife transition may be described as the significant intra-psychic changes in psychic structure; self-representations; and attitudes toward the past, present and future that occur as the result of attempts to master the developmental tasks of midlife. When changes in behavior and relationships occur as a result of the midlife transition they are usually thoughtful, limited and do not disrupt critical life structures and relationships such as work or marriage that took many years to construct (Levinson, 1978, Colarusso and Nemiroff, 1981).

A true *midlife crisis,* on the other hand, is a radical, unconsciously driven, unreasoned overthrow of vital life structures and relationships, such as work and family, often at the same time. The powerful unconscious conflicts that precipitate these irrational behaviors are centered on the inability to face and accept transience and the refusal to engage the narcissistically injurious task of accepting the fact that not all of one's goals, ambitions, and dreams have been achieved or will be realized in this lifetime, thus precipitating the frenzied attempt to throw away the present and the past and to magically begin life anew, thereby denying the truth of transience and mortality. Although relatively rare, true midlife crises are real phenomena which we, and other psychoanalysts, have observed and treated (Jacques, 1965).

However, neither of these definitions addresses large numbers of individuals who fall along a continuum somewhere between these two polarities. When used in this sense, crisis refers to a marked degree of psychic discomfort that is experienced as psychic reorganization occurs, sometimes accompanied by change in a basic life structure such as a career, marriage, or location. When such changes are made, the effect on vital relationships and life structures is considerable. The decisions that result from such crises are not always good ones, and sometimes are regretted at a later time. For example, the result may be a pathological response such as depression, precipitated by the realization that vital life structures such as marriage or career have been abandoned and cannot be reclaimed or replaced with others as satisfying in the future.

Obviously, existing degrees of health and psychopathology—determined by past developmental experience, complementary series and biological factors—-affect the psychic strengths and weaknesses that each individual brings to the developmental challenges of midlife. The degree of psychic conflict surrounding these issues pushes the individual toward either the pole of healthy transition or pathological crisis.

Thus, we propose a continuum from transition to crisis that is specific to midlife. Every midlife person falls somewhere on the continuum because of the universality of the underlying developmental issues—aging, transience, death, the maturation of children, replacement by the young in the workplace, etc.—that are the root causes of midlife transition and crisis. These definitions encourage both a developmental (chronological) and dynamic perspective, both of which frames of reference are needed to truly understand midlife patients.

THREE BASIC WAYS OF PROCESSING
THE TRANSITION-CRISIS CONTINUUM

We pose three basic ways of processing the midlife transition-crisis continuum, based on Freud's (1916a [1915]) seminal ideas in "On Transience," referred to earlier. This is not meant to imply that these are the only ways that the transition-crisis continuum may be processed or that individuals may not show a blend of coping styles. Indeed, we would expect to see blended responses. The three basic styles are presented to provide a conceptual framework that facilitates a therapeutic understanding of each individual's reaction to the challenges of midlife.

The first, most positive way of processing the continuum involves Freud's concept of "transient value is scarcity value in time" (p. 305). We understand this to mean that as one progresses through the adult years, and particularly in midlife, the growing recognition of the finite nature of personal existence propels individuals to engage the midlife developmental task of coming to terms with transience.

Normal mourning processes are the agents for these developmental processes. Beginning in young adulthood and rising to a crescendo in middle adulthood, individuals mourn for the lost body of youth and assess the consequences of life-shaping decisions such as choice of career and spouse and the advent of children that were made in more youthful times. Mourning the deaths of parents, vital internal objects associated with security, stability and permanence since childhood, (that often occur during the midlife years) shatter youthful fantasies of immortality and become irrefutable indicators of transience. In addition, past and present conflicts are reworked within the midlife crucible of transience. Cohesive ego functioning and neurotic defense mechanisms facilitate transition phenomena, while weak ego functioning with primitive defense mechanisms such as those found in borderline and narcissistic patients push the individual toward the crisis end of the continuum.

Positive results of the acceptance and integration of the transient nature of all living things include a deeper and richer—if bittersweet—understanding of human existence, and as Freud noted, an enhanced appreciation of the beauty and fragility of living things such as daffodils in the spring and autumn leaves in the fall.

The second way of processing the midlife continuum involves "rebellion against the fact asserted" (p. 305). Instead of mourning for the youthful past and integrating the midlife task of transience, some individuals fly toward their lost past in a desperate attempt to recover it. A regressive response to the confrontation (often unconscious) with the inevitability of the end of the self, flying toward the past is a fruitless, often frantic attempt to bring to life once again a more youthful existence. Such behavior is often seen in both midlife transitions and midlife crises, but at different levels of expression. Relatively benign examples that may be seen in transitions are attempts to relive the past by dressing and acting like adolescent offspring and their peers, instead of maintaining age-appropriate parental roles and attitudes. More problematic examples include searches for young lovers, as reassurance of continued attractiveness and sexual prowess, and attempts to replace current marital partners, often of many years, with first loves from adolescence and young adulthood.

Clinical Example: Mr. A., a highly successful professional man of 60, sought a consultation because he could not get out of his mind a woman he had been in love with in his teen years, but had not seen since. He was not unhappy with his wife of thirty years but his feelings for her were "boring" when compared with the excitement and passion he experienced in his fantasies about his youthful love. Mr. A. rejected a suggestion to attempt to delay any action and explore his feelings but did agree to meet periodically while he made a determined effort to find her.

Using a private detective, he was able to locate her in a small town hundreds of miles away. After learning about her daily routine from the detective he secretly observed her from afar and was once again flooded with the feelings of love and passion he had experienced as a youth and in his current fantasies.

Feigning an accidental meeting, he encountered her on the street and introduced himself. Although she recognized him immediately, Mr. A. was deeply pained by her cordial but unenthusiastic response. However, she did agree to share a cup of coffee for "old time's sake" and listened with a shocked expression as he poured out his feelings of love. Would she come away with him? He had enough money to allow them to build a wonderful life together. This prominent man, known in his community for mature judgment and behavior, had not even asked about her current life circumstances, so totally had his judgment been overwhelmed by the intensity of his feelings.

He later came to appreciate "how gently she let me down" by first reminiscing about the pleasant memories she had of their "teenage love affair" before informing him that she was a happily married woman with four children, well established in the town in which she and her husband had chosen to live.

Mr. A. had heeded the therapeutic advice not to share his feelings or action with anyone other than the analyst so there were no consequences other than a sense of emotional devastation. Upon his return he sought an immediate appointment and began a twice per week psychodynamic psychotherapy. Issues of aging, boredom with his life and relationships and a lack of pleasure in the present and future quickly came to the forefront. But so did vivid dreams and masturbatory fantasies during which his sense of reliving the teenage love affair was so intense that for brief moments "I was 17 again. It was wonderful. I've had so much success in my life [he mused painfully], great praise from colleagues, a great family life, why doesn't it hold a candle to that first love?"

Gradually Mr. A.'s associations began to alternate between fantasies about his life as a teenager—which the analyst interpreted as less gratifying in many ways and more painful than the more mundane but continually sustaining pleasures of his current life. As his thoughts and feelings about approaching the end of life without realizing his dreams, such as the "teenage love affair," as his youthful lover expressed it, became clearer, the analyst was able to interpret his difficulty in accepting the dynamic tensions and conflicts surrounding the issues of transience. Mr. A. had been attempting to avoid facing his internal conflicts about aging and transience by "rebelling against the facts asserted" and rushing toward the past rather than accepting, working through, and integrating the painful developmental tasks of the present.

Transference phenomena played an important part in the work. This material was introduced when the patient began to ask the analyst how he was dealing with aging. Was he satisfied with his present life, with his "elderly" wife; had he realized all of his dreams? Eventually the patient's need to see the analyst as the Oedipal father who would attack him for his "foolish" sexual desires toward "this stranger," and also as the wise man who could tell him how to defeat aging, but refused to do so, was interpreted.

Countertransference themes centered around two contradictory attitudes. The analyst began to experience an unusually intense curiosity about the details of the patient's encounter with his first love. This triggered self analysis and associations about the analyst's own first love who, not surprisingly, was found to be much more exciting than his "elderly wife," as the patient so crudely put it. Fantasies of seeking out the adolescent beauty—as the patient had—were followed by the painful realization that, if still alive, she was in her late 60s. So much for a fruitless "rebellion against the facts asserted."

The second, and contradictory counter-transference trend, that stemmed from the same mix of envy of the patient's ability to act and the analyst's similar need to accept transience manifested itself in a strong, fortunately contained, desire to tell the patient to stop acting like an old fool and come to his senses. At times there were two old fools in the room.

Gradually Mr. A. begrudgingly accepted "the reality of my less than perfect life" and returned to his work and his wife more accepting, but still sad about being unable to recreate the past in the midlife present.

A third way of processing the midlife continuum is suggested by Freud's words, "the aching dependency" (p. 305). Unable to engage the midlife development task regarding transience, these individuals enter a painful period of stagnation which often takes the form of a depression. Dynamically, the depression often results from superego and ego ideal recriminations for not having lived up to youthful expectations in regard to career, marital choice, children, and appearance; or for failing to bring fantasies to realization before time ran out. In performing diagnostic evaluations on midlife individuals who present with depression as a prominent symptom, analysts should make specific attempts to explore the patient's attitudes toward transience. In working with individuals who come to analysis or therapy to deal with the unsatisfactory consequences of pressured midlife behavior, careful history taking will often reveal a period of depression preceding the precipitous unreasoned outburst of action.

PATHWAYS FOR THE EXPRESSION OF MIDLIFE DEVELOPMENTAL CONFLICTS

While processing the developmental tasks of midlife, each individual operates within a framework of his or her developmental experience and intrapsychic strengths, weaknesses, and conflicts. These issues and conflicts may be expressed through one or several of the following six facilitating avenues:

1. Expression through the body: The aging body is a prime source of midlife anxiety and may become a major vehicle for expressing developmental conflicts because of the incipient signs of aging and the not infrequent onset of serious illnesses. In extreme cases, psychoso-

matic illnesses may become the expression of desperate attempts to deny the unacceptable reality of transience.

2. Expression through sexual conflicts: These may take the form of sexual avoidance or frantic expressions of sexuality in attempts to deal with difficulty in accepting the loss of procreative function in the woman and diminished performance abilities in the male. In his study of female sexuality, Jones (1927) wrote of the fear of the sudden absence of all sexual desire, something he called *aphanisis*. We have seen this fear expressed by middle aged men, as well, who incorrectly assume that the normally occurring diminution in sexual performance which occurs in midlife will lead sooner or later to a complete loss of ability. This is expressed consciously as "if I can't have sex I might as well be dead" and unconsciously through equation with death itself.

3. Expression through interpersonal conflicts: Interpersonal conflicts may become the vehicle for the expression of conflicts related to transience when the partner is blamed for unacceptable changes in the self, such as aging in the body or diminished sexual performance. The use of projection as a means of disowning aspects of the self that are unacceptable leads to a diminution of closeness and intimacy in the relationship and often to the search for new, usually younger, partners who do not, at least initially, become reminders of aging and transience. These conflicts become even more powerful when both partners use projective identification mechanisms.

4. Expression through criticism of the self: When disorders of the self are present, feelings of emptiness, helplessness, futility, and hollowness tend to be prominent, as are feelings of grandiosity and archaic exhibitionism, interspersed with narcissistic rage (Kohut, 1971). In these individuals, who often are not involved in stable relationships, the rage and anger related to the struggles with transience are directed inward rather than projected onto others. Self-esteem, which is already fragile, is further battered because of the failure to somehow magically protect the self from the awareness of time limitation and aging.

5. Expression through precipitous action: The best example of this is the full blown midlife crisis, in which basic life structures which took many years to build are suddenly abandoned. The sudden move to another city, a new job or career, and a new partner may produce, for a time, a sense of invincibility and a conquest of aging and transience. Whether the individual remains in the newly created environment or returns to his or her former world, the eventual result is the same. Aging and time limitation, like the grim reaper, are still there

and must be faced. The complications which result from the precipitous changes involved in every midlife crisis inevitably make the acceptance of transience more difficult.

6. Expression through work and professional life: Being passed over for promotion or the loss of a job confronts the midlife individual with a real-life situation that must be managed. When the reasons for the dismissal or lack of promotion are related to displacement by younger workers, the issues of aging and the passage of time are forced into consciousness and must be dealt with, or greater efforts made to avoid them. Healthier individuals will deal with the narcissistic blow and seek out new avenues for work and pleasure; those who are burdened with significant internal conflicts may not make the needed transformation and act out, become depressed, or settle into a less than satisfying early retirement.

THE EFFECT OF TRANSIENCE ON NARCISSISM AND THE EGO IDEAL

In a manner similar to that expressed by Kohut (1966, 1971) we consider narcissism to be in a continuous state of evolution and transformation throughout the life cycle. The establishment of the adult psychic organizer implies that an adaptive transformation in the way the self accepts transience has occurred. This new integration occurs when the narcissistic injury experienced by each individual as he or she struggles to accept the idea of personal death is tempered and managed. When this normative process is arrested because of pathological processes, and the individual cannot mourn the loss of imagined immortality, development is impeded or arrested, a narcissistic fixation occurs and the individual moves toward the crisis end of the continuum.

Freud (1914c) described the futile attempt of parents to deal with narcissistic injury through their affection for their children. The following comments are particularly relevant to the midlife attempts to ward off the awareness of the inevitability of mortality. "If we look at the attitude of affectionate parents toward their children, we have to recognize that it is a revival and reproduction of their own narcissism, which they have long since abandoned. . . . The Child shall have a better time than his parents; he shall not be subject to the necessities which they have recognized as paramount in life. *Illness, death, renunciation of enjoyment, restrictions of his own will, shall not touch him; the laws of nature and of society shall be abrogated in his favour; he shall once more really be the centre and core of creation*" (pp. 90–91).

However, it is also apparent that many parents are able, with some satisfaction, particularly when their children are young, to transfer their unrealized hopes to them. But by the time their offspring become young adults and have independent lives and aspirations, most often quite divergent from those of their parents, and obvious limitations and failures, it becomes clear that they cannot save their progenitors from the inevitable end of the self. The painful reality must be faced again, this time, it is hoped, with a more benign resignation.

As each individual engages the developmental tasks of midlife, the ego ideal also undergoes adaptive transformation or arrest. Expectations and ideals from childhood, adolescence, and young adulthood are critically scrutinized to determine to what degree they have been realized or have the prospect of being actualized. The struggle to accept the concept of a personal end and the narcissistically injurious realization that the future is too short to correct past mistakes or begin anew is the driving force behind this momentous, searing midlife appraisal. Reasonable success in meeting the expectations of the ego-ideal facilitates transition. Lack of success in approaching the expectations of the ego-ideal impedes the transformation of the ego-ideal and causes unmodified expectations from the near and distant past to become more entrenched, rigid and unyielding, pushing the individual toward the pole of crisis and fixation.

EVIDENCE OF THE ESTABLISHMENT OF THE ADULT PSYCHIC ORGANIZER

How can we recognize that the acceptance of transience has been achieved? What is the evidence that this midlife developmental work has been accomplished? In this section of the paper we will address these two questions by discussing four basic changes in thinking which are indicative of the intra-psychic transformation. Although the four basic changes will be addressed separately, in clinical presentation they are completely interwoven.

REASSESSING THE THREE TEMPORAL MODES

The acceptance of transience is indicated by a new appreciation of the present. Although the future may still be long, its length is not reliably predictable and becomes less so with each passing year. The past is long and contains unpleasant memories and unfulfilled wishes and ambitions. Of the three temporal modes, it is the present which contains the most promise for satisfaction, gratification, and accomplishment. The acceptance of transience brings recognition of the preciousness of time and the need to live in the present, rather than the future or the past. This transformation of thinking and feeling about the three temporal modes encourages a reappraisal of all aspects of life in the present, including self and object representation, real relationships, work, health and hobbies. To summarize, the acceptance of transience can greatly enhance the quality of life for the healthy individual by stimulating an assessment of goals, a reordering of priorities, and a greater appreciation of significant relationships and the true value of time.

TOLERATING UNCERTAINTY

As we have already stated, Freud spoke of the uncertainty of living in his article "The Uncanny" (1919), noting that uncertainty was originally tied to the fear of death. During midlife, through engagement of the developmental task of transience, the connection between uncertainty and the fear of death is reworked. As the concept of a personal end is gradually integrated, uncertainty takes on a less ominous, even sometimes enjoyable meaning, because of the awareness that, at least for now, in the vigorous midlife present, the challenges of uncertainty can be not only met but mastered. Those who are unable to engage these developmental tasks, or are less successful in mastering them, will continue to have "uncanny" experiences, viewing the unexpected as a threat rather than a challenge.

REVISING PERSONAL HISTORY

In discussing the family romance, Freud (1909 [1908]) noted that the personal history that each individual builds contains within it infantile wishes and conflicts, such as ambivalent, aggressive, and tender striving toward parental figures. During midlife, the struggle to accept transience precipitates a re-activation of pre-oedipal (abandonment anxiety) and oedipal (castration anxiety) conflicts which cause the family romance to be altered.

Kris (1956) added to our understanding of the family romance when he wrote: "The personal history is not only an essential part of the self-representation, but has become a treasured possession to which the patient is attached with a particular devotion. This attachment reflects the fact that the autobiographical self-image has become heir to important early fantasies, which it preserves" (p. 654). These narcissistically loaded memories—"treasured possessions" as Kris called them—become involved in the transformation of narcissism and the ego ideal described earlier in the paper. In order to

stress the subjective nature of this revision, Montero (2000b) proposed the name personal (private) myth.

<h2 style="text-align:center">THE RELATIONSHIP BETWEEN PERSONAL
AND GENERATIONAL HISTORY</h2>

Increased understanding of one's personal history as reinterpreted
from the vantage point of midlife and the awareness of transience
causes each individual to increasingly realize that he or she has a particular, circumscribed place in the standing among the generations,
with significant real and emotional attachments to those who came
before and those who will follow. This awareness focuses attention
and affect in two opposite directions simultaneously, toward the past
and toward the future, and stimulates the emergence of what may be
called *generational transferences*—attitudes toward past and future generations that are based on one's experiences during childhood and
young adulthood with parents and grandparents and stories and
photos of earlier generations passed on by them.

The vector pointing toward the past promotes greater awareness
and interest in generational family history, in the sense that Freud
(1912–13, p. 158, 1940 [1938], p. 207) recognized, following Goethe's
Faust: "What thou hast inherited from thy fathers, acquire it to make
it thine." Simultaneously, the vector pointing toward the future promotes the delegation of "insignias" to the next two generations (Montero 1989, 2002). These insignias, for example youthful clothes and
the popular music of the day, when allowed to exist in the lives of
their children without undue interference or competition, are concrete and abstract indicators that the elder generation recognizes the
growing prerogatives of the younger generations and their constantly
increasing role as custodians of the family's past and future. They are
indicators that those in midlife and late adulthood are accepting
transience and their diminishing role as central figures in the family's present and future.

Obvious evidence of the intra-psychic preoccupation with individual and generational history is indicated by the intense interest in
many in midlife in genealogy, family coat-of-arms and collecting verbal family history from grandparents. This interest is heightened if
one is an immigrant, with knowledge of generational history limited
to those generations who lived in one's adopted nation.

These interests and activities are not without their defensive purposes. They defend against anxiety in relationship to personal death

by placing one's personal history into a family generational chain, thereby instilling a sense of continuity in time which extends beyond one's own lifetime through a symbolic fusion with past and future generations.

DETAILED CLINICAL EXAMPLE

The following clinical example is presented as an illustration of how many of the theoretical concepts presented in this paper are extremely relevant to working with patients in midlife.

Mr. B. began psychoanalysis at the age of 37. The focus of the nearly two-year therapy was a desire to increase the degree of intimacy in his long-standing, successful marriage and curiosity about a sense of free-floating anxiety.

During the course of the treatment it became clear that he was a highly successful, neurotically organized individual who was raised in an intact, loving family. His early development was uneventful until the death of his father at age 12. This sad experience became a powerful organizing factor in his mental and emotional life, and as will be demonstrated, became a major focus of his subsequent need for additional treatment.

During the analysis, Mr. B. experienced anxiety whenever he thought of his father. "I'm fearful tragedy will strike again. Like when my father died when I was 12." At other points the free-floating anxiety was expressed through statements like "I don't know where I'm going in ten years." Although considerable time was spent analyzing his reaction to his father's death, he was primarily interested in working on relationships and professional issues.

Transference issues during the analysis were focused, not surprisingly, on strong longings for the analyst to think of Mr. B. as a good son. Desires to be praised for professional and personal accomplishments (which were many) were frequently expressed, as was the fear that the analyst would abandon him, as his father had through death, if he expressed any criticism or aggression toward the analyst. Although interpretations connected these transference themes to the patient's loss of his father, such interpretations did not have nearly the impact that they did when the patient returned to treatment as he approached fifty.

Counter-transference themes toward this very likeable, somewhat needy man revolved around wishes to take care of him and to replace the good father that he had lost. The analyst was also aware of a desire to compete with the dead father for first place in the "son's" affections. These wishes were expressed through a tendency to give advice and praise, rather than maintain neutrality and analyze.

From the vantage point of understanding the patient's dynamics after his returns to treatment at ages 45 and 49, it seems apparent, in retrospect, that the analysis should have lasted longer than it did. The analyst's failure to strongly confront the patient's desire to stop after approximately two years was also probably the result of a transference-counter-transference collusion, i.e. the successful son and the accommodating, loving father.

However, Mr. B.'s decisions to leave each sequence of analysis and therapy was interpreted repeatedly as a resistance. With the advantage of hindsight, the analyst understood the urgency to leave as a means of avoiding the great anxiety and fear that would have been generated by the emergence of murderous Oedipal wishes toward the father that were unconsciously considered to be the cause of his death. Only after Mr. B. escaped retribution, i.e. outlived his father, could the subject be approached.

Whether additional analysis in the patient's late 30s would have prevented the onset of symptoms as the patient neared 50 can never be known. But it is clear that the positive transference that emerged during the analysis facilitated the patient's return to treatment during the next decade.

Age 45: Mr. B. returned to therapy for six sessions at age 45. Six years had passed since the end of the analysis. During that time he had become highly successful professionally and very secure financially. The analysis had been extremely helpful, he said, "but I feel more vulnerable than ever." He was in fine shape physically and very happy in his marriage. Despite having "everything that would make anyone my age happy," Mr. B. still had that vague, uncomfortable feeling about the future. Much of our work centered on an exploration of options ranging from early retirement to expanding his business.

Shortly before returning to treatment, Mr. B.'s mother's second husband had died. Mr. B. did not relate his vulnerable feeling about the future or his return to treatment to his stepfather's death but quickly became less anxious when the connection was interpreted. His mother had managed the death with appropriate mourning and grace and continued to live a fully independent life.

Feeling, once again, in control of his thoughts and emotions, Mr. B. decided to stop therapy, despite analytic suggestions to the contrary.

Age 49: The clinical material from this third course of therapy will be presented in greater detail.

Mr. B. returned to treatment three months before his fiftieth birthday. This course of treatment consisted of 12 therapy sessions over an interval of nine months. Eight were concentrated during the first four months—usually on a bi-weekly basis.

First session: With a somber, depressed affect, Mr. B. related that his endocrinologist had discovered evidence of beginning osteoporosis and a significantly low testosterone level. Further, the physician felt that Mr. B. was depressed, hence the return to therapy. The endocrinologist suggested that the depression may have caused the low testosterone level or vice versa. He started Mr. B. on an antidepressant.

When asked to elaborate on his concerns, Mr. B. mentioned money and turning 50. Financially he was in superb shape but was berating himself for not selling his stocks at their peak. He felt a "driven need to save." Mr. B. was "obsessed" with turning 50. His father died at 50, he unnecessarily reminded the analyst. Father didn't take care of himself but Mr. B. worked out, had a low cholesterol and was careful about what he ate. "I think of myself as 40, not 50."

Mr. B.'s associations linked his two concerns. He feared losing his money despite having a solid business, no debt and enough funds in savings to comfortably retire. He lived "way below my means but if I spend money I feel on the edge. There is no middle ground." He might die soon, just as his father did at his age. The money was a "magical fortress" protecting him and his family against danger. His wife wanted to arrange a grand fiftieth birthday party for him, but he didn't want to "tempt fate."

In our *second session* Mr. B. immediately began talking about money. He wanted to avoid doing to his family what his father had done to him. After father died he and his mother were "very poor." Mr. B. felt intense feelings of embarrassment when relatives provided money and clothing. He went to work at age 14 and later put himself though college. History would not repeat itself, he would "bullet proof" his family.

When it was interpreted that the intensity of his feelings about money and dying were related to his approaching the age at which his father died, Mr. B. sighed, volunteered that he knew he was being irrational and thought maybe he should spend more money on a vacation.

In *session three* Mr. B. began to contrast the analyst's ability to talk calmly about his fear of dying with his own intense anxiety. The analyst's equanimity and the positive transference relationship in the past and present allowed many semi-conscious and unconscious thoughts and feelings to burst into awareness. Without his saying so, it was clear that within the therapeutic alliance Mr. B. felt safe enough to explore his thoughts.

9/11 had been a "horrible experience" for him. The analyst commented that it was a sudden, unexpected trauma for which he was unprepared—just like when his father died. "What if I don't want to die?" he said defiantly, struggling against the now fully conscious awareness of the effect of the childhood trauma. However, it was clear that he was not yet aware of the powerful, primarily Oedipal, dynamics that were determining and perpetuating the belief that he would die at the same age as his father.

He then associated to the film *Contact* in which the first human (portrayed by Jody Foster in the film) to travel to an alien civilization is addressed by them in the guise of her dead father. With increasingly confident determination he repeated that he would not do to his family what his father had done to him. The analyst sensed that he was beginning to master the trauma of his father's death.

Racing with determination from association to association Mr. B. noted that his child was approximately the same age he was when his father died. He didn't even know the exact date of his father's birth and death. He would find out. Excited by his ability to think about his Dad, he blurted out, "I'm my father. I'm just like him in the way I walk and talk." Why didn't his father get better after his first heart attack? He remembered his mother asking the doctor why he couldn't save her husband. Mr. B. thought his father died in a hospital. Maybe there were records available.

Then able to tap into the depth of his feelings for the first time since adolescence, Mr. B. cried as he related the last time he saw his father, sitting on the edge of the hospital bed in his white gown. They had been alone for a few minutes and Mr. B. was about to leave. Near the door he turned and looked at his Dad. "He was smiling from ear to ear and seemed so proud of me." Mr. B. hadn't thought of that experience in many years and sobbed with sadness and love.

He began to remember details of the death and funeral. Mother told him that his father had died and an uncle would take him to a scheduled doctor's appointment. He went to the funeral (closed casket) but not to the grave site. A relative took him for Italian food instead. As he processed this information for the first time from the vantage point of midlife, he was struck by the juxtaposition of the mundane and the tragic.

Session Four: As a result of the work during the last session Mr. B. asked his mother exactly when his father died—10 days before his 50th birthday. Mr. B. would surpass his father's lifespan in exactly 11 days!

He recalled the night of his father's heart attack. His mother's screams awoke him. He thinks his father was wheeled out and mother went to the hospital with him. Maybe there were two heart attacks?

Mr. B. missed his father during adolescence and became more of a loner, more distant from extended family, particularly when they "gave us charity." He recalled spending hours shooting basketballs, by himself.

The summer before he died, father had smiled knowingly when he saw Mr. B. cutting pictures of women out of a magazine. He felt a deep sense of sadness and loss when he imagined how supportive his father would have been of his adolescent sexuality.

Two months into the therapy Mr. B. decided to stop taking the antidepressant that had been prescribed by the endocrinologist. The depression had begun to lift soon after we began to deal directly with the memories of father's death.

As his ability to think about his father's death increased, Mr. B. began to think about his progenitor from an adult rather than a child perspective. Father had lived in a foreign country for three years in his late teens. He must have been sexually active then. Increasingly free from the early adolescent fixation point and outlook, Mr. B. said, "I'm beginning to think of him as a man, not just my Dad."

Although the subject of competitive feelings toward father and fear of retaliation had been interpreted during the analysis, they had fallen on deaf ears. The defenses against any emotional acceptance of Oedipal strivings were too strong, the day of retribution, the same age at which father had died, too far away.

Because of Mr. B.'s increasing ability to talk about his father with less anxiety and dread, the analyst chose to reinterpret the infantile, Oedipal wishes that father would die. After an initial response of surprise and dismay, Mr. B. responded, "some victory, the years after he died were the worst ones of my life."

Mr. B. avoided further discussion of his angry wishes toward father until the actual date of passing father in longevity. In our last several sessions he was more freely able to criticize father for leaving his wife and son in such a precarious financial condition, and for not being there to guide his son through adolescence.

Approximately a month later Mr. B. was feeling and sleeping much better. He was thinking about buying a bigger house. "I closed everything down. I expected to die at 50." In two weeks he would surpass his father's longevity. As he continued to discuss his abundant options for the future, the pathological identification with his father diminished and Mr. B. began to individuate, increasingly recognizing that his options and life as he approached 50 were profoundly different from his father's at the same age. No longer feeling depressed, he decided to meet less frequently.

The next session took place *two weeks after Mr. B.'s birthday.* He chose not to work the day after he surpassed his father in age. He had "an anxious celebration," as he put it. Then, proving that life is far more remarkable than fiction, he sadly reported that his mother had died two days after his fiftieth birthday. Becoming unconscious two days before death, "my mother ceased to be a person on my 50th birthday." Without prompting, he volunteered that he was sad, not depressed. He had been able to work carefully and sensitively with his family, arranging the funeral and dealing with the estate.

Mr. B.'s ability to deal with his mother's death as a middle-aged adult vs. his reaction to his father's death as a vulnerable child was contrasted by the analyst. He agreed but added that he doubted he could have managed it so well if he hadn't been working through his feelings about his father. Two weeks later, Mr. B. continued to mourn for his mother. Associations led to his wife's elderly parents' health and his own eventual demise.

Mr. B.'s ability to begin to focus on the midlife developmental tasks of transience, time limitation and personal death in relationship to himself grew rapidly, unaccompanied by the anxiety and symptoms that had surrounded his unresolved developmental fixation related to his father's death. Now that Mr. B. had survived 50, he was able to consider a future and his exciting options. He proudly declared that he had purchased a new car.

Six weeks later he announced with amazement that his testosterone levels were back to normal!

Mr. B. was extremely grateful for the therapeutic work that had been done. He felt he was ready to stop therapy, but returned three times over the next six months. In the next two sessions, he made only occasional references to his parents and focused instead on his future. "I have it all—a profession, my health back, a family, and money. I'm beginning to realize that I can admit it, and it won't go away."

Mr. B. asked to come in about *five months later.* He had some "interesting" information to share. He had been able to acquire his father's medical records from nearly 40 years ago. He learned that his father had been in heart failure for two years after his heart attack. He died of heart failure, not a heart attack. As he discussed this, and recognized that he had never manifested any signs of heart disease, and was aware of the major advances in the medical and surgical treatment of heart disease that had occurred since his father's day, Mr. B. continued to feel "liberated," certain that his father's experience was not his own. His future at 50 was bright, and long!

Discussion: The traumatic and developmental effects of Mr. B.'s father's death affected every phase of development from adolescence through young adulthood and into midlife, primarily in the form of unrecognized inhibitions and over-determined behavior. Mr. B. was driven to become highly successful financially so as to build a "fire wall" around himself and his family so they would not end up poor and dependent as he and his mother had been as a result of father's death. However, he was unable to use money in a rational manner and lived far beneath his means, unconsciously expecting financial disaster at any moment.

But it was not until approximately a year before he approached the age at which his father died that Mr. B. became depressed and experienced the significant drop in testosterone level. With little insight into the dynamics behind his behavior, he began to "close everything down" as he approached the age when he, unconsciously, expected to die.

As the therapeutic work took place during the months leading up to the anniversary of father's death and his 50th birthday, Mr. B. began to count the days and hours until he surpassed his father in longevity, hanging on to the magical, but guilt ridden, hope that once he got past the fateful day he would be safe. The Oedipal underpinnings of the fear of dying, and the hormonal castration in the form of depleted testosterone levels, were clearly related to the infantile wish to kill father off and take his place, alone with mother.

Significant is the fact that the depression—and the lowered testosterone levels—responded to an analytic exploration of the genetic and dynamic factors that had produced both the physical and psychological responses in the first place. Many non-analytically trained psychiatrists would likely have relied on antidepressant medication and testosterone replacement to treat the symptoms, never understanding or analyzing the psychological factors and conflicts that were the true determinants of the symptoms.

CONCLUSION

In this paper we have focused on the midlife reactions to transience, time limitation and eventual personal death It is our contention that the psychoanalytic and psychiatric theory of either midlife transition or crisis can be expanded into a continuum. The value of this continuum is both theoretical and clinical; theoretical because many individuals struggling with the developmental tasks of midlife fall on a broad spectrum between established concepts of transition and crisis. The continuum is clinically useful when coupled with our ideas on the three basic ways of processing the transition-crisis continuum and the various pathways through which midlife developmental conflicts are expressed.

We suggest that conceptualizing transience as an adult psychic organizer emphasizes the dynamic power and clinical importance of transience in understanding midlife patients. The concept of generational transferences is particularly useful in the analysis of patients in midlife and late adulthood when added to the traditional understanding of such phenomena.

As demonstrated by the two clinical examples, adult developmental theory does not change the classical approach to analytic technique; instead such knowledge enhances the clinician's ability to understand, relate to, connect, and interpret past and present experience; leading to an increased ability to engage and master the developmental tasks of mid and late life and a return to the developmental main stream.

BIBLIOGRAPHY

BLOS, P. (1979). *The Adolescent Passage.* International Universities Press.
BUTLER, R. N., & LEWIS, M. I. (1977): Aging and Mental Health in *Aging and Mental Health Positive Psychosocial Approaches,* Mosby.
COHLER, B. L., & GALATZER-LEVY, R. M. (1990): Self, Meaning and Morale Across the Second Half of Life, in *New Dimensions in Adult Development* (R. Nemiroff and C. Colarusso, eds.), pp. 214–263, Basic Books.
COHLER, B. L., & LIEBERMAN, M. (1979): Personality Change Across the Second Half of Life. Findings from a Study of Irish, Italian, and Polish-American Men and Women, in *Ethnicity and Aging* (D. Gelfand and A. Kutznik, eds.), Springer.
COLARUSSO, C. A., & NEMIROFF, R. A. (1981): *Adult Development: A New Dimension in Psychodynamic Theory and Practice,* Plenum Press.
COLARUSSO, C. A. (1990). The Third Individuation: The Effect of Biological

Parenthood on Separation-Individuation Processes in Adulthood. *Psychoanalytic Study of the Child.* 45:170–194.

COLARUSSO, C. A. (1992): *Child and Adult Development: A Psychoanalytic Introduction for Clinicians,* Plenum Press.

COLARUSSO, C. A. (1997): Separation-Individuation Processes in Middle Adulthood: The Fourth Individuation, in *The Seasons of Life: Separation-Individuation Perspectives,* Jason Aronson Inc., pp. 73–94.

COLARUSSO, C. A. (2000): Separation-Individuation Phenomena in Adulthood: General Concepts and the Fifth Individuation, *Journal of the American Psychoanalytic Association,* volume 48, pp. 1466–1489.

EMDE, R. N. (1985): From Adolescence to Midlife: Remodeling the Structure of Adult Development, *Journal of the American Psychoanalytical Association,* volume 33.

ERIKSON, E. (1963). *Childhood and Society.* Norton.

FREUD, A. (1965): *Normality and Pathology in Childhood,* International Universities Press.

FREUD, S. (1905). *Three Essays on the Theory of Sexuality.* SE: (J. Strachey, Ed., 1968), 7:125–243, Hogarth Press.

FREUD, S. (1909 [1908]): *Family Romances,* Hogarth Press, SE, volume 9, pp. 237–241.

FREUD, S. (1912–13): *Totem and Taboo,* Hogarth Press, SE, volume 13, pp. 1–162.

FREUD, S. (1914): *On Narcissism: An Introduction,* Hogarth Press, SE, volume 14, pp. 73–102.

FREUD, S. (1916 [1915]): *On Transience,* Hogarth Press, SE, volume 14, pp. 73–102.

FREUD, S. (1919): *The Uncanny,* Hogarth Press, SE, volume 17, pp. 219–252.

FREUD, S. (1937): *Analysis Terminable and Interminable,* Hogarth Press, SE, volume 23, pp. 216–253.

FREUD, S. (1940 [1938]): *An Outline of Psycho-Analysis,* Hogarth Press, SE, volume 23, pp. 144–207.

GUTTMAN, D. L. (1977): *The Cross-Cultural Perspective: Notes on a Comparative Psychology of Aging,* in *Handbook of Psychology of Aging,* J. E. Birren and K. W. Schaie (eds.), Van Nostrand Reinhold.

GUTTMAN, D. L. (1987): *Reclaimed Powers: Toward a Psychology of Men and Women in Later Life,* Basic Books.

GUTTMAN, D. L., GRIFFIN B., & GRUNES J. (1982):Developmental Contributions to the Late-Onset Affective Disorders, in *Life-Span Development and Behaviour* (P. Baltes and O. G. Brim, Jr., eds.), Academic Press, pp. 244–263.

JACQUES, F. (1965): Death and the Midlife Crisis, *International Journal of Psycho-Analysis,* volume 46, pp. 502–514.

JUNG, C. G. (1933): *Modern Man in Search of a Soul,* Harcourt Brace.

KERNBERG, O. (1980): *Internal World and External Reality: Object Relations Theory Applied,* Jason Aronson.

KOHUT, H. (1966): Forms and Transformations of Narcissism, *Journal of the American Psychoanalytic Association*, volume 2, pp. 243–272.

KOHUT, H. (1971): *The Analysis of the Self. A Systematic Approach to Psychoanalytic Treatment of the Narcissistic Personality Disorders*, International Universities Press.

KRIS, E. (1956): The Personal Myth-A problem in Psychoanalytic Technique. *Journal of the American Psychoanalytic Association*, volume 4, pp. 653–681.

LEVINSON, D. J., DARROW, C. N., KLEIN, E. B., LEVINSON, M. H., & McKEE B. (1978): *The Seasons of a Man's Life*. Ballantine Books.

LEVINSON, D. J. (1980): *Towards a Conception of the Adult Life Course*, in *Themes of Work and Love in Adulthood*, Harvard University Press.

LEVINSON, D. J. (1996). *The Seasons of a Woman's Life*. Alfred A. Knopf.

LIEBERMAN, M., and TOBIN S. (1983): *The Experience of Old Age: Stress, Coping, and Survival*, Basic Books.

MAHLER, M., PINE, F., & BERGMAN, A. (1975). *The Psychological Birth of the Human Infant*, Basic Books.

MONTERO, G. J. (1989): *La travesía por la mitad de la vida*, Fundación Travesía, in La travesia por la mitad de la vida. Exegesis Psicoanalitica, Rosario, 2005, pp. 197–204.

MONTERO, G. J. (2000*a*): *Las vicisitudes terminables e interminables de la mediana edad*, Asociación Psicoanalítica Argentina, Symposium Interno, in Analisis terminable e interminable y el ano 2000. La clinica, pp. 69–74.

MONTERO, G. J. (2000*b*): *El mito privado como factor estructurante de la personalidad: un caso clínico*. Paper delivered at VI Symposium about myths, Federación Psicoanalítica de América Latina, Gramado (Brasil).

MONTERO, G. J. (2002) (coordinator), Godoy, S. G., Kosack, A. M., Trovato, G. A., & Singman de Vogelfanger, L: *Comprensión psicoanalítica de la individuación en la mediana edad*, at *Interdisciplina. La escucha psicoanalítica en psiquiatría*, volume III, Revista del Capítulo de Medicina Psicosocial, Asociación de Psiquiatras Argentinos, pp. 59–72.

NEUGARTEN, B. (1979): Time, Age, and the Life Cycle, *American Journal of Psychiatry*, volume 136, pp. 887–895.

PEARSON, G. (1958): *Adolescence and the Conflict of Generations*, W. W. Norton.

POLLOCK, G. H. (1980): *Aging or Aged: Development or Psychopathology*. In *The Course of Life: Psychoanalytic Contributions Towards Understanding Personality Development*, volume III, U.S. Government Printing Office.

RANK, O. (1914): *The Double: A Psychoanalytic Study* (1971), University of North Carolina Press.

SETTLAGE, C. F., CUSTIS, J., & LOZOFF, M. (1988). *Conceptualizing Adult Development. Journal of the American Psychoanalytic Association* 36: 347–370.

SHANE, M. 1977. A rationale for teaching analytic technique based on developmental orientation and approach. *Int. J. Psycho-Anal.* 58: 95–108.

SPITZ, R. (1965): *The First Year of Life*, International Universities Press, p. 5.

VAILLANT, G. (1977). *The Adolescent Passage*, International Universities Press.

Index

AAI (Adult Attachment Interview), 83
Ablon, J. S., 296
Abrams, D., 46
Abrams, S.: on analytic process, 9–10, 92, 93; on child analysis compared with adult analysis, 93; on developmental help for children, 304; and educator-psychoanalytic partnership, 182*n*2; on M. Graf's debt to S. Freud, 121–22; on Little Hans case, 21–27, 29–30, 30*n*4, 38; on protection versus defense, 296–97; on psychoanalytical process and developmental process, 3–17, 147; on therapeutic action, 295; on transference, 104
Abuse. *See* Child abuse; Trauma
ACE (Adverse Childhood Experiences) study, 232–33
Adelphi University, 309*n*4
Adelson, E., 218
Adler, A., 53, 72*n*4, 76–77, 117
Adolescents: Aichhorn's treatment of delinquent youth and adolescents, 30, 153–75; analysis of, 30–31; delinquency of, 157–75; Diagnostic Profile for, 42; A. Freud on, 30; gender differences in treatment of, 169; Herbert Graf's adolescence, 39–42, 53, 54, 74–75, 75*n*7; group treatment with, 162; impact of, on parents' midlife transience, 335; milieu therapy for, 153–55; and transference, 155–57; violent youngsters' treatment, 171–74. *See also* Educator-psychoanalytic partnership
Adult analysis. *See* Psychoanalysis
Adult Attachment Interview (AAI), 83
Adult Development (Colarusso), 336
Adulthood: definition of, 332–33; developmental tasks of middle adulthood, 333–36; psychoanalytic view of development applied to, 330–32. *See also* Midlife transition and crisis continuum
Adverse Childhood Experiences (ACE) study, 232–33
Aggression: Aichhorn's treatment of violent youngsters, 171–74; and defenses against unwelcome affects, 292–93; of

eight-year-old boy with multiple diagnoses in foster care, 264, 266–67, 274–76; of traumatized boy, 244–47, 251–52, 258; by victims of violence, 256. *See also* Violence
Aging body, 334–35, 343–44. *See also* Midlife transition and crisis continuum
Agoraphobia, 63
Aichhorn, A.: on delinquency as mental illness and society's responsibility to delinquents, 166–69; and A. Freud, 181; on interpretation in analysis, 174–75; and Life Space Crisis Intervention (LSCI) model, 192; and Oberhallabrünn Institute, 171–74, 182; on psychoanalysis, 174–75; on responses of analysts, teachers, and society to delinquents, 162–66; theory of delinquency by, 169–71; on transference, 154, 155–62, 172–74, 174*n*2, 175; and treatment of delinquent youth and adolescents, 30, 153–75; on typology of delinquents, 157–62; on violent youngsters, 171–74
Ainsworth, M. D. S., 25, 79–80, 218, 222
Allen Creek Preschool (Ann Arbor, Mich.), 184
Alliance of Psychoanalytic Schools, 184
Alpern, L., 82
Alvarez, A., 256, 257, 277, 279
American Academy of Child and Adolescent Psychiatry, 155, 223
American Psychoanalytic Association, 39*n*9, 201, 233
Analysis. *See* Child analysis; Psychoanalysis
"The Analysis of a Phobia in a Five-Year-Old Boy" (S. Freud). *See* Little Hans case
Animal phobias: and anxious attachment, 63, 65; Bowlby on, 65; S. Freud on, 46–47; A. Freud on, 34–35; horse phobia in Little Hans case, 34–35, 51, 57–58, 62, 63, 65, 66, 68, 92, 94, 95, 97–105, 109, 126, 138, 145, 147–48
Anna Freud Centre, 183
Anti-semitism, 47–48, 114, 115–16, 133, 138. *See also* Judaism and Jews
Antisocial behavior. *See* Delinquents

359

366   *Index*

Scheeringa, M. S., 224
Schmukler, A. G., 295
School Based Mourning Project, 193
School climate, 195–96
School Development Program, 188
School refusal, 63, 65
Schools. *See* Educator-psychoanalytic partnership; Educators
Schore, A. N., 240
Schuengel, C., 83
Schur, M., 62
Schutt, E., 123
Seduction trauma, 49
Seductiveness of mother, 24, 49, 50, 51, 57, 62, 69, 70, 71, 71n3, 74, 81, 97–99, 137
Segal, H., 256
Seifer, R., 216
Self-criticism in midlife, 344
Self, disorders of, 163
Self-harming behavior, 264, 267, 274, 275–76
Self-preservation, 244
Self-psychology, 5, 163
Seligman, M. E. P., 190
Sen, A., 167
Separation: Anxiety and Anger (Bowlby), 62
Separation anxiety, 51, 57, 62, 65–68, 79, 98, 137
Separation-Individuation theory, 332
Settlage, C., 331
"The Sexual Enlightenment of Children" (S. Freud), 46, 94–95
Sexuality: S. Freud on infantile sexuality, 22, 29n2, 33, 94–95, 139; in midlife, 335, 344; and sexual knowledge of children, 52, 76n8, 95, 106–7; sexual problems in Graf marriage, 75–76, 125, 137. *See also* Oedipus complex
Shamir-Essakow, G., 80, 82
Shane, E., 198
Shane, M., 198, 331
Shapiro, L., 190
Shapiro, V., 218
Shaver, P. R., 80
Shaw, G. B., 4
Shepherd, M. J., 191
Shopper, M., 187n3
Shore, A. N., 266
Sibling rivalry, 49, 55, 69, 82, 106
Siegel, C. H., 224
Silverman, M., 56, 69, 112
Silverman, R., 214
Skinner, B. R., 164
Sklarew, B., 167, 187n3, 191, 193, 201
Slade, A., 295, 303

Slap, J., 51, 69, 100, 112
Snidman, N., 81
Social, Emotional and Academic Education, 199
Social Emotional Learning series, 199
Solnit, A., 167, 183, 188, 212, 213, 216, 222, 236
Solomon, J., 72, 80, 82
Spence, D. P., 297
Spitz, R., 62, 330, 338
Sroufe, L. A., 82
Stalin, J., 183
Steinberg, A. M., 224
Steiner, J. E., 247
Stern, D. N., 222, 264, 285
Stone, L., 175
Strachey, J., 97–98, 105, 108, 294, 310
Strange Situation, 79–80, 82–85
Strati, E., 263–86
Strauss, R., 120, 121, 128, 130
Sublimation, 302–3
Sugarman, A., 298, 304
Suicide: attachment and suicide in family history, 24, 64, 78–79, 81; of Hanna Graf, 58, 78–79, 122, 126–27; in Olga Graf's family, 24, 46, 56, 73, 78–79, 81, 82, 124; of Herbert Graf's first wife, 140
Superego: delinquents' superego failures, 170–71; A. Freud on, 299, 300; Strachey on, 294; of traumatized boy, 274
Sutton, N., 170
Symptoms, Inhibitions and Anxiety (S. Freud), 33, 34

Target, M., 257, 285, 295, 303, 304
Taylor, R. D., 190
Teachers. *See* Educator-psychoanalytic partnership; Educators
Terr, L., 255
Therapeutic action, 292, 294–96, 310. *See also* Child analysis; Interpretation; Psychoanalysis
Therapy. *See* Psychotherapy
Three Essays on the Theory of Sexuality (S. Freud), 29n2, 94
Time limitations in midlife, 333–34, 337, 340–41, 346–47. *See also* Transience
Tobin, S., 334
Toth, S. L., 226
Transference: Aichhorn on, 154, 155–62, 172–74, 174n2, 175; definition of, 9–10; S. Freud on, 9–10, 155, 255; A. Freud on, 9–10; generational transferences, 348–49; and group cohesion, 162; induction of, 154, 158–60; and Little Hans case,